HARVARD–RADCLIFFE FINE ARTS SERIES

A HISTORY OF
SPANISH PAINTING

VOLUME XI

A HISTORY OF
SPANISH PAINTING

BY

CHANDLER RATHFON POST
HARVARD UNIVERSITY

VOLUME XI
THE VALENCIAN SCHOOL IN THE
EARLY RENAISSANCE

CAMBRIDGE, MASSACHUSETTS
HARVARD UNIVERSITY PRESS
1953

KRAUS REPRINT CO.
New York
1970

Reprinted with the permission of the Licensor
KRAUS REPRINT CO.
A U.S. Division of Kraus-Thomson Organization Limited

LIBRARY OF CONGRESS CATALOG CARD NUMBER 30–7776
PRINTED IN THE UNITED STATES OF AMERICA

BIBLIOGRAPHY OF VOLUME XI [1]

Abbad Ríos, Francisco, *La colección de D. Ricardo Corredor, Boletín de la Sociedad Española de Excursiones,* LVI (1948), 233–234.

Abizanda y Broto, Manuel, *Damián Forment,* Barcelona, 1942.

Amador de los Ríos, Rodrigo, *Riquezas perdidas, La Santa Vera Cruz de Caravaca, Revista de archivos,* XXVIII (1914), 226–240.

Angulo Íñiguez, Diego, *La Virgen, el Niño y San Juan con Santa Ana y Santa Isabel, de Yáñez, Archivo español de arte,* XIX (1946), 64.

Arozena, Olimpia, *Un cuadro de Vicente Juan Macip, Saitabi (Noticiario de historia, arte y arqueología),* No. 3, April–June, 1942, pp. 6–8.

———— *El pintor Vicente Macip, padre de Joan de Joanes, Anales de la Universidad de Valencia,* XI (1930–1931), 98–121.

Bas y Martínez, Quintín, *La Santísima Cruz de Caravaca,* Caravaca, 1905.

Beltrán, Antonio, *Valencia (Guías artísticas de España),* Barcelona, 1945.

Bertaux, Émile, *Les peintres Ferrando et Andrés de Llanos á Murcie, Gazette des beaux-arts,* 1908, I, 344–350.

———— *Le retable monumental de la cathédrale de Valence, Gazette des beaux-arts,* 1907, II, 103–130.

Campos, Consolación, *El retablo de Santa Úrsula ó de las vírgenes del Convento de la Puridad de Valencia, Anales de la Universidad de Valencia,* XI (1930–1931), 187–209.

Caturla, María Luisa, *Ferrando Yáñez no es leonardesco, Archivo español de arte,* XV (1942), 35–49.

Ferrán Salvador, Vicente, *Pablo de San Leocadio y la pintura valenciana en los siglos XV y XVI,* Valencia, 1947 (reprinted from the periodical *Saitabi,* 1946, no. of October to December).

Foulkes, C. Jocelyn, *Acerca del Retablo del Bautismo, de los Masip, en la Catedral de Valencia, Boletín de la Sociedad Española de Excursiones,* XXVI (1918), 54.

Frizzoni, Gustavo, *I capolavori della pinacoteca del Prado in Madrid, Archivio storico dell'arte,* VI (1893), 180–196 (for Johannes Hispanus).

Fuente, Vicente de la, *La Santa Cruz de Caravaca, Boletín de la Real Academia de la Historia,* Madrid, IX (1886), 319–334.

Giner Ferrer, Jesús, *La santa é insigne Colegiata de Gandía,* Valencia, 1944.

[1] In addition to the works on Valencian painting listed in the bibliographies of former volumes.

González Martí, Manuel, *De la historia artística de Valencia, Las tablas de los pintores Llanos y Almedina del siglo XVI, Museum* (Barcelona), IV (1914–1916), 379–402.

———— *Joanes,* Valencia, 1926.

González Simancas, Manuel, *La catedral de Murcia, Revista de archivos,* XXIV (1911), 510–538.

Justi, Carl, *Das Geheimniss der leonardesken Altargemälde in Valencia, Repertorium für Kunstwissenschaft,* XVI (1893), 1–10. Reprinted in his *Miscellaneen aus drei Jahrhunderten spanischen Kunstlebens,* 1908, II, 135–149, with only slight changes except for an exact reversal of the attributions to Fernando de Llanos and Fernando Yáñez de la Almedina.

—— Pablo de San Leocadio, *Miscellaneen aus drei Jahrhunderten spanischen Kunstlebens,* Berlin, 1908, II, 147–149.

Llorente, Teodoro, *Valencia* (in the series *España, sus monumentos y artes*), Barcelona, 1887–1889.

Möller, Emil, *Zwei bisher unerkannte Bildnisse der Mona Lisa, Monatshefte für Kunstwissenschaft,* XI (1918), 1–14.

Orellana, Marcos Antonio de, *Biografía pictórica valentina,* edited by Xavier de Salas and published as a volume in the series, *Fuentes literarias para la historia del arte español,* Madrid, 1930.

Pano, Mariano de, *El Colegio de las Vírgenes, Pintura sobre tabla, Boletín del Museo Provincial de Bellas Artes,* Saragossa, I (1917), 18–20.

Post, Chandler R., *The Paintings of Damià Forment,* in vol. I of *Miscel·lània Puig i Cadafalch,* Barcelona, 1951.

Ros y Fillol, Godofredo, *El pintor Juan de Juanes: sus restos, Discurso leído ante el Centro de Cultura Valenciana,* Valencia, 1943.

Salas, Xavier de, *Escultores renacientes en el Levante español, Anales y Boletín de los Museos de Arte de Barcelona,* I, 2 (1942), 35–87 (important for Yáñez and Llanos).

Sánchez Cantón, Francisco Javier, review of W. Suida's *Leonardo und sein Kreiss, Archivo español de arte y arqueología,* V (1929), 126–127.

Saralegui, Leandro de, *Noticias de tablas inéditas, Archivo español de arte,* XXI (1948), 200–214.

———— *Para el estudio de algunas tablas españolas, Archivo español de arte,* XVIII (1945), 17–32.

———— *Sobre algunas tablas de particulares*, Archivo español de arte, XXIII (1950), 185–201.

Suida, Wilhelm, *Leonardo und sein Kreiss*, Munich, 1929.

Tormo, Elías, *El gran Bautismo de los Masip en la Catedral de Valencia, de 1535*, Boletín de la Sociedad Española de Excursiones, XXIV (1916), 230–234.

———— *Obras conocidas y desconocidas de Yáñez de la Almedina*, Boletín de la Sociedad Española de Excursiones, XXXII (1924), 32–39 (republished in the collection of Tormo's studies, *Pintura, escultura y arquitectura en España*, Madrid, 1949).

———— *Obras recién halladas del pintor San Leocadio*, Cultura española, IX (1908), 167–169.

———— *El presunto introductor del Arte pictórico del ya pleno Renacimiento en Valencia: Monseñor Francisco Cabañes*, Almanaque de "Las Provincias" (Valencia), 1941, pp. 399–403.

———— *Las sargas del pintor San Leocadio*, Cultura española, X (1908), 562.

———— *Yáñez de la Almedina*, Boletín de la Sociedad Española de Excursiones, XXIII (1915), 198–205 (republished in the collection of Tormo's studies, *Pintura, escultura y arquitectura en España*, Madrid, 1949).

Vian, Francisco, *Sentido artístico del Renacimiento mediterráneo*, published by the Institución Alfonso el Magnánimo, Valencia, 1951.

CONTENTS

CHAPTER I

CHAPTER VIII

The School of Yáñez and Llanos

CHAPTER IX

Valencian Paintings of the Early Renaissance but of Uncertain Affiliations

APPENDIX

Additions to Volumes I–X

CONTENTS

THE VALENCIAN SCHOOL
IN THE
EARLY RENAISSANCE

CHAPTER I

INTRODUCTION

ALTHOUGH the phase in the evolution of the Valencian school treated in the present volume and comprised generally within the first third of the sixteenth century shared partially with the contemporary pictorial production of the other regions of Spain the nature of the kind of transition between the styles of the Middle Ages and the High Renaissance which we have endeavored to define at the beginnings of volumes IX and X, yet it was differentiated by two local characteristics. One of these resulted from the fact that, despite the presence at Valencia of a certain number of Flemish paintings,[1] the art of the Low Countries had not contributed so much leaven, in comparison with its influence upon almost all the other peninsular schools, to the formation of the immediately anterior styles of the middle and second half of the fifteenth century, which had constituted partly autochthonous developments from the expression that Valencia had given to the previous modes of the "international movement." The consequence was that precedents from the Low Countries cannot be so easily detected in Valencian paintings of the early Renaissance. Doubtless it was also partly because a habit of borrowing from the Flemings had not been established in the city that its masters at the commencement of the sixteenth century betrayed scarcely any tendency to ape the artists of Flanders at this period who attracted imitation in Andalusia, the Antwerp mannerists. The neuroticism of this foreign style, moreover, was alien to the school's innate aesthetics, which from the first had shown a predilection for a serene placidity that had attained its most engaging manifestation in Jacomart and that still persisted among the Valencian painters of the Cinquecento, even to some extent among the group who derived their fashions from Leonardo da Vinci. Indeed, during the years that now concern us, Valencia provided very little congenial soil for mannerism of other sorts, whether Italian or indigenous.

[1] In addition to my vol. VI, pp. 5–7, see my articles in the *Gazette des beaux-arts*, March, 1943, and April, 1952.

Vital forces in obstructing Flemish saturation in this domain of Spanish painting had been closer artistic connections with Italy and the introduction of the Renaissance earlier than elsewhere in the peninsula, thus preparing the way for the second differentiating characteristic of the Valencian school in the first decades of the Cinquecento, an Italianism that painters in the rest of Spain did not ordinarily exhibit in so intimate a degree. We have reviewed in volume VI [2] not only the story of the continuous relationship of Valencia with the art of the sister peninsula, starting as early as the end of the fourteenth century with the sojourn of the Giottesque Starnina, but also the political as well as the geographical causes of the phenomenon; and for the precocious percolation of the Renaissance we have attached special significance to the visit from Italy of the Cardinal Rodrigo Borgia (afterwards Alexander VI) to his Valencian archbishopric in 1472, bringing with him no less than three Italian painters, one of whom, Paolo da San Leocadio, will occupy us much in the succeeding pages as having become some thirty years later an outstanding figure in the Valencian school and the fountainhead of a whole, prominent strain in the city's art at this time. Thus it had happened that even in the fifteenth century elements taken from the Italian Renaissance had begun to appear in the works of the Valencian artists before they generally showed themselves in the rest of the peninsula. The borrowings from the new movement in Italy had at first, with Jacomart, been timid and confined to details of architectural repertoire, but then, with Rodrigo de Osona the elder, his son, and his general circle, they had extended to types and compositions, although in this coterie combined with more obligations to Flanders than we generally encounter in the school.

The ground was thus ready for the more tangible dependence upon Italy which distinguished the pictorial output of Valencia in the early years of the sixteenth century from what was being achieved in the other parts of Spain, so that here the Renaissance meant rather more than the mere loosening of primitive bonds, than the desire for increased idealism, or than the introduction of settings of the new kind of architecture that the Italians had first evolved. We must reckon

---

[2] Pp. 170–173, *et passim*; and in addition, for the likelihood that the Florentine painter, the Maestro del Bambino Vispo, had begun his career as a member of the Valencian school, see my vol. VIII, pp. 647–652. I have taken up Starnina again below, p. 403.

not only with the presence of actual Italian artists, Paolo da San Leocadio and his comrades, but with the demonstrable training of native
painters in Italy. The establishers of the faction in the Valencian
school of the period that vied with Paolo and his followers for patronage were two partners, Fernando Yáñez de la Almedina and Fernando de Llanos, both of whom are proved by the internal evidence
of their works to have studied under Leonardo da Vinci and one of
whom indeed seems to be documented as an assistant of the celebrated
Florentine, although, strangely enough, it is impossible to say with
surety which, since the Italian archives describe him only by his given
name and the adjective, Spanish. Stylistic considerations, furthermore,
appear to demand the assumption that no less outstanding a painter
than Vicente Juan Masip, the father of the still more famous Juan de
Juanes, after having learned at home from Paolo da San Leocadio,
passed some time in northern Italy, especially in the Veneto. Indeed a
Spaniard who signed as "Johannes Hispanus" an Entombment once
in a nunnery at Milan reveals similarities to Masip's style, though far
from sufficiently precise to justify making the two men into a single
personality; but the intimate ties then existing between Valencian and
Italian art emerge in the fact that Berenson has ventured the tentative
hypothesis of an identification of Johannes Hispanus with the Ferrarese
master, Gian Battista Benvenuto, nicknamed L'Ortolano.[3] Another
Spaniard active at Valencia, Pedro de Rubiales, who joined with his
partner, Gaspar Requena, in creating a manner that probably had its
roots in the modes of Paolo da San Leocadio, we shall find good reason for believing to have eventually taken up residence in Italy and
there to have acquired renown for his proficiency in artistic anatomy;
but we cannot support this belief by equating Pedro, as was the old
and erroneous custom, with a painter who became practically a member of the Italian school, Francisco de Rubiales.[4] The Chinchilla
Master, whom by persuasive arguments we can attach to the Valencian *milieu* at least for a part of his career, is almost unescapably
shown by the content of his works to have profited by a visit to
central Italy.

The kinship of Valencia with the sister peninsula in art is embodied
also in such an increasing Italianism among the followers of the late
mediaeval painter, the Perea Master, that it is a question whether we

[3] See below, p. 85.
[4] See below, p. 88.

ought not to have postponed to the present our discussion of the majority of them, especially the Borbotó Master and the Cabanyes Master, but I finally decided to treat them in volume VI, which concerned itself with the ultimate stages of the Valencian Middle Ages, on account of their manifest descent from the founder of the general tendency to which they belonged. Nevertheless, a number of other artists who could trace their genealogy back to the Perea Master will find a place in an ensuing chapter for various reasons. Nicolás Falcó is reserved for this chapter not only because he was more Italian-ate than almost all his rivals in the Perea Master's progeny but also in view of his demonstrable association with Paolo da San Leocadio. The somewhat more manneristic leanings of the exponent of this style in the Balearic Isles, the Calviá Master, in comparison with his in-spirer, the Cabanyes Master, warrant his deferment to the present volume, but there was also a more practical consideration, the fact that, when I wrote volume VI, I had not yet isolated and defined his personality. It was likewise because they had not yet emerged fully to my consciousness that other members of the coterie have not ap-peared in my books until now, the Master of the Juan Family of Játiva, the Cuenca Master, and, more important, the well known sculptor, Damián Forment, in the rôle of a painter. The chapter will conclude with a few works in the circle whose authors not even a scrutiny covering many years has enabled me to specify with convic-tion. It is not impossible that the members of the group learned what they knew of the Renaissance from its early exponents at Valencia or even in the rest of Spain, above all from Paolo da San Leocadio, but nothing stands in the way of the supposition, though uncorroborated in the records, that particularly the more Italianate among them ventured the easy journey across the sea.

The foregoing paragraphs have revealed that we can distinguish clearly three strains in Valencian painting of the beginning of the Cinquecento. The first was composed of Paolo da San Leocadio and those who absorbed something of his general style; second, just as Fernando Yáñez and Fernando de Llanos could not escape the mag-netic spell that Leonardo da Vinci cast over nearly everyone with whom he came into contact, so a number of Valencians, although at least for the most part they acquired a knowledge of the renowned Florentine's attainments only at second hand through the two Fer-nandos, were fascinated to such a degree as to form, together with them, another division in the school of the city; and there are thus left, to incorporate a third strain, the men who accommodated the models of the Perea Master to the new standards of the Renaissance. It goes without saying, however, that the interpreters of any one tendency were often influenced by the qualities of their rivals who had diverse affiliations and that therefore sometimes, for instance in the cases of Miguel Esteve and Nicolás Falcó, the groups overlapped. Certain members of these subdivisions, such as Vicente Juan Masip, Martín Gómez, and the partners Requena and Rubiales, expanded their styles completely or practically into the modes of the High Renaissance, but they have been included in the present volume for the sake of lucidity of arrangement, although, generally speaking, the painters herein discussed were restricted in their pictorial fashions to the aspect of Spanish art transitional from mediaeval standards to the aesthetic ambitions of the fully evolved Cinquecento.

In the Quattrocento the acquisition of the kingdom of Naples by the Aragonese dynasty, the Italianization of the Borgia family, who had resided in Valencian territory, and particularly in 1472 the temporary return of the Cardinal Rodrigo Borgia from Rome to his see of Valencia, accompanied by a triad of Italian painters, had constituted primal concrete causes for the premature implantation of the Renaissance in the local school. The continuation of Italianism in the art of Valencia, which the intervening sea did not far remove geographically, found a reason doubtless in the fact that the Aragonese domination of southern Italy (unimpaired seriously by French interference) was expanded during the early sixteenth century into the incorporation of the kingdom in the Spanish crown, represented henceforth at Naples by viceroys; but otherwise we cannot trace in the school such definite effects of historical events, conditions, and personages as my introductions to volumes IX and X have endeavored to enumerate in Castile and Andalusia.

CHAPTER II

PAOLO DA SAN LEOCADIO [1]

1. His Life

When speaking of this still inadequately appreciated Italian immigrant into the artistic *milieu* of Valencia, the documents in Latin and in the Valencian language designate him sometimes as Paul of San Leocadio [2] and sometimes as Paul of Reggio, giving various forms to the second part of each appellation according to the fluid spelling of the period. The former title means that he came from a place called San Leocadio, and the latter, that Reggio in the province of Emilia was the nearest large town in the district and so would have been naturally employed by him in describing his provenience as better known than his native hamlet. San Valentino is the present name of the village, just south of Reggio; but, although one of its churches is dedicated to this saint, it has another under the invocation of Sant' Eleucadio,[3] which in Italian or Valencian easily was diluted to Leocadio, and in the Renaissance it must have been after this other heavenly patron that the place was denominated.[4] To the painter's name there is sometimes appended in the Valencian documents the

---

[1] Leaning upon the potent precedent of Bertaux, I bestow upon the name its Italian form, using the Italian preposition *da*. The Spanish would be, Pablo de San Leocadio.

[2] The form *Senlucha* that also occurs must represent a misreading or a misspelling of San Leocadio.

[3] I.e., St. Eleuchadius, an early, canonized bishop of Ravenna. I suspect that at least one of the reasons for the presence of the two dedications in a single hamlet is that the feasts of St. Valentine and St. Eleuchadius occur on the same day, February 14.

[4] See A. Venturi, *Storia dell' arte italiana*, VII, part 3, p. 1102, n. 1. Subsequently to Venturi but independently, the great and never resting pioneer in the realm of Spanish art, Georgiana Goddard King, discovered what Paolo's hamlet was and shortly before her death generously transmitted to me the result of her investigation. I cannot refrain from quoting her very characteristic note to me: "I found last summer the place from which Pablo takes his name — tho' so late in the campaign that I could not get there. But there would have been nothing to see. The church dedicated to S. Eleocadio is near Sassuolo and Castellarano, and the other church in the village is dedicated to S. Valentino, by which name the little place now goes. Sources contributed by the canon-archivist of Reggio, and the Post Office Administration. The men in charge at the Communal Library found me books."

adjective, Lombard, in the sense that the Spaniards would have loosely included also Emilia within the limits of Lombardy. In the contract of January 10, 1507,[5] he is once described as a *pictor latinus*, a term that I take to mean merely Italian. The careful specification of Paolo's geographical origins is more than pedantry, for they confirm the derivation of his style, revealed by internal evidence, from the schools of Ferrara and Bologna which dominated the artistic production of the region whence he took the names by which he was called in Spain.

In discussing in volume VI[6] the uninterrupted contact of the Valencian school with Italy during the fifteenth century, I have already had occasion to refer to the first emergence of Paolo to the light of history. In an entry of July 16, 1472, in the records of the cathedral of Valencia,[7] it is stated that the Cardinal Rodrigo Borgia, the future Pope Alexander VI, when he arrived from Italy on June 19 of the same year for a visit to this city of which he was the archbishop, had brought with him three painters, Paolo da San Leocadio and two others who have also engaged our attention in volume VI, Francesco Pagano of Naples and a Master Richard. Alexander VI's subsequent employment of such a secondary painter as Pintoricchio for the signal task of decorating the Borgia Apartments in the Vatican betrays that his aesthetic taste was not of the highest and that he valued opulence in decoration more than intrinsic artistic merit; but yet the three men whom he had chosen to accompany him must have enjoyed a certain degree of reputation in their own land in order to have attracted at all the great prelate's interest, and, although the attainments of Pagano and Master Richard still remain unknown quantities to us, Paolo surely deserves a more distinguished place in history than has hitherto been accorded to him. In any case, Paolo and Francesco were immediately honored, obviously at the request of Rodrigo Borgia, with the important commission of frescoing the walls about

---

[5] See below, p. 14.

[6] Pp. 171–173.

[7] For the document, see J. Sanchis y Sivera, *La catedral de Valencia*, 149, n. 2. Among "the painters whom the Cardinal had brought" only Richard and Francesco are mentioned by name in the passage quoted by Sanchis y Sivera from the entry, but we can see in the many other allusions to Paolo in the archives of the cathedral that he was one of a triad to whom reference is made on July 16, 1472. The Spanish scholar (*ibid.*, n. 1) records an arrangement for the lodging of Paolo and Francesco on May 1, 1472, but he must have made an error in the month and day, which antedate the Cardinal's arrival.

the high altar of the cathedral, since the earlier adornment of these spaces in 1432 had perished in a fire of 1469 and since Dello Delli, who at once after the conflagration had been given the order to re-decorate them, died in 1470 or 1471 before he could have proceeded very far with the undertaking.[8] The entry of July 16, 1472, in the cathedral archives has to do with the trial-pieces of fresco which all three painters had been asked to execute and one of which by Francesco and Paolo in collaboration, a Nativity, is partially preserved in the Sala Capitular Antigua of the church.

The authorities of the cathedral, in all probability because of pressure from the Cardinal, did not wait to bestow their approval upon the Nativity by Francesco and Paolo, which was not finally completed until August 20, 1476,[9] but on July 28, 1472, only twelve days after the notice in regard to this trial-piece, they signed the contract [10] with the two masters for the frescoing of the walls about the high altar or *capilla mayor*. The records of payments to them follow on during the succeeding years until December 22, 1481, when they give their last joint receipt, upon the conclusion of the enterprise,[11] for the price that they had received. Francesco Pagano then disappears from our knowledge, probably because he died or returned to Italy, and on February 13, 1483, Paolo alone signed the final quittance.[12] During the decade since the initiation of the undertaking the relations between the masters and the cathedral chapter had not always gone smoothly. As early as 1476 [13] the canons had objected that Paolo and Francesco were not working in the real Italian process of fresco, and the ecclesiastical dissatisfaction eventually reached such a pitch that a committee of Valencian painters had to be appointed to decide the merits of the

[8] See my vol. VI, p. 171.

[9] Sanchis y Sivera, *La catedral de Valencia*, 149, n. 3.

[10] The contract in the Valencian language but with a Latin preamble and conclusion is published, with a Castilian translation, by R. Chabás in the old Valencian periodical that he directed, *El Archivo*, V (1891), 380. We have seen in vol. VI, p. 171, n. 3, that the day-book of a priest who had been a chaplain of Alfonso V states that two "Florentines" were summoned in 1471 to fresco the *capilla mayor*, but, if he refers to Francesco Pagano and Paolo da San Leocadio (mistaking the date) and not to Dello Delli with an assistant or to a pair of unknown painters who might have intervened between Dello and them, the word "Florentine" can only be a looser way of describing them than the adjective "Lombard" by which we have found Paolo to be sometimes designated. See also Chabás, *op. cit.*, 379.

[11] *Ibid.*, 385, and also in Chabás's edition of J. Teixidor's *Antigüedades de Valencia*, Valencia, 1895, I, 246; and Sanchis y Sivera, *La catedral de Valencia*, 152, n. 1.

[12] Sanchis y Sivera, *Pintores medievales en Valencia*, Valencia, 1930, p. 186.

[13] Sanchis y Sivera, *La catedral de Valencia*, 152, n. 1.

question. The formal opinion of the committee, delivered on October 8, 1478,[14] was that the masters had fulfilled the terms of the contract in regard to the process but had failed to introduce the amount of gold and certain pigments demanded in the stipulations. The difficulty was in some way adjusted and the task carried in 1481 to its consummation.

In like fashion the association between the masters themselves had not continued on an entirely amicable basis, as was perhaps inevitable in such partnerships, for a document of September 23, 1476,[15] refers to disputes that had arisen between them about the division of their labor and its remuneration. Curiously enough, each fell so seriously ill, in the lapse of time during which they were engaged in the decoration of the *capilla mayor*, that, although eventually recovering, they expected to die and made their wills, Francesco Pagano on June 25, 1476, and Paolo da San Leocadio on July 4, 1478, the latter adding a codicil on the next day. Consisting of pious provisions and bequests, the testaments offer nothing of interest to the historian of art, for the difference in first names forbids us to identify the future painter, usually described as Felipe Pablo de San Leocadio,[16] with an infant [17] son whom he names as his chief legatee, Pedro Pablo (in Valencian, Peret Pau, the former name a diminutive of Pere or, in Castilian, Pedro, and the latter the Valencian for Pablo, meaning only that his father was Pablo or Paolo). The word *natural* applied to Pedro Pablo in the will has generally been taken to mean that he was a bastard, but it is clear from many documents of the time that the adjective did not then carry this significance: for example, the father of Juan de Juanes in his testament [18] couples the terms *legitim e natural* in describing his son.

An evil spell seems to have overhung the plan of frescoing the *capilla mayor* in the cathedral of Valencia, for the paintings by Francesco Pagano and Paolo da San Leocadio suffered the unhappy fate of the antecedent mural decorations, being destroyed at the end of the seventeenth century to give place to the present baroque embellishment. The stipulations of the contract of July 28, 1472, are not

---

[14] The pronouncement is published by Chabás in his article in *El Archivo*, 384.

[15] Sanchis y Sivera, *Pintores medievales en Valencia*, 182.

[16] See below, p. 277.

[17] We learn that the child was a baby from the fact that Paolo arranges for a nurse to rear him.

[18] The Barón de Alcahalí, *Diccionario biográfico de artistas valencianos*, 160.

sufficiently specific to permit an accurate mental reconstruction of
their appearance. If we leave out of account the mere polychromy of
the capitals, windows, and other pieces of the architecture, principally
comprising conventionalized *motifs* of fruit and foliage, the figure-
paintings seem to have consisted, from the top downwards, of the
enthroned Deity [19] surrounded by seraphim, then of further angels in
couples, next beneath each window a theme of sacred narrative, and
finally effigies of the Apostles. A description of the *capilla mayor*
written in the seventeenth century before its remodelling would
appear to indicate that one of the narrative themes was the Last Supper.[20] Since Miguel Esteve and Miguel del Prado were required in
a contract of 1518 for frescoes in the chapel of the Ayuntamiento at
Valencia to imitate the Pantocrator, angels, and Apostles in the cycle
of the apse of the cathedral and since Esteve seems in style to have
fallen under Paolo's influence, it is likely that the partially preserved
Apostles from the town hall reflect rather closely their effigies by the
two Italians.[21] A passage in the document of September 23, 1476, that
concerns itself with the strained relations between the two masters
probably ought to be interpreted as signifying that Pagano's chief
function was largely confined to the polychromy in pure design and
that Paolo da San Leocadio was given the lion's share of the figure-
painting, with the corollary that the former was more of a mere
craftsman and that the latter was recognized rather as the true artist
and leading spirit in the combine. Indeed, on September 13, 1476,
the ecclesiastical authorities had extracted a formal promise from
Paolo alone that he would not leave Valencia before completing the
enterprise in the cathedral, but the reason for omitting Pagano may
have been at least in part because he had not yet fully recuperated
from his malady.[22]

The employment of Paolo in the cathedral continued with the
commissions, in 1480, together with Francesco Pagano, to gild a boss
in the vault of the *capilla mayor*, and on February 13, 1484,[23] to do
by himself the polychromy of another boss in the *Arcada Nueva*, but

[19] The contract mentions only a throne, but the document of September 23, 1476,
about the dispute between the partners speaks of a *Maiestat*, a regular term for the
Pantocrator.

[20] Sanchis y Sivera, *La catedral de Valencia*, 151, n. 2.

[21] See below, p. 309.

[22] Sanchis y Sivera, *Pintores medievales en Valencia*, 182.

[23] Sanchis y Sivera, *La catedral de Valencia*, 152 and 528. The year 1484 is mis-
printed as 1884 in his *Pintores medievales en Valencia*, 186.

his name does not then emerge in the Spanish records until in 1493 he married an Isabel López (or, in Valencian, Llopis) who, since his will of 1478 shows that he already had a legitimate son, must have been his second wife. We do not hear of him again before 1501, when we find him active at Gandía, south of Valencia, the town that for the rest of his known life was to be the principal seat of his creations and honors. His early style of the Quattrocento is clearly preserved to us only in a single panel,[24] and, since his works at Gandía and elsewhere that fall within the Cinquecento exhibit a different but quite as essentially Italianate manner, we are justified in postulating that, before he attained the maturity of his expression, he had returned for a considerable time to his native land. The seventeen years that elapsed between 1484 and 1501, except for the notice of the marriage, would have given ample opportunity for such a sojourn.

His gifts had now at the beginning of the sixteenth century attracted the aesthetic discernment of Doña María Enríquez, who was not only the widow of Alexander VI's second, assassinated son, Giovanni Borgia (in Spanish, Juan de Borja), Duke of Gandía, but also the guardian of their son, the young Duke of the same name as his father; and on November 29, 1501, she contracted [25] with Paolo da San Leocadio to do the paintings of the retable over the high altar of the parish church in the town, which she had recently succeeded in having elevated to collegiate rank. Preserved until the conflagrations of the recent Spanish civil war, these paintings constituted Paolo's principal extant achievement and had been carefully studied by scholars as well as beautifully photographed by the Archivo Mas. The statue of Our Lady at the centre of the retable, the tabernacle,[26] the two angels simulated as upholding the *guardapolvos*, and the frames of Gothic carving for the pictures had been made by a Master Forment, whose Christian name is blank in the document of 1501 but who has generally and, in my opinion, wrongly been guessed to be the subsequently celebrated sculptor, Damián Forment. As Tramoyeres y Blasco justly pointed out,[27] the carver would be Damián's father, Pablo, for the son was too young at this date to have been entrusted with so signal a commission, although, as on a retable in the church

[24] See below, p. 17.
[25] The document is published by Chabás, *op. cit.*, 385.
[26] The tabernacle had been lost, and for it there was substituted a modern copy of Juan de Juanes's versions of the Salvator Mundi, holding the Eucharist.
[27] *Archivo de arte valenciano*, IV, 1918, p. 15, n. 1.

of the Puridad at Valencia no more than two years later,[28] he may have been one of his parent's helpers. Paolo agreed to do the gilding and polychromy of all the sculpture, and the clauses of the contract regarding the actual paintings we shall review on a future page in our detailed discussion of the monument.

It is further specified in the contract that he shall be provided with a house at Gandía for the three years, after June 24, 1502, within which he promised to complete the retable, and the duchess soon learned to prize his attainments so highly that on January 10, 1507, in a long and most interesting document,[29] she provided that he definitely transfer his citizenship from Valencia to Gandía and arranged with him for still further paintings. As a reward for Paolo's compliance she consents to take into her service and dower one of his daughters or, if the *señorita* wishes to become a nun, to do the same for another of his girls. The first of the three new altarpieces that he undertakes to execute we shall find to be partly preserved, a retable of themes to be selected by his patroness for the high altar of the church of the Franciscan convent of Sta. Clara at Gandía. The second commission was for a retable to be placed over the high altar of the chapel in the ducal palace, again with the subjects left to the lady's choice but probably connected with St. Michael, to whom the chapel was dedicated. Even before the civil war, we had altogether lost this altarpiece unless works of unascertained provenience by Paolo da San Leocadio in public and private collections thence derive or unless such is the origin of a separate panel of the Crucifixion that used to hang in a passageway in the Colegiata at Gandía but, like all other paintings in the church, was destroyed in the war. Bertaux [30] guesses it to come from one of the chapels in the church, but on the other hand he suggests that a panel of Christ bearing the Cross which hung close by it and which will immediately concern us may once have been in the palace. There are also the possibilities that the Crucifixion was a fragment of the retable for Sta. Clara or of the (otherwise lost) retable of the duchess's oratory which is the third among the altarpieces required from Paolo in the document of 1507 and in which the scene to be depicted is once more consigned to her arbitrament.

---

[28] See my vol. VI, p. 376.

[29] Published by Sanchis y Sivera, *Pintores medievales en Valencia*, 187.

[30] *Gazette des beaux-arts*, 1908, I, second article on *Monuments et souvenirs des Borgia*, p. 209.

Then follows the demand for a series of separate panels. The first item, a cover for a picture of the Saviour declared to have already been executed by him for his protectress, is the one to which we have just referred as conceivably the same as the Christ carrying the Cross in the Colegiata. Bertaux [31] advances the proposal that the picture the cover of which he was ordered in 1507 to paint may be the very piece until the war in the Colegiata but at the time when the French critic wrote in private possession in the town. The commissions of 1507 from the duchess conclude with four panels for unnamed destinations but perhaps again for further pious adornment of the palace, a Baptism, an Epiphany, a Nativity, and Christ of the Resurrection appearing to the Virgin, all of which have now strayed from our knowledge. On the same day, January 10, 1507, that this document was signed, another legal deed [32] records the duchess's concession of an annual salary to the master. It is stated by Bertaux [33] that the wood for the retables of Sta. Clara and the ducal chapel had not arrived by the beginning of 1508, probably on the evidence of a record published in a rare book, *Memorias de Gandía*, given to the French scholar by its author, Pascual Sanz y Forés.

We do not again come into contact with Paolo da San Leocadio until on July 5 and December 24, 1513, and on August 13, 1514,[34] he is remunerated for painting the shutters of a new organ in the cathedral of Valencia, the carpentry of which was designed by no less a person than Fernando Yáñez de la Almedina, who decorated also the instrument's "shoulders." [35] It has been generally held that the paintings on cloth from the lives of the Virgin and St. Martin in the Sala Capitular Antigua of the cathedral are the shutters of this organ and therefore works of Paolo da San Leocadio, but their style conclusively proves, as we shall subsequently find, that Nicolás Falcó executed them, thus involving us in a dilemma. Since one subject, St. Martin's encounter with the beggar, is divided between two pieces intended to meet when the shutters were folded together, we may discard the old tradition that the paintings were designs for tapestries

---

[31] *Ibid.*, 211.

[32] Sanchis y Sivera, *Pintores medievales en Valencia*, 192.

[33] *Op. cit.*, 213.

[34] For the documents, see Tormo in *Cultura Española*, X (1908), 562, and Sanchis y Sivera, *La catedral de Valencia*, 229; and for the painted shutters of earlier organs in the church, my vol. VI, p. 465, n. 3.

[35] See below, p. 181.

and likewise the suggestion of Tramoyeres Blasco [36] that the name in the documents, Paolo da San Leocadio, might be a loose way of referring to Felipe Pablo, who has been questionably thought a son of Paolo and whose now definitely ascertained style is very different. The only credible solutions, therefore, seem to be that Paolo merely planned and designed the pieces,[37] turning over the execution to Falcó as then a member of his shop, or that, like Jacomart,[38] he farmed out to Falcó the whole enterprise.

The six large panels with scenes from the story of St. James Major in the sacristy of the parish church of Villarreal are practically documented as works of Paolo da San Leocadio, since Rafael Martín de Viciana, in a Chronicle of Valencia published in 1564,[39] only about a half century after the paintings must have been done, states that our artist was the author of a retable in the church and since we may deduce that it decorated the high altar and so would have been devoted to subjects connected with Santiago, the edifice's patron. His words are, "The principal church of the town is under the title of Santiago, Apostle, with a retable of very fine workmanship by the hand of Paolo da San Leocadio," and he could scarcely have picked out any other than the specimen over the high altar for such specification, although as a matter of fact we shall find that the church contains a second retable, honoring the Salvator Mundi, which is shown by internal evidence to be Paolo's performance and hangs at the left upon the wall of entrance to the building. The transfer of pictures from their original places above altars to the sacristies of churches has been so frequent a phenomenon in Spain that it needs no comment. The notice by Viciana amounts to virtual documentation also because, evidently having before him the contract or a receipt for payment, he designates the retable's price as 1500 *escudos* and because his trustworthiness is demonstrated by his attribution to Paolo of the altarpiece in the Gandía Colegiata.[40] The style of the panels in the sacristy thoroughly bears out Viciana's declaration of Paolo as their creator, and the fact that he did one retable in the church pro-

---

[36] *Cultura española*, IX (1908), 143, n. 1.

[37] After writing this chapter, I am glad to find that Vicente Ferrán Salvador, in his short monograph on Paolo da San Leocadio, Valencia, 1947, p. 37, also doubts that the Italian could himself have actually painted the cycle.

[38] See my vol. VI, p. 14.

[39] See the modern reprint of the Chronicle, Valencia, Tercera parte, 1882, p. 334.

[40] Segunda parte, Valencia, 1881, p. 21.

vides objective support for his authorship of the other that has just been mentioned. Viciana [41] further assigns to him the principal altarpiece in the *parroquia* of Castellón de la Plana, the loss of which in the distant past is particularly to be regretted because the chronicler describes it as the largest in the realm of Valencia.

Paolo was the father of several children besides the Pedro Pablo singled out in the will of 1478,[42] but whether or not they were all the issue of his second wife, Isabel López, it is nowhere definitely stated. There were at least two girls, mentioned in his agreement of January 10, 1507, with the duchess of Gandía, and a son, Miguel Juan de San Leocadio, recorded [43] on April 12, 1513, as doing the polychromy of a statue of the Virgin in the cathedral of Valencia and on February 15, 1515, as given, for some purpose or other, one of the pieces of wood for the scaffolding employed in painting the shutters of the organ in the church, the commission for which his father received but which he did not carry out.[44] Whether he ever developed into anything more than the mere craftsman that these allusions imply, we have no means of knowing. We shall debate on a subsequent page the question whether another of his sons was the painter who has customarily been called Felipe Pablo de San Leocadio.

2. His Works

The early manner of Paolo da San Leocadio, prior to the first example of his mature style in 1501, the retable of the Colegiata at Gandía, is preserved to us with surety and satisfactorily in only one picture, the small *sacra conversazione* in the National Gallery, London, which we have had occasion to examine at length in volume VII.[1] Little information can be extracted from the ruins of the fresco of the Nativity in the Sala Capitular Antigua of the Valencian cathedral upon which he and Francesco Pagano were engaged from 1472 to 1476 in order to unfold to the authorities a sample of their talents. Although I am now disposed to think that Paolo may con-

---

[41] Tercera parte, p. 344.

[42] See above, p. 11.

[43] Sanchis y Sivera, *La catedral de Valencia*, 528, and *Pintores medievales en Valencia*, 226. On February 15, 1515, he is denominated merely as "the son of Master Paolo," but, since he was already working in the cathedral two years before, the reference is probably to him rather than to Felipe Pablo, who has only been guessed to be a second son.

[44] See above, p. 15. [1] Pp. 883–890.

ceivably have had a larger part in this joint enterprise than I believed when I wrote volumes VI [2] and VII,[3] executing perhaps at least the adoring young shepherd, our ignorance of Francesco's attainments forbids dogmatism, and indeed not enough of the Nativity is preserved to reveal a much more definite manner than a general Italianism.

On the other hand, the charming London *sacra conversazione*, which is signed by Paolo, exhibits a clearly marked style, but I have little to add to my analysis, in volume VII, of this style or of the problems that it raises. Although prophetic in certain ways of the later manner by which he is regularly known, as in the physical types and such appurtenances as the haloes and inscribed borders of the garments, it shows to us a painter bred in the more primitive modes of Mantegna and of the Squarcionesque artistic fashions that Mantegna had inspired at Ferrara and in Emilia whence Paolo had come. Kneaded into these modes there is a Flemish strain, apparent, for example, in the draperies and general technical procedure, but I am not yet any nearer an explanation of the sources of this strain in our painter, finding myself still only capable of guessing that he may have acquired it in Naples or at other centres in Italy where pictures from the Low Countries had been imported and somewhat imitated, or that he may actually have made a trip to northern Europe, or that the impregnation may have taken place after his arrival in Spain, which was dominated at the time by Flemish models. I have even suggested in volume VII that he may have owed something to contact with the distinguished interpretation of the Hispano-Flemish style displayed by Bermejo during his passage through Valencia. Likewise I continue to be unable to arrive at any certainty in an attempt to ascribe to Paolo da San Leocadio in his first or indeed in any period the works the indecisive similarities of which to his manner baffled me in volumes VI [4] and VII.[5] Within this group there belong the productions of the St. Narcissus Master [6] and the three pictures by the artist now generally called the Master of the Knight of Montesa, whom I have hesitatingly wished to identify with Rodrigo de Osona the elder.[7]

[2] P. 172.
[3] P. 890.
[4] Pp. 173, 240, and 250.
[5] P. 888.
[6] For recent additions to our legacy from the St. Narcissus Master, see my vol. X, p. 362.
[7] Vol. VI, pp. 192 ff.

Because of Saralegui's potent authority, his recent championship [8] of an equation of the Master of the Knight of Montesa with the young Paolo da San Leocadio or with an immediate follower has induced me to review once more the problem, but the process has left me quite as unconvinced as I was in volume VII [9] that we have to do with a single personality. Rather than to describe the Master of the Knight of Montesa as a follower of Paolo, I should prefer to think of him as merely participating in the same phase of the Valencian school, and I can see no adequate reason for Saralegui's repudiation of the possibility that, if he is not Rodrigo the elder, he might be Master Richard [10] or some of the other artistic individualities of the period whose names we know but whose styles we have not yet recovered. From this general subdivision of the school, the Spanish scholar publishes for the first time a panel formerly in the Collection of the Marquesa de Bermejillo at Madrid, which depicts the seated Madonna as anomalously accompanied at the left by the kneeling St. Michael holding a large cross that the Child with tragic symbolism fingers. Although one can read between the lines that he is prone to ascribe the work to Paolo da San Leocadio himself, he contends explicitly for no more than a location in the Italian's school or circle, pointing out, however, that it bridges the gap between the artist's earlier and later manners. My own feeling is that, despite the prominence of the Flemish ingredient in the stylistic amalgam, the picture is closer to Paolo than to the, for me, different personality, the Master of the Knight of Montesa. The nearest analogue for the Virgin's countenance, in the nature of the modelling, the marked cheek-bones, and the chiaroscuro, is the shepherd with a lamb in a Nativity in the cathedral of Valencia that I shall subsequently [11] endeavor to place among Paolo's authentic productions, but the evidence in general seems to me scarcely to justify a more definite attribution than Saralegui's cautious assignment merely to the painter's *milieu*.

[8] *Archivo español de arte*, XVIII (1945), 25 ff., and XXIII (1950), 194.

[9] Pp. 885–888. It is hard to question that Angulo (*Archivo español de arte*, XVIII, 1945, p. 383) rightly discerns in the Epiphany by the Master of the Knight of Montesa at Bayonne an acquaintance with Dürer's print of the subject dated in 1511 (Bartsch 3 and the volume on the German artist in the series *Klassiker der Kunst*, p. 312). We should thus be forced to believe that the picture was executed after 1511, later than the style would have led us to think, and it would be necessary definitely to discard an attribution to Paolo, who by this time was painting in a more mature and very different manner.

[10] See above, p. 9, and vol. VI, p. 250.   [11] P. 36.

Prior to the revolutionary disturbances of 1936, the developed and characteristic attainments of Paolo da San Leocadio were first securely incorporated in the retable over the high altar of the Colegiata at Gandía, soundly documented, dated in 1501, and in a sense preserved even now in the fine and copious photographs of the Archivo Mas. The topmost narrative compartment in the structure exhibited the Crucifixion for which the contract calls, and underneath, grouped about the statue from the Forment atelier, were representations of the Seven Joys of the Virgin likewise demanded in the agreement, comprising, in accord with the partial latitude permitted in the choice of such subjects,[12] the Annunciation (Fig. 1), Nativity, Epiphany,[13] Resurrection, Ascension, Pentecost, and (directly above the statue and below the Crucifixion) the Dormition. The four scenes from the Passion required by the document in the predella were aligned at the sides of the modern tabernacle, the Agony in the Garden, Via Dolorosa (Fig. 2), Deposition, and Entombment. In conformity to Valencian practice, the *guardapolvos* were very much featured, and the themes, left in the contract to the duchess's choice, were of the kind regularly encountered in the retables of the region, a bust of the blessing Eternal Father at the summit and then effigies of saints in logical pairs. Beside the Crucifixion were Michael and the Guardian Angel of the Kingdom; next, on the cross-pieces, half-lengths of the monastic theologians, Bernard and Augustine; then in full stature, balancing each other, the ascetics, Francis and Jerome; the frequent iconographic companions, Sebastian and Fabian; and finally the two St. Johns. The subjects of the painted doors at the sides of the altar, which had long been lost, are again consigned by the document to the dowager's decision, but they may very well have been the regular themes for these spots, Sts. Peter and Paul.

It has commonly been recognized that the foundation of Paolo's art is the style of Ferrara, Bologna, and Emilia in general at the end of the Quattrocentro and beginning of the Cinquecento, but what has not been realized is that he quite equals in talent, if he does not indeed surpass, the outstanding exponents of this style who remained at home, Francia and the personality usually identified with Ercole di Giulio Cesare Grandi.[14] Among the many masters active in Emilia

---

[12] Vol. VIII, p. 294.
[13] Illustrated in my vol. VII, fig. 366.
[14] Thought by some critics to be Ercole Roberti in a late phase.

FIG. 1. PAOLO DA SAN LEOCADIO. ANNUNCIATION AND ST. BERNARD,
SECTION OF RETABLE OF HIGH ALTAR. COLEGIATA, GANDÍA
(*Photo. Archivo Mas*)

FIG. 2. PAOLO DA SAN LEOCADIO. VIA DOLOROSA, SECTION OF
RETABLE OF HIGH ALTAR. COLEGIATA, GANDÍA
(*Photo. Archivo Mas*)

such as Costa, it is Francia and "Ercole Grandi" whom he most resembles, and in types, color, landscapes, and technical method he approximates very closely the works that they have bequeathed to us. The episode of the two thieves hounded on to Calvary, which was introduced into the background of the Via Dolorosa, looked as if there had hovered in his mind vague memories of the representation of the march to Golgotha, in the Gallery at Dresden, by an earlier member of the Ferrarese circle, Ercole Roberti. Bertaux has indicated the startling similarity of the separate panel of Christ bearing the Cross in the Colegiata, which will subsequently demand our study, to one of Maineri's favorite themes, but otherwise he and Paolo are interrelated only in their participation in the general Emilian manner of the period. Inasmuch as this manner, especially as embodied in Francia and "Ercole Grandi," had not been evolved by the time that Paolo betook himself to Spain in 1472, it is necessary to assume, as Bertaux also has declared, that he had made a visit or visits of some length to his native heath before he undertook the Gandía commission, and his biography has shown that the Valencian records leave sufficiently extensive chronological lacunas for such travelling.

If we look back at the *sacra conversazione* of his earlier period, we arrive at the conclusion that the Flemish strain has now at Gandía receded in his artistic make-up in favor of the new submersion in the streams of Italian painting, and it is difficult to follow Bertaux [15] in discerning a very significant, persisting indebtedness to the production of the Low Countries. Now and then he may have lifted from Gerard David suggestions for his personal types, particularly in his conception of the more aged Virgin, and once in a while he gives to a fold of cloth what may be a Flemish rather than an Italian twist; but the majority of the countenances, the draperies, and the technical procedure merely fall within the Emilian division of the Italian school. The manifest delight with which he multiplied the implements of St. Joseph's trade in the ruined chamber in the background of the Nativity does not necessarily by itself point to a dependence upon precedents in the Low Countries, and the elaborate spatial interests implied by a perspective of two apartments, one leading into the other, behind the room in which the Annunciation occurred are almost, if not quite, as characteristic of Italian as of Flemish pictorial science. The Death of Our Lady appeared to be a free adaptation from

[15] *Op. cit., Gazette des beaux-arts*, 1908, I, 209.

Schongauer's popular print of the subject;[16] but even a master active in Italy might have turned to this source for compositional ideas, and, without direct northern influence, Paolo could have been inspired to use the German cartoon by his environment in Spain, where Schongauer's engravings and particularly his rendering of the Dormition furnished many painters with ideas.

Otherwise, save in the retable's general arrangement and the composition of the Pentecost, not much was owed even to the Spanish artistic *milieu* by Paolo, who remained in essential style true to his Italian blood. Indeed the Spaniards' love of gold and of brilliant brocades in their sacred art was very largely set aside by him. For the traditional effigies of the saints on the conventional spaces of the *guardapolvos* he abided by the Spanish custom of gold backgrounds, here tooled with a brocaded design, but in the narrative scenes, if we leave out of account the haloes, such auric decoration was the exception, as on the Virgin's throne in the Pentecost, rather than the rule. As a matter of fact he used golden plaques for haloes only in the body of the retable, evidently, as we shall find also in one of his later monuments,[17] for the sake of conspicuousness at this higher level, and, when he came to the predella, he reverted to the delicate, filmy nimbuses that he had introduced into his early *sacra conversazione*. Our Lord actually wore this sort of nimbus even in the Resurrection much further above in the structure. In Italy itself the garments are often edged with golden borders, which in the Gandía retable, as habitually with Paolo, not infrequently took the form of fragments of apposite, pious inscriptions. For example, in the Via Dolorosa, there was written on St. John's tunic a verse from the first chapter of his Gospel, "Et verbum caro factum est"; in the Deposition we were able to read on his mantle, "Hic est discipulus ille" from the end of this book; and in the Entombment the bottom of the Virgin's cloak carried the familiar words from the Lamentations of Jeremiah, I, 12, referring to the Passion, "Videte si est dolor sicut dolor meus." Among his Spanish rivals, even his Valencian contemporaries appear to have impressed Paolo very little, except in so far as he adopted their programs for altarpieces.

He is partially saved from the somewhat saccharine sentiment of

---

[16] This seems to me the source rather than, as Bertaux thinks, Joos van Cleve's treatments of the theme, which indeed postdate the Gandía retable.

[17] See below, p. 36.

Francia by the serene nobility with which he invests his actors and by the greater and more incisive virility of his older men. Ordinarily he draws quite as well as his rival at Bologna, nor does he yield to him in modelling in color. The phrenetic Apostle reading in the foreground of the Pentecost betrayed that he still experienced some primitive difficulty in coping with animated or unusual postures, but he succeeded somewhat better in the soldier rushing away in terror from the risen Saviour. With the hair blown wildly behind his profile by his distracted haste, this soldier and his deeply sleeping companion in the lower right corner of the scene belonged to a series of striking and memorable figures that emerge in Paolo's creations. The affection for settings of magnificent architecture of the Renaissance that from the first had distinguished the schools of Ferrara and Bologna resulted with him in grander and more complicated edifices, sometimes conceived as Roman ruins. Relying upon his intrinsic gifts as a painter for his effects, he was usually satisfied to cling to the main outlines of the traditional compositions and to exalt these through his honest craft, but his intellect was sufficiently elastic to admit of innovations, when he wished it, as in the Resurrection where he placed off centre Christ issuing from the sarcophagus. He tended to reserve his imagination for the related scenes with which, in diminished scale, like so many of his predecessors and contemporaries, he took satisfaction in enlivening the backgrounds. In the Dormition, it was merely the episode of the Virgin dropping her girdle to St. Thomas seen through a doorway at the right, but the Via Dolorosa exhibited in the distance on Calvary the sinister and unusual theme of the preparation of the ground and crosses for the triple execution and of the thieves' previous arrival at the spot, so that the whole picture was extended to something of the epic breadth of narrative comprised in Tintoretto's Crucifixion in the Scuola di S. Rocco at Venice. Properly concentrating upon the sincere representation of the religious subjects in terms of the highest artistic gifts that he could summon into service, he did not ordinarily exploit his purely technical interests. The principal exceptions were the spatial studies in the Annunciation and his fondness for introducing among the subordinate episodes in his pleasing landscapes figures, often mounted, which he foreshortened inward with their backs toward us. The most conspicuous instance was perceived in the Crucifixion, where soldiers, thus treated, were just beginning to

disappear over the brow of the hill of Golgotha, but examples occurred also in the Via Dolorosa, Deposition, and Entombment.

The fate of the retable in Sta. Clara at Gandía for which Paolo da
San Leocadio contracted in 1507 is a somewhat complicated story.
Bertaux [18] states that at the time of his visit before 1908 its panels
were hidden from the public in the *clausura* of the convent but that
the abbess kindly had four of them brought forth for him to study
and photograph, compartments depicting the Nativity, Epiphany,[19]
Resurrection, and Death of the Virgin. The two latter panels eventually reached the Diocesan Museum at Valencia as Nos. 37 and 38,
together with a third, Pentecost, No. 39, of the existence of which the
French scholar was evidently not cognizant. Although, like almost
all the treasures of the Museo Diocesano, these paintings perished at
the outbreak of the civil war in 1936, they had survived into modern
times and thus could be scrutinized by me and other investigators, as
well as thoroughly photographed. That they belonged to the series of
which Bertaux saw four is established not only by the explicit statements of Antonio Barberá Sentamáns in his Catalogue of the Museum [20] and of Tormo in his book, *Valencia, los Museos*,[21] but also by
Bertaux's account of the curious composition for the Death of the
Virgin (Fig. 3). Instead of lying in her bed, Our Lady knelt upon it,
and Santiago was not included among the Apostles surrounding her
but appeared in his pilgrim's costume approaching in the distance,
according to Paolo's custom of introducing into his backgrounds minor
incidents. At my own sojourns in Gandía, I was not privileged to
penetrate the *clausura* and examine the pieces that there remained;
but Ferrán Salvador, in his short monograph of 1947 on Paolo da San
Leocadio,[22] declares not only the Nativity and Epiphany but also an
Ascension to have existed in the convent until the civil war, describing
the compositions in detail and giving the dimensions of the panels.[23]
Indeed, through the kind intermediation of my friend, Don Leandro
de Saralegui, I am informed that these three compartments blessedly
escaped the forces of destruction in 1936 and that, although the
Epiphany is still kept in *clausura,* the Nativity and Ascension can now

---

[18] *Op. cit.*, 212.
[19] In *op. cit.*, pp. 213 and 215, the Nativity and Epiphany are illustrated.
[20] P. 18. Barberá mistakenly calls the Death of the Virgin the Annunciation.
[21] Pp. 119 and 128.
[22] Pp. 30–31.
[23] 1.32 metres in height by .86 in width.

Fɪɢ. 3. PAOLO DA SAN LEOCADIO. DORMITION FROM STA. CLARA,
GANDÍA. DIOCESAN MUSEUM, VALENCIA
(*Photo. Archivo Mas*)

be seen by the visitor, being incorporated in the present retable over the high altar of the church of Sta. Clara.

I have suggested above that the original retable of the high altar is one of the possibilities for the source of the separate panel of the Crucifixion which hung in the Colegiata at Gandía, and we shall come upon pictures in private hands that conceivably also might have this derivation, a Lamentation over the Dead Christ in the Muntadas Collection and one of three versions of the Agony in the Garden, now belonging to the Scherer, Montortal, and Corredor Collections. In any case the known compartments from the altarpiece reveal that, strangely enough, at least the majority of its subjects were the same as those of the retable in the Colegiata.

The only real change that has taken place in his style since the creation of this retable is a very limited renunciation of the blandness of his Emilian types and a slight tendency, especially in his older, masculine actors, to the intensity and sharpness of oncoming mannerism. Again Paolo has not attempted much variation of his compositions. The Nativity and Epiphany are only insignificantly altered. In the Resurrection he abandoned the innovation that he had essayed in the retable of the Colegiata and returned to the traditional Spanish composition with Christ erect upon the sarcophagus at the middle; but he strained his abilities by filling the space with a greater number of Roman soldiers whose violent and unconventional attitudes he could not entirely manage. In the Pentecost he forewent this expression of excitement which he had sought to infuse into the version of the subject in the Colegiata, and he achieved a more compact and monumental composition. The only important innovation occurred in the Dormition. Although he reverted to the customary sidewise position of the bed, abjuring its foreshortening towards the back of the room, which in the Colegiata he had imitated from Schongauer's print, he piqued our interest by depicting the Virgin not recumbent but raptly kneeling upon the couch and by the emphasis upon Santiago that we have noted above. Tormo [24] interprets the scene as her farewell to the Apostles, but she was represented in an attitude rather of prayerful expectancy, and, as a matter of fact, in not conceiving her as lying in bed, Paolo was following very closely the first account of the Assumption in the *Golden Legend* where it is said, "In medio eorum ardentibus lampadibus et lucernis *consedit*." In any case, no matter what moment of the

[24] *Valencia: los Museos,* 128.

story he intended to embody, he departed from the regular iconography of the subject. The haloes throughout are now of the filmy sort. As a gauge of the master's eminence as a pure craftsman, we may select the delicacy with which he reverently delineated Our Lady in the Pentecost and his lovely painting of her blue mantle in this scene as well as in the Dormition.

Of the two panels separately hung in the Colegiata at Gandía, the Crucifixion, whatever its original function,[25] was similar to the example in the retable over the high altar, except that, whereas in the latter version the treatment was devotional and therefore the participants in the foreground beneath the single cross of Christ were confined to the Virgin, St. John, and the Magdalene, the detached rendering approached the tragedy of Calvary from the historical standpoint, comprising the gibbets of the two thieves and additional actors below. Paolo sought further variation by representing the Virgin and St. John as seated on the ground in the compartment of the retable and as standing in the separate panel. The use of the filmy haloes in this panel, which, if a part of an altarpiece, must have been situated at a lofty point where we should have expected the more perceptible nimbuses of solid gold,[26] may be taken for what little it is worth as implying a derivation from the assemblage in Sta. Clara.

The chief significance of the other dissociated panel in the Colegiata, a half-length of Christ bearing the Cross,[27] is that in its very intimate relation to Maineri's versions of the subject [28] and particularly to the example at Modena, it conspicuously demonstrated the fact that I have already stressed, namely, Paolo's persistent faithfulness, despite his environment, to the Italian school in which he had been trained. A repetition, apparently by his own hand, is deposited in the Sala Capitular of the cathedral of Barcelona.

My eyes are incapable of following those of Bertaux [29] in penetrating to Paolo's types and style beneath the liberal repaint upon a small panel of the Virgen de la Leche that decorated the chapel of the palace at Gandía at least by the beginning of May, 1546, but is now in

---

[25] See above, p. 14. The picture is illustrated by Bertaux, *op. cit.*, 207.
[26] See above, p. 24.
[27] Illustrated by Bertaux, *op. cit.*, 211.
[28] See above, p. 23.
[29] *Op. cit.*, 214. The panel is discussed and illustrated on pp. 46–48 of the book by Federico Cervós and Juan María Solá, *El palacio ducal de Gandía*, Barcelona, 1904.

the church of the Descalzas Reales at Madrid. The Cosmas and Damian that he ascribes to our master [30] in a private collection at Valencia are probably identical with two panels which passed into the Diocesan Museum of the city as Nos. 22 and 23 and for which I shall eventually claim the authorship of Juan de Juanes as virtual replicas of these saints in his retable in the parish church of Onda.

One must diametrically disagree with Mayer's [31] assignment of the six large and virtually documented panels [32] from the story of St. James Major in the sacristy of the parish church at Villarreal to Paolo da San Leocadio's beginnings, and instead it is necessary to classify them among his latest extant achievements, not only almost certainly subsequent to the works that we have hitherto considered but pretty clearly carried out in part by one or more assistants. The first of the series depicts Santiago delivering a sermon, while through a portal we see, as one of the episodes often introduced by Paolo into his backgrounds, the Apostle delivering his pilgrim's staff to the enchanter Hermogenes for a talisman against demoniacal attacks. Then follow the scenes of the high priest Abiathar accusing St. James before Herod and of the Apostle's decapitation. The other three compartments are concerned with events after his death. The bulls bring his body into the palace of Queen Lupa, and at the rear of the edifice there is added the representation of Santiago christening her (Fig. 4). The next panel exhibits the well known tale of the German youth, on his way to Compostela, falsely charged by the innkeeper in the presence of his parents with having stolen a cup. A rope is being tied about his neck so that he may be dragged away to be hanged, but the climax is oddly consigned merely to a subordinate scene in the landscape, the father and mother discovering on their return from the pilgrimage after more than a month that St. James has supported him alive on the gallows during all this interval. The final compartment unfolds the essentially Spanish incident in Santiago's posthumous activity, his leading of the Christians to a belated victory over the Moors in the battle of Clavijo.

It is not only the darkened condition of the series that is responsible for what Mayer stigmatizes as their dryness. He attributes this defect

[30] *Op. cit.*, 215.

[31] *Zeitschrift für bildende Kunst*, XX (1908–1909), 128, and *Geschichte der spanischen Malerei*, second Spanish edition, 1942, p. 136.

[32] See above, p. 16.

FIG. 4. PAOLO DA SAN LEOCADIO. BULLS BRINGING BODY OF ST.
JAMES MAJOR TO QUEEN LUPA'S PALACE, SECTION OF RETABLE.
CHURCH OF SANTIAGO, VILLARREAL
(*Photo. Archivo Mas*)

to the assumption that they were productions of Paolo's earlier period, but artists are not usually dry in their youth, as is charmingly evident in our master's *sacra conversazione* at London, and are likely to become so only through weariness with life and their profession as older men. Something of the freshness and incisiveness of the works done by Paolo at Gandía has died out of the Villarreal panels, but another reason for ascribing them to a late moment in his career is that larger sections were apparently turned over to his atelier, with which at the start of his career he could hardly have afforded to surround himself. For instance, at least almost all the compartment of St. James's sermon seems to have been executed on Paolo's design by an assistant who, unlike the master himself, reveals some admiration for the contemporary achievements of Fernando Yáñez de la Almedina and Fernando de Llanos, as is demonstrated especially by the woman who gazes directly out of the picture at the extreme right in the Apostle's congregation; and the intrusion of a collaborator is fairly obvious here and there in the scene of the accused German devotee of Santiago. The majority of the types, however, plainly flowed from Paolo's brush, and beneath the deterioration of the panels we can see that the tonality of color was originally the same as when he was employed at Gandía; but the forms have succumbed further in the direction of an arid classicism and of less decisive draughtsmanship. In several of the compartments he ventured the problem of depicting high activity, succeeding rather well in the case of the terrified Queen Lupa and her attendants, but the mêlée of Clavijo was above his capacity, although even greater painters than he have perpetrated quite as unconvincing representations of the difficult theme of battle when they have not been willing to fall back, like Paolo Uccello and Piero della Francesca, upon schematization. In the panel of St. James's martyrdom spectators peer or lean from upper windows as in the St. Narcissus Master's scene of the resuscitation of a dead woman, but the details are too slight to supply any indication that this Master was Paolo da San Leocadio at a prior stage in his development.[33]

The undocumented but stylistically authenticated retable of the Salvator Mundi,[34] at one time relegated to the *trasagrario* [35] of the same church at Villarreal but now set on the west wall at the left

---

[33] See above, p. 18.   [34] See above, p. 16.
[35] See Sarthou y Carreres in *Museum* (Barcelona), VI (1918–1920), 177.

FIG. 5. PAOLO DA SAN LEOCADIO. RETABLE. CHURCH OF SANTIAGO,
VILLARREAL

(*Photo. Archivo Mas*)

(Fig. 5) might give the impression to some critics of being an earlier work than the altarpiece of St. James; but this is because the main sections of the structure are occupied by single effigies of holy personages, where conservatism would be naturally expected, and we soon discover the narrative scenes in the pinnacle and predella to share in the late manner that we have found the Santiago panels to embody. The retable of the Saviour has occasionally been arbitrarily attributed to an otherwise unknown artist, "C. L. Monsó," because these letters are written in long hand between the names of the continents, Asia, Africa, and Europe, which appear in Roman capitals on the globe at Our Lord's feet in the principal panel; but the style indisputably declares for Paolo's authorship, and some other elucidation must be found for the "Monsó" inscription. It may very well be a much later addition by the kind of epigraphical maniac who wishes to perpetuate his name through scribbling it upon monuments, or, if it does come from the beginning of the sixteenth century, it is capable of many explanations, for instance, as the signature of the donor or of the rector of the church at Villarreal at the time when Paolo executed the paintings.[36]

The main body of the retable is occupied by three standing effigies, the Salvator Mundi at the centre, perhaps suggested by the cult and image of the *Longitudo Domini Nostri* in the cathedral of Valencia,[37] and in the lateral compartments, St. Ursula (at the left)[38] and St. Eulalia (at the right). The left page of the book held by Our Lord contains an adaptation of the second and ninth verses of the fifth chapter of the Apocalypse, and on the right page is written, "Ecce salvator, spes unica mundi, qui caeli fabricator ades, qui conditor [39] orbis," with the rest of the relative clause lacking. The three forms are set against backgrounds of brocaded gold, the beauty and fineness of which show that Paolo must have hired one of the most skilled indigenous exponents of this kind of work in which the Spaniards uniformly excelled. The subject of the pinnacle is the Annunciation, and the Crucifixion is thus, anomalously for Spain, relegated to the

[36] In *Boletín de la Sociedad Castellonense de Cultura*, XXV (1949), 188, Saralegui suggests that in *Monso* there may be hidden the first part of some longer surname of the donor beginning with *Mont*, since one of the charges on the escutcheons at the retable's sides seems to be a mountain (surmounted by a fleur-de-lis).

[37] See vol. IV, p. 586.

[38] Illustrated as fig. 365 in my vol. VII.

[39] Spelled *cauditor*, either through an original mistake or through an ignorant, later alteration.

middle of the predella, flanked by four other scenes from the Passion, the Agony in the Garden, Flagellation, Lamentation over the Dead Christ, and the Entombment. The *guardapolvos* are also preserved, except for the crowning piece. Beside the Annunciation are St. Agatha and (?) St. Lucy; [40] below on the cross-bits the *motif* of virgin martyrs established in the body of the retable is continued with half-lengths of Sts. Margaret and Barbara; next, of the four other, standing figures, St. Giles is opposite St. Francis; and finally St. Sebastian constitutes a balance to the Baptist.

The attribution really needs no demonstration to anyone at all familiar with Paolo's style. His easily recognizable types recur again and again, for example particularly in the central effigy of the Saviour, the St. Ursula, and the Virgin of the Annunciation. The composition for this scene is slightly varied from the rendering at Gandía, but the theophany of God the Father sending the dove is managed in just the same curious way. The Agony in the Garden was very similarly treated at Gandía, where practically the same person acted the part of St. John. The redeemed thief in the Crucifixion actually repeats the corresponding figure in the version of the theme that hung separately in the Gandía Colegiata, and in the distance we descry two soldiers, one again mounted, turning their backs on us in the attitude in which Paolo so liked to depict his subordinate actors. It is even to be doubted whether he consigned so much to his shop as in the altarpiece of Santiago. Certain passages, particularly in the predella, look as if they might be the work of an assistant, but the effects are probably due, at least largely, to the impaired condition of the panels and to retouching. The Flagellation suggests, perhaps fortuitously, that Paolo might be remembering the treatment of the subject from Signorelli's early period now in the Brera at Milan, but the two scourgers betray even more clearly than his other attempts at movement that he could not vie with the great Central Italian master in the representation of violent activities. In the formal images in the principal section of the retable and on the *guardapolvos*, the haloes are gold plaques, but the employment of this kind of nimbus in the high placed Annunciation, whereas the specimens in the predella

[40] At my visit to Villarreal I failed to note who the pendant to St. Agatha is; but she would naturally be St. Lucy, as in a panel of the circle of the Perea Master also at Villarreal (see below, p. 423), and, so far as the darkness of the Mas photograph reveals, the figure seems to carry a plate containing eyes.

are of the filmy class, tends to confirm the theory [41] that it was for greater visibility that he retained the traditional Spanish sort at the tops of his structures.

The one relic of Paolo da San Leocadio's developed manner that still remained in a sacred edifice at Valencia itself until its destruction [42]

Fig. 6. PAOLO DA SAN LEOCADIO. ADORATION OF SHEPHERDS.
CATHEDRAL, VALENCIA
(*Photo. Archivo Mas*)

in the civil war, a rather large, horizontal panel of the Adoration of the Shepherds in the chapel of the Trinidad at the left of the entrance in the cathedral (Fig. 6), brings us to the separate, single pictures in various places or collections that must be ascribed to him on internal evidence. Conforming very obviously to his style and methods, it exhibited such actual repetitions of his types as: the vigorously de-

[41] See above, p. 24.
[42] So far as I can inform myself, it is not among the objects of art in the cathedral that survived the war.

lineated figure of the kneeling shepherd, who should be compared, for instance, with the Apostle in profile at the right in the Ascension in the retable of the Colegiata at Gandía and the Apostle in the lower right corner of the Dormition from Sta. Clara; the St. Joseph who reiterates the man on the left arm of the cross assisting in the lowering of the sacred body in the Deposition in the Colegiata; and the curly-headed shepherd holding the lamb for whom direct counterparts are forthcoming in the kneeling rustic in the Nativity of the Colegiata and especially in the standing youth at the extreme left in the version of the theme done for the Sta. Clara altarpiece. The Virgin also, with her undulating tresses, fell within the norm to which he clung when he represented her in her youth. The composition was only slightly and pleasantly varied from his other treatments of the subject. The shape of the panel was scarcely such as to have fitted into an ordinary Valencian retable, and its original function is an unsolved problem. The evidence was not sufficient for determining whether the date lay just before, during, or after his employment at Gandía.

In any case he did a very little altered replica as the principal section of an altarpiece now in private possession at Barcelona (Fig. 7). The constitution of the structure is peculiar in one or two respects, but I can see no valid reason for refusing to believe that it has come down to us in its original arrangement and frames of the Renaissance. The whole main body of the altarpiece is occupied by the Adoration of the Shepherds, extended beyond the scope of the version in the cathedral of Valencia into a vertical rectangle so as to fill properly the space. Above this and above the intervening and elaborate top of the frame of the Adoration a representation of St. Jerome doing penance in a landscape forms a pinnacle (not included in the illustration), and there is a predella displaying in half-lengths at the centre the Dead Christ in His tomb, at the left the Visitation, and at the right a second figure of the penitent St. Jerome paired with another hermit, St. Onuphrius. It is indeed odd that Jerome should be twice honored in the retable, but, since the double introduction of the same saint into an altarpiece, once in a narrative scene (as in the pinnacle) and again as a mere subordinate effigy, is not an absolutely unparalleled phenomenon,[43] we are forbidden to take this factor as proof that the

---

[43] I am not referring here, of course, to the common custom of representing a sacred personage in the body of an altarpiece and under him in the predella an episode from his life but to the much more unusual occurrence of both an effigy and an episode in secondary sections of the structure.

FIG. 7. PAOLO DA SAN LEOCADIO. RETABLE OF ADORATION OF THE
SHEPHERDS. PRIVATE COLLECTION, BARCELONA
(*Photo. Archivo Mas*)

pinnacle or the predella was not a part of the assemblage, as first conceived. Still stranger is the insertion of half-lengths of the two participants in the Annunciation, in simple frames like those of the predella, filling the upper corners of the Adoration in the body of the altarpiece and thus hiding bits of the landscape, but internal evidence shows that these insertions were executed by Paolo or at least by some member of his atelier and so would probably have been parts of the original enterprise and intended to be thus placed.

The St. Jerome in the pinnacle betrays nothing discordant with an attribution to Paolo himself, who painted exactly similar figures of bearded old men in the Dormitions of the Gandía retable and of the Diocesan Museum, Valencia, and in the Pentecost of this Museum. The analogy of the Dead Christ of the predella to the Saviour both of the Deposition in the retable in the Colegiata at Gandía and of the separate Crucifixion in this church would appear to place the panel likewise in the category of Paolo's own creations. Parallels may be easily found also to the figures in the other subordinate compartments. The participants in the Annunciation, for instance, were nearly duplicated in the rendering of the theme in the Gandía retable, and the Magdalene of the Crucifixion in this retable incorporated the type used for the Virgin of the Visitation; but, if one thinks that he discerns in the Annunciation, Visitation, and the half-lengths of Sts. Jerome and Onuphrius in the altarpiece at Barcelona a somewhat less delicate and drier craft than in Paolo's own handiwork and a slightly farther advance into the modes of the full Renaissance, no harm would be done by acceding to the theory that the master might have turned over these sections to an assistant.

Although no document has been discovered recording the fact, Paolo must have done a capacious retable for the town of Villar del Arzobispo, west of Valencia, from which a single, large panel representing the Dormition was preserved until the civil war as No. 43 in the Valencian Diocesan Museum (Fig. 8).[44] Since, as with the Adoration of the Shepherds in the cathedral, the attribution has not hitherto been made, it is necessary to tax the reader's patience with a few of the most convincing pieces of proof, which even the ruinous condition of the picture, as it was to be seen in the Museum, did not hide. The Apostle holding the processional cross was practically the

[44] I have not discovered whether it was one of the meagre number of pieces in the Museum saved from the iconoclasm of 1936.

FIG. 8. PAOLO DA SAN LEOCADIO. DORMITION FROM VILLAR DEL
ARZOBISPO. DIOCESAN MUSEUM, VALENCIA
(*Photo. Archivo Mas*)

same person as the kneeling shepherd in the cathedral Adoration, so that we can use for him the same parallels in Paolo's other works. The one of the Twelve directly behind him incorporated a recurrent type in the master's production, illustrated, for instance, by the Apostle in profile at the left in the Ascension of the Gandía Colegiata. For the St. Peter with the aspergillum he used the same individual as in the Dormition from Sta. Clara, where, in the upper left corner, this Apostle held, instead, a candle and a book of offices, and this compartment from Sta. Clara furnished, in another Apostle looking downward at the right and away from the Virgin, an exact analogue for the mystically intense glance so peculiar to Paolo da San Leocadio that was illustrated in the panel from Villar by St. Peter's foremost companion. Our Lady, as in the subordinate episode in the background she was received into heaven, displayed a countenance regularly used by Paolo for women and young men, for example in one of the disciples of St. James in the Villarreal representation of the scene at Queen Lupa's palace, but the principal figure of the Virgin upon her bed looked as if it might have suffered somewhat from repaint. In contrast to his other treatments of the subject, he abided by the traditional composition, with Mary recumbent upon a bed stretched horizontally across the space, as in the renderings of the Dormition by his Valencian predecessor, Juan Rexach. The lessened serenity of the types implied that the Villar panel should be classified among Paolo's latest achievements.

Of a number of his most memorable creations that have strayed into private hands, one belongs to the great Muntadas Collection at Barcelona, a Lamentation over the Dead Christ the comparatively small size of which implies a predella as its source (Fig. 9).[45] He has not bothered to vary much the composition that he devised for the subject in the predella of the retable of the Saviour at Villarreal but once more seems to say to us that his mere craft is enough to give the picture distinction. The presence of this personal craft at its highest is so obvious that, without need of analysis, his authorship is self-apparent.

[45] No. 226 on p. 61 of the Catalogue. The dimensions are 90 centimetres in height by 67 in width. Quite independently of me, Saralegui perceived Paolo to be the author: *Archivo español de arte*, XVIII (1945), 24. Ferrán Salvador (monograph on Paolo da San Leocadio, 31, n. 1), writing in 1946, states that the picture was then kept in the family's near-lying country estate at Badalona.

FIG. 9. PAOLO DA SAN LEOCADIO. LAMENTATION OVER THE DEAD
CHRIST. MUNTADAS COLLECTION, BARCELONA
(*Courtesy of the Heirs of Don Matías Muntadas, Conde de Santa María de Sans*)

The inevitableness of the attribution to Paolo da San Leocadio is quite as manifest and his gifts are quite as finely demonstrated in no less than three separate versions of the Agony in the Garden. Since the subject naturally found a place in countless altarpieces, it is probable that so many treatments by Paolo are preserved through chance and not through any predilection for the theme on his part or that of his patrons. Again he refuses to descend to an appeal by mere innovations in the composition, which is much the same in all three examples, following very closely the cartoons of the subject that he utilized at Gandía and Villarreal. In the panel of the Agony in the Garden once in the Collection of Carl W. Scherer at Lucerne,[46] but purchased originally in Italy (Fig. 10), the style, however placidly beautiful, betrays slightly more primitive limitations than the Gandía and Villarreal renderings, and yet it is far more advanced than the still somewhat Squarcionesque manner of the early *sacra conversazione* at London, giving evidence of acquaintance with the developed attainments of Francia and "Ercole Grandi." The likelihood is that the Scherer panel was executed at the very beginning of Paolo's mature period immediately prior to his sojourn in Gandía, but, since the differences from the retable of 1501 in the Colegiata are almost infinitesimal and in any case chronological judgments based upon subtle degrees of stylistic progress in artists, who may vacillate somewhat at a given moment, are very delicate, untrustworthy affairs,[47] it is not out of the question that the picture should have been a part of either of the lost works commissioned in 1507, the retable for the chapel of the palace at Gandía or the altarpiece of the duchess's oratory.[48] The use of gold plaques as haloes would seem to exclude the picture from the altarpiece for Sta. Clara, although the retable in the Colegiata and that of the Saviour at Villarreal show that sometimes he varied his practice in this respect within a single monument; and the manner of the Dormition from Villar del Arzobispo is definitely too advanced to have admitted the Scherer panel within the precincts of the same assemblage.[49]

[46] The dimensions are 1.65 metres in height by 1.25 in width.

[47] See vol. X, pp. 66 and 402.

[48] See above, p. 14.

[49] After writing this paragraph, I am glad to be confirmed in the attribution by finding in the Catalogue of the Sales at the Fischer Gallery, Lucerne, on May 25–27, 1944, where the picture is entered as No. 695, that August L. Mayer suggested that it should be "brought into connection with Paolo da San Leocadio."

FIG. 10. PAOLO DA SAN LEOCADIO. AGONY IN THE GARDEN. SCHERER
COLLECTION, LUCERNE

With entire justice Saralegui [50] has consigned to Paolo the second separate version of the Agony in the Garden, a panel belonging to the Collection of the Marqués de Montortal at Valencia. As exhibiting perhaps slightly greater maturity in drawing and modelling than the Gandía and Lucerne treatments, it would tend to substantiate not only Saralegui's desire to seek a date after the first Gandía retable but also his surmise that it could have been a piece of one of the retables ordered by the duchess of Gandía in 1507, achievements that, as I stated in the last paragraph, seem to me less likely to have comprised the Lucerne picture. I should be loath to believe that it was executed subsequently to the example in the Villarreal predella, but a year at least as late as this predella may legitimately be guessed for the third separate version, a panel in the Collection of Don Ricardo Corredor de Arana at Madrid.[51]

So far as the rather limited evidence goes, I am very strongly inclined to subscribe to Saralegui's [52] attribution to Paolo of a fragment in the Collection of Don José Navarro Alcácer at Valencia aligning as half-lengths Sts. Thaddaeus and Philip. The former Apostle reproduces one of the artist's recurrent types of old men, and the St. Philip seems too closely analogous in features to such a figure as the Saviour in the Montortal Agony in the Garden to admit any other possibility of authorship. Saralegui perceives resemblances to the productions of the Master of the Knight of Montesa, but they appear

---

[50] *Arte español*, XVII (1947), 36.

[51] In an account of the Collection in the *Boletín de la Sociedad Española de Excursiones*, LVI (1948), 234, the Agony in the Garden is wrongly placed in the school of Toledo and incorrectly supposed to be a companion-piece of a Flagellation by Fernando de Llanos also belonging to Señor Corredor: see below, p. 255. The classification in the school of Toledo was doubtless provoked by an alleged provenience of both panels, as I am informed by my eminent friend, Don Leandro de Saralegui, from the monastery of San Martín de Valdeiglesias, one of the principal focuses of the activity of the Toledan painter, Juan Correa de Vivar (cf. my vol. IX, p. 305); but I refuse to believe that Paolo and Llanos could have worked for so distant a Castilian site, and the provenience, as in so many other, demonstrable instances, must be falsely reported. The dimensions of the two panels are now identical, 1.99 metres in height by 1.31 in width, but it is highly probable that they have been cut to the same size in order to serve as companion-pieces. After ascribing the Corredor picture to Paolo, I was heartened by Saralegui's independent arrival at the same conclusion in an article published in the *Archivo de arte español*, XXIII (1950), 195.

[52] *Archivo español de arte*, XXIII (1950), 194. He identifies the former figure as Matthias, but, although the emblems of certain of the Apostles are sometimes confusedly interchanged, the halberd carried by the saint in question in the Navarro panel regularly belongs to Thaddaeus, whereas Matthias has the axe or lance: see my vol. IX, p. 864, n. 2.

FIG. 11. PAOLO DA SAN LEOCADIO(?). PREDELLA. COLLECTION OF MRS. FRANCISCA REYES, NEW YORK

(Courtesy of the owner)

to me as indeterminate as the other correspondences in which I have failed [53] to discover enough concreteness to substantiate the theory that this Master could be equivalent to the yet immature Paolo da San Leocadio. The halberd of St. Thaddaeus displays a series of letters which, like so many others in the Spanish paintings of the period, carry for us no sure sense but for which Saralegui most tentatively suggests several ingenious interpretations.

After a diligent search through the several schools of Spain at the beginning of the sixteenth century, the output of Paolo provides the most probable spot to which I can consign a whole, small predella formerly in the possession of Mrs. Francisca Reyes at New York (Fig. 11). The Christ of the Mass of St. Gregory occupies His frequent place at the centre, and in the lateral compartments are half-lengths of the mourning Virgin, St. John Evangelist, the Baptist, and St. Peter, relieved against gold backgrounds patterned with a design of lozenges. There is an unsupported tradition that it comes from a church at Valladolid, but the only painter active in this city or its region with whose manner it exhibits any affinity whatsoever is the Portillo Master, who is inconceivable as its parent. The attribution to Paolo cannot be made categorical, and yet the ties with his authenticated works are very persuasive. The flesh and countenances are modelled in just his fashion, and all the types are practically duplicated in his production. The Redeemer, for example, was remarkably similar in the separate Crucifixion once at Gandía; the Baptist vividly recalls the Saviour of the Resurrection that belonged to the Diocesan Museum at Valencia; and — still more arresting — the St. John Evangelist in face, bend of the head, and pious expression scarcely differs from the same Apostle in the separate Gandía Crucifixion and the St. Eulalia in the retable of the Salvator Mundi at Villarreal.

[53] See above, p. 19.

CHAPTER III

MASIP AND JOHANNES HISPANUS

1. Vicente Juan Masip

The personality whom I shall consider under this heading involves us in the difficult and still not wholly solved problem of whether he may not, instead, merely constitute an early phase of the more renowned Juan de Juanes. There certainly existed a painter, Vicente Juan Masip, who was Juan de Juanes's father, but it is not entirely beyond the range of credibility that the one extant work which is now generally assigned to him on documentary grounds, the retable of Segorbe, and the other productions which on internal evidence can be attributed to the same hand are early creations of the son and that the father's individuality and manner are unknown quantities. The style of all these paintings, though somewhat diverse from that of Juan de Juanes, is not so far removed as to make it absolutely impossible that their author could eventually have developed Juan de Juanes's typical traits, but the combined witness of their partial stylistic difference and of what biographical data about the father and son are preserved to us incline me strongly to ascribe them to the former. I am therefore so designating them in the text as well as under the illustrations; but the reader must always remember that some very slight doubt remains and ought not to be completely surprised if future discoveries in the archives should, by revealing the young Juan de Juanes to have been the creator of the group of pictures, plunge Vicente Juan Masip into obscurity.

Until a fairly recent date the existence of the father was not realized, and the paintings in question were claimed for the son because of the confusion occasioned by the fact that he also was sometimes denominated in the records as Vicente Juan Masip, whereas in other instances he described himself or was described as Juan de Juanes or even by other appellations. Our first notice of the father, whom I shall henceforth call simply Vicente Masip, occurs in 1501, when he is mentioned as residing in Valencian territory and as performing legal acts possible only for a man in his majority, and this Vicente cannot be Juan de Juanes, who did not die until 1579.[1] In his will of 1545 [2] the father states his wife's Christian name to be Isabel, and Sanchis y Sivera [3] declares, without revealing his authority, that her surname was Fornes and that the marriage took place between 1503 and 1506, whereas Tramoyeres y Blasco [4] gives the surname as Navarro. We shall immediately find that the year of the birth of Juan de Juanes is in dispute, but, even if, with Tramoyeres, we grant as early a date for the event as *c.* 1500, he would have still been too young to permit an identification with the Master Vicente Masip, painter, of the parish of Santa Cruz at Valencia who in 1513 is recorded as paying a tax,[5] so that the reference must have to do with the father. For the same chronological reason it would probably be the father who in 1522 and 1525 was paid for jobs of mere gilding in the cathedral of Valencia.[6]

José María Pérez Martín [7] has proposed that the father may be the "Juanes" who, in an unpublished chronicle of the great Carthusian monastery of Valdecristo, near Segorbe, written by two successive monks between 1658 and 1790, is stated to have executed a now lost retable of Sts. Sebastian, Bruno, and Vincent Ferrer in the institution. Since Pérez does not actually quote the passage in full but only summarizes it rather vaguely, we cannot control his surmise. In the first place, it is not absolutely apparent whether the passage designates the painter as Vicente Masip or merely as Juanes. The father seems never to have been known as Juanes, but writers of the seventeenth and eighteenth centuries, unaware of his existence, would have thought Juan de Juanes was any Vicente Masip whose name they found in a document. Furthermore, Pérez fails to make it clear whether a date in the twenties, to which he assigns the retable, is copied from the

---

[1] Tormo, *Desarrollo de la pintura española del siglo XVI*, Madrid, 1902, p. 81.

[2] Published by the Barón de Alcahalí, *Diccionario biográfico de artistas valencianos*, Valencia, 1897, p. 158.

[3] *Pintores medievales en Valencia*, 231.

[4] The Valencian newspaper, *Las Provincias*, September 26, 1909.

[5] T. Llorente, *Valencia* (in the series *España, sus monumentos y artes*), Barcelona, II, 1889, p. 239. According to M. González Martí (*Joanes, Valencia*, 1926, p. 32), there was another painter called Vicente Juan Masip and recorded in 1513 as living in the parish of San Martín.

[6] Sanchis y Sivera, *La catedral de Valencia*, 536, and *Pintores medievales en Valencia*, 230–231; and the article on Vicente Masip by Olimpia Arozena in the *Anales de la Universidad de Valencia*, XI (1930–1931), 120.

[7] *Archivo español de arte y arqueología*, XII (1936), 256.

chronicle or only forms his own guess; but the way in which he quotes other dates from the manuscript would imply that the twenties of the sixteenth century are actually specified in it, and, if this be the case, Juan de Juanes, whenever he was born, could scarcely as yet have attained the prestige to receive so important a commission. One factor tends to support the contention that the Juanes of the retable at Valdecristo was the father, a statement in some printed notes at the end of the manuscript to the effect that "the celebrated Juanes, the painter," was a native of the town of Andilla, not far from the monastery or from Segorbe. The adjective "celebrated" suggests that the writer of the note was thinking of Juan de Juanes; but, although there is a doubt whether this artist was born in the Valencian house of the family or at Fuente la Higuera, south of Valencia, no one else has ever advanced Andilla as the place of his birth, and the likelihood is that the writer took the name of Andilla from some document in the monastery in which the author of the retable was described as coming from this town, so that the painter would be not the son but the father. We should thus acquire the information that Vicente Masip, the father, originated in Andilla, and we should be provided with a partial explanation of his patronage at Segorbe and Valdecristo, both of which are located near to the town. The manuscript adds that Juanes did also in the monastery a Salvator Mundi, one of the favorite subjects of the son, but the extant example at Villatorcas[8] demonstrates that the father was also in demand for the theme.

The crux of the whole problem of the existence of a style attributable to the father rather than to the youth of the son lies partly in the question whether the latter was old enough to have painted the retable over the high altar of the cathedral at Segorbe, the parts of which are now distributed about the church; but I will eventually adduce evidence which has not hitherto been brought to bear upon the question and which goes very far towards deciding the dilemma in the parent's favor. Villagrasa, writing in the seventeenth century a book on the cathedral of Segorbe,[9] stated that a Vicente Juan Masip received the commission for the retable prior to 1522 and at some time during the long period from 1500 to 1530 when Gilaberto Martí was bishop of

---

[8] See below, p. 54.

[9] Francisco de Villagrasa, *Antigüedad de la Iglesia Catedral de Segorbe y Catálogo de sus obispos*, Valencia, 1664, chapter XLI. I take the references from Llorente, *op. cit.*, I, 348, and II, 240, since Villagrasa's work is inaccessible to me.

the see; Villanueva [10] saw in the church Masip's receipts, which he declares to be dated in 1530, for 16,000 *sueldos*, the sum of the artist's remuneration; and items from the records of the cathedral, published in modern times, show that the main body of the retable was completed and installed in 1531, the *guardapolvos* were added in 1532, the altar was prepared for the relics in 1534, and the painter given his final payment on May 1, 1535.[11] The date 1523 is ordinarily given for the birth of Juan de Juanes, since he died in 1579 and Palomino [12] asserts him to have been scarcely fifty-six years old at the time of his decease, so that, if this reckoning is correct, he could not possibly have been the creator of the panels at Segorbe. Palomino, however, is far from a trustworthy authority on chronology, and as early as the end of the eighteenth or beginning of the nineteenth century, the old Valencian scholar and man of letters, Marcos Antonio de Orellana, in his *Biografía pictórica valentina*,[13] believing Juan de Juanes to have done the Segorbe cycle, realized that in such case he must have been born before 1523 and suggested a date some eighteen or twenty years prior to this year for his entrance into the world. Following in Orellana's footsteps, Tramoyeres Blasco [14] created a mild sensation in 1909 by pushing back the birth of Juan de Juanes to 1500, without giving his reasons, but González Martí [15] and Tormo [16] appear to be right in declaring it probable that he was motivated merely by the desire to credit to the son the cycle at Segorbe, like Orellana, and, in addition, the Baptism in the cathedral of Valencia, which seems securely dated in 1535 and which we shall perceive to incorporate the same style as the Segorbe retable. After Tramoyeres had once thus established the habit of guessing, Mayer and González Martí, wishing to retain only the Baptism for Juan de Juanes, hypothetically

[10] *Viaje literario*, III, Carta XVIII, pp. 17–18.

[11] Señorita Arozena, *op. cit.*, 120–121, and José María Pérez Martín in *Archivo español de arte y arqueología*, XI (1935), 301–302. On another page (109) in her article the Señorita gives the date of the actual consecration of the retable as May 7, 1533, but I deduce that Pérez is correct in stating the year to have been 1535, since the ceremony would scarcely have taken place before the altar received its relics.

[12] New edition of *El Parnaso Español* in Sánchez Cantón, *Fuentes literarias para la historia del arte español*, IV, 56.

[13] Madrid, 1936, edited by Xavier de Salas in the series *Fuentes literarias para la historia del arte español*, p. 65.

[14] The Valencian newspaper, *Las Provincias*, September 26, 1909.

[15] *Op. cit.*, 21.

[16] *Boletín de la Sociedad Española de Excursiones*, XXIV (1916), 232.

advanced the time of the birth somewhat, the former to 1505–1507,[17] the latter to c. 1510.[18] Tormo, however, points out that, although Palomino is not a good chronological guide and indeed wrongly sets down the vicinity of the year 1596 for the death of Juan de Juanes, there would have been preserved at Valencia a tradition of the painter dying at an unusually great age, if he had been born c. 1500 and came to the end of his life in 1579, and that Palomino therefore may well be reporting an authentic remembrance of the span of the painter's days, especially in view of the consideration that his rather careful modification of "fifty-six" by the world "scarcely" (apenas) would imply that he had some precise information at hand.

One item, moreover, in the records of the payments for the Segorbe retable makes it all but certain that the author was the father and that Juan de Juanes acted as no more than his assistant at this time. In 1531 it is stated [19] in the list of disbursements that "the son of Master Maçip, painter," was given ten ducats for the retable's inauguration (with reference clearly to the setting up of the structure's main parts prior to the final consecration in 1535 [20]). The only escape from the belief that the son was a child of the principal creator of the altarpiece is the very unlikely proposition that this creator is here himself described as "the painter, the son of Master Maçip," although in the other published Segorbe documents he is called Master Vicente Maçip. The natural deduction would be that the principal painter had with him a son who was paid for a minor task (since ten ducats is not a large sum) either in connection with mechanical labor in the installment of the panels or for assisting his father in their execution, the remuneration being made logically at the moment of the completion of the chief part of the commission and when "Master Vicente Maçip" is registered as receiving a large amount for his activity upon the commission.[21] Juan de Juanes would reasonably be identified with this son, since we are not informed that the father had other male offspring and since, even if there was such offspring, Juan is definitely known to have been a painter. Here again, therefore, we cannot avoid the conclusion that the father did the retable, with the son still a sub-

[17] Second German edition of his Geschichte, 122.

[18] Op. cit., 26.

[19] See the documents as published by J. M. Pérez in Archivo español de arte y arqueología, XI (1935), 302.

[20] See above, p. 51, n. 11.

[21] See the reference, just cited, to Pérez's publication of the documents.

ordinate helper, unless we are willing to suppose that Juan de Juanes was born as early as *c.* 1500 and that he married at so youthful an age as to have had by 1531 a son who, about twelve years old, might already have been of some aid to his parent. Even the precocity of the Renaissance, however, would have to be stretched to its utmost limits in order to allow either Juan de Juanes or a son such premature powers; and yet, since I myself have not read the original entry in the Segorbe documents but know it only in its quotation by another and since there are the loopholes, insignificant though they may be, that I have indicated in the evidence, I hesitate to press the entry to what would seem its full implication, namely that it was Juan de Juanes's father who painted the retable of Segorbe, or to use the entry for putting the seal upon the series of arguments.

In any case, inasmuch as there exist a number of works in a style both earlier than the surely ascertained manner of Juan de Juanes and somewhat different, and as the style would naturally be supposed to belong to a separate personality if these works had not been loosely attributed to Juanes, the burden of proof lies with those who, lacking any documentary evidence whatsoever, would wish to extend the term of his existence backward to the first years of the Cinquecento; and, until such evidence is forthcoming, the safest course is to ascribe the group of paintings to the father, whose methods the son would have acquired and evolved to a slightly diverse expression.

The Vicente Masip who in 1533 was remunerated for a minor task in connection with the retable of the Guardian Angel on the "Portal del Mar" at Valencia [22] would thus be the father, and if, as appears to me likely, the son was born in the region of the year 1523, it would still be the elder artist who was paying the taxes in 1542.[23] The principal interest of the will of 1545,[24] in which he declares his wife to have predeceased him and specifies Juan de Juanes as his chief legatee, is that, since he describes himself as of advanced age, it suggests a date of about 1470 for his birth. He must have been dead by October 10, 1550, when the will was probated.[25]

Inasmuch as the documented retable of the cathedral of Segorbe

---

[22] Sanchis y Sivera, *Pintores medievales en Valencia*, 231.

[23] T. Llorente, *op. cit.*, II, 239. Although he is called in the entry of 1542 Juan Masip, he could nevertheless be identified with the Vicente Masip who was paying taxes in 1513, since the full name was Vicente Juan Masip.

[24] See above, p. 49.

[25] The Barón de Alcahalí, *op. cit.*, 160.

was a vast affair and its parts are wholly or almost wholly preserved in the church and in the *parroquia* of the adjacent village of Villatorcas, we are provided with abundant material for an estimate of the style of the father, Vicente Masip. Only the paintings from the tabernacle have been relegated to Villatorcas, small panels of a half-length of the Salvator Mundi, the standing Melchizedek, and the seated and weary Elijah fed in the wilderness by an angel who carries a scroll with the words from III Kings, XIX, 7, that he uttered on this occasion to the Prophet, "Surge et comede, grandis enim tibi restat via." Melchizedek was commonly taken as prefiguring the institution of the Blessed Sacrament, which was reserved in the tabernacle, but I do not recall another instance of Elijah's miraculous nourishment employed with the same symbolism. The other numerous and main sections of the retable are in the cathedral of Segorbe and have constantly been moved about: at my visit in 1926 to study them, many of the compartments had been gathered in a dependency of the church where the intent was to form a diocesan museum. Dedicated to the Virgin, the structure displayed at the centre her sculptured image, which also still exists in the church, and round about were the large, painted, preserved compartments from her life and her participation in events of the New Testament — her Nativity, the Adoration of the Shepherds (Fig. 12), the Epiphany, Via Dolorosa, Crucifixion, Lamentation over the Dead Saviour (Fig. 13), Resurrection, Ascension, Pentecost, and Dormition. The Meeting at the Golden Gate, Annunciation, and Visitation are consigned to narrow, horizontal panels, with the figures reduced to busts or half-lengths, probably parts of the *guardapolvos*. The assembly comprises also large effigies of saints in full length and in iconographic pairs, the Apostles Peter and Paul, the deacons Stephen and Vincent, the pilgrims Christopher and Roch, the ascetics Giles [26] and Bernard, and the virgin martyrs Apollonia and Quiteria.[27] The remains of the altarpiece conclude with a panel of the same size and shape as the Annunciation, a half-length of Solomon who holds a volume inscribed with verses from the book of Proverbs, VII, 1–4, IX, 10, and I, 7, and who is also accompanied by a banderole with the well known words from the beginning of the book of Ecclesiastes, "Vanitas vanitatum, et omnia vanitas."

What are in all probability early works of Vicente Masip, prior to

[26] With the attribute of the fawn.
[27] With the emblems of a knife and chained mad dog: see vol. VII, p. 264.

Fig. 12. VICENTE JUAN MASIP. ADORATION OF SHEPHERDS, SECTION
OF RETABLE. CATHEDRAL, SEGORBE
(*Photo. Archivo Mas*)

FIG. 13. VICENTE JUAN MASIP. LAMENTATION OVER THE DEAD
CHRIST, SECTION OF RETABLE. CATHEDRAL, SEGORBE
(*Photo. Archivo Mas*)

his activity at Segorbe, demonstrate that he began as a follower of Paolo da San Leocadio, but from the first with an innate tendency to larger forms and a more monumental manner. It is hard or impossible to believe that the Segorbe cycle and his other later achievements could have been produced without an interval of study in northern Italy, not at Venice itself but in territory dominated by the Venetian school. The master in the Venetian region whom he most resembles is Pordenone. It is perhaps not absolutely out of the question that he should by himself have evolved independently a style similar to the manner of north Italy and in particular to the modes of Pordenone through developing the lessons from Paolo da San Leocadio in accord with his natural fondness for the grandiose, but certain of his qualities and especially his types reproduce those of Pordenone and other north Italian artists so precisely that by far the most likely explanation is to predicate a definite contact with this *milieu*. Nearly an exact contemporary of Vicente Masip, Pordenone attained his characteristic style by the second decade and early twenties of the sixteenth century, and it is this style that the creations of Masip irresistibly recall; but both his Spanish sobriety and his partial provincialism forestalled in him an attempt to imitate the Italian master's sensational inventiveness in composition and premature velleity for the ways of the baroque.

In his types, he reminds us of many painters of north Italy — of the Lombard, Pier Francesco Sacchi, the Ferrarese L'Ortolano, and the Brescian Savoldo, though without their peculiarities of chiaroscuro — and he reveals also resemblances to the Brescian Moretto, who, however, hardly matured early enough to have had much influence upon the Segorbe series; but it is with Pordenone that the ties are most intimate. Not only does Masip embody this master's general traits, the predilection for big forms, accentuated by massive draperies, the affection for the gaiety of contemporary costume, derived from the Giorgionesque tradition, and a Venetian warmth of color, but the countenances of his actors often seem to reflect Pordenone's influence. Too much stress should perhaps not be laid upon the analogies in aged, bearded masculine persons, since they are likely to be similar among all the artists of the period; and, as a matter of fact, the parallelisms are even more striking in the representation of other figures. Masip's preferred feminine type, as in the midwife next to St. Joachim in the Birth of the Virgin, Our Lady in the Adoration of the Shepherds and the Epiphany, and the woman facing us in the Ascension, constantly emerges in Pordenone's production, witnessing again to the Italian's ultimate sources in the circle of Giorgione. Examples are the Madonna of Mercy between Sts. Christopher and Joseph in the Duomo of the town that gives Pordenone his name and the Madonna in the altarpiece of the Duomo of Cremona. The Spaniard's youths also are handsomer and serener versions of those whom we meet in Pordenone's extensive output. The most signal instance of this phase of Masip's creations, the young man above St. Joseph in the Adoration of the Shepherds, should be compared with the first of the disappointed suitors in the Marriage of the Virgin in the Duomo of Spilimbergo and with two heads in the fresco of the Epiphany in the Duomo of Treviso. The mounted horseman at the left in this fresco supplies a counterpart for the dapper and brilliantly garbed cavalier at the right in the Segorbe Via Dolorosa. Even more persuasively, the type of the Baptist in the altarpieces at Susegana and Torre is a favorite with Masip, as in the St. Joseph of the Adoration of the Shepherds, the Christ of the Lamentation and Resurrection, and above all, in both the Saviour and St. John in the Baptism of the cathedral at Valencia. It may have been Paolo da San Leocadio who advised him to perfect his education by betaking himself to the sister peninsula, and yet it was not the district of northern Italy whence Paolo had come, Emilia, that was the eventual seat of his studies but the Venetian provinces.

Although perhaps any Spanish artist who had the privilege of an Italian journey could scarcely have failed to be attracted to Rome, there is no real evidence that Masip owed anything of significance to the circles of Raphael and Michael Angelo. It is just possible that the woman with her back toward us in the Birth of the Virgin was suggested by the figure carrying an urn on her head in Raphael's fresco of the Burning of the Borgo, but it is quite as likely that the resemblance is fortuitous. Now and then his types, for example the two large angels at the right in the Adoration of the Shepherds and the angel consoling Elijah, appear to derive not so much from Paolo da San Leocadio as from the fashions popularized at Valencia by Rodrigo de Osona the younger. Curiously enough, however, Masip seems to have been practically untouched by the contemporary activity of Fernando de Llanos and Fernando Yáñez, and he did not imitate with any definiteness the cartoons for the sacred themes evolved by them or even by Paolo da San Leocadio or his other Valencian predecessors and contemporaries. Not much importance attaches to the consideration that, like Paolo at Gandía, he introduces in smaller scale into the background of the Via Dolorosa the ominous representation of the preparations on Calvary for the Crucifixion. Although he does not endeavor, in the mode of the two Fernandos, to renounce the long established, general European outlines of the compositions by spurts of inventiveness and to devise new conceptions, such panels as the Adoration of the Shepherds and the Lamentation reveal that, within the self-imposed, traditional limits, he was capable of welding the forms into arrangements that are as interesting as they are compact. He set before himself, indeed, as his principal aim in composition the monumental effect of heroic figures in solid masses almost entirely filling the spaces. The Elijah and, as a matter of fact, all the separate effigies of saints conform to this ideal of burly forms in voluminous draperies. Not that he could not gird himself, when he so cared, for introducing details of invention into the regular compositions by which he chose to abide. The Adoration of the Shepherds is particularly notable in this respect. At the left the comely young shepherd turns to discuss reverently the mystery with one of his comrades; the two Osonesque angels naturalistically seek to improve their vocal performance by beating time together in close unison over a book of music; and a white dove is symbolically perched upon a tie-rod in the architectural background of the Renaissance. In the Lamentation, Joseph of Arimathaea points out to one of the holy women the sepulchre in the distance that he has offered as a resting-place for the sacred body, and Nicodemus, holding in one hand the "mixture of myrrh and aloes" in a round vessel (which is a fine example of the craft of the Renaissance), touches with the other the linens that she carries and counsels her in regard to their mortuary use.

The draughtsmanship of Masip is incisive and for the most part correct, tending to a virile hardness of outline that distinguishes him from his son. The inclination to fill his compositions with ample forms permitted him only bits of landscape in the settings, but in his appreciation of the beauties of nature and in the ability to transmit to us their effects he quite equals Paolo da San Leocadio and the two Fernandos, exhibiting as one of his peculiarities a fondness, perhaps under Venetian influence, for the hours of sunrise and sunset and for somewhat darkened heavens.[28] Proceeding further along the ways of the High Renaissance than almost any of his Valencian contemporaries, he abjures gold in the narrative scenes and retains it only for the backgrounds of the separate effigies of sacred personages, thus continuing to enhance their religious character in the mode of mediaeval Spanish art. The gold behind Sts. Peter and Paul and in the pieces of the tabernacle at Villatorcas is tooled with a pattern, suggested by the tiling of pavements, that he employs also in other works.

The panels of Vincent the Martyr and Vincent Ferrer which, since both saints are patrons of Valencia, appropriately serve as doors beside the high altar of the cathedral must definitely be numbered among Vicente Masip's productions, and both internal evidence and what objective suppositions we may venture about them indicate that they belong to an early period in his career (Fig. 14). Once mistakenly believed to be relics of a retable of 1483–1484 by Rodrigo de Osona the elder or the younger, they were subsequently assigned by Tormo merely to the school of the Osonas and tentatively, but, in my opinion, wrongly, to the Master of the Knight of Montesa.[29] There is much to be said, however, for his surmise [30] that they were probably painted for their present destination about the time, 1507, when Fernando de Llanos and Fernando Yáñez did the shutters for the silver retable over the altar, and that they were not imported from some other spot and coerced into functioning as portals. The proof for the attribution to Masip is unescapable. Although the representation of St. Vincent the Martyr is varied in the Segorbe retable, both figures in the doors of the altar conform to a placid, youthful type often emerging in this retable, and their faces exhibit the artist's distinctive mode of modelling in light and shade. The St. Vincent Ferrer, for example, finds close analogues in the attendant women in the Birth of the Virgin and in the separate effigy of St. Stephen, whose arms are stretched across his body to hold his emblems of the stones with the very gesture employed by St. Vincent Ferrer in clasping his book. Moreover, the buildings depicted in the bits of landscape behind the figures are almost duplicated several times in the compartments of the Segorbe assem-

[28] Tramoyeres y Blasco (*Archivo de arte valenciano*, IV, 1918, p. 52) descries in the background of the Crucifixion the now ruined castle of Segorbe as he believes it then looked, and others have seen it also in the landscape of the Lamentation (Arozena, *op. cit.*, p. 104, n. 1).

[29] See my vol. VI, p. 175, and above, p. 18.

[30] *Archivo español de arte y arqueología*, IX (1933), 186.

FIG. 14. VICENTE JUAN MASIP. STS. VINCENT THE MARTYR AND
VINCENT FERRER. CATHEDRAL, VALENCIA

(*Photo. Archivo Mas*)

blage. A certain lingering degree of primitive rigidity coincides with the possibility of the panels' connection with the two Fernandos' enterprise to induce the hypothesis of a classification at the beginning of Masip's activity, which obtains some corroboration from the maintenance of the old conventions of ensconcing the saints under formal canopies of textiles and of accenting these textiles and the orphreys of the Martyr's dalmatic with gold. The types still plainly reflect a dependence upon Paolo da San Leocadio, and, although the pictures may have been executed before Masip's sojourn in Italy, they already incorporate, especially the Martyr, something of his feeling for monumental stature and breadths of drapery.

At either side of a statue of St. Joseph in a chapel at the right of the nave in the Colegiata of Gandía there were to be seen, prior to the destruction of the edifice's contents in the civil war, panels of the two St. Johns which are very similar in general manner to the St. Vincents and which the types clearly show Tormo [31] to be right in claiming for Masip (Fig. 15). Implications of an early moment in his development were not quite so manifest, but it is very possible that such was their date and that he owed the commission to the friendship of the artistic dictator at Gandía in the first decade of the sixteenth century, Paolo da San Leocadio, whose conceptions of bearded young men the St. Johns closely resemble facially.

Mayer [32] tentatively suggests that the young Masip may have been the author of the retable of Martin and other saints in the Musée de Cluny at Paris which I [33] have ascribed to the Cabanyes Master or an intimate follower; but the more I study the retable, the readier I am to vote for the Cabanyes Master himself, although some resemblances to Masip's modes, especially in the women in the compartment of the Crucifixion, are not lacking. If perchance Juan de Juanes's father did have anything to do with the monument, he would only be exemplifying what we should expect, contact with Valencian art in general at the beginning of the Cinquecento.

The cathedral of Valencia harbors a work by Masip which, like the two St. Vincents, has not hitherto been perceived to incorporate his craft and must have been executed at about the same time, a large panel of the Crowning with Thorns that before the civil war hung on

[31] *Levante*, 230.
[32] Second Spanish edition of his *Geschichte*, 1942, p. 146. I do not know whether he was right in stating the retable to have been moved to the Louvre.
[33] Vol. VI, pp. 414–420.

the right side of the nave (Fig. 16). The artist has painted a small placard at the bottom with the words, "Sit nomen Domini benedictum," but the original function of the picture has not been discovered. Every factor in the work agrees with Masip's practices. The persecutor of Christ at the right, for instance, reiterates his oft re-

FIG. 15. VICENTE JUAN MASIP. THE TWO ST. JOHNS. COLEGIATA, GANDÍA
(*Photo. Archivo Mas*)

peated type for youths, and both this figure and his balancing companion at the left are clad in the smart, contemporary costumes that Masip owed to his contact with the Venetian tradition. The Saviour recalls the Gandía St. John Evangelist, and His draperies, as well as those of Herod, are disposed in the narrow, almost plaited folds that, as in the loin-cloth of Christ in the Segorbe Resurrection, the master tended to cultivate. For an example of the detailed pieces of invention often inserted into the long sanctioned compositions that he retained, we may point here to a group of women and children, prettily composed as spectators in a round opening in the architectural setting, and in these also there appear his characteristic countenances, the

FIG. 16. VICENTE JUAN MASIP. CROWNING WITH THORNS.
CATHEDRAL, VALENCIA
(*Photo. Archivo Mas*)

elderly profile like the St. Anne in the Segorbe Meeting at the Golden Gate and the boy like the St. John in the Dormition. The general nature of the architecture is paralleled in the backgrounds of the documented retable, and Masip's lively interest in the minor arts of the Renaissance finds the same sort of outlet in the ornamentation of the armor of Christ's youthful tormentor as in the embellishment of Nicodemus's urn in the Segorbe Lamentation.

In the panel displaying a bust of the Man of Sorrows belonging to Monsieur Guillaume Bernstein at Madrid, the features of Christ in the Crowning with Thorns are almost duplicated, so that, when we take into account the general conformity with Masip's style and the resemblances to such other figures by him as the St. Roch of the Segorbe retable, there is no reason, it seems to me, for questioning the attribution to our master that has been proposed.

He is manifestly the author of the retable of St. Vincent Ferrer in the Iglesia de la Sangre at Segorbe that I discussed and illustrated in volume IV [34] for the sake of demonstrating the artistic connection of the schools of the eastern Spanish littoral and Naples. I should no longer wish to take as proof of this relationship the compositional analogy of the central effigy of the saint to the similarly placed figure of Vincent Ferrer in Colantonio's altarpiece in the Neapolitan church of S. Pietro Martire, since the representations of the great, canonized Dominican preacher by the Sant Quirse Master [35] and Pedro García de Benabarre [36] show that there were even more exact precedents in the iconography of eastern Spain itself. The general structure of the retable in the Iglesia de la Sangre and even the pattern in the gold background of the principal compartment, which is identical with a design employed by Masip in several sections of the cycle for the cathedral of Segorbe, are practically and curiously duplicated in the Cabanyes Master's altarpiece of St. Peter in S. Esteban, Valencia.[37] The same model is used for St. Vincent in the main panel as on the door of the *capilla mayor* in the cathedral of Valencia, but he is depicted at a more mature age, so that he finds a closer counterpart in the St. Bernard of the series in the cathedral of Segorbe. Anyone at all familiar with Masip's productions would realize at almost first sight that in the retable of the Iglesia de la Sangre he was in the artist's presence, but he could bolster up his feeling with many further bits of concrete evidence, such as the repetition, on the uprights, of the St. Roch in the Segorbe cathedral and the resemblance, in types as well as composition, of the Lamentation in the middle of the predella to the cathedral version. Although the central image is still petrified into an object of cult, a date about contemporary with his commission in the cathedral of Segorbe is implied by the retable's general manner.

Until the discoveries of Sanchis y Sivera, the large and celebrated

---

[34] P. 57, n. 2, and fig. 7.
[36] *Ibid.*, pp. 275–276.

[35] Vol. VII, p. 207.
[37] Vol. VI, p. 412.

panel of the Baptism above the font in the cathedral of Valencia had been attributed to Juan de Juanes, but the stylistic evidence seems to me to corroborate the Spanish scholar's contention [38] that the honor belongs rather to the father (Fig. 17). He found that the panel must have been painted by 1535, for an entry of this year in the cathedral book of accounts prescribes payment to two stone-cutters for perforating the wall over the font so that it might receive the picture, and the reference can be only to the panel in question since the entry describes it as the "retable of Master Bautista," namely the Venerable Juan Bautista Agnesio, who is actually introduced as donor in the lower left corner of the extant work. A humanist and teacher as well as a magnanimous and pious member of the cathedral chapter, proficient in Greek and Hebrew, it is certainly he who is here portrayed, because he carries a book with Greek on one side and Hebrew on the other and because he is the same person at an earlier age as the donor, indubitably Agnesio, in Juan de Juanes's famous painting of the Madonna with Sts. Agnes and Dorothy in the Provincial Museum, Valencia. Not only is the recognition of Agnesio as the ecclesiastic in Juan de Juanes's picture preserved by Valencian tradition, but the identity is definitely proved by the fact that he is conceived here as mystically marrying St. Agnes, under whose protection his surname naturally placed him.[39] The learned cleric was thus a patron of both Vicente Masip and his son, and the endowment of the cathedral with a representation of the Baptism was a reflection of his devotion to the saint after whom he took his Christian name. Sanchis y Sivera points out, furthermore, that the age at which he is depicted, in the neighborhood of forty, coincides with the years that he attained about 1535.

The orthodox date for the birth of Juan de Juanes, *c.* 1523, would, as Sanchis y Sivera argues, render his authorship of the Baptism unthinkable, but, if we break with orthodoxy and are willing to extend his life to the beginning of the sixteenth century,[40] there would be no chronological obstacle to maintaining the old attribution to the son. As so often, then, in the history of art, the criterion in the end

[38] *La catedral de Valencia*, 352–353.

[39] Tormo (*Boletín de la Sociedad Española de Excursiones*, XXIV, 1916, p. 233, n. 2) supposes that the picture may have been the predella of the Baptism, but, if so, the father must have left it to be subsequently executed by his son. As a matter of fact, there is no reason for refusing to believe that the panel by Juan de Juanes may derive from some other donation of Agnesio in the church.

[40] See above, p. 51.

FIG. 17. VICENTE JUAN MASIP(?). BAPTISM. CATHEDRAL,
VALENCIA

(*Photo. Archivo Mas*)

must be stylistic, posing in this instance a difficult problem because
the manner and types of Juan de Juanes, particularly in his early
period, are so similar to those of his father. Nevertheless, my eyes
see in the Baptism, despite a date that might fall at the beginning of
Juan de Juanes's career, the more primitive and harder modes which
we have associated with the father and which the son, in his surely
authenticated productions, always softened and veiled with increased
sfumatezza. All of the types in the panel may be observed again
and again in the works that we have assigned to Vicente Masip.
The Christ, if stripped of His beard, would turn out scarcely distinguishable from the St. John in the Segorbe Via Dolorosa and
Lamentation, and there are even many bearded countenances at
Segorbe virtually identical, for instance the Saviour of the Lamentation, the profile at the extreme right in the Pentecost, and the
Apostle with clasped hands in the foreground of the Dormition.
The Baptist merely repeats the Christ in features. The Eternal
Father above in the clouds is not differentiated from the aged
shepherd in the Segorbe Adoration of the Child. Of the four
Fathers of the Church set on either side immediately behind the two
principal actors in order to make the subject into a devotional rather
than historical conception, the St. Gregory belongs exactly within the
class of human beings embodied in the St. Joachim of the Virgin's
Birth; the head of the St. Augustine, standing next, is so commonly
encountered in the figures at Segorbe that it is not necessary to specify
examples; the St. Ambrose, opposite, is paralleled by the shepherd
with the lamb in the Adoration and the soldier at the left in the
Resurrection; and the St. Jerome is intimately affiliated with the
Nicodemus of the Lamentation. Even the children are treated in the
same way as at Segorbe, the pair of *putti* at the extreme left in the
heavens recalling the Baby adored by the shepherds, just as the one
in the upper right corner reminds us of the infant Mary. The dove
itself reproduces line by line the bird in the Segorbe Pentecost. After
having in 1916 [41] ascribed the picture to Vicente Masip alone, Tormo
in 1923 [42] modified his opinion so far as to admit the collaboration of
the son, whose birth he thus would probably have finally decided to
set at least somewhat earlier than 1523, but it is difficult to ferret out
any passage of which the unassisted father would have been incapable.

[41] *Boletin de la Sociedad Española de Excursiones*, XXIV, 233.
[42] *Levante*, 86.

C. Jocelyn Foulkes [43] has championed the dependence of the composition of the Baptism upon the rendering of the theme by Cesare da Sesto last reported as in the possession of the Principe di Molfetta at Milan, but the hanging locks of the Saviour and the introduction of God the Father in an aureole of clouds at the top create a closer parallel in the version by Cesare's pupil, Andrea da Salerno (ascribed by some to Cesare himself), in the Badia della Trinità at Cava dei Tirreni near Naples. Whether or not Masip had either of these works in mind or some other, yet undiscovered, corresponding treatment of the subject by a Lombard artist, all that the resemblances indicate is that, as we already surmised, he had passed some time in northern Italy or that he was impressed by the painting at Cava in touring in the region of Naples on his travels from Spain to Italy or *vice versa*; and his fundamental style was not derived from the Lombard school or its offshoots but from another section of Italy of the north, the Veneto. The Baptism by Gaudenzio Ferrari at Casale Monferrato, dated in 1534, would probably be too late for Masip to have known it before he started his own altarpiece, and if, as is generally held, Gaudenzio's rendering in S. Maria presso S. Celso at Milan was executed at least no earlier than *c.* 1538, it certainly could not have inspired the Spanish master; but in any case these versions are not so close to that of Masip as necessarily to imply a relationship.

There can be no doubt that we have to do with an achievement of Masip and with probably almost, if not quite, as late a moment in his life as that of the Baptism when we come to the panel of the actors at the Crucifixion used as a background for the sculptured image of the Cristo de la Buena Muerte that of old was to be seen in one of the rooms leading to the Aula Capitular Antigua in the cathedral of Valencia but has now been consigned to the ambulatory (Fig. 18). The statue, manifestly a work of the seventeenth or eighteenth century, has been loosely claimed for Alonso Cano, but Tormo [44] ascribes it to the Valencian sculptor of the first half of the seventeenth century, Juan Muñoz; and in any case it must replace an earlier image of the Crucified for which Masip did the setting. St. John is again one of his grave and tranquil youths; the Virgin proves to be identical in the Segorbe Ascension; and her companion at the extreme left is a

---

[43] *Boletín de la Sociedad Española de Excursiones*, XXVI (1918), 54.
[44] *Valencia: los Museos*, 109.

Fig. 18. VICENTE JUAN MASIP. BACKGROUND FOR A CRUCIFIX.
CATHEDRAL, VALENCIA
(*Photo. Archivo Mas*)

FIG. 19. VICENTE JUAN MASIP. VIA DOLOROSA. MADRID, PRADO

(*Courtesy of the Museum*)

replica of the woman conversing with Joseph of Arimathaea in the Lamentation.

Another sure work of Vicente Masip, a panel of the Via Dolorosa in the Prado, derives from the church of El Temple at Valencia, the seat of the Order of Montesa in the city (Fig. 19), but it was probably not done originally for this edifice, since it was a gift of a private owner to the Order.[45] Registered as No. 849 in the Prado, it is assigned in the Catalogue to the son, Juan de Juanes, but everything bespeaks rather the father, for instance a confrontation with Juanes's version in the Valencian church of S. Nicolás. The pleasant variations from the father's rendering in the Segorbe retable are only matters of detail, and in general the stylistic correspondence with the high degree of attainment in this retable is so exact that the date must be about contemporary. Some of the subordinate actors are actually repeated: the Virgin is precisely the same person as in the Lamentation; and the St. John in the Segorbe Via Dolorosa and Lamentation incorporates the type employed for the Magdalene in the picture from El Temple. More than the Segorbe rendering, the Prado treatment suggests the possibility that Masip may have known directly, or indirectly through an engraving, Raphael's composition for the subject in the canvas, also belonging to the Prado, called Lo Spasimo, which, however, did not reach Spain from Sicily until 1661; but once more [46] it should be emphasized that an indebtedness to Raphael for one or two occasional ideas in composition does not mean that the Spaniard underwent his influence in any stylistic or otherwise significant degree.

Quite as lovely as the Adoration of the Shepherds in the Segorbe retable is a variant in the Valladolid Museum, manifestly executed by Masip's own hand (Fig. 20). Among the differences, all of them minor, we descry in the background the approach of the Wise Men's cavalcade.

Not only by reason of the iconographical content but also because of the light that it throws upon his sources, an important place in our painter's production is occupied by a retable once belonging to the long since dissolved firm of Cooper and Griffith at New York (Fig. 21). The profound debt to Italy is shown by its very formation, with the sacred personages not consigned to a number of separate compartments according to the Spanish mode but, as in Italian altarpieces, with

FIG. 20. VICENTE JUAN MASIP. ADORATION OF THE SHEPHERDS.
MUSEUM, VALLADOLID

(*Photo. Archivo Mas*)

FIG. 21. VICENTE JUAN MASIP. RETABLE. FORMERLY BELONGING
TO THE FIRM OF COOPER AND GRIFFITH, NEW YORK
(*Courtesy of Dr. John Maxon*)

angels and saints grouped about the enthroned Madonna and Child in a single space. The upper tier of surrounding figures consists of the archangels (reading from left to right) Michael, Gabriel, the Guardian Angel of the Kingdom,[47] and Raphael; and the saints below are Sebastian, Mary Magdalene,[48] Roch, and Martha.[49] The systematic iconography was carefully planned, comprising four captains of the heavenly host, two saints invoked against the plague, Sebastian and Roch, and the sisters Martha and the Magdalene. The structure includes also a lunette displaying, between half-lengths of Sts. Cosmas and Damian, the frequent Valencian theme for the summits of retables, the Trinity, here enclosed in a mandorla girt with the heads of cherubim.

The attribution needs no demonstration to anyone who has scanned the preceding illustrations, and I will bore the reader only so far as to ask him to note the conformity of the Madonna to the representations of the Virgin in the retable of the cathedral at Segorbe, especially in the Epiphany, or a more exact identity of Roch and his dog with the effigy of the saint and his canine companion in this retable than we observe on the uprights of the altarpiece of St. Vincent Ferrer in the Iglesia de la Sangre in the same city.[50] The gold background is diapered with Masip's characteristic design of lozenges.[51] An aspect of the significance of the retable for the understanding of his style emerges in the fact that the analogy of the countenances of the angels to types of the Martínez Master, the Cabanyes Master, and their circle demonstrates very tangibly what we are likely to overlook amidst Masip's personal qualities, namely his participation in the general contemporary artistic *milieu* of Valencia.

With practically the same certainty the father of Juan de Juanes may be declared to have painted a large Pietà [52] in the Collection of the eminent scholar in the field of the art of his own city, Valencia, Don Manuel González Martí (Fig. 22). The concordance of the two angels at right and left with Vicente Masip's types would seem sufficient to reveal him as the painter, especially the one with the crown

[47] With the emblems of the crown and scourge: see vol. VI, p. 154.
[48] In addition to the usual box of ointment she carries her peculiarly Valencian attribute of the crown of thorns and protects both of them with a ritualistic veil: see vol. VI, p. 75.
[49] With the emblems of the pot of holy water and the aspergillum.
[50] See above, p. 65.
[51] See above, p. 65.
[52] The dimensions are 1.50 metres in height by 1.10 in width.

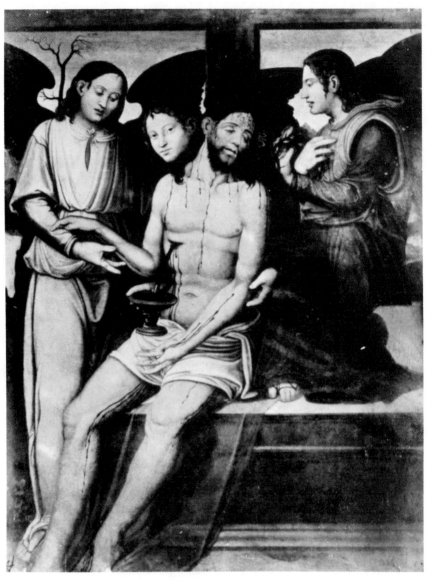

FIG. 22. VICENTE JUAN MASIP(?). PIETÀ. GONZÁLEZ MARTÍ
COLLECTION, VALENCIA

(*Photo. Sanchis*)

of thorns, who is not differentiated from the similarly placed angel in the Nativity or the St. John in the Crucifixion of the Segorbe retable. Other correspondences, of course, are not lacking, such as the predilection for powerful legs in the representations of Christ in the scenes of the Passion. The whole picture, moreover, is pervaded with the kind of vernal freshness that generally distinguishes the work of the father from that of the son.[53]

It is difficult, if not impossible, to see who else but Vicente Masip could have executed a panel in the Mateu Collection at Barcelona (Fig. 23) depicting, as the inscription on the parapet declares, St. Sennen and constituting, on the authority of Don Diego Angulo,[54] the companion-piece to a representation of his inseparable iconographic partner, St. Abdon,[55] which the Spanish scholar once saw at a dealer's in Madrid but with which I am unacquainted. The countenance and expression are the same, though perhaps painted at a later moment in the artist's life, as those used for the Christ in the Crowning with Thorns in the cathedral of Valencia, and there are many other similar bearded faces in his output, for example the second Apostle from the right behind the bed in the Segorbe Dormition and the Solomon from this retable. The contemporary costume has the splendor of attire that Masip sought, and the aged shepherd in the background of the Segorbe Adoration reveals how he liked to put this kind of cap upon his personages' heads. The hanging against which St. Sennen stands is decorated with the *motif* of a checker of lozenges that he is shown by other works to have favored. Angulo has descried in the building represented in the right piece of landscape an architectural element unusual for the Valencian school, an arcade like that of the maksurrah in the Mosque at Cordova.

The St. Sennen constitutes an exception to the rule that the evidence afforded by a single figure is too slight for a persuasive attribution

[53] In *Archivo español de arte*, XXIII (1950), 199, Saralegui, independently of me, ascribes the Pietà to the painter of the two St. Vincents in the cathedral of Valencia and of the retable of St. Vincent Ferrer in the Iglesia de la Sangre at Segorbe, but he does not yet thoroughly agree that this painter is Masip. As I shall point out on p. 365, I cannot, strive as I may, follow Saralegui in attributing to the painter a Lamentation over the Dead Christ in the Museum of Barcelona. He may be right, however, in discerning in the angel with the crown of thorns in the Pietà belonging to González Martí one of the rare instances in which a consciousness of the achievements of Yáñez and Llanos modified slightly a specimen of Masip's standard types.

[54] *Archivo español de arte*, XVII (1944), 237, n. 1.

[55] Vol. VI, p. 130, n. 1.

FIG. 23. VICENTE JUAN MASIP(?). ST. SENNEN. MATEU COLLECTION,
BARCELONA

(*Photo. Archivo Mas*)

unless both it and the proposed author have marked idiosyncrasies, which were certainly alien to Masip's wholesome nature, and the rule is particularly true when the figure is St. Peter, whose general outlines were more or less established by a long iconographical tradition, so that he was treated in much the same way by all Valencian artists of the early sixteenth century; but the manner of Masip is certainly the niche into which there most neatly fits a large panel depicting the Apostle against a gold background in the parish church at Bañeras, west of Alcoy (Fig. 24). The representation of Peter in the Segorbe series is only slightly varied, and in both paintings there is to be seen the peculiar detail of the saint resting his right arm upon a narrow piece of wall. The head is of a sort that we often encounter in Masip, for instance with virtual identity in the same Apostle as he appears in the lower left corner of the Segorbe Pentecost.

In volume VI [56] we registered the phenomenon of the repainting in the sixteenth century of a Valencian panel executed some hundred years earlier, and either Vicente Juan Masip or his son Juan de Juanes was called upon to perform a similar task, likewise within the limits of the school of Valencia, in the case of a Lamentation over the Dead Christ in the possession of the firm of William Hallsborough at London (Fig. 25).[57] The composition and the still primitively articulated poses and gestures practically duplicate those of the same subject formerly in the Demotte Collection at Paris that in volume IX [58] we provisionally claimed for the Valencian painter of the first half of the Quattrocento, the Martín de Torres Master, and it may very well be that the Hallsborough panel was originally also his creation. The gold background, tooled only at the border according to the Valencian practice, and the nature of the patterning in the gold haloes are likewise retained from the original of the early fifteenth century, but the repainter in the Cinquecento has modernized the countenances, hands, and the majority of the draperies. That this repainter could have been none other than Juan de Juanes or his father is plainly revealed by the types of personages, and I am inclined to believe, although without dogmatism, that it was rather the father to whom the job was assigned. Juan de Borgoña's retouching of the retable in the chapel of S. Eugenio in the cathedral of Toledo [59] supplies still further evi-

---

[56] P. 336.
[57] The dimensions are 52 inches in height by 39½ in width.
[58] P. 761.   [59] *Ibid.*, p. 171.

FIG. 24. VICENTE JUAN MASIP(?). ST. PETER.
PARISH CHURCH, BAÑERAS
(*Photo. Archivo Mas*)

FIG. 25. LAMENTATION OVER THE DEAD CHRIST, VALENCIAN WORK
OF THE FIRST HALF OF THE FIFTEENTH CENTURY REPAINTED
BY VICENTE JUAN MASIP(?). HALLSBOROUGH COLLECTION,
LONDON

(*Courtesy of the owner*)

dence that, by reason either of deterioration of older works or of change of taste, it was not entirely uncommon for artists of the Renaissance to be asked to renovate the productions of the Middle Ages.

Tormo and others have ascribed to Vicente Masip, either definitely or in some cases provisionally, a series of works (besides the Baptism) that hitherto had been placed under the name of Juan de Juanes, but my study of the problem forces me to abide by the traditional view and to attribute them to the son, though to his youthful period when he was still very much under the spell of the paternal achievements. They include the *tondi* of the Visitation and the martyrdom of St. Agnes in the Prado,[60] the Holy Family and conversion of St. Paul in the Sala Capitular Moderna of the cathedral of Valencia,[61] the Last Supper in the Provincial Museum of this city,[62] and the retable of the Immaculate Conception at Sot de Ferrer.[63] The types in these paintings still often resemble those of the father, but they have been slightly modified in the direction taken by the style of Juan de Juanes, especially in a tendency to a greater softness and a more obvious striving for prettiness rather than for a noble beauty. There is already evidence of a desire for melodramatic posture and for a *sfumatezza* resulting from less firm contours. The fundamental question becomes then whether we have any right to believe that the father ultimately thus altered his manner, and, since no work assignable to him with security, not even the Baptism of the Valencian cathedral, justifies this belief and since the qualities lead immediately into the kind of art embodied in the son's mature creations, I postpone the consideration of the group of pictures until in a subsequent volume I shall treat the attainments and development of Juan de Juanes. The oval-shaped Coronation of the Virgin in the Prado, the so-called Gloria, is another piece for which the father has been proposed [64] rather than the son, but in this case, while decisively rejecting the ascription to the former, I cannot yet convince myself that even the latter was the author.

[60] Tormo, *Desarrollo*, etc., 83–85.
[61] Tormo, *Valencia: los Museos*, 103 and 106. I am not informed whether the Holy Family survived the war.
[62] *Ibid.*, 33.
[63] Tormo, *Levante*, 60.
[64] Tormo, *Desarrollo*, etc., 84.

2. Johannes Hispanus

Among the painters of the early Spanish Renaissance, Vicente Juan Masip is the one whose style most nearly approaches that of the hauntingly beautiful Entombment formerly belonging to the Collection of the Marchese d'Adda at Milan and signed on one side of the Saviour's sarcophagus IOAES (= Johannes) ISPANUS (with the initial aspirate omitted according to the fluid spelling of the period), followed by the letter P, standing for *pinxit* [1]; but yet the distance between the two styles is almost a chasm, and I am so far from willing to ascribe the panel to Masip as to venture nothing more definite than the assertion that it is not *absolutely* inconceivable that he should have thus painted when a student in Italy, although it is my rather decided opinion that he does not deserve the honor of being credited with the picture's execution (Fig. 26). In the first place, we should have to imagine, without any other authority, that the father anticipated the son in employing as a surname Juan or Juanes, for which the Johannes would stand, since no stretch of one's critical sense could propose the son as the author and since the father would scarcely have used the second of his two given names, Juan, in a signature, especially when the contemporary documents customarily designate him only as Vicente Masip. It would be necessary to suppose also that the picture was done during an Italian sojourn by Masip, who in the exercise of his profession at home would not have felt it requisite to describe himself as a Spaniard.

We should be obliged to make the further assumption that, while in Italy, he painted in a more Italianate manner than on returning to Spain, indeed in a manner practically indistinguishable from that of a native Italian master. Mayer [2] relates this manner to the school of Vicenza at the end of the fifteenth and beginning of the sixteenth century, having in mind such painters as Bartolommeo Montagna or Giovanni Buonconsiglio, il Marescalco, and Berenson, as we shall see, with keener perception, finds its analogue in Masip's contemporary at Ferrara, L'Ortolano; but it is questionable whether the type of the Magdalene, the chiaroscuro on the countenances of Joseph of Arimathaea and Nicodemus, and their subtlety of expression are enough

---

[1] The inscription on the other side of the sarcophagus reads, Sepulcrum Christi.

[2] *Geschichte*, second German edition, 110.

to substantiate Carlo Gamba's [3] assertion of the influence of Leonardo, although the panel was once in the church of the nuns of the Gesù at Milan and thence passed into the Collection of the Marchese d'Adda. [4] If one wishes to interpret the Magdalene as Leonardesque and to hazard the guess that Masip could have executed it, her partial resemblance to the women of·Fernando de Llanos and Fernando

FIG. 26. JOHANNES HISPANUS. ENTOMBMENT. FORMERLY IN THE COLLECTION OF THE MARCHESE D'ADDA, MILAN

Yáñez might suggest the hypothesis that he picked up from them at Valencia any trace of Leonardo's style in the panel, before he betook himself to the sister peninsula. One objective argument for the attribution to Masip would be that, as we have found, he certainly studied in northern Italy, where the D'Adda picture seems from the first to have been located.

Since I know the picture only in photograph, I can make no comparisons of color, but at any rate the best internal evidence for Masip's

[3] *Arte toscana in Spagna, il Marzocco* (Florence), February 1, 1925, p. 2.
[4] G. Frizzoni in *Archivio storico dell' arte*, VI (1893), 183.

authorship would be found in the facial analogies to the figures that he painted in Spain. Approximations to the Joseph of Arimathaea and Nicodemus emerge throughout his production, as notably in the representation of these two actors in the Segorbe Crucifixion and in the Sts. Gregory and Jerome of the Valencian Baptism. Indeed the Virgin and the woman supporting her in the Crucifixion provide the nearest parallels, among many in his output, to the sorrowing Mother and Magdalene of the Entombment. The conception of the suffering Christ, however, in the Segorbe series is very different in its grimness and realism from the ideal, Giorgionesque beauty that the painter of the Entombment bestowed upon the Saviour, and Masip nowhere treats the landscape with such Giorgionesque *sfumatezza* and poetry, not even in the Crucifixion. None of these correspondences is, as a matter of fact, convincing, and the Entombment is carried out in a mood of dreamy, Giorgionesque gentleness and with softened outlines that are alien to what we surely know of Masip's style. A slight Giorgionesque tinge he acquired from Pordenone's early manner, and Pordenone at his beginnings could have endowed his imitator with types of bald-headed old men of the sort depicted in the Entombment; but, if by a remote chance Masip painted the work, he never again actually recaptured its essential spirit or technique.

It is possible that we owe the Entombment to some gifted young Spaniard who, perhaps after being touched with the art of the two Fernandos at Valencia, found an atmosphere congenial to his nature in northern Italy but was one of those geniuses who, like Masaccio and Lorenzo da Viterbo, died at an early age, leaving as a testimony only the Entombment and possibly a few other works that have not yet been recognized. Another "Johannes," Juan de Borgoña, despite the fact that he too passed some time in nothern Italy,[5] is unthinkable as having any connection with the picture, and the Peruginesque Giovanni di Pietro, Lo Spagna, must, of course, be categorically excluded. For Von Loga's [6] attempt to discern Andalusian affiliations, there are no apparent grounds. A proposition that is at first startling but on examination becomes more and more intriguing has been tentatively advanced by Berenson,[7] namely, that Johannes Hispanus might

[5] Vol. IX, p. 186.
[6] *Die Malerei in Spanien*, 92.
[7] In the heading to his list of L'Ortolano's works in *Italian Pictures of the Renaissance*, Oxford, 1932, p. 403.

conceivably be the painter active at Ferrara, L'Ortolano, whose real name in Italian was Gian Battista Benvenuto and who thus would have signed his Christian name in Latin as it appears in the Entombment. No document tells us that L'Ortolano was Italian-born, and not only does his manner closely correspond in general with that of "Johannes" but it even reveals a number of detailed analogies. The type, for instance, that he employs for the dead Christ is very similar, and his old men, particularly the foster-father of Our Lord in the Nativity of the Doria Gallery, possess a very persuasive facial resemblance to the Joseph of Arimathaea at the head of the sarcophagus in the perplexing picture that now concerns us. As in our attempt, however, at identification of Johannes with Masip, the evidence stops short of certainty.

CHAPTER IV

GASPAR REQUENA AND PEDRO DE RUBIALES

FROM the circle of Paolo da San Leocadio rather than of Fernando de Llanos and Fernando Yáñez de la Almedina there emerged a style that cumbersomely once again [1] must be ascribed to a partnership of two artists rather than to a single personality, since it is impossible to distinguish the individual contributions of each to their one documented work, which indeed is entirely homogeneous in character, and since we cannot identify any separate achievements by either. To Señorita Consolación Campos [2] belongs the credit of enabling us to give names to the exponents of this phase of the Valencian school through her recognition of a series of five panels in the Provincial Museum at Valencia as the remains of a retable from the convent of the Puridad in the city, for which she publishes also the contract of the painters Gaspar Requena and Pedro de Rubiales, dated April 20, 1540. She includes in her article the information that we possess about the two masters, but, as her little monograph is found in a periodical accessible to very few readers and as one or two of her statements need modification, I will summarize the ascertained data, with some slight comment.

Gaspar Requena, coming from the town of Cocentaina, south of Valencia, is usually alleged, without definite proof, to have been a brother of the somewhat better known painter, Vicente Requena, who will concern us in a subsequent volume. He must have been still a fairly young man in 1540 when he collaborated in the retable for the nuns of the Puridad, since in 1580 and 1583 he was still strong enough in mind and body to be called in as an expert to assess the proper price of certain Valencian works of art. The Baron de Alcahalí, in his Dictionary of Valencian artists,[3] tells us (without giving his authority) that Gaspar did not venture matrimony until 1555, and he confirms the high estimation in which the painter's aesthetic judg-

---

[1] See, for example, vol. X, p. 134, and below, p. 307.
[2] In *Anales de la Universidad de Valencia*, XI (1930–1931), 187–202.
[3] Pp. 254–255.

ment was held in his later years by declaring that other masters did not consider their productions to be really finished until they had submitted them to Gaspar's "friendly and paternal criticism." The only record that has come to light in regard to his productive activity, other than upon the retable of the Puridad, has to do merely with a job of gilding in the governmental building at Valencia, the Palacio de la Generalidad, in 1576.

Pedro de Rubiales enjoys a modest but wrongly acquired renown because Ceán Bermúdez and others have confused [4] him with Francisco de Rubiales, called in Italian Francesco Ruviale or Roviale and nicknamed il Polidorino, the assistant of Francesco Salviati and Vasari. The confusion was made the more possible because both Pedro and Francisco de Rubiales hailed originally from Estremadura and presumably belonged to the same artistic family. The writer of the Dictionary of the famous men of Estremadura, Nicolás Díaz y Pérez,[5] says that Pedro was born on April 3, 1511, and, although he too labors under the delusion that Pedro was the associate of Salviati and Vasari, he could hardly have copied the date of Francisco de Rubiales's birth from some record and put it down as that of Pedro. He goes on to assert that Pedro died at Rome in 1582, but once more he fails to reveal the source of his information. Inasmuch as the companion of Salviati was not Pedro, it cannot be securely demonstrated, as Señorita Campos has followed her predecessors in alleging, that Pedro ever went to Italy; but it is highly likely that such was the case, for Juan de Valverde in his *Historia de la composición del cuerpo humano*, published at Rome in 1556,[6] does a Spanish artist whom he specifically dubs "Pedro Rubiales of Estremadura" the tremendous honor of coupling him with Michael Angelo not only as an expert in the science of anatomy but also as one of the world's greatest painters, and he would scarcely have conceived such superlatives if Pedro had remained in the comparative obscurity and provincialism that must be admitted to have beclouded Valencia at this period. In any case Pedro undoubtedly dwelt for a considerable time at Valencia prior to betaking himself to Italy, for he entered into a partnership with a painter of

[4] See the entries *Pedro de Rubiales* and *Francesco Ruviale* in the Thieme-Becker *Lexikon.*

[5] *Diccionario histórico, biográfico, crítico y bibliográfico de autores, artistas, y estremeños ilustres*, Madrid, 1884, II, 309.

[6] F. J. Sánchez Cantón, *Fuentes literarias para la historia del arte español*, V, 333-334.

the region, Gaspar Requena, he is called in the contract of 1540 "Valentiae habitator," and, if he continued to collaborate with Requena in the other works in which I shall endeavor to prove the existence of the same manner, he would have had time to execute commissions as far distant in the range of the Valencian school as Murcia and Orihuela. I have had occasion in volume IX [7] to observe that no works either of Pedro or of Francisco de Rubiales have been recognized in their native Estremadura.

The subjects of more than one of the panels in the Museum that now concern us are so unusual that their identity with themes mentioned in the contract for the retable of the convent of the Puridad makes certain their derivation from this source. The contract describes the altarpiece demanded as a "retable of the virgins," and its further stipulations show that by the term "virgins" was meant virgin martyrs. The principal compartment was to represent "St. Ursula, with the sea and [8] a ship, disembarking," and on either side of her were to be compartments with figures of Sts. Catherine, Agnes, Angelica, and Margaret. To the predella were consigned Sts. Lucy, Agatha, and Cecilia; to the lateral *guardapolvos*, Sts. Barbara, Emerentiana, Quiteria, and Apollonia; and to the upper pieces of the *guardapolvos* three other canonized young women whose names the document does not specify.

Of the five pieces preserved in the Provincial Museum at Valencia, one is fortunately the principal compartment depicting, exactly in the way prescribed in the contract, St. Ursula and five of her maidens as just landed upon the beach, with the sea and their ship in the offing (Fig. 27). Señorita Campos understands that they are oddly imagined as making their first disembarkation on the shore of the ocean before proceeding up the Rhine to the chief place with which they are connected, Cologne; but, as Shakespeare bestows a coast upon Bohemia, so the nuns and their two painters may have had such a vague idea of northern geography that they thought of Cologne as a maritime port. Although I can recall no other instance in which this scene is made the centre of an altarpiece, Señorita Campos carries scholarly prudence to an extreme but admirable point by cautioning that such altarpieces

[7] P. 720.
[8] Señorita Campos, in reproducing the contract, gives the words as "sea or a ship"; but this must be a misprint, and on an earlier page (196) she puts it rightly as "and a ship."

FIG. 27. REQUENA AND RUBIALES. ST. URSULA
AND HER MAIDENS LANDING AT COLOGNE,
SECTION OF RETABLE. PROVINCIAL
MUSEUM, VALENCIA

(From an article by Consolación Campos)

might have existed and that therefore the final confirmation of the identity with the retable of the contract is that the preserved parts include the figures of the very rare saints, Emerentiana and Angelica, so labelled on little scrolls in the lower right corners of the panels. The two other preserved effigies are Sts. Catherine and Agnes, and this set of four virgin martyrs, since their panels are only slightly smaller than the main compartment of St. Ursula, would have been ranged in horizontal pairs on each side of it, or, if there was a (lost) piece above the St. Ursula, in vertical pairs. The original intent had been to relegate St. Emerentiana to the *guardapolvos*, but there are many examples of more drastic changes in iconographic programs than her transfer to the body of the structure.[9] She finds a place in the retable as the foster-sister of St. Agnes. The name of a martyred St. Angelica does not occur in any of the ordinary hagiographical compilations, but we may surmise that she is identical with the St. Angelina whose day is October 21 and the invention of whose body is celebrated at Valencia on April 29.[10] Since the feast of St. Ursula also occurs on October 21 and since a St. Angelina is one of her many companions to whom tradition has given a name,[11] the likelihood is that is was this St. Angelina or Angelica who was honored at Valencia and ensconced in the retable of the Puridad.[12]

The style is one of considerable competence, developing farther towards the High Renaissance the purer, serener, and more idealistic Italian manner implanted by Paolo da San Leocadio in the Valencian region, as contrasted with the sterner modes of the two Fernandos

[9] The language of the contract does not make it clear whether the figures of the virgin martyrs adjoining the principal compartment were to be aligned horizontally or set in vertical pairs. The latter arrangement is followed in the present installation in the Museum, which goes back at least to the beginning of the last quarter of the nineteenth century and may reflect the form in which the remains of the retable were found in the church, whether or not this form preserved alterations made while the retable was in process of execution.

[10] J. E. Stadler and F. J. Heim, *Vollständiges Heiliger-Lexikon*, I, 208.

[11] See the Bollandists under October 21, p. 259.

[12] By indefatigable search through the purlieus of the Museum, my friends, Don Manuel González Martí and Don Leandro de Saralegui, have finally ferreted out the only fragment, a pinnacle representing the First Person of the Trinity with the dove of the Holy Spirit, that Tormo (*Valencia: los Museos*, 62) could have meant by the panel of the "Eternal Father" that he catalogues as a part of the retable of the virgin martyrs; but (cf. the recent photograph by the Archivo Mas, Barcelona, No. 19702) I seriously doubt whether the panel belonged to the retable or was executed by the partners, particularly when I compare it with the same subject at the summit of their presumptive altarpiece of St. Catherine at Orihuela (see below, p. 92), and I should judge it a work of the later sixteenth or even of the seventeenth century.

and their satellites, but unexpectedly at so late a date a good deal of primitive restraint still pleasantly remains. If Pedro de Rubiales constituted an important stylistic factor in the partnership, he must have accommodated himself to the artistic fashions of this part of Spain. One of the distinctive qualities incorporated in the retable of the virgins is a predilection for very delicate youthful types and a captivating nicety in the drawing and modelling of their countenances. In other works in the same manner, we shall find the fondness for bleak landscapes, studded with jagged cliffs, that may be descried behind the Sts. Agnes and Angelica.

These other works are almost wholly confined to the cities of Orihuela and Murcia, close to each other and far south of Valencia, yet well within the domain of the Valencian school. My long study of the paintings at Orihuela and Murcia and my frequent returns, at intervals, to the problem have eventually convinced me that they are productions of Requena and Rubiales; but I will cautiously place a question-mark in the captions under the illustrations, waiting until time shall have established the justness of my opinions. We noted at the beginning of the chapter that we cannot, with our present knowledge, dissociate the personalities of the partners but are obliged to attach both their names to the aspect of Valencian art that now occupies our attention.

An eminent example of this aspect is a retable of St. Catherine of Alexandria in a chapel on the south side in the cathedral of Orihuela. The central effigy of the virgin martyr matches, now in the modes of the early Renaissance, the delicate loveliness with which the mediaeval Juan de Leví had represented her a century or more before at Tudela,[13] and she is indeed still archaically relieved against a gold canopy (Fig. 28). In the compartment at the left is depicted her ordeal of the wheels (Fig. 29), and at the right her final decapitation. The subjects at the next higher range are three figures of saints, in the middle Paul (also placed in front of a textile, according to the older fashions of Spanish art) and at the sides James Major and Christopher. The theme of the *remate* is the usual one, the Crucifixion. The Pietà at the centre of the predella is set between busts of four worthies of the elder dispensation, all still conforming to the practices of the mediaeval altarpieces in that they are accompanied by scrolls with sentences from their writings (in this case with reference to the Pas-

[13] Vols. III, p. 186, and IV, p. 628.

FIG. 28. REQUENA AND RUBIALES(?). ST. CATHERINE, CENTRE OF
RETABLE. CATHEDRAL, ORIHUELA
(*Photo. Archivo Mas*)

FIG. 29. REQUENA AND RUBIALES(?). ST. CATHERINE'S ORDEAL
OF THE WHEELS, SECTION OF RETABLE. CATHEDRAL,
ORIHUELA

(*Photo. Archivo Mas*)

sion), Jeremiah, Isaiah, Daniel, and David.[14] The summit of the *guardapolvos* is decorated with the Eternal Father bestowing His benediction; at the next level, beside the Crucifixion are the seated forms of Sts. Lucy and (?) Apollonia; then come the cross-pieces with busts of Sts. Agatha and Quiteria; and the principal uprights in these accessories of the retable are reserved for full-lengths of the four Fathers of the Church.

The facial analogy of the central St. Catherine to the maidens in the retable from the Puridad, especially to the girl just behind St. Ursula, the exquisiteness lavished upon her delineation, and the mode of shadowing the countenances are nearly enough to establish the attribution; but there are further correspondences. The partners reveal a fondness for a congeries of small folds of drapery, as over the arms of the Valencian Sts. Catherine and Agnes, and this peculiarity is even more obvious in such parts of the Orihuela retable as the lower sweep of the central St. Catherine's mantle, the vestments of the Father of the Church at the upper right, and the winding-sheet of Christ in the Pietà. Throughout the retable, also, the settings are the stern and rocky landscapes of the panels at Valencia. The number of virginal saints included in the thematic material, considered in conjunction with the subjects of the altarpiece from the Puridad, might be interpreted as suggesting that the shop of Requena and Rubiales was famous for the representation of such personages.

Whether or not the array of evidence is judged by the reader, as well as by me, to place the retable of St. Catherine definitively under the aegis of the partners, he cannot deny that the author or authors of the retable painted also another, rather large altarpiece in the cathedral of Orihuela, at the time of my visit in 1934 consigned to the Sala Capitular (Fig. 30).[15] In its present condition, the altarpiece preserves: in its main body, three standing effigies, at the middle the Madonna with the Child and at the sides St. Peter and (?) St. Anne; the central pinnacle of the Crucifixion; and in the predella four busts of sacred personages set against a continuous landscape, Joachim (?), Catherine, John Baptist, and (?) Anthony Abbot. Curiously enough, the three principal figures and the Crucifixion argue neither for nor against the same attribution as the other retable in the church, al-

---

[14] Jeremiah, XI, 19; Isaiah, I, 6; Daniel, IX, 26; and David, Psalms, XXII, 16 (Foderunt manus meas et pedes meos).

[15] Shown in the Barcelona Exposition of 1929 as No. 164.

FIG. 30. REQUENA AND RUBIALES(?). RETABLE. CATHEDRAL,
ORIHUELA

(*Photo. Archivo Mas*)

though the Crucifixions in both monuments possess analogous simple
compositions and sorts of landscape; and it is only the Sts. Catherine
and John, together with the setting, in the predella that leave no
doubt. The faces of the virgin martyr here and in the principal compartment of the other retable are almost replicas, and the Baptist
exactly duplicates in neurotic excitement, particularly of the eyes, the
stricken executioner directly behind St. Catherine in the ordeal of the
wheels. Nor are the affiliations confined to the human types, but the
cleft and slanting rock in the background of the ordeal of the wheels
is repeated well-nigh line for line between the Baptist and Catherine
of the predella.

A precariously injured panel of St. Michael that from the Colegio
de Sto. Domingo at Orihuela has recently passed to the Diocesan
Museum (Fig. 31) reveals less manifest links with the other works in
the city than with the Valencian altarpiece from the Puridad, as well
as with a retable at Murcia which we shall soon analyze; and it thus
assumes the importance, since after all it surely enjoyed the same authorship as the other Orihuela productions, of compactly tying these
productions and the Murcia retable to the documented altarpiece. The
archangel's countenance, elegant inclination of the head, and even the
gesture of the right arm are so nearly reiterated in the St. Ursula in
the Valencian series that I do not see how anyone could bring himself
to believe in execution by two different artists. Not only is St. Michael
framed in the background by the threatening geological formations
characteristic of Requena and Rubiales, but architectural monuments
punctuate these formations exactly as behind the Sts. Agnes and
Angelica of the Museum at Valencia. Resemblances in the other
paintings at Orihuela are, of course, not far to seek, although of
slightly less specific a nature — grim landscapes, identical modelling
and chiaroscuro in the male actors in St. Catherine's ordeal of the
wheels, or, in the altarpiece in the Sala Capitular of the cathedral,
analogous facial traits in the Madonna and similarly mannered droop-
ings of the heads in the busts of the predella.

The affinities with the productions of Requena and Rubiales at
Orihuela and Valencia are so precise in a retable in the chapel of S.
Juan, now the Sala Capitular, in the cathedral of Murcia that, in my
opinion, they conclusively proclaim the same authorship (Fig. 32).
Flimsy documentary evidence has hitherto ordinarily been taken as

FIG. 31. REQUENA AND RUBIALES(?). ST. MICHAEL. DIOCESAN
MUSEUM, ORIHUELA

sufficient to credit an Andrés de Llanos [16] with the retable's paintings. Fernando de Llanos eventually found employment at Murcia,[17] and Andrés is generally and probably with correctness supposed to have been a relative, perhaps his son or nephew. Among our records of Fernando at Murcia, we find that he was remunerated in 1520 for the addition of paintings or possibly just polychromy to the no longer extant sculptured retable over the high altar of the cathedral, and further work on this retable, consisting in polychromy and gilding, was done from 1526 to 1545 by Andrés de Llanos, at first in collaboration with a Miguel Jerónimo de la Lanza.[18] The lost paintings of the organ and its shutters in the church provided another commission that fell to the partners' lot.

The retable that particularly concerns our investigation, in the chapel of S. Juan, has been attributed to Andrés de Llanos because González Simancas in 1911 [19] baldy stated, without quoting the document, that the financial records of the cathedral in 1545 proved him to have executed it, but Baquero Almansa [20] in 1913 modified this statement by purporting to quote the entry in the records as specifying that Andrés was paid only for *assisting* in the painting of the retable 6240 *maravedís*, decidedly too small a sum to allow the general assumption that he was the retable's chief master and certainly implying that, as in the case of the *retable mayor*, he was responsible only for the polychromy of its architectural and sculptural frames. It is true that Baquero Almansa is an untrustworthy guide in the archives, making what seems the error of referring here the entry of 1545 to Fernando de Llanos instead of Andrés and alleging that the document mentions as the place of the retable the chapel of the Cabildo (i.e.,

---

[16] See below, p. 184.

[17] See below, p. 184.

[18] Bertaux (*Gazette des beaux-arts*, 1908, I, 345 ff.) believed that the retable included painted panels and that the commission to Andrés de Llanos and Miguel Jerónimo de la Lanza to complete the polychromy included the execution of these; but he did not know the documents afterwards published by González Simancas (*Revista de archivos*, XXIV, 1911, pp. 535–536) in regard to the sculpturing of the retable by a Master Antonio, and the very document of 1526 that he quotes in regard to the activity of Andrés de Llanos and Miguel de la Lanza upon the retable, as well as the subsequent records of 1528, 1534, and 1545 (González Simancas, 537), must, in my opinion, be interpreted as referring only to the polychromy and gilding. That earlier in 1520 *Fernando* de Llanos had made painted panels as companion-pieces to the sculpture, cannot be absolutely denied. See also A. Baquero Almansa, *Catálogo de los profesores de las bellas artes murcianos*, Murcia, 1913, p. 46.

[19] *Op. cit.*, 537.

[20] *Op. cit.*, 47.

FIG. 32. REQUENA AND RUBIALES(?). RETABLE. CATHEDRAL,
MURCIA

the Sala Capitular), into which the chapel of S. Juan had not then been transformed; but it is hardly possible that he would have introduced into the document out of the whole cloth the amount of the sum or the word implying that the artist merely assisted on the retable. The joint testimony of Bertaux, González Simancas, and Tormo [21] would appear to establish that Baquero Almansa is wrong in substituting Fernando for Andrés as the man engaged on the retable in the chapel, but the lack of absolute surety on this point is a further reason for refusing to put down Andrés as the creator of the retable's paintings. The gist of the whole matter is that the uncertain witness from the archives is far outweighed by the stylistic arguments for an attribution to Requena and Rubiales. The activity of the Italian Jacopo Torni, called by the Spaniards Jácobo Florentín, at Murcia in 1521 as architect and sculptor might suggest the idea of seeking his hand, since he was also a painter, in the retable's panels which we are now considering and which, after all, are carried out in a style hardly differing from that of the High Italian Renaissance, but no suppposition of this kind is justified on the basis of our scantily preserved record of his pictorial manner. [22]

Although the Baptist was included in the chapel's original dedication, St. John Evangelist is the personage honored in the retable's principal compartment, and he is flanked in the lateral spaces by Sts. Peter and Paul. The only other paintings in the structure occur in the predella, at the centre the dead Christ supported by two angels and at the sides half-lengths of the four Fathers of the Church disposed in pairs.

The searcher for proof of the attribution to Requena and Rubiales should look first at the St. John, who intimately resembles in countenance and in technical delicacy not only the central St. Catherine at Orihuela but also, among the figures at Valencia, especially the same virgin martyr. His drapery also is soon perceived to exemplify the characteristic treatment that we have analyzed on a former page. When we compare the faces of the angels in the Pietà and of the St. Michael in the Diocesan Museum at Orihuela, we arrive at practical identity. Nor are correspondences lacking in the delineations of the Fathers at Murcia and in the Orihuela retable of St. Catherine. The second Father from the left (Augustine ?) in the former monument does not vary much from the St. Gregory on the Orihuela *guarda-*

---

[21] *Levante*, 344.   [22] Vol. X, p. 273.

polvos; the bishop at the extreme right (Ambrose ?) is even more like the prelate on the *guardapolvos* at the upper left; and the two St. Jeromes are interrelated. The St. Paul is differently conceived in the two retables, and yet the representation at Murcia finds a fairly exact parallel on the Orihuela *guardapolvos* in the effigy of God the Father. The landscapes display once more the rocky bleakness to which Requena and Rubiales have accustomed us, and behind the St. John, with even a nearer approximation to some of their backgrounds, the austerity of the vista is relieved by accents of clustered buildings.

The compositions for the Pietà are very similar in the Murcia retable and the Orihuela altarpiece of St. Catherine, stirring vivid memories of Giovanni Bellini's treatments of the theme, but in view of the closely corresponding arrangements of the subject by the Cabanyes Master, as notably in his retable of Sts. Dionysius and Margaret,[23] the analogy to the Venetian examples may be fortuitous, the result of a separate, local Valencian development. The types of the Fathers in the Murcia predella could be interpreted as bespeaking rather clearly the relations of Requena and Rubiales to the tradition established at Valencia by Paolo da San Leocadio.

The style of all these works that we are associating with Requena and Rubiales declares itself unmistakably in a panel in the Museum at Murcia depicting the miraculously entombed body of Santiago lying on the Galician shore as one of his disciples brings the cart drawn by the tamed bulls to take the sacred remains to Queen Lupa's palace (Fig. 33). The type of the disciple at once stirs memories of figures in the Orihuela retable of St. Catherine, especially of the St. Christopher and the discomfited executioner behind the martyr in the ordeal of the wheels. The St. Paul in the retable and again the executioner provide counterparts for the way in which the disciple's hair is blown forth from the side of his face. The Apostle's two followers in the background conform in general to the sort of personages depicted in the predella of the second altarpiece at Orihuela, and the landscape is precisely of the nature that we have so often had occasion to describe in the preceding paragraphs. Furthermore, the panel supplies an additional tangible link between the Orihuela-Murcia group and the documented retable of Requena and Rubiales in the Valencian Museum, since the twisting *contrapposto* of the disciple with the cart is

[23] Vol. VI, p. 397.

repeated almost line by line in the St. Ursula. Unusual in this whole series of paintings is such a naturalistic touch as the companion of St. James reading beside the body while he patiently awaits its transportation.

FIG. 33. REQUENA AND RUBIALES(?). PREPARATION FOR TRANS-
PORTATION OF ST. JAMES MAJOR'S BODY TO QUEEN LUPA'S
PALACE. MUSEUM, MURCIA
(*Photo. Archivo Mas*)

It is hard to resist the temptation to see the partners' style in a Nativity in the Diocesan Museum at Tarragona, which Saralegui [24] has provisionally ascribed to the Cabanyes Master (Fig. 34). The analogies to this artist's manner discerned by the Spanish scholar have much validity; but they are explicable on the ground of a partial interconnection between his creations and the works that we are now

[24] *Archivo español de arte*, XVIII (1945), 18.

FIG. 34. REQUENA AND RUBIALES(?). NATIVITY.
DIOCESAN MUSEUM, TARRAGONA
(*From an article by Saralegui*)

considering, and we have indeed discovered one indication of such affinity in the Murcia retable. Saralegui himself admits in the Nativity a somewhat more mature phase of the Valencian school than the authenticated achievements of the Cabanyes Master incorporate. We can force our eyes into seeing vague correspondences to the manner of Damián Forment, whose pictorial achievements are similar to those of the Cabanyes Master;[25] but many factors seem to pull the picture pretty definitely into our legacy from Requena and Rubiales. The facial resemblance of the Virgin and some of the angels in the Tarragona panel to the central St. Catherine at Orihuela is very persuasive; the masculine types can easily be reconciled with the attribution, especially the St. Joseph, who recalls the St. Joachim in the predella of the smaller retable at Orihuela; and the landscape of Palestine has assumed the defining mountainous severity. No more is known of the panel's history than that it existed in one of the dependencies of the cathedral of Tarragona before the formation of the Diocesan Museum in the first part of the twentieth century; but, if it was originally done for Tarragona and not, with some other ultimate provenience, merely presented to the church by a pious donor, its acceptance as an example of the modes of Requena and Rubiales would mean that their popularity stretched as far north of Valencia as we have found it to reach at the south to Murcia and Orihuela.

[25] See below, p. 143.

CHAPTER V

THE CHINCHILLA MASTER (PEDRO DELGADO?)

If we could entirely neglect other possibilities, chiefly the consideration that the very interesting artist who now concerns us might conceivably embody merely a late stage in the development of the painter of Toledo, Pedro Delgado, both stylistic and circumstantial evidence would naturally place him in the Valencian school. After we have analyzed his recognizable, extant works and thus are provided with material upon which to base an examination of the problem, we shall return and weigh the other possibilities, but the fact that I include him in the present volume indicates that in my opinion the hypothesis of a connection with the artistic *milieu* of Valencia must very seriously be taken into account.

The name that I have chosen for covering his anonymity comes from the town, Chinchilla de Monte-Aragón, southeast of Albacete, where he has left us a work *in situ*, a large *Noli me tangere* in the church of Sta. María del Salvador (Fig. 35). One of his peculiarities at once appears, the multiplication, in the landscape, of small, subordinate events, usually connected with the main theme. In the centre of the background is enacted the scene of the Magdalene (here, as in the twentieth chapter of St. John's Gospel, without any other holy woman) arriving on the morning of the Resurrection at the empty sepulchre and beholding there the "two angels in white." On a path at the edge of a knoll at the left, there stands poised a young female saint in wind-blown draperies, who can scarcely be anyone else than again the Magdalene, represented, according to the original iconography with which the painter treats these secondary episodes, as on her way to the sepulchre with the spices for the sacred body and as obliged by the geography to descend from an eminence to the plain where the tomb lies. Just beneath, in one of the pieces of architecture of the Renaissance in which, as we shall find in another of the painter's works, he is prone to set the subordinate incidents, we look upon a still prior event in her story, a very strange treatment of her washing of Christ's feet at the meal in the house of Simon. It is possible that the panel has been cut at both sides, but, since the other work reveals that

FIG. 35. THE CHINCHILLA MASTER. *NOLI ME TANGERE.* STA.
MARÍA DEL SALVADOR, CHINCHILLA DE MONTE-ARAGON
(*Photo. Archivo Mas*)

he had a predilection for depicting edifices parts of which are conceived as extending beyond the frame and the picture's space, we probably have not lost much of the open apartment where the feast takes place. In any case, all that the panel at least now exhibits of the Magdalene, as she kneels to wash Our Lord's feet, is a bit of her drapery outspread in front of the table, and only three Apostles are visible, two seated at the board and a third, for some queer reason, shown as issuing from the door with a jar to fetch water. In the actual scene of the *Noli me tangere* in the foreground, the Magdalene's box of ointment is inscribed at the top with the letters M A D A, which may be an abbreviation of the beginning of her name, and at the bottom with what is perhaps the word, *Surrexit*, thought of as partly concealed by her hand. Exhibiting his characteristic alertness to new ideas in illustration as well as in technique, the painter has sought, like Piero della Francesca, albeit with far less ability, to transmit the effect of the earliness of the morning at the first Easter stressed in the accounts in the New Testament. Whereas Piero marvellously spreads through his great Resurrection the diffused light just before dawn, the Chinchilla Master displays the blazing edge of the sun commencing to emerge above the distant line of the horizon.

The underpinning of the Master's style is ultimately derived from the Low Countries, so that he must have originated in the Hispano-Flemish manner of the end of the fifteenth century or at least have come intimately into contact with this manner. It is particularly in the elaborately puckered folds of the draperies that the Flemish affiliations are strongly pronounced, in the red cope of Christ and in the copious and intricate masses of the Magdalene's garments. The crinklings in the sleeve of her right arm seem Flemish rather than Squarcionesque; but a belief in the painter's fruitful acquaintance with the Italian Renaissance, especially with the circle of Piero della Francesca, will be forced upon us by the extensive architectural studies in the background of the Madonna in the Barcelona Museum that we shall claim for him, and an example of such interest is prominent in the building that shelters the feast of Simon in the left distance of the *Noli me tangere*. Although in the Barcelona picture the tendency to use the sacred scenes in the background as mere excuses for representations of architecture insistently suggests that the artist enjoyed some sort of familiarity with phases of the modes established by Piero della Francesca in Umbria and central Italy in general, yet it must not be forgotten that architecture plays a large rôle in the school of Ferrara, and the notes which I took when examining the Chinchilla panel at the Seville Exposition of 1929–1930 reveal that I derived from it the impression of a kind of Ferrarese overtone.

The Chinchilla Master betrays a curious dichotomy: in the main subject in the foreground, he projects at us great, hulking forms, but, when he comes to the lesser scale of the figures in the background, he manifests bewitching delicacy both in feeling and in execution. The posture of Christ in the *Noli me tangere* is even awkwardly articulated, and it is in the little actors, made filmy in acknowledgement of the demands of aërial perspective imposed by their remoteness from our vision, that he attains to the ability to give true aesthetic delight. He is also a landscapist of no mean talents, spreading out for us a vista of quite Umbrian depth that extends to a far-off horizon and is pleasantly punctuated, not only by romantic towns, castles, trees, and shrubbery, but also in the extreme distance by small, conventionalized hills like those of Piero della Francesca and nearer at hand by loftier eminences. Among his several idiosyncrasies is his habit of dividing a picture into halves by a most obvious and arbitrarily placed vertical axis, in the case of the *Noli me tangere* by the thin trunk of a palm tree rising from the ground without foliage until it begins to break into leaf at the top of the panel.

Inasmuch as the works in the following of Fernando de Llanos and Fernando Yáñez at Albacete prove that the domain of the Valencian school extended even further west in this region than Chinchilla and as the latter town belonged to the diocese of Murcia which depended for its art upon Valencia, the objective evidence, however slight, would imply, other things being equal, that the painter was a member of this school. The coalition of Flemish with Italian traits of the kind that at least in some degree may have emanated from the territory of the Ferrarese school would guide us for the painter's origins to the phase of the Valencian school which was inaugurated, or at least greatly stimulated, by Rodrigo Borgia's importation from Italy, in 1472, of the artists Paolo da San Leocadio, Francesco Pagano, and Master Richard [1] and which focused partly in the Osonas and their *entourage*. Indeed Saralegui, before he proposed an attribution of the Chinchilla picture that we shall subsequently ponder, was minded [2] to place it in

[1] Vol. VI, pp. 170 ff., and above, p. 9.
[2] *Boletín de la Sociedad Española de Excursiones*, XL (1932), 53.

the Osonas' circle. In one work preserved from Paolo da San Leocadio's early period, the *sacra conversazione* in the National Gallery
at London,[3] the subordinate figures of Sts. Joseph, Catherine, Agatha,
and Lucy are distributed through the landscape and architecture of
the background in much the same way as in the Chinchilla Master's
creations. Even if the *sacra conversazione* was executed by Paolo during a temporary return to Italy, he probably painted in Spain other lost
productions of the sort that our Master could have seen. The Osonas
and their circle exhibited keen interest in architecture of the Renaissance, especially Rodrigo the younger and the St. Narcissus Master,
but not to the point that we shall discover in the Chinchilla Master's
Barcelona Madonna, where the scenes from the New Testament in
the background are dwarfed by the enthusiastic concern with the edifices in which they are enacted. We are virtually compelled by this
characteristic to postulate a sojourn of our painter in Umbria and
among the works of Piero della Francesca and his pupils in other
parts of central Italy, for, even if Tormo was right in assuming an
influence of Piero upon Rodrigo de Osona the elder,[4] it did not inspire
him, so far as we can judge from his extant paintings, to any such all-
consuming study of architecture as will surprise us in the Chinchilla
Master's panel at Barcelona.

The provenience of this panel is unknown, since until very recently
it lay unregarded in the storerooms of the Museum of Catalan Art
without any record concerning its previous history and has only in
these last years been placed on exhibition (Fig. 36). The foreground
is occupied by the Madonna holding the Child, enthroned in a curule
chair of rich marbles, and accompanied by the infant Baptist, who
with his emblem of the lamb sits at the right upon an opulent oriental
rug laid over the dais that supports the chair. The composition for
the Madonna and Child is taken directly from Dürer's engraving of
the Virgin with a Monkey, dated about 1498; but the print does not
include the Baptist, and the Chinchilla Master, with his typical whim-
sicality, has added to the monkey at Mary's feet a little white poodle
seeking to frighten the beast by its bark. Four angels flutter above her
head carrying a queer canopy that looks as if were made of a striped
and tasseled shawl and billows with the wind. At the top of the panel
the Eternal Father sheds upon the sacred group the dove of the Holy

[3] Vol. VII, p. 883, and above, p. 17.
[4] See my vol. VI, p. 182.

Fig. 36. THE CHINCHILLA MASTER. MADONNA, CHILD, AND INFANT
JOHN. MUSEUM OF CATALAN ART, BARCELONA

(*Photo. Archivo Mas*)

Spirit, which, again according to the artist's eccentric imagination, oddly flies between the Virgin's head and her peculiar, platter-like halo and is connected with the First Person of the Trinity by three rays of light, materialized as if they constituted a ladder without rungs descending from the Father through the clouds and miraculously piercing also the canopy.

Numerous episodes of the Birth and Infancy take place in diminished scale in the emphasized pieces of architecture and in the landscape of the background. A chamber of the fine mansion at the left is chosen as the scene of the Annunciation, and its courtyard constitutes the setting for the Adoration of the Child by the parents and shepherds. The even statelier palace at the right becomes the locality of the Adoration of the Wise Men and a shelter for their suite, among whom a servant is naturalistically depicted as unpacking one of the chests containing the royal gifts. In front of the palace the Holy Family plod onward in their Flight into Egypt, and below they rest in a forest while their donkey grazes in a near-lying field. Far-off, in the country just above and to the right of the mansion at the left the pursuing soldiers of Herod are misdirected by the husbandman in regard to the time of the Family's passing. The landscape below the mansion is reserved for a representation of the Massacre of the Innocents, unusually conceived as happening beside a charmingly romantic river, at the edges of which, further forward in the picture, there are distributed the four early Fathers of the Church, who thus extraordinarily but not inappropriately increase the iconographic repertory surrounding the Mother, her Son, and St. John. Other small figures and groups are scattered in the extensive landscape, but they are probably the bits of *genre* frequent in the backgrounds of other painters of the time, although it is possible that some of them are intended as enacting incidents from the Bible that I fail to recognize. To complete the cycle from the Virgin's life, her participation in Pentecost is limned in the book of hours or missal that she fingers. The sky is quite as alive with activity as the earth. Amidst the symmetrically disposed puffs as of smoke into which the capricious painter conventionalizes the clouds, sundry angels perform various offices, the majority making music, as, for instance, in the choruses at the centres of two wreaths of such puffs at the borders of the picture or as in the cluster of *putti* sporting about the ladder of rays directly above the canopy. Close to the Eternal Father at the left, however, there may be descried St. Michael worsting the dragon.

The attribution to the Chinchilla Master gradually but convincingly imposes itself. In essential nature, the picture agrees exactly with the *Noli me tangere*. Burly forms at the front are set against a landscape differing from that of the Chinchilla panel only in a still greater impressiveness. Small figures are engaged in episodes from Holy Writ in this landscape and in its buildings according to the fashion illustrated in the setting to the encounter of Christ with the Magdalene. The face of Christ in the Chinchilla panel, if relieved of the beard, would emerge as almost identical with that of the Barcelona Madonna, but it is particularly in the types of actors in the background and in their vaporous delineation that the styles of the two pictures coincide. The factor which the Barcelona picture brings more into relief than the other and which obliges us to assume the artist's knowledge of certain works produced in the circle of Piero della Francesca and in Umbria is the greater stress upon the pieces of architecture in the background than on the episodes occurring in their precincts. Outstanding among the Italian examples, whoever were their authors, are the Birth and Presentation of the Virgin from the Barberini Palace, Rome, now in the Metropolitan Museum, New York, and the Museum of Fine Arts, Boston, respectively, and the series of the Miracles of St. Bernardine in the Gallery, Perugia.

Don Diego Angulo [5] has wished to credit the Barcelona picture to the school of Catalonia by reason of the resemblances that he discerns to the manner of the Catalan painter of the early Renaissance to whom he tentatively follows some other critics in giving the name of Porta but whom, as I shall argue in my next volume, the evidence seems insufficient for so designating and will leave me with the unhappy alternative of calling only the St. Felix Master. He does not believe the picture to be a work of the St. Felix Master (Porta ?), and the analogies, which certainly exist, do not appear to me concrete enough even to locate it in the Catalan school. The striking similarity of the landscapes is one of the two really significant analogies of this sort. The other applies actually only to a single example among the St. Felix Master's many panels, the representation of the tearing of St. Felix's body upon the *eculeus* in the retable, in the church of S. Félix at Gerona, that gives the Master his pseudonym. Here subordinate incidents in the story are enacted in the background, but there is an

[5] *Archivo español de arte*, XVII (1944), 358. See also another article by him in the same year of the periodical, 329.

important difference from the Chinchilla Master's method in that they take place in front of or beside architectural masses and not within sections of buildings that obviously are of primary interest to the Chinchilla Master and much more emphasized, more clearly defined, and more affectionately studied than in the St. Felix Master's productions. The landscapes (though not the pieces of architecture) correspond also in another Catalan painter of the period, the author of the retable of the Magdalene which has entered the Provincial Museum at Tarragona (not the Diocesan Museum) from one of the near-lying monasteries of Poblet and Santas Creus. Angulo thinks that the Crucifixion in this retable and probably indeed the rest of its compartments were executed by the personality whom he calls Porta, but its author seems to me a separate, though related, artist, for whom in my next volume I shall coin the title of the Master of the Trees and who shares with the Chinchilla Master lingering and pronounced Flemish traits that "Porta" fails to reveal. None of the affinities to the St. Felix Master and the Master of the Trees is of adequate concreteness to attract the Chinchilla Master into their Catalan school, and indeed this Master's style diverges in many fundamental respects. On the other hand, some slight influences may easily have been interchanged between the three painters along the east coast, particularly at Tarragona, for the cathedral of which the Master of the Trees also worked and where in the Middle Ages and early Renaissance there are many traces of artistic contact with Valencia, the Chinchilla Master's presumptive residence. As a matter of fact, Angulo might have adduced as further witness to a connection between the St. Felix and Chinchilla Masters the existence of sections of a retable of St. Andrew by the former in the church of Nuestra Señora del Milagro at Valencia, although it cannot be proved that they were not made rather for Catalonia, whence they might have been brought and presented to the church.

The suggestions of Angulo, however, possess, in my opinion, less validity than Saralegui's [6] eventual contention that Pedro Delgado or a member of his immediate circle was the author of the *Noli me tangere* and therefore, by implication, of the Madonna in the Barcelona Museum. Saralegui arrived at this attribution in 1944, changing, as we have seen, from his earlier assignment of the picture to the circle of the Osonas. It was perhaps in too cavalier a fashion that I tended in vol-

[6] *Boletin de la Sociedad Española de Excursiones*, LII (1944), 28.

ume IX [7] to dismiss his second idea, and I must state at once, at the beginning of my return to the problem, that I do not consider it entirely incredible that the two pictures embody a phase of Delgado later than in his hitherto recognized achievements or that we owe them to an artist who had fallen rather directly under his spell. Even if we confine ourselves to the pair of panels that Saralegui knew, the Chinchilla *Noli me tangere* and Delgado's St. Michael in the Adanero Collection, somewhat arresting similarities emerge, as I admitted in volume IX. There is much the same kind of combination of a Flemish legacy with such Italianate qualities as particularly a love of architecture of the Renaissance, and the Flemish contribution to the amalgam becomes peculiarly analogous in the nature of the puckerings in the Magdalene's and the archangel's widespread draperies. A certain correspondence exists even between the countenances of St. Michael and the Magdalene. Little secondary figures are disseminated also in the landscape behind St. Michael, partly engaged in activities connected with the main theme, but this custom is common in the paintings of the Hispano-Flemish style and of the early Spanish Renaissance and by no means confined to Delgado and the Chinchilla Master. A notable Hispano-Flemish instance in Delgado's own district of the peninsula is the altarpiece of the Virgin of Montserrat in the Museo de Sta. Cruz at Toledo.[8] The pretty landscape itself in the panel of St. Michael lacks the rugged grandeur and sense of distance that the Chinchilla Master fuses with the charm of his vistas.

Nevertheless, when we add to the count the Barcelona picture, not known to Saralegui or at least not ascribed by him to the author of the *Noli me tangere*, still further parallelisms loom to our cognizance. The serenading child-angels on the ladder of rays and their playfulness recall Delgado's marked affection for sporting *putti*. The curious detail of the canopy of cloth over the Barcelona Madonna reminds us of the spread of fabric above the St. Michael and beneath the architectural *baldacchino*. Even Delgado's velleity for inscriptions of enigmatically formed letters is reflected in the canopy of the Barcelona picture; but I am unable to wring from the examples in the canopy any such abbreviation of Delgado's name as Lafuente Ferrari believed that he had extricated from the jumble on the archangel's *baldacchino*, and in fact I cannot descry in them any recognizable words whatsoever.

[7] P. 374, n. 17.   [8] Vol. IX, p. 810.

The Madonna once at Amsterdam, if in volume X [9] I have rightly claimed it for Delgado, adds a few more links with the modes of the Chinchilla Master. The Holy Child in countenance and curly hair is quite surprisingly like the infant Saviour and especially the young Baptist at Barcelona; the small and lovely Virgin of the Coronation inserted in the architecture of the *baldacchino* over the Amsterdam Madonna is treated with a delightful *sfumatezza* precisely conforming to that of the figures in the Chinchilla Master's backgrounds; and the note of caprice that echoes all through this Master's works is perhaps more pronounced in the Amsterdam panel than in Delgado's other creations.

We are ignorant of the place from which the Barcelona Madonna originally came, but Chinchilla de Monte-Aragón is perhaps not too far distant from the province of Toledo, at least the principal seat of Delgado's activities, to have commanded his services. We possess practically no information about his biography, but we have conjectured in volume IX [10] that he might have eventually wandered as far as Saragossa in Aragon. The *Monte-Aragón* added to Chinchilla does not mean that this town is in Aragon, but, if he travelled to such a distance as Saragossa, he might have included Chinchilla in his peregrinations in another direction. Indeed, we have observed in volume X [11] that the author of the Amsterdam Madonna, whom I provisionally identify with Delgado, did a replica of the picture the present existence of which in a collection on the east coast of Spain may signify that it was actually ordered for this region of the peninsula. I cannot, however, bring myself to the definite conviction that Delgado and the Chinchilla Master are one. Although I have mustered a number of analogies between them, I have suggested that the landscape of the St. Michael is still mediaeval in character in contrast to the open, Umbrian breadth of the Renaissance in the Chinchilla Master's settings. Moreover, Delgado's Italianate architecture is confined to the foregrounds and (except in the case of the tentatively attributed St. Anthony of Padua in the Prado) fantastic in its nature, whereas the Chinchilla Master's serious studies of rational edifices of the Renaissance are distributed through his backgrounds. To put the whole matter more generally, the style of Delgado belongs in essence still to the late Middle Ages, despite the decorative furbelows of the

[9] P. 420.

[10] P. 368.

[11] P. 424.

Renaissance, and it retains much of the punctilious method of an illuminator; but, although something of the Hispano-Flemish manner lingers on in the Chinchilla Master, the more magnanimous ambitions of the Renaissance have taken a definite hold upon him and impressed upon his paintings a grander and more modern effect. It would be presumptuous to assert that Delgado did not possess the genius to have developed into such a less precise and less primitive artist, possibly through an emigration to Valencia, whither the meagre evidence about the Chinchilla Master would seem to direct us; but, until further data emerge, it is quite as hazardous to equate the two painters. With our present knowledge the most reasonable conclusion is that the Chinchilla Master derived his manner from the circle of Paolo da San Leocadio and of the Osonas in the Valencian school, possibly modifying what he learned from this circle by contact, in some way as yet obscure to us, with the achievements of Pedro Delgado.

If we could with absolutely easy consciences augment our legacy from the Chinchilla Master by a large [12] panel of the Nativity in the Musée National des Beaux-Arts at Monte Carlo (Fig. 37), we should be provided with one or two more shreds of evidence for contending that he incorporates a late phase in Pedro Delgado's evolution. In the midst of a *general* agreement with the Chinchilla Master's style which would render an attribution to him at least plausible, it is the background that most *specifically* implies him to have been the actual painter. Here at the left we have ledges of whimsical geological formations built up as in the settings to the *Noli me tangere* and the Barcelona Madonna, and upon them, also correspondingly, are enacted in much diminished scale subordinate episodes in the story, at the upper level the proclamation to the shepherds and through the underlying tunneled rock the approach of the Magi's cavalcade. High at the right in the Barcelona picture, a forbidding cliff is similarly pierced, and the low trees in the Nativity grow and are touched with spots of light quite according to the Master's arboreal practices. One could argue that his architectural preoccupations are illustrated by the prominence given to a portal of the Renaissance, intended to represent a bit of a Roman ruin, jutting forth behind the Holy Family, and above the entablature there rises a broken fragment of an arch precisely as in the edifice of the Nativity depicted in the background of the Madonna at Barcelona (although the composition itself of the Birth of

---

[12] The dimensions are 1.45 metres in height by 1.35 in width.

FIG. 37. THE CHINCHILLA MASTER(?). NATIVITY. MUSÉE
NATIONAL DES BEAUX-ARTS, MONTE CARLO
(*Courtesy of the owner*)

Christ is different). The parallelisms extend also quite impressively to the types. The Virgin and St. Joseph, to be sure, are not duplicated in either of the other paintings, but we must remember that these works afford very limited evidence of what the Master's range in conception of human beings may have been. The Child, however, quite startles us by the very close resemblance to the infants grouped with the Barcelona Madonna, and the analogy is almost as tangible between this Madonna and the angel who faces us in the panel at Monte Carlo. I toyed more than once with the idea that the Sardinian Castelsardo Master [13] might be the artist for whom we were here seeking, but in the end I have been obliged to reject him by reason of the more exact similarities in the Chinchilla Master's creations.

The attribution of the Nativity to this Master would add not only another example of a Child intimately akin to the babies depicted by Pedro Delgado but also additional specimens, in the Virgin's and St. Joseph's haloes, of his mysterious inscriptions of capricious letters. As a further indication that Delgado might, after all, be the Chinchilla Master in an early stage of the latter's development, the Monte Carlo panel would furnish an instance of the unexpected embossings of the gold in the former's presumptive Madonnas. [14]

[13] Vol. VIII, pp. 488 ff.
[14] Vol. X, p. 423.

CHAPTER VI

THE HEIRS OF THE PHASE OF VALENCIAN PAINTING INITIATED BY THE PEREA MASTER

1. Nicolás Falcó

In the current of the Perea Master's following started by the Martínez Master [1] there was trained a painter who eventually underwent the influence of Paolo da San Leocadio and, while always giving clearer evidence of his first education, yet united the two streams. His identity with a Nicolás Falcó who figures in the documents of the sixteenth century is a practical surety, and, although, for the sake of absolute honesty, we must modify the noun "surety" by the adjective "practical," the doubt in regard to the identification is so infinitesimal that I will henceforth call him Nicolás Falcó in order not to have to resort to the process of inventing a sobriquet which would designate him as the Master of something or other. The work that may be regarded as revealing his name is the panel of the Virgen de la Sapiencia built into the later baroque retable of the chapel of the University at Valencia. We have had occasion in volume VI [2] to illustrate this panel and to amass the cogent evidence ascribing it to Nicolás Falcó. There exist both his contract of March 12, 1516, for a retable in the chapel of the University and his receipts of March 15 and October 20 for the payments,[3] and, although the documents do not specify the subjects of the retable or particularly the extant panel of the Virgen de la Sapiencia as the principal compartment, the elaborate content of the panel which we have analyzed in volume VI as suited to an educational institution and the correspondence of the style to the date render it virtually impossible to question that the panel derives from Falcó's altarpiece.

[1] Vol. VI, p. 268 and chapter LXXIII.
[2] Pp. 380–384.
[3] Tramoyeres Blasco (*Archivo de arte valenciano*, IV, 1918, p. 21) prints the year as 1516 in the contract and record of the first payment that he publishes, but later (p. 22) he refers to 1516 as one year subsequent to the painting of the retable. Sanchis y Sivera (*Pintores medievales en Valencia*, 220) gives 1515 as the date of the retable but does not make it clear whether he thinks the final payment of October 20 to belong to this year or to 1516.

In volume VI we have debated at length and without conclusive results the difficult and unsolved problems surrounding the personality of Nicolás Falcó, and it continues uncertain whether the author of the Virgen de la Sapiencia was a first or second painter of this surname and this Christian name and whether either of them should be identified with the Martínez Master. Luckily we do not need to return to these vexatious questions, for it is sufficient for our purpose to establish the artistic personality of a Nicolás Falcó, the author of the altarpiece in the University and of many other Valencian works of the early Cinquecento which must be ascribed to him on internal evidence, and it is not really essential that we should know whether he had a homonym who preceded or followed him.

Not that many perplexities do not remain! First, we have asked ourselves in volume VI whether the Martínez Master (or the painter of the retable of the Puridad, if he be not this Master) merely equals an early stage in the career of the author of the Virgen de la Sapiencia, and we tended to answer in the negative.[4] The other works that we shall here attribute to Nicolás Falcó perhaps make the identity a little more plausible, but it is still to be doubted whether even the influence of the Renaissance and specifically of Paolo da San Leocadio could have changed the Martínez Master into the artist who is the subject of the present pages. A far more delicate problem of connoisseurship is raised by the striking stylistic similarities existing between Falcó and another member of the Martínez Master's coterie, the St. Lazarus Master. We have not even been able in volume VI [5] definitely to set aside the proposition that the St. Lazarus Master is only one aspect of the Martínez Master, but in any case the St. Lazarus Master, whoever he was, approximates Falcó so much more closely as to render their identity at least credible. The fact, however, that I give Falcó a separate chapter in my volumes distinct from my earlier discussions

---

[4] P. 382.
[5] Pp. 387 ff. I am disposed, though without conviction, to agree with Saralegui (*Arte español*, XVII, 1947, p. 27) in ascribing to the Martínez Master rather than to the St. Lazarus Master two scenes from the life of St. Lucy in the Collection of the Marqués de Montortal at Valencia; and I am practically ready to follow his guidance (monograph on *El Maestro de Sta. Ana*, Valencia, 1950, p. 62) in crediting the St. Anthony of Padua in the Provincial Museum of this city, which I had been unable to classify exactly (vol. VI, p. 446) and which he has found to have possibly come from the Valencian church of Sto. Domingo, to the painter of the small retable in the Benlliure Collection that (*ibid.*, p. 370) I have placed in the Martínez Master's *entourage*.

of the St. Lazarus Master betrays my leaning towards the opinion that there is enough divergence between them to justify the provisional belief that the latter did not develop into the former. I have often [6] had occasion to point out the desperate puzzles created by the almost inextricable way in which Valencian painters at any given moment in the evolution of the school resemble one another, whether we look at Pedro Nicoláu and his circle or at Jacomart and his imitators or attempt to discriminate between the Artés Master and the Borbotó Master; [7] but Nicolás Falcó appears to be removed from the St. Lazarus Master by the same subtle shades of difference as, let us say, the Master of Martín de Torres from Pedro Nicoláu, although I am bound to admit that documentary discoveries of the future securely proving their identity would not absolutely surprise me.

Many of the events and dates referring to the one, two, or even three (!) painters called Nicolás Falcó in the sixteenth century I have recorded in volume VI. The interested reader will find the other details in Sanchis y Sivera's *Pintores medievales en Valencia*, pp. 220–221, and in Tramoyeres Blasco's article in the *Archivo de arte valenciano*, IV (1918), pp. 3–22. The only fact germane to our present investigation that I did not stress in volume VI is the very continuous employment of a Nicolás Falcó in the decoration of the cathedral of Valencia during the first third of the sixteenth century.

The reason for emphasizing this patronage by the authorities of the cathedral is that it provides some objective substantiation, however slight, for what internal proof plainly reveals, i.e., that Nicolás Falcó, the author of the Virgen de la Sapiencia, executed the series of paintings on cloth in the Sala Capitular Antigua of this church which originally served as organ-shutters and have hitherto been almost universally attributed to Paolo da San Leocadio. We have seen [8] how cogent are the documentary considerations for naming Paolo as their creator in 1513–1514, but stylistic evidence demonstrates conclusively that he could not have done them, thus supplying one of many instances in the history of art where internal proof must supersede what the archives would seem to teach us. In my biography of Paolo [9] I have suggested explanations of the contradiction. The compositional

---

[6] See especially vol. IX, p. 833.

[7] Saralegui (*Arte español*, XV, 1944, p. 84, n. 1) has persuasively ascribed to the Borbotó Master a small panel of the Visitation belonging to the Barón de San Petrillo at Valencia.

[8] P. 15.   [9] P. 16.

similarity of the scenes from the lives of Christ and the Virgin to his authenticated renderings of the themes may be taken for what it is worth as implying that he may have made the general designs for the organ-shutters and given Falcó the task of carrying out the sketches. The likelihood that Paolo so did or instead farmed out the whole order to Falcó finds corroboration in the possibility that on another occasion we shall discover the latter linked with a commission of the former, thus demonstrating the intimate relationship between them and providing a reason for Falcó's stylistic debt to the Italian master. An otherwise unknown Diego de Mallorca is recorded at the time as painting upon the organ-shutters,[10] but his task could have been only that of a very subordinate assistant to Falcó, a mere mixer of pigments or a gilder, since it is hard to descry in the pictures the intrusion of an apprentice's hand.

Of these twelve pictures, one half display six of the Seven Joys of the Virgin that Paolo da San Leocadio had incorporated in his retable in the Colegiata at Gandía, the Annunciation, Nativity, Epiphany, Resurrection, Ascension, and Pentecost. The others are devoted to St. Martin. The episode with the beggar is divided between two pieces, showing plainly that the series were folding shutters, on one side the mounted saint cutting his cloak and accompanied by a pair of soldiers and on the other side Our Lord in the guise of the mendicant with two further members of the military forces as spectators (Fig. 38). A third painting represents the story included by Jacomart[11] and the Sant Quirse Master[12] in their retables of St. Martin, the appearance of the Madonna, Sts. Peter, Paul, and Agnes to him in his cell (Fig. 39). His other celestial visitor, St. Thecla, is absent from Falcó's version; St. Martin is conceived as writing (in Gothic characters), "Beata es, Maria"; and one of his followers witnesses the supernatural occurrence in a dream. The fourth piece is consigned to the rare theme of St. Martin causing the horses of the soldiers attacking him to sink prostrate and motionless upon the ground. The event enshrined in the fifth compartment is almost as infrequent in art, although Simone Martini includes it in his cycle of frescoes in honor of the saint at Assisi: the emperor Valentinian, having refused to open to him the door of the palace, finds himself on his throne

---

[10] Sanchis y Sivera, *La catedral de Valencia*, 229, and *Pintores medievales en Valencia*, 226.

[11] Vol. VI, p. 33.   [12] Vol. IX, p. 850.

FIG. 38. NICOLÁS FALCÓ. CHRIST AS BEGGAR, PART OF SCENE OF
ST. MARTIN'S CHARITY, SECTION OF ORGAN-SHUTTERS.
CATHEDRAL, VALENCIA

(*Photo. Archivo Mas*)

FIG. 39. NICOLÁS FALCÓ. ST. MARTIN'S VISION OF THE VIRGIN, STS.
PETER, PAUL, AND AGNES, SECTION OF ORGAN-SHUTTERS.
CATHEDRAL, VALENCIA

(*Photo. Archivo Mas*)

enveloped, as a punishment, by miraculously created flames. The subject of the last section I have not been able to unearth in the classic account of St. Martin by Sulpicius Severus or in any other source. In the presence of a potentate who, by reason of his identity in features and costume with the sovereign depicted in the former compartment, should be Valentinian, he blesses three kneeling pilgrims, one of them in rags and the third perhaps a woman rather than a youth.[13]

Nicolás Falcó is so far restricted within a certain number of norms and so unfailingly true to these norms that his hand can be easily recognized. Thus in the organ-shutters he literally repeats the types that we see in his panel of the University. The Virgen de la Sapiencia, for instance, reappears unchanged as Our Lady of the Annunciation and Nativity and in her manifestation to St. Martin. The St. Luke is used again for the Apostle at the extreme left in the Ascension and for the Saviour as the beggar. Falcó does not alter the type of the St. Nicholas when he wishes to delineate the excited soldier in the upper right corner of the Resurrection or St. Martin as bishop, especially in the scene of Valentinian's fiery chastisement. Of the six angels girding the throne of the Virgen de la Sapiencia, the one at the extreme right acts the part of St. Agnes visiting St. Martin; the next heavenly spirit is compressed into service as the younger of the two men whose horses St. Martin immobilizes; and the central angel at the left may be perceived again as the shepherd carrying the lamb upon his shoulders in the Nativity.

The organ-shutters disturb us with the possibility of Nicolás Falcó's identity with the St. Lazarus Master more insistently than the panel of the Virgen de la Sapiencia. The types of the two artists are often like brothers or sisters. Most significant is the resemblance of the jaunty youth just behind St. Peter in the burial scene of the retable that gives the St. Lazarus Master his name to the first soldier accompanying St. Martin dividing his cloak; but in this scene the St. Peter also should be compared with the same Apostle appearing to St. Martin, and the kneeling, tattered figure beside the candle-bearer recalls Christ as the recipient of St. Martin's charity. St. Joseph in the Epiphany of the Sala Capitular Antigua is only a very slight modification of a kind of old man frequently emerging in the St.

---

[13] Tormo (*Valencia: los Museos*, 110) cannot be right in his tentative guess that it represents the closing of the doors of Valentinian's palace to the saint.

Lazarus Master's works, as in the worshipper next to St. Peter in the scene of the interment or the Abraham contemplating Dives in hell in the same retable. Further confrontations of this sort could be multiplied almost *ad libitum*, and yet, in addition to other divergences, there is a more rough-hewn primness about the St. Lazarus Master's draughtsmanship that gives me pause when I try to persuade myself that admiration for Paolo da San Leocadio could have transformed him into the personality incorporated in the productions of Nicolás Falcó.

If we set Falcó's works beside those of the Martínez Master and the St. Lazarus Master, we note at once that, while true to the types of their tradition, he has tempered them by an Italian idealization and formal beauty of countenance that the contact with Paolo has inculcated in him. He is an entirely competent supplier of the religious market, but, though freer in manner than the Martínez Master or the St. Lazarus Master, he remains, in comparison with Paolo, somewhat dry, rigid, and uninspired. To a greater degree than Paolo he tends to fill his spaces with large figures, but, when he does leave himself any space for landscape, he exhibits, like the majority even of the provincial Spanish painters of the period, unexpected charm and ability, stimulated doubtless by a study of Paolo's distinguished achievements in this phase of his profession. The view of the hills sloping to the water in the compartment depicting Our Lord as the beggar quite rivals or even surpasses the setting of Ghirlandaio's fresco of the Calling of Sts. Peter and Andrew in the Sistine Chapel.

The painting by Falcó in which there is a possibility that he again labored together with Paolo da San Leocadio was a panel of the Annunciation that until the desolation caused by the Spanish civil war existed as No. 88 of the Diocesan Museum at Valencia (Fig. 40). In all probability it came from the convent of Sta. Clara at Gandía, and, although the curator of the Museum, Don Antonio Barberá Sentamáns, acknowledged to me verbally that he was not *absolutely* certain, he declares in his Catalogue [14] that such was the provenience. It is indeed not out of the question that it should have been a part of the retable for the convent from which three compartments by Paolo himself also reached the Diocesan Museum and three further pieces can still be seen at Gandía.[15] An Annunciation is not mentioned by Émile Bertaux as shown to him in the convent, but neither is

[14] P. 21.   [15] See above, p. 26.

FIG. 40. NICOLÁS FALCÓ. ANNUNCIATION. DIOCESAN MUSEUM,
VALENCIA

(*Photo. Archivo Mas*)

the Pentecost, one of the three parts of the retable that were lodged in the Museum. The measurements of the Annunciation were slightly larger than those of the triad, but the compartments of a retable are by no means always uniform in size. It remains, of course, only in the status of a conjecture that Paolo might have turned over the Annunci-ation in the retable to Falcó in the rôle of an assistant, just as he may have consigned to him the execution of the organ-shutters in the cathedral, but in any case, if Barberá is right in his statement of the provenience, the picture and its style establish Falcó's activity in the same institution where Paolo was working and at the same general period.

The identical relaxation and idealization of the inheritance from the Martínez Master that we have studied in the Virgen de la Sapi-encia and in the organ-shutters stood forth in the Annunciation. In imitation of Paolo's procedure, Falcó even edged the Virgin's mantle with inscriptions, in part from the account of the mystery in the first chapter of St. Luke's Gospel. The words written in the book on her prie-dieu were the well known prophecy of the Incarnation in the fourteenth verse of the seventh chapter of Isaiah. The introduction of a legion of angels in Gabriel's train, though not infrequent in the iconography of the subject, was probably in this instance suggested, as Saralegui [16] has perceived, by the description of the Annunciation in the book, published in 1497, that gives expression to so many of the peculiarities of Spanish and especially Valencian iconography in the late Middle Ages and early Renaissance, the *Vita Christi* of Isabel de Villena,[17] who was indeed the first abbess of the Franciscan convent of the Trinidad at Valencia, a daughter-house of Sta. Clara at Gandía.

The same Ermita de las Santas at Játiva that supplied the Museum in this city with the retable of the Transfiguration by the partners, the Artés Master and the Borbotó Master,[18] endowed the collection also with a large panel of the paired Sts. Nicholas and Dionysius the Areopagite by Nicolás Falcó (Fig. 41). Tormo, in his book *Las tablas de las iglesias de Játiva* published in 1912,[19] mentions it as still over an altar on the right side of the Ermita, and in his *Levante* of 1923,[20] recording it as transferred to the Museum and stating his belief that

[16] *Boletín de la Sociedad Española de Excursiones*, XXXIX (1931), 229–230.
[17] Cf. especially my vol. VI, p. 75, n. 2. For this detail of the Annunciation, see the modern edition of the *Vita Christi* by Miquel y Planas, Barcelona, 1916, vol. I, chapter XX, p. 113.   [18] Vol. VI, p. 320.
[19] Pp. 101–102.   [20] P. 212.

FIG. 41. NICOLÁS FALCÓ. STS. NICHOLAS AND DIONYSIUS.
MUSEUM, JÁTIVA
(*Photo. Archivo Mas*)

FIG. 42. NICOLÁS FALCÓ. CANONIZED BISHOP AND ST.
ANTHONY OF PADUA. ONCE IN THE ERMITA DE
LAS SANTAS, JÁTIVA

it was once the centre of a retable, he ascribes it to Nicolás Falcó, whether or not meaning the personality that I connect with the name. Its subjects do not, like those of the retable of the Transfiguration, show that it was painted after 1514 when the Ermita was taken over by the Augustinians,[21] but the style reveals that its date cannot be much before or after this year. Dionysius carries a book inscribed with a slightly different version of the same statement in the letter on the Passion to Polycarp, then still wrongly attributed to him, which Rodrigo de Osona the younger used correspondingly to distinguish the saint in the altarpiece in the cathedral of Valencia.[22] To be convinced that Falcó was the painter, one need only compare the Dionysius with the St. Nicholas kneeling before the Virgen de la Sapiencia or set the St. Nicholas of the Játiva panel beside the various representations of St. Martin as bishop in the organ-shutters. The old practice of accentuation by gold lingers on to a greater degree than Falcó or his Valencian contemporaries customarily admit, being lavished upon the two bishops' vestments and the textile against which they are relieved.

His style is recognizable likewise in another panel of paired saints which is said to have once been also a part of the pious decoration of the Ermita de las Santas at Játiva but is no longer registered there or in the Museum to which the rest of the paintings from the chapel have been consigned (Fig. 42). The photograph, however, is quite enough to substantiate the ascription. Before a background of gold tooled with a brocaded pattern, St. Anthony of Padua stands at the right holding his regular emblem in the art of eastern Spain, the vessel with the grape vine,[23] and his companion at the left is a canonized bishop whom the absence of attributes prevents us from naming. The St. Anthony reproduces such types of Falcó as the Magdalene and the woman next to her in the Lamentation over the Dead Christ at Morella, which will immediately concern us, and the episcopal worthy not only is scarcely varied from the representations of St. Martin as a prelate in the organ-shutters or from the St. Nicholas in the University

[21] Vol. VI, p. 320.

[22] *Ibid.*, 208–209. In Falcó's panel the inscription reads: "Aut deus naturae patitur aut tota mundi machina destruetur. Ego, Dionysius, in Passione scripsi." On p. 209 of vol. VI, following the opinion of others, I said that the panel in the Játiva Museum should *perhaps* be ascribed to "Felipe Pablo de San Leocadio" (see below, p. 277), but my own study has plainly demonstrated to me that we owe it to Falcó.

[23] Vol. VI, p. 156.

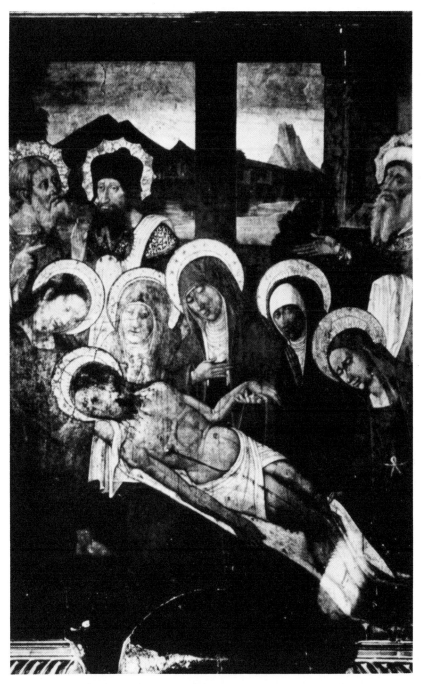

FIG. 43. NICOLÁS FALCÓ. LAMENTATION OVER THE DEAD CHRIST,
SECTION OF RETABLE. STA. MARÍA, MORELLA

retable and in the Játiva Museum, but also he wears a mitre identical with that of St. Martin in the scene of the miraculous fire.

The claims of Falcó to a small altarpiece at the left of the nave in the church of Sta. María at Morella are so palpably manifested in every figure, every touch, and every detail as to require no analysis, and indeed Tormo [24] has once more, albeit in this case only tentatively, brought him forward as the author, although again I am not sure that he would define Falcó as just the personality whom I understand him to be. The altarpiece consists merely of one large panel of the Lamentation over the Dead Christ (Fig. 43) and, at a reliquary's sides in the predella, of figures of Sts. John Baptist and Jerome in landscapes. Since the carvings of the frames or at least their gildings seem to be documented as done in 1524, Tormo assigns the paintings to this year, but Saralegui [25] deems them too primitive and Gothic for so late a date, escaping the dilemma, I suppose, by assuming that the frames were made for already existing works. Conditioned, however, by his training under the still mediaeval Martínez Master, the none too ambitious Falcó might easily have maintained without much change through the first quarter of the sixteenth century his somewhat conservative fashions, which are here signalized also by the retention of gold in some of the garments as well as in the haloes and by no endeavor to vary an established composition for the Lamentation in the Valencian school, which was favored particularly by the Játiva Master.[26] The most advanced factors in the altarpiece, as in the organ-shutters of the cathedral at Valencia, are the delightful, partially aquatic landscapes in the predella as well as in the principal compartment.

The more Italianate phase of Nicolás Falcó was unmistakably embodied, before the civil war, in a small panel of the Virgen de la Leche which entered the Diocesan Museum at Valencia from the parish church of S. Pedro, attached to the cathedral,[27] and which, by reason of its use as an object of cult, was eventually marred by additions of superimposed silver haloes (Fig. 44).

[24] *Levante*, 28, and *Boletín de la Real Academia de la Historia*, Madrid, XC (1927), 34.
[25] *Boletín de la Sociedad Española de Excursiones*, XXXIX (1931), 231.
[26] For the Játiva Master, see vol. VI, p. 345, and the indices of the succeeding volumes.
[27] See the Catalogue of the Museum by Antonio Barberá Sentamáns, p. 16, no. 16. The companion-piece of St. Joseph with the Holy Child (no. 17) is a much later creation.

Fig. 44. NICOLÁS FALCÓ. VIRGIN OF THE MILK. DIOCESAN
MUSEUM, VALENCIA

(*Photo. Archivo Mas*)

Fig. 45. NICOLÁS FALCÓ. ANNUNCIATION. CALABUIG COLLECTION,
VALENCIA

(*Photo. Archivo Mas*)

The mere publication of a photograph (Fig. 45) is sufficient to ensconce in Falcó's canon an Annunciation in the Calabuig Collection at Valencia, which nearly repeats in composition his version for the organ-shutters.

To the Seminario Conciliar at Tudela there belongs a panel displaying the Valencian composition for the Lamentation over the Dead Christ retained by Falcó in his altarpiece at Morella; and of the several Valencian painters of the late fifteenth and early sixteenth centuries who adopted the composition he provides the closest stylistic analogies to the Tudela picture, although he is by no means the author (Fig. 46). Since its history has not been discovered, there are no means of determining whether it was executed in the territory of Valencia and merely presented by someone to the Seminario at Tudela, or whether it is a relic of an otherwise unknown Aragonese or Navarrese artist who had enjoyed a Valencian training or of an actual Valencian master, an immigrant into this region. Large medallions of Sts. John Baptist and Peter are baldly inserted against the sky at the picture's summit.

In the problem debated by Saralegui in an article [28] as to where in the group of works by the Martínez Master and his circle we should place a large panel of St. Catherine of Siena in the Collection of Doctor Jimeno Márquez at Valencia that he illustrates, my inclinations would lead me to our Nicolás Falcó. Behind the beggar upon whom St. Martin, in the organ-shutters of the cathedral, bestows his cloak there spreads out a nearly identical landscape, and beside the St. Catherine there are introduced in the foreground not only two of the partridges that so frequently fill the interstices of Valencian paintings of the period [29] but also a pheasant and, on the parapet, a smaller bird. Saralegui rightly explains the unusual emblem for St. Catherine, a heart (upon the book that she holds) by reference to her vision of an exchange of hearts with Christ.[30] I quite agree with him that the author of the St. Catherine, and therefore, in my opinion, Nicolás Falcó, executed little panels of the heads of Christ and the Virgin which have recently entered the Provincial Museum at Valencia from an unknown source and of which also he publishes reproductions. Although in their present condition they look like veronicas, the fact

[28] *Archivo español de arte,* XXI (1948), 203.
[29] See my vol. X, p. 364.
[30] See my vol. VI, p. 410.

FIG. 46. CIRCLE OF NICOLÁS FALCÓ. LAMENTATION OVER THE
DEAD CHRIST. SEMINARIO CONCILIAR, TUDELA

(*Photo. Archivo Mas*)

that parts of the haloes and other details have been cut off may indicate that originally the panels were sections of larger compositions.

2. The Master of the Juan Family of Játiva

Since with a high degree of probability at least two known works can be ascribed to a craftsman who embodied less competently somewhat the same stylistic fusion as Falcó, it is necessary to devise a name for him, and, inasmuch as these works are not distinctive in location, manner, or subjects, I am obliged to resort to the unwieldy appellation printed above, which is derived from the noble family that the Barón de San Petrillo [1] has shown to have ordered the craftsman's basic achievement, one of the monuments of painting at Játiva that survived the disasters of the civil war, a retable which may be seen in the church of S. Félix and has long contained two alien pieces, the panel of St. Ursula by the Borbotó Master [2] and a compartment with a pair of scenes from St. Peter's life contemporary with the sections by the personality who now concerns us but still weaker in quality. It should be pointed out at once that the Juan family of Játiva was not the same as the Juan family of Valencia, who commissioned the retable of the Perea Master's school once in the church of S. Juan del Hospital at Valencia.[3] The Barón de San Petrillo suggests as mere possibilities that the panel of the patrons of the Juan family of Játiva, the two St. Johns, now at the summit of the retable in S. Félix may have once constituted the principal compartment and that therefore the retable perhaps originally decorated the chapel of the Juan family in the Colegiata of the city. Since figures of Sts. Jerome and possibly Louis of Toulouse [4] are comprised in the retable, we may venture the guess that it might have owed its genesis to a Jerónimo Juan and his son Luis who were prominent at the beginning of the sixteenth century. The Master of the Juan Family of Játiva reveals close similarities to the Calviá Master,[5] but, after a careful study of the problem, I cannot bring myself to assert their identity.

---

[1] *Archivo español de arte y arqueología*, XII (1936), 102.
[2] See my vol. VI, p. 335.   [3] *Ibid.*, p. 440.
[4] It is only on the authority of Tormo (*Las tablas de las iglesias de Játiva*, 89) that I state the figure at the left end of the predella to be St. Louis of Toulouse, since in my notes taken on the spot I failed to specify the subject at this point; and I am bound to say that we cannot entirely rely upon the Spanish scholar's denominations of the sacred personages, since in this retable he demonstrably mistakes St. Quiteria for St. Agnes and St. Thomas Aquinas for St. Dominic.
[5] See below, p. 148.

Of the pieces by our painter in the main body of the retable, the St. Quiteria forming a pendant in the lowest row to the St. Ursula by the Borbotó Master needs comment, since the architectural niche in which the figure is ensconced so resembles the setting of the St. Ursula as to suggest that the retable might just possibly have been begun by the Borbotó Master and, except for the panel with scenes from the story of St. Peter at the centre in the same row, have been left to the Master of the Juan Family to complete. The themes of the second row are the Dormition in the middle and the Resurrection and Ascension at the sides. To the topmost compartment with the effigies of the two St. Johns, we have already had occasion to allude. The tendency of the Valencian school to emphasize the *guardapolvos* is carried to the point of relegating to them, except for Sts. Jerome and Thomas Aquinas on the cross-pieces, the important subjects of the seven Joys of the Virgin, in this case [6] comprising the Annunciation (Fig. 47), Visitation, Nativity, Purification, the young Christ among the Doctors, Pentecost, and the Coronation. The Crucifixion at the centre of the predella is flanked by four other scenes from the Passion, the Betrayal, Flagellation, Crowning with Thorns, and Via Dolorosa, and at the ends are separate little figures of the putative St. Louis of Toulouse and of St. Anthony Abbot.

The painter is one of the lesser exponents of the general Valencian manner of the beginning of the sixteenth century apart from the Leonardesque style that was launched by the two Fernandos. He derives his inspiration from such a follower of the Martínez Master as the Cabanyes Master and from Paolo da San Leocadio, but he rather debases his composite borrowings to the level of the mere craft of a purveyor to religious trade.

The Master of the Juan Family of Játiva is the most likely candidate whom I can find to father a painting on cloth in the church of Santa María at Morella representing the Madonna enthroned on clouds between angels with instruments of the Passion and worshipped by the kneeling Sts. Martin and Agatha (Fig. 48). The face of the St. Quiteria in the Játiva retable is practically repeated in the St. Agatha, and there may be also observed in the retable analogues for the angels that are only slightly less persuasive.

[6] For the latitude in the choice of the seven Joys, see vol. VIII, p. 294.

FIG. 47. THE MASTER OF THE JUAN FAMILY OF JÁTIVA.
ANNUNCIATION, SECTION OF RETABLE. S. FÉLIX, JÁTIVA
(*Photo. Archivo Mas*)

FIG. 48. THE MASTER OF THE JUAN FAMILY OF JÁTIVA(?).
MADONNA AND SAINTS. STA. MARÍA, MORELLA
(*Photo. Cardona*)

3. Damián Forment as a Painter

On this subject I have contributed an article to the first volume of the book published in 1951, *Miscellània* in honor of the great scholar, Puig i Cadafalch, so that in the present volume I need only summarize its contents. The style of Damián Forment in painting, an art that he practised less than sculpture, is divulged by four panels of a predella, now in the Museum of Saragossa, the remains of those sections of a retable which were demanded from him for the nearlying town of San Mateo de Gállego in an agreement of March 31, 1523.[1] It is explicitly stated in the document that Forment is not obligated by its terms to do the statue of the peculiarly Aragonese virgin martyr, St. Engracia, at the structure's centre, whether he received the order for this piece of sculpture in a separate contract, now lost, or whether it was made by another artist; and the stipulations cover only the other sections, all paintings, of which every piece except the four compartments of the predella has perished or degenerated into such hopeless dilapidation as to be valueless for an appraisal of style. The document prescribes four scenes from the story of St. Engracia in the predella, without specifying their themes, which turn out to be her arraignment before Dacian, flagellation (Fig. 49), dragging behind a horse, and laceration on the *eculeus*.[2]

Our purposes do not require that we should rehearse the details of Damián's life, which belong preponderantly to the history of sculpture and comprise the beginnings of his artistic career at Valencia in the opening years of the Cinquecento, his long, busy, and honorable residence in Aragon whither he had moved at least by May 1, 1509, and his employment at the end of the thirties on the carved retable of the high altar in the cathedral of the Castilian town of Santo Domingo de la Calzada, where on December 22, 1540, he made his will, dying shortly thereafter. The style incorporated in the panels from San Mateo de Gállego reveals little or no awareness of his Aragonese environment but is part and parcel of the fashions in the contemporary Valencian school, so similar especially to the manner of the Cabanyes Master as to be scarcely distinguishable from it. A slightly diverse cast in the female countenance is almost the sole factor differentiating

---

[1] For the contract see M. Abizanda y Broto, *Documentos para la historia artística y literaria de Aragón*, II (1917), 192–195.

[2] For the passion of St. Engracia, see my vol. IX, p. 819, and Alonso de Villegas, *Flos sanctorum*, I, Madrid, 1593, p. 624.

the faces delineated by the two painters, but it should be very definitely pointed out that the nude of St. Engracia's body in the scourging, probably by reason of Forment's essentially sculptural nature, is sturdier than the Cabanyes Master's naked forms and the object of more anatomical attention. Although the types and draperies of his carvings and paintings are in general analogous, the style of the latter

FIG. 49. DAMIÁN FORMENT. ARRAIGNMENT AND FLAGELLATION
OF ST. ENGRACIA, SECTIONS OF PREDELLA. MUSEUM,
SARAGOSSA
(*Photo. Mora*)

is decidedly gentler, since he appears to have sensitively felt the distinction between the two arts.

I shall have to ask the reader to examine in my above-mentioned article the internal evidence by which other paintings may be ascribed to Forment tentatively but very persuasively. Two of them must have been done either before he sought new opportunities for his chisel and brush in Aragon or thence dispatched subsequently to the old district of his activity. The one of whose exact provenience we are informed has passed from the ownership of Don Francisco Díaz de Brito of Valencia to the Viñas Collection, Barcelona, but derives from the great Carthusian monastery of Valdecristo near Segorbe in Valencian territory, displaying the Madonna holding the Child and worshipped by her kneeling parents as well as by a pair of angels (Fig. 50). Other sacred *motifs* are consigned to medallions simulated as inlaid in the Virgin's rich marble throne of the Renaissance, at the top the Blessing Father and dove of the Holy Spirit between the participants in the Annunciation, and at the bottom busts of three white-habited monastic saints, of whom one is identified by the accompanying inscription as Bernard of Clairvaux and the two others (the inscriptions being illegible) may depict the patrons of the Carthusian Order, Bruno and Hugh of Grenoble. If, as I am strongly inclined to believe, the picture is the work of Forment, it throws further light upon him in the guise of a painter, for we perceive not only the relationship to the Cabanyes Master but also, especially in the St. Joachim, an acquaintance with the achievements of Vicente Juan Masip, the father of Juan de Juanes. Almost certainly, likewise, he should be credited with a panel in regard to which [3] I was loath to follow Saralegui in an attribution to the Cabanyes Master himself, a version of the *Anna Selbdritt* in the Provincial Museum, Valencia, and therefore presumably the result of a commission for the city or its domain.

Of two paintings in which I should wish to see Forment's hand after his departure from Valencia, one has disappeared from my knowledge after, from the Collection of Don Luis Ruiz of Madrid, it was offered for sale in January, 1929, at the American Art Association, New York.[4] The subject is the characteristically Aragonese theme of the Virgin of the Pillar appearing to St. James Major with a companion (Torquatus?),[5] and the stylistic ties with the predella of San Mateo de Gállego are perhaps more numerous and tangible than in any of the other instances.

To the second picture executed in Aragon the anomalous iconography adds a particular interest (Fig. 51). There can hardly be a doubt that, now in the Museum of Saragossa, it once decorated a no longer existing pious institution of the city, the Colegio de las Vírgenes, and that it represents Our Lady enthroned and surrounded by women of the lay, religious Order who comprised the institution,

---

[3] Vol. VI, p. 430, n. 1.
[4] When I wrote my article, I had not traced the picture even so far.
[5] See my volume VIII, pp. 288–290.

FIG. 50. DAMIÁN FORMENT(?). MADONNA, ANGELS, AND SAINTS.
VIÑAS COLLECTION, BARCELONA
(*Photo. Archivo Mas*)

Fig. 51. DAMIÁN FORMENT(?). OUR LADY AND THE COLEGIO DE
LAS VÍRGENES. MUSEUM, SARAGOSSA

(*Photo. Archivo Mas*)

seated on the pavement and wearing what became eventually their habit, a white wimple and a blue mantle, on one shoulder of which was a red cross. The style shows that it must have been painted about the time of the papal confirmation of the Order in 1531, shortly after its foundation. The men seen in the view of a city in the left distance may be the Deputies of the Realm, who had charge of the Colegio de las Vírgenes; and at the back of the still Gothic church in which the chief persons in the picture are imagined as ensconced there are introduced, in the same diminished scale as the supposed Deputies, women in the coarse cloth of the Order's original habit, four of them in standing devotional attitudes but a fifth, at the extreme right, kneeling in prayer before a gold tabernacle of the Blessed Sacrament, a group probably to be interpreted as occupied in the Eucharistic cult of the Forty Hours, which was one of the society's privileges. Since Our Lady is reading in a book while the nuns in the foreground, also holding tomes, gesticulate in ways that imply discussion with her, it is to be surmised that they are engaged in a conference upon some sacred topic, perhaps the evidence in theological literature for the Immaculate Conception, which may have been another principal devotion of the Colegio de las Vírgenes as well as of the at least partly affiliated and more widely disseminated Order of the Conceptionists. In the lower part of the panel, beneath and in front of the pavement of the simulated church, there is featured a garden of various flowers, seemingly the *hortus conclusus* of the Song of Songs, IV, 12, which was regularly taken as a symbol of Mary's perpetual virginity, an idea intimately connected with the opinion that she herself had been immaculately conceived.

4. The Calviá Master

We may designate by the above pseudonym a painter who in the early sixteenth century carried to the Balearic Isles the modes that he had learned at Valencia in the shop of the Cabanyes Master and who takes his sobriquet from the location of his most comprehensive work over the altar of a chapel in an estate in the district called Valldurgent within the municipality of Calviá west of Palma on the island of Majorca. Since we are ignorant of his real name and therefore of his history, we have no means of determining whether he was a Valencian by birth or whether, like his predecessor in the fifteenth century, Martín Torner, who also had Valencian affiliations of a sort,[1] he was a native of the Balearic Isles but spent a part of his life in the city on the mainland. At the end of the chapter, it will be incumbent upon us to examine a painting which, if it was indeed executed by the Calviá Master, would reveal that he received at least one commission in Valencia itself, prior to the inauguration of his insular career. No evidence has been discovered to show whether perchance he was identical with a Perot lo Mallorquí[2] or a Diego de Mallorca[3] who are recorded as performing minor pictorial tasks at Valencia in 1512 and 1513.

The main body of the retable at Valldurgent consists of three arched compartments, equal in height, in the centre the Visitation and in the lateral pieces, slightly less wide, at the left St. Michael and at the right St. Anthony Abbot. Behind both participants in the Visitation are inscribed sentiments that they uttered at the time of the event, though not in the customary way upon banderoles but as Roman letters directly upon the background. The words chosen for the Virgin are from the beginning of the Magnificat, and those for St. Elizabeth from Luke I, 42. St. Michael is not represented in the usual fashion of the time as a winged knight but in an angel's dalmatic, and he not only crushes the Satanic dragon but also weighs souls in his scales. The spandrels of the three arches are embellished with cherubs' heads. Above these principal compartments the fine architecture of the Renaissance in which the retable is framed forms an entablature with a painted frieze of half-lengths of a canonized pope set between Sts. Agnes, Cosmas, Damian, and Agatha; and the *motif* of the child-angels' heads appears also on the entablature's *ressauts*. The central compartment of the predella is devoted to an odd modification of the subject that the Germans call *die heilige Sippe*, the representation of the infant Christ's family in the broadest sense (Fig. 52).[4] The Virgin and Child are strangely absent, and instead in the middle there sits St. Anne (or St. Elizabeth) between, at the right, Mary Salome, with her boys who were to be Sts. John Evangelist and James Major, and at the left Mary Cleophas with her offspring for whom religious preëminence was also in store, Sts. Simon, Jude,

[1] Vol. VI, pp. 464–465.
[2] Sanchis y Sivera, *Pintores medievales en Valencia*, 228.
[3] See above, p. 123.
[4] Vol. VI, p. 276.

Fig. 52. THE CALVIÁ MASTER. *DIE HEILIGE SIPPE*, MIDDLE OF PREDELLA OF RETABLE. VALLDURGENT, CALVIÁ, MAJORCA

(*Photo. Amadeo*)

James Minor, and Joseph the Just (the rival of St. Matthias for the place of Judas among the Twelve). The children and their mothers are accompanied by banderoles of identification with their names in Latin and in Roman letters. The lateral sections of the predella under the Sts. Michael and Anthony exhibit St. Sebastian's ordeal of the arrows and the flaying of St. Bartholomew in symmetrical and balancing compositions. The latter, with an avoidance of bloody realism uncommon in the theme, depicts merely the approach of the two executioners with their knives in lieu of the actual removal of the Apostle's skin. The predella ends at its extremes, on the bases of the colonnettes that enclose the altarpiece, with little, standing figures of Sts. Elizabeth of Hungary and Margaret. The presence of St. Elizabeth, the Baptist's mother, in the main panel of the retable, the Visitation, and possibly also in the *heilige Sippe* combines with the introduction of her later namesake into the predella to suggest that at least one of the donors may have been named Isabel, the equivalent of Elizabeth in Spanish.

The Calviá Master is a rather close imitator of the Cabanyes Master's style, but, while he is somewhat harder, less fresh, and less technically expert, he nevertheless now and then betrays, as in the two scenes of martyrdom in the predella, a slightly greater tendency than his teacher to succumb to oncoming mannerism. The modifications do not mean that he has lost any of the Cabanyes Master's agreeable tenderness: instead perhaps he accentuates it, without, however, any mawkish exaggeration. The types occasionally suggest, as was to be expected, that he was familiar with the productions of such other Valencian colleagues of the dawning Renaissance as the Borbotó Master and Miguel Esteve. Far more than in any other of his creations he clings in the Valldurgent altarpiece to the brilliant brocades of the Spanish painters of the fifteenth century as formalizing accents in a picture, displaying them in the Visitation and on the St. Michael with the loud and gorgeous patterns of even his most ostentatious predecessors.

Another pivotal work of the Calviá Master is in the Museo Arqueológico at Palma, a panel of the Madonna of the Rosary (Fig. 53). Enthroned at the centre she is worshipped beneath by the institutor of the devotions of the Rosary, St. Dominic, and by the great nun of the Dominican Order, St. Catherine of Siena. Round about in small circular compartments, like magnified beads, are repre-

FIG. 53. THE CALVIÁ MASTER. MADONNA OF ROSARY. MUSEO
ARQUEOLÓGICO, PALMA
(*Photo. Archivo Mas*)

sented: the five joyful mysteries of the Rosary, beginning with the Annunciation; the five sorrowful mysteries, beginning with the Agony in the Garden; and four of the five glorious mysteries, the Coronation being omitted. The authorship would be sufficiently established merely by the single factor of the entire affinity existing between the head of the Madonna and that of the Valldurgent St. Michael. Even her slickly combed and parted hair repeats one of the constantly recurring characteristics by which the Master may be recognized. Further proof, however, could be amassed almost *ad libitum*. The Child held by the Madonna, for instance, belongs artistically as well as actually to the same family as those of the *heilige Sippe*, turning out to be especially comparable to the young St. Simon. The St. Catherine embodies just the insinuatingly gentle loveliness of the Valldurgent Virgin of the Visitation. The student whose vision is good will find, if he has patience, the painter's unmistakable types and methods likewise in the appropriately reduced distinctness of the little sacred scenes of the mysteries of the Rosary.

In a panel of St. Bernardine in the church of Sta. Eulalia at Palma (Fig. 54), the purposed idol-like rigidity and the desire to preserve the haggard likeness of the canonized Franciscan that had become a tradition in Christian iconography might have concealed from us the Calviá Master's hand; but he declares himself very clearly in the Gabriel and Virgin of the Annunciation who are introduced in much smaller scale in apertures at the effigy's sides, since not only do both of them accord with one of his feminine types but they also have several direct counterparts in the mysteries of the Rosary in his panel in the Museo Arqueológico.

His countenances and forms emerge at their most characteristic in two companion-pieces of Sts. John Evangelist and Michael in the Casa Rectoral at Alcudia, in the northern part of Majorca (Fig. 55). Differently from the representation at Valldurgent, the archangel is now clad in armor according to the normal iconography of the period.

The activity of the Calviá Master extended to the island of Ibiza where at the top of the structure over the altar of the Blessed Sacrament in the cathedral he has left us another version of the *heilige Sippe*, which, however, was so far truncated at some time in its history as to leave only the central St. Anne, Virgin, and Child, St. Joseph, and the infant Baptist, with parts of other figures and in the lower left corner the final OR of an inscription revealing that at this spot there

Fig. 54. THE CALVIÁ MASTER. ST. BERNARDINE. STA. EULALIA, PALMA

(*Photo. Archivo Mas*)

FIG. 55. THE CALVIÁ MASTER. STS. JOHN EVANGELIST AND
MICHAEL. PARISH CHURCH, ALCUDIA
(*Photo. Archivo Mas*)

has been lost the form either of the young St. James Major or St. James Minor (Fig. 56). The Virgin and the two holy children at once stir such vivid memories of other paintings by the Master that I will not insult the reader's intelligence by itemizing any additional evidence.

The discovery of the Calviá Master's personality provides me with the author of a Last Judgment in the Collection of the Marqués de Santillana at Madrid for which I had long vainly sought the exact affiliations (Fig. 57). The general composition betrays no departure from the iconographical norm, but certain details need to be noted. Of the sacred personages surrounding the judging Saviour, many of whom can be recognized by their costumes and emblems, a few exhibit peculiarities. Very strangely the only one who is specified by an inscription on a banderole is Zacharias, the Baptist's father, in the first row at the right, and whereas he properly wears the polygonal halo of the elder covenant, David (with a harp) higher in the row behind him possesses anomalously the round nimbus of a Christian saint. Inasmuch as St. Benedict (with his attribute of the aspergillum) just above St. Dominic in the first row at the left is clad not in the black habit of the original Benedictines but in the white of the Carthusians, a reformed Benedictine Order, we may guess that the picture was painted for a Carthusian institution, since in works of art done for the several reformed Benedictine Orders it was the practice not to dress St. Benedict in the black that he actually wore but in the garb of the commissioning Order. In Our Lord's mandorla are written in Latin at one side, "Venite, benedicti," and on the other side the single word "maledicti"; but the sentence accompanying the trumpeting angels beneath is in the language of the east coast of Spain and the Balearic Isles, "Sortiu a judici" (Come forth to judgment). I cannot explain what seems to be the Castilian form, "Santo," thrice written on a scroll issuing from the mouth of a monk who has risen from the dead to be received by an angel at the lower left, unless someone has tampered with an original Latin "Sanctus," in which the *c*, as often, was omitted and the final *us* was represented by the frequent abbreviating sign looking like the numeral 9, which the tamperer perverted into an *o*; but the stanza in Castilian at the very bottom of the picture in the middle is certainly a subsequent superimposition:

Fɪɢ. 56. THE CALVIÁ MASTER. *DIE HEILIGE SIPPE.* CATHEDRAL,
IBIZA

(Photo. Archivo Mas)

F̲ı̲g̲. 57.   THE CALVIÁ MASTER.   LAST JUDGMENT, DETAIL.   SANTILLANA COLLECTION, MADRID

(*Photo. Moreno*)

Hombre, en este espejo
Algún día serás visto:
Si eres bendito, con Cristo,
Si maldito, con Luzbel.

The Calviá Master is so completely true to himself in the Last
Judgment that I will again leave to the reader the detective's pleasure
of verifying the attribution. I confine myself to starting the process
by pointing out such absolute identities, among many, as exist between
the angel with the instruments of the Passion and the Valldurgent
Michael, between the first saint at the top in the second row at the left
and the Joseph in the Ibiza picture, or between the next saint in the
same row and the Gabriel in the panel of Bernardine in Sta. Eulalia at
Palma. In general, we discern everywhere in the Santillana panel
the Calviá Master's somewhat dry interpretation of the Cabanyes
Master's style.

The painting that I adduced in the first paragraph of this section as
perhaps demonstrating the Calviá Master's employment, in addition
to his study, at Valencia before his establishment in the Balearic Isles
is a large and deteriorated panel, somewhat truncated at the top, which
represents Our Lady in the midst of angels and virgin martyrs giving
the Carmelite scapular to St. Simon Stock and which passed into the
Provincial Museum in the city from the possessions of the institution
in whose very buildings the Museum was until recently housed, the
Carmelite monastery (Fig. 58). I have always found the picture a
baffling puzzle, and my discussion of it must be prefaced by the con-
fession that I myself am by no means convinced of the Calviá Master's
authorship and that I advance him only as the most likely candidate
among the artists of the period whose personalities have been defined,
always keeping in my mind the proviso that we may some day discover a painter whose right to the panel will be entirely obvious.

At first sight we seem to have before us merely the ordinary theme
of the Madonna and Child enthroned among angels and saints, but
we soon see the Carmelite of the thirteenth century, Simon Stock,
kneeling and experiencing the most celebrated episode of his life, his
reception from the Virgin of the scapular that henceforth was to be a
part of his Order's habit. As his symbol, like the emblems that usually
identify sacred personages in art, the painter has placed on the pavement a plate of the crude herbs and roots to which the accounts constantly emphasize that he ascetically confined his diet. Beside him an

FIG. 58. THE CALVIÁ MASTER(?). THE VIRGIN GIVING THE
CARMELITE SCAPULAR TO ST. SIMON STOCK. PROVINCIAL
MUSEUM, VALENCIA

(*Photo. Archivo Mas*)

unhaloed Carmelite is depicted, also on his knees and probably the picture's donor. All the six sacred personages ranged in the foremost tier of Our Lady's attendants bear emblems that enable us to recognize them. Next to the throne stand St. Michael, and as a natural pendant, the Guardian Angel of the kingdom (with his regular symbols, a crown and a scourge). The four virgin martyrs at their sides prove to be, from left to right, Apollonia, Ursula (with her arrow only visible in part), Catherine, and Barbara. The bevies of angels at the upper levels offer flowers, sound instruments of music, lift a crown above Mary's head, or, curiously conventionalized to look almost like vases, raise their voices in song as they stand upon the parapet which continues the staid architecture of the Renaissance that is used for the throne. The letters inscribed in the pavement, some of them Roman and others Gothic (or intended as Hebrew?), are as undecipherable to me as in so many other similar cases in the Spanish paintings of the fifteenth and early sixteenth centuries.

I have long floundered about in a struggle for an attribution, re-jecting one possibility after the other, until I have been almost driven by a process of exclusion to the Calviá Master. From my earliest examination of the panel in 1926, I have been impressed by its unusually Italianate character, so that I naturally have compared it with another work from the domain of the Valencian school in which the affinity with the art of Italy is very tangible, the Madonna once at Murcia but now in the Collection of Mr. Aldus C. Higgins at Worcester, Massachusetts;[5] but the links with this Madonna are less close than with the Calviá Master's achievements, and I am cognizant of no Italian painter to whom the Carmelite panel could be reasonably ascribed. I have likewise tried in vain to relate the panel to such men as the Borbotó Master,[6] the Cuenca Master,[7] or the partners Gaspar Requena and Pedro Rubiales,[8] but, as soon as I review the Calviá Master's productions, I feel myself in an atmosphere congenial to the personality whom we are seeking.

If it were only a question of the single figure of Our Lady in the panel, I should have few or no reservations in championing the Calviá Master's cause, for she is practically identical with the Virgin

---

[5] Vol. VI, p. 264. Saralegui (*Archivo español de arte*, XVI, 1943, p. 33, n. 73) finds it hard to believe that the Murcia panel was not painted by an Italian.

[6] Vol. VI, p. 320.   [7] See below, p. 162.

[8] See above, p. 87.

of the Visitation, with Mary Salome, and with Mary Cleophas in the Valldurgent retable, as well as with the St. Catherine of Siena, in the Palma Museum, represented at the feet of the Madonna of the Rosary, and there seems to be no other Valencian or Majorcan painter of the period who creates just this delicately tender type of woman. The other resemblances, however, are not quite so persuasive. At Valldurgent, the infants in the *heilige Sippe* afford partial analogues for the Child in the picture in the Valencian Museum, and the St. Michael could easily be supposed to have been executed by the artist who as a younger man did the same archangel and even some of his winged companions grouped round the Madonna appearing to St. Simon Stock. The analogy of the Virgin of the Rosary in the Palma Museum to the Valencian St. Michael is perhaps a little more arresting. In any case, it is possible to assign the panel of the Museum at Valencia to the Calviá Master only on the understanding that it was painted earlier than his thoroughly authenticated works, which have taken on something of the harder, drier, and more mannered fashions of the Cinquecento. In making the very tentative attribution, I am encouraged by the consideration that Tormo,[9] with what reason I do not know, describes the panel as in the manner of either Valencia or Majorca.

5. THE CUENCA MASTER

Apart from the more or less interrelated, regular lines of descent [1] from the Perea Master there existed a painter formed under his influence but fusing with it additional strains and thus rather sharply distinguished in style from the homogeneous group of his other artistic heirs, as well as by a more vivid nature. It is only recently that his personality has defined itself in my mind through the realization that a single painter, namely the man who now concerns us, created the retable in the Mateu Collection at Peralada which I published in volume VII [2] (Fig. 59) and a retable now hanging on a wall of the *capilla mayor* in the episcopal palace at Cuenca which I have long known but had hitherto been unable to attribute with exactitude (Fig. 60). I acknowledged in volume X [3] that I had once toyed

---

[9] *Valencia: los Museos*, 26, no. 158.
[1] Vol. VI, p. 268.
[2] P. 905 and fig. 378, illustrating the whole retable.
[3] P. 17.

FIG. 59. THE CUENCA MASTER. STS. JOHN BAPTIST, MICHAEL,
JAMES MAJOR, AND ANDREW, SECTIONS OF RETABLE.
MATEU COLLECTION, PERALADA

(*From an article by Folch on the Collection*)

FIG. 60. THE CUENCA MASTER. RETABLE. EPISCOPAL PALACE,
CUENCA

(*Photo. Pando*)

briefly with the idea that the latter retable might explain the trip of Alejo Fernández to Cuenca in 1522 but only to reject very quickly the possibility of his authorship. At my own first visit to Cuenca in 1926 I was told that the retable had originally graced one of two churches in the city, either Sta. María or S. Martín, and we often perceive that Cuenca, by reason of its geographical situation, divided its artistic patronage between the schools of Toledo [4] and Valencia.[5] Since this retable is the only recognized work of the painter remaining in the town for which it was made, I can invent for him no more distinctive a pseudonym than the Cuenca Master, but it is less inexact than it would at first seem because the other paintings of the period at Cuenca can generally be parcelled out among nameable artists and their following, Juan de Borgoña, Fernando Yáñez, and Martín Gómez.[6]

When I described in volume VII the retable in the Mateu Collection and its style, I should have noted that the painter had perhaps modified his dependence upon the Perea Master through contact with Bermejo during the latter's presumptive sojourn at Valencia. Several characteristics can be selected to support the hypothesis. The Magi in the Epiphany in the pinnacle and the St. Sebastian of the predella illustrate how the costumes are enriched to a sober magnificence, in the case of the Wise Men actually continuing Bermejo's predilection for trimmings of fur. It may have been because of Bermejo's influence that our artist exhibits more Flemish qualities than he could have acquired from the Perea Master, as particularly in the Virgin and St. John of the predella; and once again it is the St. Sebastian who interests us as the figure that exemplifies Bermejo's use of heavier shadows in countenances than was the Perea Master's wont. Some of the human types might be interpreted to imply that the author of the Mateu altarpiece had derived something from his Valencian predecessor, the Alacuás Master, and this impression suggests itself more insistently when we contemplate, in the retable at Cuenca, the conspicuous brilliancy of the brocades.

The three compartments in the main body of this retable are occupied by standing effigies of life-size, at the centre the Madonna of the Milk, at the right Santiago, and at the left a papal saint; and the likewise triply divided predella displays in three-fourths length

---

[4] Vol. IX, pp. 222 and 234.   [5] See below, p. 193.
[6] See below, p. 337.

Christ as the Salvator Mundi and the aligned twelve Apostles. At the feet of the papal saint there kneel in miniature size the unidentified [7] donor, his wife, and two adolescent sons. Since, except for a slight alleviation of primitive severity, the style of the paintings remains essentially mediaeval, the only thing indicating that the work was executed as late as the very early sixteenth century is the delicate Plateresque ornamentation sculptured on the uprights in the retable's main body, which combines with the entirely unusual employment of a great, monumental carved crown, stretching across the whole summit of the retable, to form one of the handsomest frames of altarpieces in the whole range of Spanish art.

The factor that at once strikes the student as inevitably revealing the same painter as in the Mateu retable is the close similarity of many of the masculine types, modifications of the Perea Master's models in the direction of greater gentleness. Not only does this similarity prove to be general in nature, resulting in part from the analogous, marked contrasts of light and shade in all the countenances in both altarpieces, but the features in a number of cases are practically identical. In particular, the Santiago in the main body of the structure and the Sts. Simon and Jude (second and third from the left) in the predella should be compared with the Baptist in the Mateu retable, who illustrates also the Cuenca Master's habit of allowing stray locks of hair to dangle down over the forehead. The stern visage of St. Andrew in the Mateu retable is repeated as a profile in the same Apostle (fourth from the left) in the Cuenca predella. There are even counterparts for the Madonna's face, narrowing rapidly to the chin, in such figures in the Mateu assemblage as the Sts. Michael, Sebastian, and John Evangelist. The fixed, piercing glance of the eyes that often stares forth at us from the Mateu retable seizes upon our attention at Cuenca especially in the papal saint and several of the Apostles. A preference for an elongated canon of the human form is characteristic of both altarpieces, as well as a tendency to cast the body and its drapery in an undulating curve, exemplified at Cuenca by the Virgin and pope and in the Mateu panels particularly by the St. Bernard on the *guardapolvos*. The Virgin is more reminiscent of Flemish precedents than ordinarily in the Valencian school; and to a greater degree than in the Mateu retable not only the facial types but

---

[7] The escutcheon twice employed on the *guardapolvos* has been recognized neither by me nor, so far as I know, by anyone else.

also the boldness of the auric brocades of the backgrounds seem to indicate some sort of contact on the author's part with the Alacuás Master.

Many things imply that we probably have a further work of the Cuenca Master preserved to us in a Pietà, the central compartment from a predella, formerly in the Collection of Mr. James W. Barney of New York and now in the Louvre, Paris (Fig. 61).[8] Again the most determinative element is the reappearance, in the Saviour, of his favorite type of masculine countenance, finding its nearest analogue in the Baptist of the Mateu retable. The suffering Christ conforms to a cartoon for this figure diffused through the production of the Perea Master and his following, but it incorporates the Cuenca Master's proclivity to attenuation of the body. The theme of the Pietà is treated with more emotion in the predella of the Mateu retable, and yet in the angels, despite the grieving distortion of their visages, it affords parallels for the kind of face that we see in their more placid brothers in the Barney picture, whose cheeks, however, are fuller than those generally encountered in the Cuenca Master's output. The picture reiterates also the unusual restriction of the gold background to a strip at the top of the panel, as in the principal sections of the Mateu retable. The Hebrew inscription on the sarcophagus, the interpretation of which defies the Semitic scholars to whom I have submitted it, possibly denotes once more the influence of Bermejo, who is prone to decorate his paintings with legends in the Jewish language. The serenely beautiful countenances of the angels and the nature of the gold brocades of their tunicles witness to the ultimate genesis of this whole phase of Valencian art in the shop of Jacomart.

6. Paintings of Indeterminate Attribution in the Class Comprised in the Present Chapter

A capably executed panel displaying the figures of Sts. Cosmas and Damian against a landscape (Fig. 62), which used to exist in the cloister of the cathedral of Segorbe but disappeared during the Spanish civil war, should in all probability be related to a benefice founded on January 16, 1514, in honor of these hallowed physicians in the chapel of St. Catherine in the church.[1] The style obviously places

[8] The dimensions are 25 inches in height by 20 in width.
[1] I take this notice from a Latin list of the benefices of the cathedral of Segorbe and of the churches of the diocese written in 1596 and most generously copied for me

Fɪɢ. 61. THE CUENCA MASTER(?). PIETÀ. LOUVRE, PARIS

Fig. 62. VALENCIAN SCHOOL, SIXTEENTH CENTURY. STS. COSMAS
AND DAMIAN. CATHEDRAL, SEGORBE

(*Photo. Archivo Mas*)

FIG. 63. VALENCIAN SCHOOL, SIXTEENTH CENTURY. RETABLE.
FORMERLY IN THE ERMITA DE S. FRANCISCO, NÁQUERA
(*Courtesy of Don Leandro de Saralegui*)

the picture in the immediate vicinity of the Martínez Master, the Cabanyes Master, and Miguel Esteve, but my eyes cannot discover sufficiently distinctive factors to reveal which of the three artists, if indeed any one of them, deserves the credit.

After even more intense study and frequent returns to the problem through a period of many years, I fail likewise to arrive at a specific author for a retable [2] formerly in the Ermita de S. Francisco at Ná-quera (west of Sagunto) or at a more definite allocation than in the Cabanyes Master's immediate circle (Fig. 63). Effigies in full length occupy the three compartments that constitute the structure's main body, St. Francis of Assisi at the centre, Sts. Michael and Margaret at left and right respectively. The middle division of the predella shows the dead Christ supported by two angels, and the panel directly at its left depicts the Visitation; but the other three parts are reserved for seated pairs of saints, at the extreme left the two Johns, at the Pietà's right Peter and Paul, and finally Valerius with his deacon, Vincent. The pilasters that frame the principal section of the altar-piece are surmounted by sculptured escutcheons of later date, the one at the right displaying the arms of the town of Náquera and its pen-dant at the left embellished with a charge that has been identified with surety [3] neither by me nor anyone else. The painter who in 1922 was assigned the task of restoration stated that he retouched the St. Fran-cis and the two St. Johns but allowed the rest to remain intact.

Saralegui, to whom I owe, like so much else, my knowledge and photograph of the retable, may very well have been right when in his first letter to me about an attribution he tentatively supported the candidacy of the Cabanyes Master himself. Undoubtedly the general stylistic affinity emerges, to say the least, as very intimate, and not only is practically the same cartoon used for the St. Margaret as in the central panel [4] of the Master's altarpiece from the church of S. Juan del Hospital, but also the Pietà in the predella repeats, albeit with simplifications, the composition of the correspondingly placed version of the theme in this altarpiece; and yet the sum of the evi-dence is perhaps, possibly by reason of the restorations, not quite conclusive. Indeed Saralegui eventually wrote me proposing as an-

---

by Don Leandro de Saralegui from a transcription that itself had been made for him by the learned cleric and archaeologist of Segorbe, Don José María Pérez Martín.

[2] The height is 1.50 metres and the width 1.16.

[3] Saralegui suggests to me that it might be the shield of some local confraternity devoted to the Passion.   [4] Vol. VI, fig. 166.

other choice the Cabanyes Master's close imitator, the Gabarda Master.[5] If it were only a question of the virtual identity of the St. Margaret with such types of the latter as the figures of the Virgin in the retable that gives him his name, we could accept Saralegui's second hypothesis wholeheartedly, but much of the workmanship in the Náquera panels seems to lie above the Gabarda Master's rather meagre talents. The personality in the Cabanyes Master's *entourage* whom we have recently come to know, Damián Forment, can be set aside with somewhat more conviction. I once even sought the authorship in another, though related, phase of the Valencian school, fondly but in the end futilely cherishing the hope that Requena and Rubiales might prove the solution to the puzzle.

Some not too skilful follower of the Artés Master was responsible for an iconographically characteristic Valencian retable in the Collection of the Condesa de Alcubierre at Madrid (Fig. 64). Vague resemblances to the Last Judgment in the Provincial Museum, Valencia, by another anonymous imitator [6] are detectable, as well as to further works in the same general circle, such as the retable of the stigmatization of St. Francis in the Diocesan Museum of the same city [7] or the productions of the Master of the Juan Family of Játiva,[8] but in no case do the analogies reach such a point of concreteness as to permit the assertion that we are in the presence of the same artist. The principal compartment shows the Madonna enthroned between a pair of adoring angels; next above, there appears the favorite Valencian theme of Christ bringing to His mother the redeemed of the old dispensation;[9] and in the pinnacle the usual Crucifixion is replaced by another frequent subject in the school, the Trinity. The four lateral, standing figures in the body of the altarpiece are St. Jerome, the Magdalene, and the two St. Johns. The predella comprises in half lengths the dead Christ, supported by an angel, and effigies of Sts. Cosmas, Peter, James Major, and Damian. The *guardapolvos*, employed, as commonly at Valencia, for an aggregation of further sacred forms, display in the apex two angels with instruments of the Passion, then, flanking the Trinity, the actors in the Annunciation, next, in the cross-pieces, St. Sebastian and a canonized monk whom I cannot identify, and finally, on the main uprights, Sts. Christopher, Onuphrius,

[5] *Ibid.*, p. 430.
[7] *Ibid.*, p. 440.
[9] Vol. VI, p. 270.

[6] Vol. VI, p. 342.
[8] See above, p. 139.

Fig. 64. SCHOOL OF THE ARTÉS MASTER. RETABLE. ALCUBIERRE
COLLECTION, MADRID

(*Photo. Moreno*)

Anthony Abbot, and Dominic. Each side of the *guardapolvos* is decorated also with an escutcheon that my mentors in Spanish heraldry are unable to recognize. The dependence of the altarpiece upon the Artés Master is patently revealed by such figures as the angels in the principal compartment or the St. John Evangelist.

CHAPTER VII

FERNANDO YÁÑEZ DE LA ALMEDINA AND FERNANDO DE LLANOS

1. Their Lives

THE earliest certain notices of these exponents of Leonardo da Vinci's insinuating influence find them as partners at Valencia; but eventually their association was disrupted, and each painted separate extant works, which enable us to distinguish their individual manners and even to a large extent their respective contributions to productions that they executed in collaboration. The former of the twain is designated in the Valencian and Catalan documents only as Fernando de la Almedina, revealing that he came from the town of Almedina, southeast of Valdepeñas in the province of Ciudad Real and therefore in the region of Spain immortalized by Don Quixote, La Mancha. Juan de Butrón, publishing his *Discursos apologéticos* in 1626,[1] was aware that the surname of the painter was Yáñez, stating him to have been a native of Almedina, and this writer's words carry weight because he probably obtained his data from a discussion of Yáñez that was certainly included in the important book of the second half of the sixteenth century, *Arte de la pintura* by Hernando de Ávila, of which we know a little through the references to it in Diego de Villalta's *De las estatuas antiguas* of 1590. Hernando de Ávila is quoted by Diego de Villalta [2] as calling our painter only Fernando Yáñez and not as declaring Almedina to be his birthplace, but he may nevertheless have included this fact in his book. In a document of 1531 relating to the painter's activity at Cuenca, he is described merely as Fernando Yáñez.

Chabás [3] interprets the "Llanos" of the other Fernando's name as

[1] F. J. Sánchez Cantón, *Fuentes literarias para la historia del arte español*, II (Madrid, 1933), 30. Palomino (new edition of *El Parnaso Español*, the third volume of his *Museo pictórico*, in Sánchez Cantón, *op. cit.*, IV, Madrid, 1936, p. 58) merely echoes Butrón, adding impossibly, seemingly as a mere guess, that Yáñez died about 1600.

[2] Sánchez Cantón, *op. cit.*, I (1923), 295 and 299.

[3] *El Archivo* (Valencia), V (1891), 394.

signifying that his town was Santa María de los Llanos just south-west of Belmonte in the province of Cuenca, also comprised within La Mancha and not too far distant from Almedina. The surmise of this old Spanish scholar has ever since been pretty generally taken for granted; but "llanos" as a common noun in Spanish means merely "plains," and there are many towns in other provinces of Spain with this word as a part of their titles. It is not indeed absolutely incredible that "Llanos" should have been no more than a simple surname, without geographical implication, at least any longer in Fernando's time, and we must not overlook the peculiarity that, if he really came from Santa María de los Llanos, he should not have been called in the documents Fernando de *los Llanos*, instead of only *Llanos*, where-as the end of his companion's name appears consistently as de la *Alme-dina*. Tormo [4] points out that St. Mary of the Plains (Santa Maria de los Llanos) was the patroness of the important town of Albacete, which lies south of Cuenca and west of Valencia and contains a work of the two partners' school. The likelihood, however, would remain that the pair had originated in the same district of the peninsula in order to explain their partnership, especially since we are virtually bound to believe that not one but both of them as youths enjoyed the adventure of a trip to Italy and a sojourn at Florence. Once in the documents regarding their designs for a sculptured retable by Onofre and Damián Forment in 1510 they are definitely denominated not as Valencians but as Castilians.[5]

It has been wrongly maintained that Yáñez is less dominated than Llanos by Leonardo, but, as a matter of fact, both are so saturated in the style and compositions of the Florentine whose personality over-powered everyone with whom he came into contact that an elucidation can scarcely be sought in the assumption that only one of the Fernandos had been in Italy and that the other derived the Leonardesque man-ner from his Valencian partner. Moreover, the tangible differences in their interpretations of Leonardo's modes render most unlikely either's acquisition of these modes merely by the channel of his asso-ciate's mediation. In our discussion of the shutters of the retable over the high altar in the Valencian cathedral and of their many additional works we shall find, besides, that each of them reveals knowledge of other Italian masters apparently inexplicable save on the supposition

---

[4] *Boletín de la Sociedad Española de Excursiones*, XXXII (1924), 39.

[5] See below, p. 181. The page of the article by X. de Salas there mentioned is 61.

of residence in the sister peninsula. There is much to be said for the customary conjecture that one of the partners was identical with the *Ferrando spagnuolo* who is recorded as paid on April 30 and August 30, 1505, for assisting Leonardo in his ill-starred painting of the Battle of Anghiari in the Palazzo Vecchio at Florence;[6] but it remains odd that only a single *Ferrando* should be listed in the Florentine documents. Certainly neither of them can be equated with the Spanish painter whom Vasari, without naming, declares in his life of "Bartolommeo della Gatta" to have aided Domenico Pecori at Arezzo in the opening years of the Cinquecento, for in a subsequent volume it will be shown, without a shadow of a doubt, that this painter was a Manuel Ferrando, active in Majorca.

Tormo[7] has proposed as a possibility that the Valencian prelate, Francisco Cabañes, a favorite of Alexander VI at Rome, was responsible for the summons of Yáñez and Llanos from Italy to Valencia, but he bolsters up this mere hypothesis with an argument in which it is very difficult to concur, the provisional ascription to both the then young partners of the fresco in the monastery attached to the Roman church of Sant' Onofrio representing the Madonna adored by a cleric whom he believes to be Cabañes himself. Leonardo's Lombard pupil, Boltraffio, is the painter to whom the fresco has long and very generally been assigned, and so authoritative a connoisseur as Berenson still maintains this attribution. Tormo makes the good point that there is no other evidence of the activity of any member of Leonardo's Milanese following in Rome at the very beginning of the Cinquecento, the period in which he places the picture; but it is not certain that the ecclesiastic depicted is Cabañes or that the fresco was done in the first years of the sixteenth century, and it is true that the Lombards very soon after journeyed to the eternal city, Bramantino in 1508 and Boltraffio himself in 1513, a quite conceivable, later time stylistically for the painting's execution. Judgment is hampered by liberal retouching, and one can ferret out, if he tries, analogies of a sort to the creations of the two Fernandos in Spain; but these result from their participation in the general Leonardesque inheritance, and I find it hard to escape the justice of the attribution to Boltraffio. In

[6] G. Gaye, *Carteggio d'artisti dei secoli XIV, XV, XVI*, Florence, II (1840), 89–90.
[7] *Almanaque de "Las Provincias"* (Valencia), 1941, pp. 399–403, and also his large work, *Monumentos españoles en Roma, y de portugueses y hispano-americanos*, Madrid, 1942, II, 105–107.

1480 the proper sum to be paid to Francesco Pagano and Paolo da San Leocadio for gilding the sculptured boss in the vault of the apse of the cathedral of Valencia [8] was estimated by a Master Ferrando, whom Sanchis y Sivera [9] guesses to have been perhaps either Llanos or Yáñez. If there is any validity in the surmise, at least one of the pair would have established his connection with the Valencian artistic *milieu* before going to Italy.

We first surely become acquainted with them when in 1506 [10] they are paid as partners for painting in the cathedral a retable (until the Spanish war partly preserved) for the chapel of Sts. Cosmas and Damian, now under the invocation of St. Catherine. Having evidently given satisfaction in this commission, they were honored, on March 1, 1507, with the contract [11] to paint their best known achievement, the extant wooden shutters for the silver retable over the high altar of the cathedral. The earlier retable of silver, dedicated to Our Lady, the patroness of the church, had perished in the conflagration of the year 1469; a new one in substitution had just been completed; and it was for this, in the general process of renovation of the *capilla mayor* then being carried out, that the two Fernandos decorated the shutters, the wood of which had already been prepared in 1506. Even the second silver retable succumbed in 1812 during the Napoleonic disturbances, and its place was taken by a modern Gothic specimen of copper manufactured in 1867,[12] which itself disappeared in the recent war, now leaving only a statue of the Virgen de Portaceli by the sculptor of the eighteenth century, Ignacio Vergara; but the shutters have blessedly survived and remain in their original position. The contract definitely specifies the six of the Seven Joys of the Virgin that are depicted on their exterior surfaces, the Nativity of Christ, the Epiphany, Resurrection, Ascension (Fig. 65), Pentecost (Fig. 66), and Assumption (although in the actual compartment this scene is enacted only in the distance and the Dormition occupies the foreground). The intention obviously was that, when the shutters were

[8] See above, p. 12.

[9] *La catedral de Valencia*, 152, and *Pintores medievales en Valencia*, 224.

[10] Sanchis y Silvera, *La catedral de Valencia*, 322–323 and 533, and *Pintores medievales en Valencia*, 224.

[11] The contract is published by R. Chabás in *El Archivo* (Valencia), V (1891), 390.

[12] For a more detailed account of the series of retables, see R. Chabás, appendix to his edition of *Antigüedades de Valencia* by J. Teixidor, Valencia, 1895, II, 455, and E. Bertaux in *Gazette des beaux-arts*, 1907, II, 105 ff.

FIG. 65. LLANOS. ASCENSION, SECTION OF SHUTTERS OF RETABLE
OF HIGH ALTAR, CATHEDRAL, VALENCIA
(*Photo. Grollo*)

FIG. 66. YÁÑEZ (AT LEAST IN VERY LARGE PART). PENTECOST,
SECTION OF SHUTTERS OF RETABLE OF HIGH ALTAR,
CATHEDRAL, VALENCIA

(*Photo. Grollo*)

closed, the faithful should see upon them six of the Seven Joys that were represented in the concealed silver retable, and the seventh Joy, the Annunciation, was omitted from the outer sides of the shutters probably because there was no room for it in the half-dozen spaces. The six themes on the inner faces, which were left to the choice of the cathedral chapter, naturally turned out to be more subjects from the Virgin's life, the Meeting at the Golden Gate, her Birth, her Presentation in the Temple (Fig. 67), the Visitation (Fig. 68), Purification, and the Rest on the Flight into Egypt. The records of remunerations to them for the enterprise continue in the archives of the church [13] from December 6, 1508, until the final payment on December 18, 1510. Moreover, in 1507, they had been employed in renewing the polychromy of the statue of Our Lady at the centre of the silver retable and in ornamenting the structure's *guardapolvos*.[14]

Recently [15] another item has been added to their activity at Valencia, the fact that in 1509–1510 they made the designs for the lost, sculptured retable of St. Eloy by Onofre and Damián Forment in the chapel of the silversmiths in the church of Sta. Catalina. Yáñez alone was soon at work, from 1511 to 1513, upon a further job for the cathedral, making the sketches for the decorative carvings, by Luis Muñoz, of the preserved wooden case of the new organ, the likewise extant shutters of which were painted by Nicolás Falcó,[16] and himself actually painting what are called in the document its "shoulders," [17] whether with pure design or sacred episodes it is now impossible to determine, since this embellishment has disappeared.[18] Both masters

[13] Sanchis y Sivera, *La catedral de Valencia*, 533, and *Pintores medievales en Valencia*, 225.

[14] Same references in Sanchis y Sivera's books, except p. 224 in the latter.

[15] See the article by X. de Salas in *Anales y Boletín de los Museos de Arte de Barcelona*, I, 2 (1942), 36, 41, 45, 47, 49, 50, 54, 55, 57, 58, 61, 69, 70, 71, 78, and 80.

[16] See above, p. 122.

[17] See the next paragraph.

[18] Sanchis y Sivera, *La catedral de Valencia*, 229 and 532–533, and *Pintores medievales en Valencia*, 225. His somewhat obscure language in the latter book might appear to refer to Llanos, and on page 224 he declares that Yáñez is not recorded as doing any work at Valencia after 1511; but the clearer statements in *La catedral de Valencia* show that, at least when he wrote this earlier book in 1909, he definitely meant Yáñez, and I assume that the words in his later volume of 1930, *Pintores medievales en Valencia*, are not corrections but mistakes. The same confusion occurs even in his first publication of the *Pintores medievales* in serial form, *Estudis universitaris catalans*, VII (1913), 65–66. X. de Salas, however (*op. cit.*, 41), interprets Sanchis y Sivera's data about the organ as referring to Llanos.

FIG. 67. YÁÑEZ (AT LEAST IN VERY LARGE PART).
PRESENTATION OF THE VIRGIN, SECTION OF
SHUTTERS OF RETABLE OF HIGH ALTAR,
CATHEDRAL, VALENCIA
(*Photo. Grollo*)

Fig. 68. YÁÑEZ AND LLANOS. VISITATION, SECTION OF
SHUTTERS OF RETABLE OF HIGH ALTAR,
CATHEDRAL, VALENCIA

(*Photo. Grollo*)

are registered as still residing at Valencia in 1513 in the parish of S. Andrés.[19]

After this year they are not mentioned at Valencia again, and the partnership must soon have been dissolved, each seeking by himself a new market for his products. In 1520 [20] a Master Hernando was paid for painting (perhaps only with polychromy) the "shoulders" [21] of the sculptured retable which had just been set up over the high altar of the cathedral of Murcia but was destroyed by fire in 1854, and for several reasons it is impossible to doubt that he was none other than Fernando de Llanos. In the first place a painter fully denominated as Fernando de Llanos is recorded in 1525 as remunerated for an unspecified task at the near-lying city of Cartagena.[22] Second, the existence at Murcia of an artist, Andrés de Llanos, who, among other tasks between 1526 and 1545, continued the work on the retable over the high altar with polychromy and gilding,[23] bears out the identification of the Hernando of 1520 with Fernando de Llanos, who would naturally be surmised to have been an older relative of Andrés, and it may even be deduced that the reason for the assumption of the polychromy by Andrés was the death of Fernando, which would then have occurred in 1525 or 1526. Finally, we shall subsequently discover that works are still to be seen in Murcia and its territory which are undocumented but precisely in the manner of certain parts of the shutters of the retable of the Valencian cathedral and therefore attributable to Fernando de Llanos by reason of his activity at Murcia which may be predicated on the grounds that we have just enumerated. One of these works, a retable of the Marriage of the Virgin in the cathedral of Murcia, reveals that he had moved to this more southerly city at least by 1516.

[19] Sanchis y Sivera, *Pintores medievales en Valencia*, 225.

[20] See M. González Simancas in *Revista de archivos*, XXIV (1911), 536, and A. Baquero Almansa, *Catálogo de los profesores de las bellas artes murcianos*, Murcia, 1913, p. 46.

[21] As the retable has perished, we cannot tell whether the word "shoulders," describing Hernando's employment upon it, refers to its back or merely to its upper borders. Bertaux understands "shoulders" as signifying "le revers des volets." We have just perceived that the parts of the organ in the cathedral of Valencia painted by Yáñez are also enigmatically described as "shoulders."

[22] Bertaux (*Gazette des beaux-arts*, 1908, I, 345), probably because he did not know the documents at first hand, describes the payment of 1525 as coming from the cathedral of Murcia, but González Simancas (*op. cit.*, 536) definitely refers it to Cartagena.

[23] See above, p. 99.

Fernando Yáñez, after we lose him at Valencia, reappears in 1515 at Barcelona [24] on a committee of experts chosen to pass judgment on paintings by Joan de Burgunya in the retable over the high altar of the church of Sta. María del Pino. The next sure seat of his labors was Cuenca, whither he may have gone as early as 1523,[25] but we cannot fix him there with certainty until some years later, when we find him employed, with greater *éclat* than his erstwhile companion, by no less a personage than the Italianate canon and treasurer of the chapter in the cathedral of the city, Gómez Carrillo de Albornoz, to do in this church the extant paintings of the chapel of the Albornoz family which the cleric remodelled and redecorated during the first third of the sixteenth century. In his will of May 23, 1531,[26] he states that he had contracted with Yáñez for the principal retable in the chapel as well as the lateral retable of the Pietà, and the date 1526 inscribed on the frieze of the architectural frame of the former shows that at least this part of the structure had been made five years before and, it may be guessed, also the paintings. Gómez Carrillo, however, survived to make a second will in 1536, the language of which reveals that by this time he enjoyed the gratification of having brought entirely to completion the magnanimous enterprise of reconditioning the chapel. The other lateral altar, over which there is a retable of the Epiphany, was under the patronage of the canon's brother, Luis Carrillo de Albornoz; but in one of his testaments [27] Gómez Carrillo exhibits his interest in the retable by making a point of remunerating his brother for what he had spent upon it, and as a matter of fact the style proves that his favorite, Yáñez, was the author.

The canon in his first will goes out of his way to distinguish the artist by the words *singular pintor* (an extraordinary painter) and even gives him the aristocratic title, *señor pintor*. Indeed from the partnership only the fame of Yáñez lived on in subsequent Spanish literature about the Fine Arts, gracing the writings of Hernando de Ávila, Juan de Butrón, Vincencio Carducho, and Palomino.[28] The statement that the great satirist and poet of the early seventeenth cen-

---

[24] See in an article by J. M. Madurell in *Anales y Boletín de los Museos de Arte de Barcelona*, I, 3 (1943), 82–84.

[25] See below, p. 244.

[26] Ceán Bermúdez, *Diccionario*, VI, 15.

[27] Ceán Bermúdez (16) does not make it clear which testament — probably the second since he mentions the fact in the same paragraph in which he discusses this will.

[28] See above, p. 175, and Sánchez Cantón, *op. cit.*, II, 84.

tury, Quevedo, dedicated an epigram to him rests only on the not too sound authority of Palomino, since the verses have never been discovered;[29] but, among the artists of the early Renaissance, Yáñez would have been particularly known to Quevedo, who had estates and partly dwelt at La Torre de Juan Abad in La Mancha. Butrón, probably deriving his information from Hernando de Ávila, who was more nearly the contemporary of Yáñez and therefore would be more trustworthy as a source, declares that he did a retable for the church of his birthplace, Almedina, from which a panel in the Prado may be a relic; but he is wrong in making him an imitator of Raphael, although in the last creations of Yáñez some rather indeterminative borrowings from the Umbrian master are superimposed upon the Leonardesque foundation.[30]

2. Their Individual Manners and the Problem of their Collaboration in the Retable of the Cathedral of Valencia

We arrive at a divorce of the styles of the two Fernandos by taking as a basis paintings that they are known or demonstrated by geographical situation to have done separately from each other at the end of their lives and by applying the distinctions thus obtained to works which are documented as executed by them in partnership or which, though not authenticated by any record, are proved by internal evidence to be the creations of one or the other of the twain or, in a few possible instances, of both together. It should be stated at once that this criterion for discriminating between their respective manners avoids the partial fallacy of what has hitherto been almost the general practice, namely, the assignment of sets of *whole* compartments to each of the Fernandos in their most celebrated achievement, the shutters of the retable over the high altar in the cathedral of Valencia, for which the archives show them in association to have received the commission. It is true, as we shall find, that in a number of cases each did paint wholly or at least very largely an entire compartment, but the fundamental and important point which has until now been missed by nearly all critics is that in other instances they

---

[29] See Sánchez Cantón, *op. cit.*, IV, 58, and V, 450.
[30] See below, p. 229.

divided between them the labor upon a single panel, each taking in it certain figures or sections for himself.

It was Bertaux [1] who definitely established the mode of partitioning the shutters that has enjoyed virtually universal acceptance ever since. To Yáñez he allocated six compartments, the Meeting at the Golden Gate, Presentation of the Virgin in the Temple, Visitation, Nativity of Christ, Purification, and Dormition. In the Ascension he held that Yáñez was assisted by Llanos, thus in one case foreshadowing my belief in collaboration in certain panels, and he therefore left to the latter alone five pieces, the Birth of the Virgin, Epiphany, Rest in the Flight into Egypt, Resurrection, and Pentecost. Justi had already in 1893 [2] distributed the shutters between two painters in the same way as Bertaux, except that he perceived only one hand in the Ascension and this the hand of the artist whom the French scholar identified with Llanos; but the danger of holding that the partners always took whole compartments for themselves is unmasked when we find that the German gave to Llanos the panels which Bertaux ascribed to Yáñez and *vice versa*, nor is the implication of this divergence in connoisseurship completely removed by the considerations that Justi was relying only on visual memory and that later, in republishing the article in his *Miscellaneen* of 1908 [3] and having seen Bertaux's illustrations from photographs, he changed his opinion and concurred in the Frenchman's attributions to the two names. Moreover, María Luisa Caturla, writing in 1942,[4] further exhibited the insecurity of the allotment of entire panels in all cases between the masters by partially abandoning the categories of Bertaux and Justi and by claiming for Yáñez the Resurrection and Pentecost that they had bestowed on Llanos and conversely for the latter the Purification in which they had seen the craft of his companion.

There are only two scholars, so far as I know, who subsequently have dared to question explicitly the custom, sanctioned by Bertaux, of apportioning complete panels of the shutters between the Fernandos. The first, in 1929, was Allende-Salazar, but only in a sentence hidden away in the brief notice that he devotes to Llanos in the Thieme-Becker *Lexikon*, where, referring to the shutters, he says: "Probably both painted in closest collaboration on all twelve panels of

[1] *Gazette des beaux-arts*, 1907, II, 103ff., and 1908, I, 344ff.
[2] *Repertorium für Kunstwissenschaft*, XVI, 1–10.
[3] II, 135–149.
[4] *Archivo español de arte*, XV, 35ff.

this fine altarpiece, and each did not, as commonly asserted, undertake six of the pictures." Tormo followed in 1941, putting the matter somewhat more timidly in an affirmation, likewise concealed because included in a not easily accessible article: [5] "The two Hernandos collaborated very closely at Valencia in the twelve compositions of the high altar, even working at times on the same panel." Berenson *implicitly* accords with Tormo's and Allende-Salazar's attitude, for, in his *Italian Pictures of the Renaissance*,[6] inserting lists of the works that he ascribes to Llanos and Yáñez, he groups them altogether, without attempting to specify, in the shutters or even in their further productions, which are by one and which by the other, and this although ordinarily he subtly separates the manners of artists who are intimately allied.

A comparison of the paintings by Yáñez at Cuenca and in the region with those by Llanos at Murcia and its district plainly shows, as Bertaux contended, that the former was the more talented. His memory alone survived,[7] and the usual [8] occurrence of the other Fernando's name before that of his colleague in the Valencian documents concerned with their joint output could be explained by Chabás's [9] assumption that he was the elder or by the supposition that he conducted the business of the partnership. Although we shall find it probable that the greater gifts of Yáñez extended to matters of composition, treatment of architecture, and the like, his actually demonstrable superiority consists in a usually livelier imagination and in elements of pure craft, such as draughtsmanship and modelling in color. This superiority is one of the criteria by which I have arrived at my own convictions in regard to the division of labor on the shutters, but much more they are based on frequent, long, and scrupulous comparison with the assured, separate attainments of each Fernando after the dissolution of the partnership. So far as possible, I have endeavored thus to study the panels freshly and unbiased by what my predecessors have written on the matter, but I am confident that Bertaux would have subscribed to my apportionment of the masters' activity in the shutters, if he had been able to utilize the more copious and better photographs of the works at Cuenca and Murcia

[5] *Almanaque de "Las Provincias"* (Valencia), 1941, p. 401.
[6] Oxford, Clarendon Press, 1932, p. 289.
[7] See above, p. 185.
[8] The exception is in one of the deeds referring to their designs for the Forment retable: X. de Salas, *op. cit.*, 45.   [9] *Op. cit.*, 394.

now at our disposal and if his knowledge of the productions of Llanos in Murcia and its territory had not been confined to the single retable of the Marriage of the Virgin in the cathedral of the city. The individual contributions of each painter seem to me, generally speaking, plain to discern, but there are, of course, passages in which it is impossible dogmatically to decide between the claims of the two participants, since, engaged simultaneously upon a common enterprise, they would be subject to interinfluence, now and then naturally imitating each other's forms and methods, and since in certain ways their styles, to begin with, are analogous. In outlining my conclusions about their respective efforts in the shutters, I shall have to resort to irksome details of comparison, but I will limit these to the lowest terms feasible, transferring to the reader the task of pursuing the proof in my subsequent analysis of the works at Cuenca and Murcia and in his own examination of the photographs or better, if possible, of the originals.

I am glad to be able to concur with Bertaux in so far as to assign very largely, if not wholly, seven of the compartments to the candidates whom he proposes. In the case of Yáñez these are the Meeting at the Golden Gate, Presentation of the Virgin, Nativity of Christ, and Dormition. My eyes can perceive no passages in the last three that definitely suggest intervention of his partner, but in the Meeting at the Golden Gate the St. Anne, her attendant in profile, and the other with a basket on her head look as if Llanos had executed them. The Marriage of the Virgin at Murcia provides a parallel for the St. Anne in Our Lady's matron of honor and for the profile of the attendant in the bridesmaid next to Mary, a type that, when we study the separate works of Llanos, we shall find to be peculiarly characteristic and recurrent in his production. The girl with the basket prophesies the Virgin herself in the Marriage as well as in another authentic panel by Llanos in the cathedral of Murcia, the Adoration of the Shepherds. In the Presentation of the Virgin, the woman behind St. Anne is a somewhat less pronounced example of Llanos's much loved profile, but, nevertheless, she may be by Yáñez, who sometimes employs a similar countenance, so that she would constitute an instance of the phenomenon which I have noted above, the occasional adoption by one artist of the forms of his associate.

The three compartments in which I agree with Bertaux in descrying at least the predomination of Llanos are the Birth of the Virgin, Epiphany, and Resurrection. The last fails to reveal anything conclusively due to Yáñez, but in the other two there are passages in which I frankly confess that I cannot decide between the respective claims of the partners. The Marriage of the Virgin at Murcia furnishes counterparts for the parturient St. Anne in the man reading a book and for the woman carrying a plate of fruit in Mary's older attendant. The St. Joachim embodies precisely the same unsuccessful struggle for an abnormal, Leonardesque kind of visage as the episcopal saint at the right in a predella at Barcelona which we shall attribute to Llanos, and the two men, in diminished scale, conversing in the right background are types entirely characteristic of the master. The maiden holding the newborn Virgin is disfigured by his fondness for lankiness of physique and straggling locks, and the woman next to her has a face so like the countenance of the Virgin in the panels at Murcia that I incline to ascribe her to Llanos despite the elaborate foreshortening, in Yáñez's mode, of the hands. I rather think that he did also the midwife spreading out a cloth, but I am obliged to admit my inability to determine whether Yáñez might be responsible for the other two feminine assistants at the event.

Bertaux has amassed some of the reasons for giving the Epiphany to Llanos, and other arguments could be added, provided, for instance, by the master's retable at Caravaca, near Murcia, with which the French scholar was not acquainted. The clumsy drawing and poor articulation of the prominent negroid Magus at the right (whose face, oddly enough, if the moustache were obliterated, would reproduce the type used for the Virgin in the panels in the cathedral of Murcia) are found again, almost line for line, in the henchman at the left among the walking captors in the scene, at Caravaca, of the priest's arrest,[10] and an analogue for the countenance of the older of the two kneeling Wise Men may be seen in the head at the extreme right in the compartment depicting the Moorish king's baptism. The Madonna, however, is not duplicated in any of the unquestionable creations of Llanos, and constitutes a version in full face of the type appearing in her representation in the Nativity, a figure that there is no reason for doubting that Yáñez executed, as well as the rest of the compartment of Christ's birth. The countenance occurs also in paintings other than the shutters, attributable to Yáñez on internal evidence and without, so far as one can see, any intervention of Llanos. In no other work, moreover, does the latter show that he was capable

[10] See below, p. 249.

of rising to such heights of expressiveness as in the very youthful Magus, who is most successfully imbued with intense Spanish religious devotion.

With Justi I fail to discover in the Ascension the traces of the participation of Yáñez noticed by Bertaux, and indeed the whole picture appears to me eminently consistent with the norms of Llanos, especially his affection for lank and haggard human beings crowned by tousled hair.

My real quarrel with Bertaux begins with what I am convinced is the necessity of transferring in entirety from Llanos to Yáñez the Rest in the Flight into Egypt (if we can speak of entirety without having actually watched the partners paint) and of the Pentecost at least in very large part (in this instance in agreement with Señora Caturla). All the types in the former compartment look directly forward to the modes that Yáñez was to display at Cuenca, the Virgin especially incorporating a kind of feminine countenance which he much affected and which receives its perhaps most emphatic expression in Our Lady of the Cuenca Epiphany. In the Pentecost the nearest approximations to Llanos's conceptions of mankind are the two Apostles in the upper row at the extreme left and right, another Apostle next to the haloed woman at the right (by comparison with the suitor at the extreme left in the Murcian Marriage of the Virgin), and the upgazing youthful Apostle at the left (by comparison with the similarly placed, unbearded, kneeling Apostle in the Ascension of the shutters), but these figures are better executed than the analogous ones by Llanos and may very well provide examples of the likelihood that I have already pointed out, the almost inevitable, occasional imitation by one partner of the specialties of the other. Rapturously upturned faces are far more characteristic of Yáñez than of his associate, and the youth at the right with such a head (in distinction from his comrade at the left whom I have just mentioned) will be more than once virtually repeated at Cuenca. The stern Apostle at the left (with his hand upon his chest) is a type to which both Fernandos resort, but its employment by Llanos in the Birth of the Virgin in the shutters is a weak performance by contrast with the figure in the Pentecost and with the other examples in Yáñez's production. If we were right in assigning to the latter the Virgin in the Epiphany, he must have done also the arresting form of the woman in the lower right corner, who expresses the infusion of the Holy Spirit by dumbfoundedly raising her hand to her head. We could not expect Yáñez, in the representation of the event commemorated on Whitsunday, to duplicate every actor in his other works, but the figure who most clearly witnesses to his craft is the *haloed* woman at the right, a further specimen of the type to which I have referred in discussing the Virgin of the Flight into Egypt. Above all, Llanos scarcely shows himself equal anywhere to the general standard, in the Pentecost, of draughtsmanship and dramatic effectiveness in posture and gesture.

Both the Visitation and Purification, deemed by Bertaux works of Yáñez, present us, in my opinion, with a dichotomy, the Frenchman's candidate in each case doing the persons in the left half and Llanos those at the right. Among all the figures in the shutters, the handmaid at the extreme right in the Visitation is the nearest to an actual replica of the Virgin in the Marriage at Murcia; in the same section of the compartment, the other attendant and Our Lady herself are close enough to the type to be credited also to the account of Llanos; and I discern no obstacle to assigning to him likewise the St. Elizabeth. Of the participants at the right in the Purification, the priest and Simeon behind him conform precisely to Llanos's representations of haggard old men, whereas the other attendant at this side belongs to the class of his unmistakable profiles, which I have stressed in analyzing his contribution to the Meeting at the Golden Gate. Simeon, like one of the midwives in the Birth of the Virgin, would provide an example of his aping of his partner's interest in the foreshortening of hands. The figures at the left, Mary, the Child,[11] and their companions may be safely regarded as the contribution of Yáñez to the picture. It is significant that in both the Visitation and Purification, as well as in the limited additions of Llanos to Yáñez's compartment of the Meeting at the Golden Gate, the passages by the former are found at the right.

We possess no absolutely infallible means of determining whether each partner planned the compositions of the panels in the shutters that he painted wholly or largely by himself, nor to which of the twain we owe the compositions in the pieces exhibiting more of a dichotomy, nor whether one of them assumed the important task of making the sketches for all the compositions, delegating to his associate only the actual execution of entire compartments and of certain figures in other panels; but, if the last alternative is the right one, the likelier choice would be Yáñez, who, when working alone, shows invention as a com-

[11] See below, p. 267.

poser more frequently than Llanos. A similar query must be put in regard to the architectural settings, and a similar hypothetical answer given in Yáñez's favor.[12] When we do find Llanos either in the shutters or in his later, separate achievements more interesting in these respects, we shall perhaps not do him an injustice by saying that he was profiting by lessons conned from his companion. Analogous impressive landscapes, with the outlines in the distance often vaporously softened, seem to have been equally the property of both.

3. Their Works Executed in Partnership

We may now turn to what is more a labor of love, the analysis not only of the place of the two Fernandos in the history of art but also of their aesthetic attainments, first using as examples their most comprehensive achievement, the shutters of the retable over the high altar of the cathedral of Valencia, the documentation and subjects of which we have already had occasion to review. Several of the characteristics that emerge in this monument, such as the indebtedness to Leonardo, the landscapes, and the interest in the representation of still life and animals, we must, with our present knowledge, ascribe to both the painters in common by reason of their intermingled collaboration and of what we shall find in commissions carried out by them apart from each other; but with a good deal of confidence I will credit to Yáñez other and higher qualities on the basis not only of the compartments in the shutters attributable wholly or almost wholly to him but also of the works that he did at Cuenca after the sundering of the partnership. Our eventual scrutiny of the paintings executed by each separately will amplify our understanding of their individual qualities and, together with our study of the shutters, will reveal, as I have already urged, that Yáñez was the enterprising and original spirit in the combine and that Llanos, when not coöperating with him, at times, though by no means always, sank to the status of a rather humdrum exponent of Leonardesque fashions.

Until, as we shall subsequently see,[1] María Luisa Caturla, in my judgment, strained at a gnat and sought vainly to prove that Yáñez owed more to Giorgione than to Leonardo da Vinci, all have agreed to the perfectly obvious truth, i.e., that the foundation of the Fernandos' style derives from this over-celebrated Florentine inaugurator of the

---

[12] See below, p. 195.   [1] P. 196.

manner of the Cinquecento. Indeed, in types, chiaroscuro, and general methods they are as thoroughly subject to Leonardo's compelling influence, to say the least, as any of his Milanese followers, even Luini or Ambrogio dei Predis; and this element is so all-pervasive in their output that the other winds which blew upon them are subservient. It would be only an insult to the reader's intelligence to irk him by amassing the overwhelming number of examples, when he will find it mere child's play to observe them everywhere plainly for himself, and when, for instance, the Mona Lisa or the faces of the *Anna selbdritt* in the Louvre stare at us from the visages of so many of the partners' women. Actual compositions of Leonardo have been carried by them to Spain. The Epiphany in the shutters is a faithful adaptation of his unfinished version of the theme in the Uffizi, even retaining the mysteriously brooding spectator at the extreme left; and in the Rest in the Flight into Egypt, there is chosen an arrangement of the Virgin and Child and their postures often repeated among Leonardo's north-Italian pupils such as Luini, Boltraffio, and Sodoma,[2] thus pointing to a lost Madonna by the famous Florentine himself. Suida[3] has singled out an instance of Leonardesque dependence that had not yet been noted, the relation of one of the Roman soldiers at the left in the Resurrection to the warrior crouching under a shield in the Battle of Anghiari.

The two Fernandos could not have failed to be touched also by other great artists active in Florence during their sojourn in the city. The occasional emergence of solid, stocky physiques, exemplified by the three prominent spectators in the foreground of the Presentation of the Virgin in the Temple or by the St. Joseph in the Rest in the Flight, may very well embody a misunderstood adaptation of Fra Bartolommeo's monumental forms. The robust, racial strain of La Mancha would perhaps have stimulated them naturally to the creation of such bodies, but an interest in Fra Bartolommeo is almost incontrovertibly demonstrated by the very probable knowledge of his composition for the Last Judgment evidenced in Yáñez's rendering at

[2] Bertaux (in Michel, *Histoire de l'art*, IV, 2, p. 912, n. 1) mentions the example by Sodoma (now in the Reford Collection, Montreal), referring to the reproduction in Reinach, *Repertoire de peintures du Moyen Âge et de la Renaissance*, IV, 421, no. 2. See also W. Suida, *Leonardo und sein Kreiss*, Munich, 1929, pp. 251 and 272, and figs. 132 and 133. I cannot follow Mayer (Spanish edition of his *Geschichte*, 1942, p. 145) in seeing much relation to the drawing in the Ashmolean Museum, Oxford, illustrated on p. 126 in the volume on Leonardo in the *Klassiker der Kunst*.

[3] *Op. cit.*, 251.

Játiva.[4] Not enough attention, however, has been paid to their debt, particularly in the sections of the shutters by Yáñez, to another Florentine painter with whom they would have come into contact, the whimsical Pier di Cosimo. They often essay Leonardo's subtle transitions from light to shade and within the shadows, but almost as frequently we espy Pier di Cosimo's more violent contrasts of light and dark, which anticipate the fashions of Caravaggio and the *tenebrosi*. Among the many instances, the most tangible are the shepherd extracting a thorn from his foot in the Meeting at the Golden Gate and the dazed woman in the lower left corner of the Pentecost. The admiration for Pier di Cosimo also sometimes conflicts in another way with the legacy from Leonardo, so that the Fernandos do not always seek to reproduce the latter's *sfumatezza*. The very type of the Madonna in the Nativity of Christ appears to be inspired by such personages of Pier di Cosimo as the St. Catherine in his altarpiece in the Florentine Galleria dell' Ospedale degl' Innocenti or the two feminine saints kneeling beneath the Virgin of the Immaculate Conception in the Uffizi. In view of the many precedents, even in the artistic history of Spain, it is to be doubted that Angulo [5] is right in deriving the composition of the Birth of the Virgin from Ghirlandaio's fresco of the Baptist's Nativity in S. Maria Novella at Florence, which it resembles only in certain details.

Whether the ecstatically upturned faces in the Ascension and Pentecost are borrowed from Perugino or incorporate the partners' own interpretations of religious transport, there are no means of determining; but they would have seen in the paintings of Perugino, who was much at Florence at the end of the fifteenth and the beginning of the sixteenth centuries, serene, chaste, and classical architecture of the Renaissance which might have been the starting-point for their own backgrounds of the same noble class. We shall subsequently [6] cite further evidence that at least implies an appreciation by Yáñez of this Umbrian painter. Since the feeling for architecture marks especially not only the parts of the shutters attributable to Yáñez but also his other sure separate achievements and since, almost without exception, it is not conspicuous in works done by Llanos alone, we may deduce the former

---

[4] See below, p. 207.

[5] *Archivo español de arte*, XVII (1944), 346, and his monograph, *Pedro Berruguete en Paredes de Nava*, Barcelona, 1946, p. 17.

[6] P. 221.

to have been the one who was highly endowed with architectural curiosity and imagination and so could have evolved from the suggestions in Perugino such original amassments of buildings as pique our interest in the Presentation of the Virgin in the Temple and in the Pentecost. We need not, therefore, accompany Señora Caturla [7] in her peregrinations through the Italian peninsula and especially to Venice in order to seek the explanation. The colored marbles in the niches of the hall of the Dormition suggest, rather than Señora Caturla's Venice, Alberti's Santo Sepolcro in the Rucellai Chapel at Florence or the settings to Castagno's Last Supper and, at Urbino, Piero della Francesca's Flagellation. Indeed the travels of one or both of the Fernandos in Umbria and central Italy would seem to be proved by the probable dependence of the splendid figure of the sleeping soldier in the lower right corner of the Resurrection in the shutters upon the correspondingly placed actor in Piero della Francesca's supreme rendering of the subject at Borgo San Sepolcro. The lively concern with architectural setting creates an analogy to Bramantino, who at least owed something in his forms to Leonardo; but the resemblances are probably accidental, and Bramantino may not have developed his characteristic manner by 1507.

It is indeed difficult to follow Señora Caturla [8] in her principal contention, a determinative debt of Yáñez to Giorgione; and in studying her article I glean that she really did not fully mean her sensational title, "Ferrando Yáñez is not a Leonardesco," and that she would not deny altogether the great Florentine's influence upon him, but only that she deems the obligations to the Venetian more vital. If the obligations exist at all, however, this is just what they are not, vital, since they fail to affect in any way his mode of painting but would merely have supplied him with one or two ideas for composition and poses. It is quite credible that he never visited Venice or knew Giorgione's works and that the similarities are fortuitous, but no harm is done if we wish to think that he journeyed widely in the Italian peninsula and with his alert mind picked up here and there pictorial, though nonessential, ideas that interested him. I select for discussion only the analogies brought forward by Señora Caturla that seem to have any validity. The composition of the Nativity of Christ is certainly very close to Giorgione's rendering now in the National Gallery at Wash-

---

[7] See the next paragraph.

[8] *Archivo español de arte*, XV (1942), 35–49.

ington; but the examples by Ghirlandaio in the Trinità at Florence, by Perugino in the Villa Albani at Rome, and especially by Pier di Cosimo in the Museum at Berlin display almost as many resemblances, and it is not impossible that on such precedents Yáñez could by chance have evolved a composition like that of the Venetian master. A still less plausible argument adduced by her is the fact that both in the Visitation [9] of the Valencian shutters and in Sebastiano del Piombo's altarpiece in S. Giovanni Crisostomo at Venice there happens to be a group of three standing young women, and, moreover, it must be remembered that no ground exists for her belief in Giorgione's planning of the altarpiece and that it may not have been executed before the return of Yáñez, in 1505 or 1506, to Spain. She would trace to Giorgione's pastoralism the standing shepherds with their staffs in the Meeting at the Golden Gate and in the Nativity of Christ; but they would occur spontaneously to the mind of anyone called upon to paint these rustic themes of sacred story, and Perugino introduces into his fresco of the Nativity in the Collegio del Cambio at Perugia, dating from about 1500, shepherds who hold their staffs, although in distinction from the figures in the shutters, they kneel in adoration.

Even if we should grant that her comparisons establish a visit to Venice, the fundamental manner of the partners was not significantly affected by the experience, but she does make an important point by indicating an at least possible dependence of the Pietà by Yáñez at Cuenca upon Sebastiano del Piombo's great treatment of the theme at Viterbo. The hands of the prostrate body of the Saviour take the same positions; the Mother clasps her hands at her side correspondingly; and the St. John at Cuenca looks tragically upward in the mode of the Virgin in the Viterbo picture. In Sebastiano's rendering of the subject at Leningrad, the Christ is also nearly identical, and here it is the Magdalene who analogously joins her hands together. It is to be noted, however, that the body of the Redeemer is almost as similar and that one of the mourning women thus clasps her hands in the Lamentation, almost certainly by Yáñez rather than Llanos, until recently preserved in the Sala Capitular Moderna of the cathedral at Valencia, which, if, as is generally believed, it constituted a section of the partners' retable of Sts. Cosmas and Damian documented in 1506, was executed before Sebastiano's pictures, so that the correspondences

---

[9] She accepts the whole compartment of the Visitation as by Yáñez, whereas I assign to him only the left half comprising the three young women to whom she refers.

in the Cuenca version may again embody an independent arrival at parallel results. Since the Leningrad picture is definitely dated in 1516, and the Viterbo version must fall at least as late, in Sebastian's Michelangelesque period, the relationship of the Lamentation by Yáñez at Cuenca to these works by Sebastiano, if valid, would combine with other questionable evidence which we shall subsequently ponder [10] to suggest that he perhaps made a second journey to Italy after his activity in the cathedral of Valencia. Señora Caturla admits the possibility of such a second trip, but, with her velleity for discovering traces of Giorgione's influence upon Yáñez, she is forced to think that the Viterbo Pietà is a work of the Venetian master only finished by Sebastiano, and she stands, therefore, in unenviable isolation in assigning it, despite the obvious debt to Michael Angelo and against the unanimous consent of other critics, to Sebastiano's early, Venetian period.

The panels over the high altar of the Valencian cathedral embody a considerable degree of original imagination which, as the examples are found almost entirely in passages that I have claimed for Yáñez, may be generally supposed expressions of his more alert intellect. Indeed, if he does deserve the honor, he stands almost alone among Spanish artists of the early Renaissance in often inventing new compositions for the time-worn sacred themes. In the Presentation of the Virgin in the Temple the originality consists in three things, all of which tend to transform the religious subject naturalistically into a scene from every-day life. In the first place Mary is not isolated as a miraculous object of reverence, but Joachim, Anne, and the spectators are given almost as much prominence. Second, the foreground and background disclose much stressed and charmingly treated urchins of the streets dallying about the Temple and directly prophesying Murillo's affection for such figures of *genre*. Finally, according to one of Yáñez's frequent practices, his concern with architecture has interestingly created a series of levels in the Temple on which the characters, even the priest who is usually depicted as formally awaiting the maiden, can be casually disposed. I note a similarity in posture between the child in the lower right corner and the correspondingly placed boy in Cima da Conegliano's rendering of the theme at Dresden, but the parallelism is probably just a chance and not another indication of an excursion to Venice, since in other respects the compo-

[10] See below, p. 229.

sitions are not analogous and it is quite possible that the Dresden picture was painted after 1507. More daringly new is the Pentecost. Tradition is violated by the transplantation to outdoors; the compact mass of the habitual composition that even Paolo da San Leocadio retains is broken up into deceptively accidental little groups, one of which is even assigned, in diminished scale, to the distance; and several women, besides the Virgin, are the recipients of the gifts of the Holy Spirit. The novelties in the shutters sometimes consist in mere little touches as when, in the Rest in the Flight, the Holy Child turns and fingers a palm held by a *putto*.

We are also constantly meeting impressive, fresh dramatic conceptions of individual actors. So, the psychological study of the half timid, half precocious little Virgin looking out at us too demurely and somewhat too conscious of her pious preëminence as she climbs the stairs at her Presentation. In the Pentecost much is made of the contrasted effects of the infusion of the Holy Ghost into the two women who in the foreground are the objects of more attention than the traditional participants in the scene — the one at the left felled to the ground by the divine force, the other clasping her brow with her hand in perplexed amazement. In the background of the Nativity of Christ a shepherd falls prostrate with awe, in another memorable attitude, at the proclamation of the angels, and his companions, although thus removed from our first sight, are effectively represented as not yet cognizant of the vision and given varied, finely rendered postures demanded by their rural occupations. We have already had opportunity to observe the profound and entirely convincing expression of adoration in the young Magus of the Epiphany. Another new study of mentality occurs in the priest of the Purification who, partly frightened and partly perplexed, seems not yet to have arrived at a full comprehension of the august ceremony that he is about to perform. Considerable and successful effort is expended even upon the secondary form of the shepherd extracting a thorn from his foot in the Meeting at the Golden Gate. Bathed in the violent chiaroscuro of Pier di Cosimo, he may have been suggested, not by any ancient, classical treatment of the *motif*, but by the attendant in Brunelleschi's trial-relief of the Sacrifice of Isaac, thus again demonstrating awareness of important achievements in Italian art besides those of Leonardo.

The greatest examples of dramatic expressiveness mark the Dormition. The painter clings to the stereotyped horizontal composition, transferring to the smaller scale of a subordinate episode seen through an archway St. Thomas's reception of the girdle, for some unexplained reason endowing only six of the Apostles and not even the Virgin with haloes, and, as in the Pentecost, anomalously introducing other women; but he magnificently elevates the event above the ordinary conceptions of the scene by the differentiation and incisive individualization of the three Apostles in the foreground who are not standing. St. John, holding the palm brought to the Virgin by the angel, sits at the left bowed in sorrow; in the centre, on a projection of her couch, another Apostle is rapt in the pondering of the mystery; and just beyond him at the right a more aged member of the college of the Twelve sinks over a book upon the ledge profoundly absorbed in conning the prophesies of the Assumption. In the Resurrection, the commonly less acute Llanos, if he planned as well as executed the panel, hits upon the idea of depicting a soldier (in the lower left corner) drawing his sword as if to combat the supernatural powers that coöperate in the stupendous miracle.

The anatomy of the half-nude Christ of the Resurrection has been the object of greater care than the ordinary Spanish painter of the period possessed enough knowledge to exert, but we shall come upon more outstanding examples of this interest which runs all through the Fernandos' production and reflects their absorption of the Italian academic attitude and especially the instruction of the scientifically minded Leonardo. The naturalistic approach to art, indicated by the endeavors to treat the sacred subjects in terms of ordinary existence upon which I have commented, manifests itself also in a sphere where they definitely, even Llanos separately at Murcia, surpassed almost all their Spanish contemporaries, namely in the delineation of animals. Bertaux has singled out for praise the trussed lamb in the Meeting at the Golden Gate, and to this we may add the cow facing inward in the Nativity of Christ, the reposeful beasts in the Rest in the Flight into Egypt, and, above all, the two cats in the lower right corner of the Birth of the Virgin, especially noteworthy because so few artists of any period have been able to catch successfully the shape and postures of this elusive creature.

If we set aside the naturalism, there is little in the shutters that is essentially Spanish or connected with the past aesthetic tradition of the peninsula. Now and then, especially in their representations of still life, the Fernandos seem cognizant of modes of painting derived from the Low Countries, since they were possibly trained in the Hispano-Flemish manner of the late Middle Ages before they went to Italy and were transmuted by Leonardo and his *confrères*. Both the Spaniards and Italians of the time, for example Paolo da San Leocadio, introduce incidents in smaller scale into their backgrounds. In addition to the instances that we have already observed in the shutters, we may register the vision of Joachim at the left in the Meeting at the Golden Gate, the actual journey of the Holy Family in the distance behind the Rest in the Flight into Egypt, and the women approaching with their ointments in the Resurrection. Under the influence of Leonardo and the Italian Renaissance, the prodigal accentuation with gold and the brilliant fabrics of the older Spanish school have vanished, the only conspicuous exception being the robe of Simeon in the Purification. We should possibly regard as an indigenous quality a slight degree of provincialism that denies to the Fernandos and especially to Llanos the facility of Leonardo's Italian pupils and is betrayed, for instance, by the standing Magus at the right whom Bertaux so vituperates and by the failure to attain the desired, subtle expression on the face of the midwife who holds the newborn Virgin; but they quite compensate and really achieve greater vitality than their Italian rivals because they are able to transcend the potent effect of contact with Leonardo and infuse the borrowed style with the freshness and vigor that emanated from the very provincialism of their origins and environment.

Little is added to our understanding of the Fernandos by the effigies of Sts. Cosmas and Damian which, before their destruction in the civil war, formed part of the collection in the Sala Capitular Moderna of the cathedral at Valencia but originally were paired in the central panel of the partners' documented retable of 1506 in the chapel of these canonized physicians[11] in the church and then were sawed asunder; nor can I perceive *conclusive* criteria by which to determine whether they were both done by one of the twain or whether each chose a figure for himself and, if so, which. It has been customary to assign to Llanos the Cosmas who would be the figure turning his head towards the right according to the practice of recognizing this saint, when we have to do with pairs of the hallowed brothers, in the one who looks in this direction and therefore would have been placed at the left; and Yáñez has been called the author of the Damian (Fig. 69). It seems probable to me indeed that the Damian was executed

[11] See above, p. 178.

FIG. 69. YÁÑEZ AND LLANOS. STS. COSMAS AND DAMIAN.
CATHEDRAL, VALENCIA

(*Photo. Archivo Mas*)

by Yáñez because of the facial analogy to the Virgin of the Pentecost and because his extended left hand, involving a purposed problem in foreshortening, is repeated almost line for line in the Christ of a painting formerly in the Cremer Collection at Dortmund with the creation of which this master should obviously be honored;[12] but I see no reason why Yáñez should not have been responsible likewise for the Cosmas. The Damian was a pronounced and not unsuccessful example, like the young Virgin in her Presentation on the shutters, of the desire for the psychological subtlety of expression in which Leonardo's followers sought to reproduce the exaggerated extreme to which their inspirer pressed this quality.

It would be a hard task even for an artist endowed with the originality of Yáñez to make much of the stereotyped subject of cult-figures in the middle of an altarpiece, but, when we encounter another casualty of the war, the Lamentation over the Dead Christ once in the same Sala Capitular, which is universally stated (on no divulged evidence, however) to have come from the predella of the retable of Sts. Cosmas and Damian and which, by comparison with his achievements at Cuenca, I judge him to have executed all or practically all by himself, it is a different story (Fig. 70). In the first place, the panel was not one of the small compartments into which Spanish predellas were customarily divided but, even if not originally the whole predella, it stretched to a long horizontal space so as to give scope for an adequate visualization of the tragedy. The scene, furthermore, comprised some of the author's most memorable individualizations and characterizations, in this instance various expressions of grief, whether we looked at the bowed and seated woman at her Lord's feet, at her companion who, clasping her hands beside the Virgin, provided a precedent for a figure in the rendering at Cuenca,[13] or even at the group in diminished scale in the background gathered about the Holy Sepulchre. In the atmospheric effects that Yáñez permitted himself to a greater degree than in the large panels of the shutters, where a clear and striking impression upon the somewhat distant worshipper was desirable, he cultivated more sedulously Leonardo's *sfumatezza*, allowing the forms to melt off into the circumambient penumbra. The past of the Valencian school found a reflection in

[12] See below, p. 227.
[13] See above, p. 197, and below, p. 236.

Fig. 70. YÁÑEZ. LAMENTATION OVER THE DEAD CHRIST.
CATHEDRAL, VALENCIA

(*Photo. Archivo Mas*)

little else than the Magdalene's brocade, the gold of which, however, was not actual but simulated in yellow pigment.

Tormo [14] justly dignifies with the title of a masterpiece the undocumented panel of the *Anna selbdritt* about which a congeries of works by Juan de Juanes have been grouped over an altar at the left side of the apse in the church of S. Nicolás at Valencia and which happily survived the civil war (Fig. 71). The Spanish scholar ascribes it to Yáñez alone, but it is difficult to avoid the impression that Llanos was allowed to do the St. Anne who is practically a replica of the person reading a book in the Murcian Marriage of the Virgin. If, however, as we have deduced, Yáñez painted the thunderstruck woman in the lower right corner of the Pentecost in the shutters of the retable in the cathedral, he must have executed the figure of Our Lady in the panel in S. Nicolás; and no achievement of Llanos justifies the idea that he possessed the competence incorporated in the Child. The probability is that we owe to Yáñez also the unusual composition, since his partner almost never interests us in this phase of his profession. The only defect of the picture is that, under the corrupting influence of one of Leonardo's most fatal proclivities, the sleeping Child is *too much* an object for academic display. Much skill in drawing and painting is expended upon the Infant's form, upon the rendering of the lassitude and unconsciousness of slumber, and upon the cloth spread beneath Him; but the success with which these aims have been realized goes a long way towards compensating for the parade of artistic talents. The type of the Child is perhaps — quite fortuitously, of course — rather Correggesque than Leonardesque, but the Fernandos never created personages more indebted to Leonardo than the St. Anne and especially the Virgin, who seems an even closer transcription of the Mona Lisa than is the analogous woman in the Pentecost. Amidst the borrowings, nowhere else has the originality of Yáñez manifested itself more palpably, evolving a new and beautiful composition for the theme and this in face of the fact that he may have known Leonardo's cartoon of the subject, though not the painting, which was executed after the Spaniard's repatriation. The three figures are separated from one another, the Virgin sitting above her Son and tenderly conceived as dropping flowers upon Him, St. Anne seated at a still higher level and intent upon her book; but, despite this disintegration, the composition is unified because the forms make a kind of rising and continuous

[14] *Levante,* 121.

FIG. 71. YÁÑEZ AND LLANOS. *ANNA SELBDRITT.*
S. NICOLÁS, VALENCIA
(*Photo. Archivo Mas*)

pier the base of which is constituted by Our Lord's bed. The picture is saved from sentimentality by the nobility and restraint of the Mother and Grandmother, and this restraint is echoed in the architectural setting, in which the most prominent feature is an arcade treated with the chastity of Brunelleschi.

4. Works Solely by Yáñez, or with Very Little Assistance from Llanos, before the Former's Establishment at Cuenca

With the exception of the Játiva Last Judgment, the examples comprised in the present division of this chapter are of unascertained original provenience, but their existence now or at least formerly in public or private collections at Valencia implies that they were ordered by patrons there or in the vicinity and that they thus antedate the activity of Yáñez at Cuenca, unless we are to presume that he returned at intervals to the seat of his first honors. On the grounds of similarity in style we must place also in this class a Last Judgment now in Majorca and a panel once at Dortmund. The absence or virtual absence of the collaboration of Llanos in the commissions suggests that Yáñez was well understood to be the really important member of the partnership and that Llanos may have abandoned Valencia shortly after the last mention of him in the city in 1513 and considerably before he is definitely recorded at Murcia in 1520.

We may safely abide by the traditional attribution to Yáñez (with little, if any, intervention from Llanos) of a Last Judgment that until its destruction in the civil war existed in a chapel on the north transept of the Colegiata at Játiva (Fig. 72). Its primal significance is that it established with approximate certainty his interest also in one of Leonardo's contemporaries at Florence, Fra Bartolommeo.[1] The indebtedness, however, to the Italian's ruined fresco of the subject, begun in 1499 and now in the Museo di San Marco at Florence, has been much exaggerated. With the exception of the composition of the blessed in a monumental semicircle foreshortened inwards, all the elements that the retable shared with the fresco are present in the many other earlier or contemporary Valencian renderings of the theme by the Artés Master and the Cabanyes Master and their followers [2] and in the painting of Roger van der Weyden's school that graced the Ayunta-

[1] See above, p. 194.
[2] Vol. VI, pp. 297, 342, 420 ff., 432, and 436.

FIG. 72. YÁÑEZ (WITH THE COLLABORATION OF LLANOS?).
LAST JUDGMENT. COLEGIATA, JÁTIVA
(*Photo. Archivo Mas*)

miento of Valencia at least as early as 1494.[3] Before the partners left Italy, Raphael had evolved the idea of such a celestial semicircle in the Coronation of the Vatican Gallery and in the Trinity in S. Severo at Perugia, in the latter instance himself under obligations to Fra Bartolommeo, and after their departure he was to develop it gloriously into the epic amplitude of the Disputa. It is not absolutely unthinkable that Yáñez might independently even of Raphael have arrived at this factor in the composition, but the greater likelihood is that it was a product of his memories of Fra Bartolommeo's arrangement of the redeemed in the same subject that he was commissioned to paint. Tormo[4] believes that the general composition is derived from the practically contemporary retable of the Last Judgment by the collaborators, the Borbotó Master and the Artés Master,[5] which from Torre de Canals has now entered the Játiva Museum. Although the two altarpieces for the most part resembled each other only in the constituents owned by all the Valencian Last Judgments of the period and although there were marked divergences in content and in the absence, at Torre de Canals, of the great semicircle, they did both display the peculiarities of a symbolization of the heavenly Jerusalem in the *remate* and of a person at the bottom who might be a donor or merely a representative of the class of redeemed souls, in the case of the example by Yáñez a very Luinesque lady, under the patronage of an angel, kneeling to the left of St. Michael; but, if any interrelation thus actually existed between them, the influence would more naturally have proceeded from the decidedly more masterly and cosmopolitan work in the Colegiata.

In accordance with Yáñez's less local and ecclesiastically dominated ideas of art, the detailed representations of purgatory and hell at the lower left and right respectively were simplified in comparison with the treatments by the Cabanyes Master and his school; but yet the cave of the unbaptized infants in limbo was much featured, and two nudes of a younger and older man in purgatory were made, perhaps for academic reasons, rather conspicuous. Mona Lisa looked forth at us, still with her sinister allurement, as one of the women in the purgatorial flames. The unappreciated capacity of Yáñez was signalized in the remarkable solution of a problem that has baffled so many of his

---

[3] *Ibid.*, p. 297.
[4] *Un museo de primitivos, Las tablas de las iglesias de Játiva*, Madrid, 1912, pp. 30–31. [5] See my vol. VI, p. 328.

colleagues at all times, the difficulty of endowing St. Michael with an ideal beauty and of yet maintaining his masculinity.[6]

For the loss of this painting there is partial compensation in another large rendering of the same theme attributable to Yáñez, although the assistance of Llanos perhaps ought to be discerned more surely and in larger degree than in the Játiva version. Of undisclosed original provenience but now belonging to Don Juan March at Sa Vall on the island of Majorca, it exhibits several rather extraordinary variations from the destroyed treatment. Except for the absence of the *remate*, the upper half of the March picture is very like this division of the other version, and the general arrangement of the lower section is also similar, even with a repetition of the postures of two among the babes in limbo, although the disposition of the figures in purgatory and hell is different; but to a further extent than at Játiva, the lower section contains elements of a pronounced Italian academicism which is foreign to the temper of Spanish art of the period and of which other works of the partners reveal only traces. The most obvious example is the representation of one of the purgatorial sufferers as an unblushing study of a feminine nude, quite in the spirit of Giorgione's and Titian's addiction to such themes (Fig. 73). The masculine nude is likewise exploited in a figure given an even more undue prominence for the purpose, standing in the very foreground of the picture beside St. Michael and pointing to the infernal regions. It is hard to see how this figure can depict anyone more definite than a redeemed man drawing attention to the punishments of the damned, with the corollary that the clothed, kneeling lady on the other side of St. Michael should be understood as likewise singled out to represent the blessed of the gentler sex. We should thus be justified in deducing that neither this lady nor the corresponding woman in the Játiva panel, despite the fact that, in distinction from her analogue in the March picture, she is presented by an angel, was conceived as a donor. The Italianate and academic concern with ideal feminine comeliness is extended from the nude in purgatory to the kneeling lady's fully clad form, but the St. Michael constitutes a less successful effort than the Játiva archangel in a study of pulchritude and was perhaps one of the few passages, like possibly even the judging Christ, handed over to Llanos. The

---

[6] For the introduction of St. John Evangelist instead of the Baptist as an intercessor for mortals in the Last Judgment, see Saralegui in *Archivo de arte español*, XIX (1946), 138.

FIG. 73. YÁÑEZ (WITH THE COLLABORATION OF LLANOS?).
DETAIL OF LAST JUDGMENT. MARCH COLLECTION,
SA VALL, MAJORCA
(*Photo. Archivo Mas*)

great majority of the types, however, accord with the norms of Yáñez.

In a Resurrection, which belongs to the group of works of art given to the Provincial Museum at Valencia by Don Juan Martínez Vallejo (Fig. 74), the close similarity of the Saviour to the judging Christ of Játiva is enough to assign the panel to Yáñez, but the other figures also conform to the differences of his manner from that of Llanos. Moreover, he practically repeated the composition in one of his works at Cuenca,[7] and, although he might have imitated an achievement of his erstwhile partner, it would be more natural for an artist to turn back to one of his own performances. The attribution is further driven home by the variations that Bertaux perceived in the figure of Our Lord and in other details from the rendering in the shutters, which I have agreed with the French scholar in believing that Llanos executed.

The Lamentation over the Dead Christ, supposed to derive from the predella of the Fernandos' documented retable of Sts. Cosmas and Damian, reveals certain correspondences to a Crucifixion that, obviously a creation of Yáñez, has long belonged to the Provincial Museum, Valencia, but was only recently put on exhibition (Fig. 75). Of unascertained original provenience, it embodies, like the Lamentation, an unusual treatment of the theme in a horizontally extended composition, and it contains similarly two of the masters' memorable emotional poses. One is incorporated in the Virgin with her hands clasped beside her face, practically duplicating the holy woman who has stirred our admiration in the Lamentation and thus demonstrating, like the later iteration at Cuenca,[8] that Yáñez was proud of the expressiveness which he achieved in the figure. Indeed in another actor, the Magdalene, the manifestation of despairing sorrow is so convincingly realized that he repeated her also at Cuenca in his large panel of Calvary, crouching at the foot of the cross as she shrouds her face with a handkerchief in profound but not hysterical grief. The St. John unhappily strikes a false note as one of the too numerous instances in the artist's output, under Leonardo's influence, of expressiveness strained to the point of the mawkish. Nor must we forget, in our justifiable admiration for many of his qualities, that after all he cannot be ensconced among the greatest painters and that a degree of provincialism is likely to be betrayed by such slight defects as the unnaturally elongated right leg of the Virgin. In the background,

[7] See below, p. 231.
[8] See above, p. 203, and below, p. 236.

FIG. 74. YÁÑEZ. RESURRECTION.
PROVINCIAL MUSEUM, VALENCIA
(*Photo. Archivo Mas*)

Fig. 75. YÁÑEZ. CRUCIFIXION. PROVINCIAL
MUSEUM, VALENCIA

(*Photo. Archivo Mas*)

nevertheless, there stretches one of his frequent lovely vistas, here largely of a city and a bridge spanning a river, the whole veiled in the lighter tones of the mists in which he likes to envelop his landscapes. Rescued from a private collection at Valencia during the storm of the civil war, there have entered the Provincial Museum four fine panels which to my eyes contain nothing not ascribable to the unassisted Yáñez and which may be judged to have once constituted parts of a single altarpiece because they were deposited in the Museum as a group and because they are all approximately of the same small size.[9] Their style, especially a kind of freshness, implies a moment in his career little, if at all, later than the first documented achievements at Valencia, but it may have been only the reduced proportions of the panels that caused him to indulge in a greater nicety of brushwork than he ordinarily cultivated.

His originality is illustrated by a composition for the *Anna selbdritt* very different from that of the rendering in S. Nicolás, although nothing could be more thoroughly characteristic than the types themselves. The iconography also exhibits distinctive elements. Since the cult of the Virgin of the Milk is superimposed upon the theme, Our Lady has delicately bared one of her breasts, from which the Child, however, has momentarily turned away to toy with His grandmother's fingers, and, according to the variations in level typical of the treatment of space by Yáñez,[10] there is introduced at the right kneeling on the pavement, below the dais of the holy triad, a saint who is probably Bernard, thus perhaps meaning that the altarpiece was done for Cistercians. It may even be that the *motif* of the Virgin's milk has here to do, not with the Child, but with St. Bernard's vision of her bestowal of it upon him. The covering of the bench upon which St. Anne, Mary, and her Son are seated is one of the artist's favorite striped fabrics. The subject of the second compartment is the Ecce Homo, confined to the figures of Christ, Pilate, and a handsome guard, who is very like a replica in front view of the soldier with his back to us in the Resurrection that we have studied as also in the Museum. The three are again set on a somewhat elevated platform, and the classical *milieu* of Pilate's palace is suggested by its adornment with two simulated ancient statuettes on pedestals.

The third and most appealing panel of the set depicts the somewhat

---

[9] They measure, with slight variations, somewhat more or less than fifty centimetres both in height and width.   [10] See above, p. 198.

Fig. 76. YÁÑEZ. APPEARANCE OF CHRIST TO HIS MOTHER AFTER
THE RESURRECTION. PROVINCIAL MUSEUM, VALENCIA
(*Photo. Archivo Mas*)

rare theme [11] of Christ granting to His mother His first appearance after the Resurrection (Fig. 76). Although conceived in a tenderer mood — indeed with a gentleness unusual in the Fernandos' production — the picture has a composition rather similar to that which we shall study in the Annunciation by Yáñez in the Colegio del Patriarca at Valencia, with the Virgin's curtained bed carefully delineated behind her kneeling form; and in addition to the same two levels as in the *Anna selbdritt* and Ecce Homo, a third is created by an elevated oratory at the left of Mary's chamber. It is particularly this panel of the series that in the pronounced contrasts of light and shade indicates the admiration for Pier di Cosimo's attainments which we have wished to descry especially in the sections of the shutters that we have classified as Yáñez's handiwork. The only compartment in which the principal figures are not placed upon a low dais is the fourth, which merely aligns the standing effigies of two saints, a canonized bishop, recognizable by no distinctive emblems, and Vincent Ferrer, about whom there flutters the inscription, on a banderole, that constitutes his regular attribute and begins, "Timete Deum." [12] A window to the rear of the episcopal worthy looks out upon one of the partners' nobly simple pieces of architecture, analogous to the building seen behind the *Anna selbdritt* in S. Nicolás and meant to represent a classical ruin, but the prelate violates, as in a few other instances, their ordinary sobriety in the nature of costume by retaining one of the brilliant brocades of Spanish mediaeval painting in his chasuble, the morse of which consists of a simulated medallion of Christ of the Passion rendered with an intelligent comprehension of the *sfumatezza* required for the delineation of such a more dimly seen object.

An Annunciation in the collection of works of art assembled in the Colegio del Patriarca at Valencia (Fig. 77) is assigned by Tormo [13] to Llanos, but even the single factor of the type of the Virgin seems to demand an ascription to Yáñez, according, as it does, with one of his favorite sorts of feminine countenance, as in Mary of the Epiphany at Cuenca, rather than with the other Fernando's oft repeated representation of women, illustrated in the Murcian Marriage of Our Lady. Moreover, she duplicates Mary's gestures and costume in the *Anna*

[11] See vols. VII, p. 527, n. 2, and IX, p. 240. Not the commoner Valencian theme of Christ bringing to her from limbo, just *before* the Resurrection, the redeemed of the old dispensation.
[12] Vol. IV, p. 57, n. 2.   [13] *Valencia: los Museos*, 131.

selbdritt of S. Nicolás so exactly as to suggest that the two pictures were painted at about the same time. The closest counterpart for the angel is found in the Virgin in that part of the Purification in the shutters which I deem to be Yáñez's craft. Denied by the iconographic scheme the opportunity of depicting in the shutters the Annunciation, it is as if in the version in the Colegio del Patriarca he wished to show himself capable of rejuvenating even this countlessly repeated theme by innovations in composition paralleling those that in the cathedral panels elicited our praise. The Virgin sits, by a most unusual arrangement, almost directly facing us at the right. She is fingering her book of prayers, rapt in religious meditation and turning her head only slightly toward the angel as if not yet quite cognizant of his presence. In conformity with the characteristic desire of Yáñez for varied elevations, she is represented as seated before her bed with a foot upon a stool beside the table that holds her book, and this whole section of her apartment is imagined as itself raised upon a dais. Gabriel, likewise lost in contemplation of the mystery rather than intent upon his message and holding the herald's staff as well as a banderole inscribed with the angelic salutation, stands at a still lower level, assuming a novel posture by finding upon the dais a support for one of his feet.

Tormo [14] has discussed four panels once in the Collection of Colonel Montesinos at Valencia and, at my last knowledge, distributed among his heirs, judging them, if I understand him rightly, to derive from a single retable, although ascribing only two, the Agony in the Garden and the paired Sts. Michael and Jerome, to Yáñez himself and debasing the others, the *Noli me tangere* (Fig. 78) and the paired Sts. John Baptist and Sebastian,[15] to the rank of works of his school; but I can discern no traits in the *Noli me tangere* and its companion-piece that would really militate against a belief in Yáñez's own personal execution. Inasmuch as one compartment includes two patrons of the Hieronymites, Sts. Jerome and Michael, Tormo logically deduces that the panels were probably parts of a retable in some institution of this religious Order in the Valencian region, but, as in the case of the scenes from the life of St. Jerome by the Artés Master two

---

[14] *Boletín de la Sociedad Española de Excursiones,* XXXII (1924), 35–36.
[15] Tormo illustrates the Agony in the Garden and the Sts. Michael and Jerome; Saralegui has published a reproduction of the Sts. John Baptist and Sebastian (*Museum,* VII, 324); and I include an illustration of the *Noli me tangere.*

Fig. 77. YÁÑEZ. ANNUNCIATION. COLEGIO
DEL PATRIARCA, VALENCIA
(*Photo. Archivo Mas*)

Fig. 78. YÁÑEZ. *NOLI ME TANGERE*, BELONGING TO THE HEIRS
OF COLONEL MONTESINOS, VALENCIA
(*Photo. Archivo Mas*)

of which were once in the same Collection,[16] there seems to be no sure means of determining whether this institution might have been San Jerónimo de la Murta or San Jerónimo de Cotalba, although Tormo favors the former alternative on grounds that he does not disclose. The phase of the style of Yáñez embodied in the series is so precisely like the clean, fresh manner of the other four panels saved for the Provincial Museum from the war [17] that I have sometimes wondered whether they do not derive from the same altarpiece, but arguments against the supposition, albeit not conclusive, are the much larger dimensions [18] of the Montesinos set and the possibly different proveniences of the two cycles.

The principal purely archaeological interest of the Montesinos series is that the Sebastian, standing against a pier, may quite possibly stem from such representations by Perugino of the saint as the one in the Uffizi altarpiece of 1493 and the virtual replica of this figure in the Louvre, thus contributing to the evidence which we have already amassed for the theory that the Fernandos could have learned something from the Umbrian master. Their superiority, at least in the factors that they acquired from an academic Italian tutelage, to the majority of their Spanish contemporaries is revealed by another [19] instance of their anatomical studies, the good nude of the Sebastian, which exposes, by comparison, the inadequacy of even so competent an artist as the Borbotó Master in the same theme [20] and outdoes Perugino in its masculinity. Likewise, Yáñez manages to maintain in the St. Michael, as at Játiva, a balance between virility and angelic comeliness. The meditating reader, St. Jerome, adds another, and one of the best, to his long array of unforgettable successes in putting over to us impressive realizations of varied psychological states, and the lion, an animal much less familiar to the Fernandos than their cats, sheep, and cattle, is perhaps the most unexpected witness in their whole output to their primacy in a zoological curiosity that they may well have owed to Leonardo's passion for every phase of science. One of the touches of originality by which Yáñez constantly enlivens tra-

---

[16] See my vol. VI, p. 314, and below, p. 425. Saralegui discusses with perspicacity the still unsolved problem of the provenience of the Artés Master's panels in *Archivo español de arte*, XXI (1948), 278, n. 4.

[17] See above, p. 215.

[18] The Agony in the Garden and the panel of Sts. Michael and Jerome are 2.27 metres in height and 1.94 in width.

[19] See above, p. 200.   [20] Vol. VI, p. 330 and fig. 134.

ditional scenes is the partial hiding of St. Peter's body in the Agony
in the Garden behind the fragment of a conspicuously featured, ruined
wall. The scene enacted in the background of the *Noli me tangere* is
a dramatic rendering of the three holy women receiving the glad
tidings from the angel at the empty tomb.

González Martí [21] properly claims for the Fernandos, and Berenson
also accepts, a panel of the Madonna, Child and an angel in the Collection of Hugo Brauner at Valencia, which, with the greater precision
made possible by the segregated personality that we are succeeding
in building up for Yáñez, we may credit to his solitary brush (Fig.
79). Its unusually small size, extending only to about thirty centimetres in height, probably means that it was done for a destination
not customary in Spain of the period, a shrine in a private house, but
its dimensions are not at all in proportion to the singularly important
position that it occupies in his career. Separate, little representations
of the Madonna are very rare in Spanish painting of the Middle Ages
and early Renaissance, and not only the Brauner specimen but also the
few further examples by Yáñez and other native artists [22] witness to
a potent Italian influence. We should have expected the cartoon to
have been based upon one of Leonardo's paintings or drawings of the
subject, but, although there are distant suggestions here and there in
the works of the great Florentine, I am familiar with no direct and
complete source either in him or in the other Italians of the period,
so that we are again provided with an instance of the master's originality in composition. The Virgin sits with a reversal of the *contrapposto* of Leonardo's St. Anne in the Louvre; the Child is placed
in high animation far to the right, for the sake of balancing the bend
of His mother; and they both seem more naturistically than piously
absorbed with the objects displayed on a table featured in the foreground, roses, pottery, and fruit, including a melon exactly like that
in the Birth of the Virgin in the shutters of the cathedral. Possibly in
lingering homage to the old Flemish tradition of Spanish art, still
life stands forth now and then in the Fernandos' output [23] but never
again to the extent to which it is emphasized in the Brauner panel.
The St. Joseph seen in the offing through a window rests upon his staff
in an attitude which Yáñez was to repeat for the foster father of our

[21] *Museum* (Barcelona), IV (1914–1916), 398–399.
[22] See vol. IX, pp. 122 and 127.
[23] See above, p. 200.

FIG. 79. YÁÑEZ. MADONNA, CHILD, AND ANGEL.
BRAUNER COLLECTION, VALENCIA

Lord in the Cuenca Epiphany and which both the Fernandos were fond of using for shepherds.

Since it has an eventual provenience from private possession at Valencia,[24] we may register at this point a work that takes a high place in the production of Yáñez or indeed the highest from the standpoints of an unexaggerated ideal, girlish beauty and a fineness of craft to match this loveliness, the panel of St. Catherine of Alexandria that passed into the Collection of the Marqués de Casa-Argudín at Madrid and thence to the Prado (Fig. 80). As the picture is large, with the figure of life-size, it perhaps once constituted the centre of a retable, and we may amuse ourselves with guessing that it might have originally adorned at Valencia the church of Sta. Catalina, where the partners are recorded at least to have drawn the designs for another, sculptured altarpiece by the Forment atelier.[25] While the type once more reflects the Mona Lisa, Leonardo's immoderate subtlety in expression, which often impairs the Fernandos' creations, is by a miracle eluded, and we find, instead, an embodiment of much of the essence of a delightful and simple maidenhood. In the new and inevitably somewhat more substantial terms of the early Renaissance, she retains the fair and ethereal mysticism with which a century earlier the Aragonese exponent of the international style, Juan de Leví, had invested at Tudela the same virgin martyr.[26] The other qualities of the picture are keyed to this exquisiteness. The gloom of Leonardo's color is abandoned in a greater degree than Yáñez's potent memories of the Florentine master ordinarily permitted, and the whole panel is attuned to a lighter tonality. In harmony with this mood the figure rises to a delicacy of pose, gesture, and general draughtsmanship unusual for him. The nicety of feeling imparts an even more Flemish touch than in their other bits of still life and appurtenances of costume to St. Catherine's emblems, the fragment of the wheel at her feet, the book, palm, and crown prettily disposed upon the parapet behind her, as well as to the jewelled pendant that hangs from her neck. The gown that she wears is made of a geometrically patterned fabric that Yáñez much affected, as on the back of a soldier in the Resurrection in the Provincial Museum at Valencia and as on the

[24] See the article by Tormo, to whom belongs the honor of having first recognized the affiliations of this masterpiece, *Boletín de la Sociedad Española de Excursiones*, XXIII (1915), 201 n. 2.

[25] See above, p. 181.

[26] Vols. III, p. 186, and IV, p. 628.

FIG. 80. YÁÑEZ. ST. CATHERINE. PRADO, MADRID
(*From an article by Tormo*)

prominent Magus in the Epiphany at Cuenca, and it is trimmed with the borders of Arabic lettering that Bertaux takes to be a token of Yáñez in distinction from Llanos.

The Catalogue of the Prado at Madrid seems correct in labelling as a work of Yáñez, rather than Llanos, a half-length of St. Damian [27]

FIG. 81. YÁÑEZ. ST. DAMIAN. PRADO, MADRID
(*From an article by González Martí*)

(Fig. 81) which has entered the Museum from the possession of Doña Isabel Orellana at Valencia and lost its companion-piece of St. Cosmas [28] long before it became known as in the Valencian Collection. Though rather different from the St. Damian in the documented re-table of 1506 and certainly not so much marred by a Leonardesque leer, the figure is securely attached to Yáñez by its intimate resem-

[27] For the criterion for distinguishing a St. Damian from a St. Cosmas, see above, p. 201.
[28] For what the St. Cosmas may have looked like, see below, p. 284.

blance to the second spectator from the left in the foreground of the
Presentation of the Virgin in the shutters.

The panel of the Salvator Mundi between Sts. Peter and John
Evangelist formerly in the Cremer Collection at Dortmund must,
with the St. Catherine now in the Prado, rank among Yáñez's master-
pieces (Fig. 82). The sort of composition, with the figures in half
length behind a parapet, was much favored by Leonardo's Lombard
followers, and indeed the panel reveals analogies to the achievements
of Andrea Solario; but none of these elements is sufficiently distinctive
or pronounced to establish the hypothesis that Yáñez had begun his
training under Leonardo at Milan and then accompanied him to
Florence or that at any time during an Italian sojourn he had included
Milan within his possible travels.[29] It is, however, no more a Spanish
composition than the Madonna of the Brauner Collection and supplies,
like many other productions of his, tangible evidence of persistent
loyalty to Italian precedent after returning to his native country. The
more than usual care lavished upon the execution, as well as the nature
of the composition, may be interpreted as implying that the panel was
not a part of a retable but a separate effort painted, like the Brauner
Madonna, for a shrine in a private residence.

The Saviour's hands, as in the case of the St. Damian in the partners'
documented retable, have been the objects of the most deliberate attention, especially the left one, in which the painter has purposely and
academically created a problem of elaborate foreshortening. In Our
Lord's face, he has admirably grappled with the difficult task of incorporating benignity divorced from insipidness, and he has imbued
it with a startling degree of the lifelike alertness that is habitually
one of his most distinguished attainments in the treatment of countenances. The St. Peter is the kind of Leonardesque type of old man
used, for example, in the Apostle at the extreme left in the Pentecost
of the shutters of the Valencian retable, but, according to the constant
desire of Yáñez to break with tradition, he has represented him
centrifugally as turned away from the Redeemer toward the outside
of the picture and looking at us in an attitude of *contrapposto*. As in
other actors in scenes depicted by both Fernandos, animated expressiveness, under the spell of Leonardo's example, is much stressed in
the Apostle's visage. The unforgettable figure in the panel is, however, St. John, perhaps the most remarkable embodiment by Yáñez

[29] See above, p. 196.

FIG. 82. YÁÑEZ. THE SAVIOUR BETWEEN STS. PETER AND JOHN
EVANGELIST. FORMERLY IN THE CREMER COLLECTION,
DORTMUND

of pensive poetry in a youth, inspired by Leonardo but obtained, because of the artist's healthy Spanish blood, without the Florentine's morbidity and without the effeminacy that vitiates, for instance, the St. Philip in his Last Supper. The actual type of the Evangelist is a modification of a kind of face often appearing in Yáñez's production, as in the Virgin of the Cuenca Epiphany.

5. Works Done by Yáñez in Cuenca and the Region

Among the new factors that the paintings of this class by Yáñez add to our knowledge of his scope is the superimposition of some interest in the achievements of Raphael upon the still fundamentally Leonardesque character of his style. Be it said at once, however, that the borrowings from Raphael do not absolutely compel the postulation of a second sojourn in Italy on his part, since they are all derived from productions of the Umbrian master that are surely or possibly dated before the return of Yáñez to Spain in 1506 after his Italian training; nor are any of the other arguments that could be proposed for a second journey entirely conclusive. We have seen [1] that it cannot be definitely asserted that the Pietà by Yáñez at Cuenca reveals acquaintance with paintings which Sebastiano del Piombo executed in 1516 or later. One could contend that the sudden appearance of Raphaelesque reminiscences in his art would naturally have been motivated by a renewed contact with the Italian atmosphere, even though they are affected by the Umbrian's earlier creations; but, on the other hand, they may represent only memories of Raphael's works that had long been fermenting in his mind and now came to the surface, stimulated by the contemporary Spanish and indeed European enthusiasm for the great Italian's attainments. The pictures of the Cuenca period, to be sure, exhibit a decided advance beyond the works of Yáñez's Valencian years toward the standards of the High Roman Renaissance, but the tendencies in this direction were sufficiently well established in the Iberian peninsula itself by the time of his activity at Cuenca, the beginning of the second quarter of the sixteenth century, to account for the further development in his art without attempting to explain it by direct familiarity with Raphael's productions.

Of his documented works [2] in the Albornoz chapel on the ambulatory in the cathedral of Cuenca, the retable over the principal altar

[1] P. 197.
[2] See above, p. 185. The sculptured frames were made by Antonio Flórez.

Fig. 83. YÁÑEZ. CRUCIFIXION, CENTRE OF RETABLE OF
PRINCIPAL ALTAR IN THE ALBORNOZ CHAPEL,
CATHEDRAL, CUENCA

(*Photo. Pando*)

displays: at the centre a large treatment of the Crucifixion, with St. Dominic (identified by his habit and his emblem of the lilies on a book beneath him) as a kneeling worshipper of the mystery (Fig. 83); set in the architectural and sculptural crown of the altarpiece, a miniature version of the Nativity; in the narrow compartments between the pilasters at the sides of the Crucifixion, standing effigies of St. Clement and a canonized bishop [3] and, above them, medallions of Isaiah and Habakkuk; [4] in the predella, at the middle the Resurrection, in the presence of the kneeling donor, Gómez Carrillo de Albornoz (whose dignity is somewhat sacrilegiously indicated by a magnification to a size out of all proportion to the risen Christ and the one soldier) (Fig. 84), and at the sides, compartments of half-lengths of the paired Sts. Peter and Paul and of the two St. Johns; and finally, on a level with the predella but in larger spaces at the bases of the lateral pilasters, the scenes of St. Catherine's ordeal of the wheels and decapitation. The two subordinate altars in the chapel are surmounted only each by a single, capacious panel, with the figures of greater dimensions than in the main retable, in one instance the Epiphany (Fig. 85) and in the other, the Pietà (Fig. 86).

Bertaux believed that Yáñez may have done the chief retable before the two others, perhaps because it seems to contain fewer signs of a partial change to the manner of the Roman Renaissance; but the divergence between the retables is due at least in some degree to the larger size of the figures over the lateral altars, which gave more scope to monumental breadth. The master's essential qualities remain the same as in his Valencian period, but to a certain extent even in the retable of the Crucifixion they have been emancipated from primitive restrictions. Although the little Nativity at the summit does not follow closely the composition in the shutters of the Valencian cathedral, the Resurrection in the predella, as we have seen,[5] is no more than an actual simplified replica of the version in the Valencian Museum. We have already [6] noted also that the Magdalene's posture and gesture in the Crucifixion had been used for her figure in Yáñez's Calvary in the same Museum, one of the most remarkable in the long

---

[3] They have usually been called Sts. Gregory and Augustine; but St. Clement is identified by the emblem of the anchor as well as the papal regalia, and the balancing bishop has no distinguishing attribute.

[4] The banderole of Isaiah reads, from LIII, 4, of his prophecy, "Vere languores nostros (ipse tulit)"; that of Habakkuk, "Cornua in manibus eius" (III, 4).

[5] P. 212. [6] P. 212.

FIG. 84. YÁÑEZ. RESURRECTION, WITH GÓMEZ CARRILLO DE ALBORNOZ AS DONOR, SECTION OF PREDELLA OF RETABLE OF PRINCIPAL ALTAR IN THE ALBORNOZ CHAPEL, CATHEDRAL, CUENCA

(*Photo. Pando*)

FIG. 85. YÁÑEZ. EPIPHANY OVER LATERAL ALTAR IN THE
ALBORNOZ CHAPEL, CATHEDRAL, CUENCA
(*From an article by Tormo*)

Fig. 86. YÁÑEZ. PIETÀ OVER LATERAL ALTAR IN THE
ALBORNOZ CHAPEL, CATHEDRAL, CUENCA
(*From an article by Señora Caturla*)

series of impressive realizations of unique characterizations enshrined in his extant output. The effectively rendered serenity of the redeemed thief is strongly contrasted with the agonized contortions of his companion. The attitudes of St. Catherine's executioners, wounded by the very wheel with which they had meant to torture her, are objects of studies not only in foreshortening but also in the same sort of dramatic poses as the two awe-stricken women in the Pentecost of the shutters. The children who enliven the *milieu* of the Presentation of the Virgin in the shutters reappear, somewhat more accommodated to the standards of the High Renaissance, as figures of *genre* indifferent to the grimness of St. Catherine's decollation; and in the Nativity the pair of rustics advancing from the background, one with a staff and the other carrying a lamb as in the early Christian statue of the Good Shepherd in the Lateran Museum at Rome, are literally repeated from the rendering of the theme in the shutters, thus adding another item to the evidence that Yáñez retained this compartment in the joint enterprise for himself.

Certain passages disclose the outstanding position enjoyed by Yáñez as a mere technician among his Spanish contemporaries, for instance the head of St. Dominic in the Crucifixion and the whole figure of the potentate before whom St. Catherine receives the *coup de grâce*. The effigy of Gómez Carrillo de Albornoz possesses the importance of exhibiting the painter's incisive talents in a phase that his other certain extant works do not illustrate, the field of portraiture.

In proposing that the Epiphany is the later of the pictures over the altars at the sides of the chapel, Bertaux was probably moved by the consideration that the commission for it was given to Yáñez by Luis Carrillo de Albornoz as well as by his distinguished clerical brother; but, if there was any interval of time between the two pictures, the more obvious conformity to the ideals of the full Renaissance would seem, in my opinion, to give the posterior date to the Pietà. The Virgin in the Epiphany, especially in the attitude of the legs, very plainly embodies a recalling, on the master's part, of the same figure in Leonardo's cartoon for the *Anna selbdritt* in Burlington House, London, and the pose of the head may have been suggested by that of the St. Anne herself; but the general composition, with the standing Child, was in all likelihood inspired by some of the celebrated Madonnas of Raphael's Florentine period. Señora Caturla[7] has

---

[7] *Archivo español de arte*, XV (1942), 43.

pointed out the resemblance to his drawings for the Madonna im Grünen at Vienna, dated in 1505 or 1506, but the analogy is quite as close in the Madonna del Cardellino in the Uffizi, which belongs to the same moment in Raphael's career. Even in the facial type of the Virgin (Fig. 87), which constitutes merely a modification of a kind of countenance that Yáñez had employed more than once at Valencia, he cannot escape fusing with the Leonardesque features some degree of homage to the quality that has caused the phrase, "as beautiful as a Madonna of Raphael," to become a commonplace in all the languages of Europe. The rest of the picture is all still preponderantly Leonardesque. The indelible recollections, for instance, of the cavaliers in the Florentine's Epiphany are maintained in the forms, nicely painted in smaller scale, who amuse themselves with equestrian exercises in front of a city in the right background.

Like the main altar in the chapel, the Adoration of the Kings offers to our aesthetic enjoyment fine specimens of the author's capabilities. The most featured actor, the standing Magus at the left, is a more memorable realization of the ideal of monumental manhood than the closely analogous figure in the background of the Virgin's Presentation in the shutters, and, conceived as a Moor accoutred in magnificent contemporary costume, he would make a better Othello than any tragedian whom I have ever had the privilege of seeing in the rôle. The kneeling Wise Man at the right, however (Fig. 88), is a less ostentatious but actually quite as great an achievement, garbed in the rich armor of the early sixteenth century and embodying an aged expression of the same intense devotion that makes it hard to forget the adoring youthful Magus in the Valencian version of the theme. The St. Joseph just above the Holy Child, like the St. Peter in the Cremer panel, incorporates a successful endeavor for an unusual expression in the countenance, here that of quizzical surprise. The man behind the standing Magus at the left closely resembles the shepherd with a staff beside St. Joachim in a section that, in the compartment of the Meeting at the Golden Gate in the shutters, I have desired to allot to Yáñez.

The merits of the Pietà over the other lateral altar are sadly obscured by the desperate blackening that it has suffered in the course of the centuries, but in any case no points of significance occur to me beyond those which I have attempted to bring into relief on former

FIG. 87. YÁÑEZ. DETAIL OF EPIPHANY OVER LATERAL
ALTAR IN THE ALBORNOZ CHAPEL,
CATHEDRAL, CUENCA

(*Photo. Pando*)

FIG. 88. YÁÑEZ. DETAIL OF EPIPHANY OVER LATERAL
ALTAR IN THE ALBORNOZ CHAPEL,
CATHEDRAL, CUENCA

(*Photo. Pando*)

pages,[8] especially its possible indebtedness to Sebastiano del Piombo. The cathedral of Cuenca is packed with retables and separate panels attributable both by document and by internal evidence to Yáñez's pupil, Martín Gómez, who will concern us in a later chapter, but there is only one other work in the church that can be given to Yáñez himself, a retable in the Capilla de los Pesos. The body of the structure is occupied wholly by a large representation of the Adoration of the Shepherds, and the only other panel is a Visitation in the crown of the altarpiece, with St. Elizabeth on her knees as in the rendering on the shutters of the cathedral at Valencia. Since, however, the paintings have been practically destroyed by an inexpert cleaning with potash, I could perceive little else, in my visit to the cathedral to study them, except that they must have been executed by Yáñez and that the Virgin in the Adoration, who is varied but slightly in type from her representation in the Cuenca Epiphany, quite vies with the St. Catherine now belonging to the Prado in a wholesome purgation from Leonardo's morbidity in favor of an unsophisticated loveliness that improves upon Luini's assuagement of the lessons which he had learned from the same Florentine teacher.[9]

Internal evidence assigns to the same, late phase of Yáñez's development as the series at Cuenca a simplified treatment of the subject that the Germans denominate as *die heilige Sippe*,[10] recently acquired by the Prado (Fig. 89). It comes indeed from the same general region of the peninsula, the parish church of the town of Infantes, just north of the village of Almedina, the painter's birthplace, whither he may have returned to end his days, a prophet, after a distinguished career elsewhere, finally to find honor and commissions in his own country. Butrón[11] alleges that he did a retable for Almedina itself, and it has been thought that the picture in the Prado may be a remaining panel from this work rather than, as is quite as likely, a fragment of some altarpiece at Infantes ordered by a patron in the place.

At the right the Virgin sits in front of St. Anne, or perhaps, as in Leonardo's cartoon for the theme,[12] she was meant to be understood as seated on her lap. St. Elizabeth stands next with the Holy Child

---

[8] Pp. 197, 198, 203, and 212.

[9] In the lower right corner of the plate opposite p. 200 in Tormo's article in the *Boletín de la Sociedad Española de Excursiones* of 1915, there is an illustration made from a drawing of the Virgin's head.

[10] See above, p. 149. [11] See above, p. 186.

[12] See above, p. 205.

FIG. 89. YÁÑEZ. *DIE HEILIGE SIPPE*. PRADO, MADRID
(*From an article by Señora Caturla*)

erect before her and with her own son, the infant John Baptist, sprawled in a playful attitude upon the ground. The scene enacted in miniature in the left distance is the Meeting at the Golden Gate. The composition for his *heilige Sippe* Yáñez doubtless developed on the basis of the kind of arrangement employed by Raphael in the renowned series of Madonnas belonging to the first years of the Cinquecento, although the posture of St. John is probably the Spaniard's own invention. The dependence upon Raphael ends with this, for it is difficult to follow Señora Caturla [13] in discerning a likeness of the Virgin to the portrait of Maddalena Doni except in so far as the Umbrian master was here obviously Leonardo's debtor. Like all the other personages in the panel, she reveals how Yáñez continued even at the conclusion of his life essentially true to his first instructor, and Leonardo's cartoon of the *Anna selbdritt* may very well be the source of the juxtaposition of her head with that of her parent. The countenance and questioning expression of the St. Anne by Yáñez are exactly repeated in the St. Joseph of the Cuenca Epiphany; and, in Señora Caturla's vain struggle to empty the Spaniard of his obligations to Leonardo, I can see no force whatsoever in the argument that in the Florentine master's preserved works there do not happen to occur any visages of old women and that he preferred to depict Our Lady's mother as still rather young instead of in the more advanced years with which in the Prado panel she and St. Elizabeth are burdened.

Amidst Diego Angulo's many recent demonstrations of the incredibly large and hitherto scarcely suspected rôle that German prints played in Spanish painting of the early Renaissance, he has pointed out [14] that even such a convinced Italianate as Yáñez lifted almost every detail of the composition and setting of the Meeting at the Golden Gate in the background of the Prado picture (which abandons the treatment used in the Valencian shutters) from Dürer's woodcut of 1504 in the series on the Life of the Virgin.

The production of small representations of the Madonna by Fernando Yáñez for private devotional use according to Italian fashions is exemplified not only by the Brauner rendering but also by a panel in the Collection of Don Carlos Grether at Buenos Aires (Fig. 90), [15]

[13] *Op. cit.*, 43.
[14] *Archivo español de arte*, XIX (1946), 64.
[15] Formerly in the Collection of the Señora Sara Larco de Palacio in the same city. For the photographs of the illustration that I publish and of the inscription on

FIG. 90. YÁÑEZ. HOLY FAMILY. GRETHER COLLECTION,
BUENOS AIRES
(*Courtesy of Professor Buschiazzo*)

FIG. 91. INSCRIPTION ON BACK OF PAINTING OF HOLY FAMILY IN
THE GRETHER COLLECTION, BUENOS AIRES
(*Courtesy of Professor Buschiazzo*)

which has the very great interest of displaying on its back what we
can scarcely doubt is either the master's signature and the date or an
authentication by someone else contemporary with the painting:
"Hernandiañes (= Hernando Yáñez) . . . (an illegible word or
words) año 1523 (in Arabic numerals)" (Fig. 91).[16] Since the picture
is entirely in the manner of his works at Cuenca, it suggests that he
had established himself in the city before the late twenties or thirties,
the earliest time at which the documents allow us to place him there,
but it is, of course, possible that he had already developed these modes
in some other unascertained locality after 1515, the last year of his
known presence on the east coast. Only a bit higher (36½ centimetres) than the Brauner version, the panel adds St. Joseph to the
Mother and Child to form the subject of the Holy Family. The
composition of the two principal figures follows the same lost Madonna
by Leonardo as the corresponding group in the Rest in the Flight
into Egypt on the Valencian shutters, but the activity of the Child is
accommodated more to that of the Infant in Leonardo's cartoon for
the *Anna selbdritt* at London. The St. Joseph in type and in the effort
for expressiveness practically duplicates the corresponding figure in
the Cuenca Epiphany; and the Virgin's upraised hand repeats, perhaps
a little less successfully, the similar academic study of foreshortening
that we have noticed in the Cremer panel.

6. Works Solely by Llanos

We have already [1] reviewed the grounds on which we can con-
fidently ascribe to Fernando de Llanos alone certain paintings in
Murcia and its vicinity, and to these must be added a few other pieces
of undiscovered provenience which stylistic identity proves him to
have executed separately, whether or not before he left Valencia. In
order to uncover the fallacy of attempting to divide the shutters of the

---

the back, I am indebted to the kind and unflagging efforts of Professor Mario J.
Buschiazzo of the University of Buenos Aires, who also examined for me both the
inscription and the whole picture.

[16] The handwriting is reconcilable with the date; and a person of a subsequent
period would surely have spelled the name as Hernando or Fernando Yáñez instead of
the approximation to the archaic form in which it appears in the Cuenca documents,
Hernand Yañes, and probably would not have arrived at a date concordant with the
style or else would have guessed a year in the thirties when the master is *known* to
have been at Cuenca. The inscription quoted above was originally followed by other
words of which only the dimmest, undecipherable traces remain.

[1] P. 184.

Valencian cathedral into two sets of six panels for each partner, I have had something on former pages to say of the retable of the Marriage of the Virgin which, in the chapel of the Communion in the cathedral of Murcia, bears an inscription on the lower molding of the frame recording that it was a commission of 1516 from the prebendary, Juan de Molina (Fig. 92). Besides the large, main panel of the Marriage, it includes only a crowning piece which Llanos has devoted to a formal and ritualistic representation of the blessing Eternal Father. Our Lady and her two attendants are pronounced examples of types that occur in the passages of the Valencian shutters attributable to the master, and in general the retable illustrates some of his other individual characteristics in contrast to those of his erstwhile partner. The composition, entirely traditional in its retention of mediaeval Spanish symmetry and not necessarily revealing any cognizance of Raphael's *Sposalizio*, betrays, like his other works, that he did not have ordinarily at his control Yáñez's powers of invention. The velleity of Llanos for emotional expressiveness in the face carried almost to the point of caricature and more pronounced, as well as less subtly rendered, than the similar endeavors of his former associate is strikingly illustrated by the snooping old woman who peeks through her fingers behind St. Joseph, a detail suggesting, as Bertaux realized, that the artist may have seen, during travels in Italy, Benozzo Gozzoli's proverbial figure of "La vergognosa di Pisa." The analogy in face and gesture to the man with a finger upon his lips in the background of the Epiphany by Yáñez at Cuenca affords an example of a fact to which I have before alluded, the participation of both Fernandos in certain types and practices, thus warning us once more against dogmatic distribution of absolutely every figure in their joint undertakings. Some cognizance of the "Squarcionesque" school is possibly betokened by the hanging festoon of fruit and vegetables adorning the temple of the espousals, but such an assumption is not really obligatory, since corresponding botanical decorations occur, perhaps without influence from north Italy, in the contemporary frescoes of the vestibule of the Sala Capitular in the cathedral of Toledo.[2] It may have been the proximity of Llanos at Murcia to Andalusia that led him to use for the priest's tunic the spotted kind of brocade preferred by the painters of this region.[3] The altarpiece provides one of the instances in which, although in less degree than Yáñez in the St. Catherine in

---

[2] Vol. IX, p. 194.   [3] Vol. X, p. 24 *et passim*.

FIG. 92. LLANOS. RETABLE OF MARRIAGE OF VIRGIN.
CATHEDRAL, MURCIA
(*Photo. Archivo Mas*)

the Prado, he substituted clearer and brighter color for Leonardo's sombreness of hue.

Internal evidence likewise conclusively sets in Llanos's canon an Adoration of the Shepherds in the chapel of S. Juan, now the Sala Capitular, in the cathedral of Murcia, a panel apparently not known to Bertaux but rightly attributed by Tormo [4] (Fig. 93). Whether or not it is a relic of the pieces painted in 1520 by a "Master Hernando" for the "shoulders" of the sculptured retable of the high altar in the cathedral,[5] there appear to be no trustworthy means of determining. We now perceive in the St. Joseph and shepherds a trait of Llanos which the Marriage of the Virgin fails to exemplify but which is conspicuous in the sections of the Valencian shutters that I have claimed for him, a predilection for rather gaunt and haggard masculine types and for a fluffy treatment of the hair. Indeed, the St. Joseph and the foremost shepherd practically repeat the standing soldier at the left in the Resurrection in the shutters. Perhaps the pleasantest and most freely executed of his preserved, separate works, the panel constitutes an exception to his comparative poverty of imagination, incorporating a charmingly fresh composition for the theme, in which, for instance, the rustic with a lamb upon his shoulders, whom Yáñez in the shutters and at Cuenca depicted walking toward us, is given an easy position of rest in profile. The captious critic might object to the inordinate emphasis upon the shepherds' dog through isolating the beast under an arch in the background, but in any case this bit of *genre* witnesses to the fondness for the animal world that so often delights us in the productions of both Fernandos.

The most unusual work that Llanos has bequeathed to posterity consists in the remains of a retable telling the engaging story of the cross venerated at Caravaca, a town that lies at a considerable distance west of Murcia. At the time of my visit to the place in 1930, they were scattered about the present church of Santa Cruz in the town, a grandiose structure of the seventeenth century that succeeded to earlier edifices built to house the precious relic, but the panels almost certainly derive from a retable over the high altar in one of these prior churches and were not destroyed in the Spanish war. The tradition is that the retable was ordered by Don Pedro Fajardo, first Marqués de los

---

[4] *Levante*, 344.
[5] See above, p. 184.

Fig. 93. LLANOS. ADORATION OF THE SHEPHERDS.
CATHEDRAL, MURCIA
(*Photo. Archivo Mas*)

Vélez, in 1521,[6] a year that cannot be far wrong for the date of the extant paintings. The story runs that in 1232 the Moorish king of Valencia and Murcia, Zeit abu Zeit, became curious about the practices of the Christian religion and, still an unbeliever, asked a priest whom he had captured to celebrate mass in his presence. Having obtained the vestments and ornaments of the altar by means of a messenger whom the sovereign had dispatched on this errand, the priest found to his consternation, as he commenced the liturgy, that the cross was lacking, when suddenly the monarch, looking towards the altar, perceived that a cross had miraculously there appeared. Inasmuch as subsequently during the canon of the mass the Moor beheld the Christ Child within the elevated Host, he was converted and baptized, with the result that the cross has ever since at Caravaca been an object of intense devotion. As the centuries passed, the account of the miracle inevitably received embellishments,[7] such as the denomination of the priest as a cleric of Cuenca, Ginés Pérez Chirinos, but the detail of *angels* bringing the cross to the mass in the presence of the Moorish king must be at least as early as the preserved panels, since it is included in the compartment depicting the Eucharistic scene.

Four of the panels have ordinarily been hung in the transepts of the church, but two of these at the time of my visit had been removed to the schoolroom attached to the building. The subjects of the four are: the capture of the cleric by the Moors (Fig. 94); his religious discussion with Zeit abu Zeit (Fig. 95); the appearance of the cross in the hands of angels at the mass, with the king's wife [8] prominent among the spectators; and his baptism (in a font of the Renaissance) again with the queen as a conspicuous onlooker. Of four further panels assigned by Tormo [9] to the same original retable as the other quartet, the two that in 1930 were to be seen in the *Coro alto* certainly have this provenience and incorporate Llanos's craft. In the first [10] a young man in front of an altar is exhibiting a small chest to a group of surprised worshippers, including an infant upon the pavement, and

[6] Vicente de la Fuente, *La Santa Cruz de Caravaca, Boletín de la Real Academia de la Historia*, Madrid, IX (1886), 326, 327, and 331.

[7] *Ibid.*, and R. Amador de los Ríos, *Riquezas perdidas, La Santa Vera Cruz de Caravaca, Revista de archivos*, XXVIII (1913), 226–240.

[8] One of the later fanciful additions to the story was the account of his estrangement from her because of his passion for bullfights.

[9] *Levante*, 381.

[10] Quintín Bas (*La Santísima Cruz de Caravaca*, Caravaca, 1905, p. 10) says that it is painted on cloth, but Tormo must be right in describing it as a panel.

FIG. 94. LLANOS. THE CAPTURE OF THE CHRISTIAN PRIEST BY
ZEIT ABU ZEIT, SECTION OF RETABLE. CHURCH OF
SANTA CRUZ, CARAVACA

(*Photo. López*)

FIG. 95. LLANOS. RELIGIOUS DISCUSSION OF THE CHRISTIAN PRIEST
WITH ZEIT ABU ZEIT, SECTION OF RETABLE. CHURCH OF
SANTA CRUZ, CARAVACA

(*Photo. López*)

the intent seems to have been to depict the messenger arriving with the Eucharistic ornaments, except the cross. The second panel in the *Coro alto* shows St. John Evangelist on Patmos, with his symbol of the eagle, as occasionally elsewhere in Spanish art, obligingly holding for him an inkwell. Of Tormo's other twain, relegated in 1930 to a stairway, the representation of the seated Christ of the Passion is so entirely repainted as to make impossible a trustworthy decision in regard to its alleged association with the retable. The final piece, a Virgin of the Immaculate Conception holding the Child and with the moon at her feet, is less disfigured by retouching and appears to have been originally a creation of the early sixteenth century; but, although the draperies are like those in the certain remains of the retable, the Child is less Leonardesque than the infant in the panel that depicts the arrival of the vestments, and, when I was at Caravaca, I could not determine to my own satisfaction whether it was by the same hand that did the series of the story of the Caravaca cross.

In the matter of attribution Tormo hesitates between Llanos, Yáñez, or one of their followers, but the first of the three alternatives, at least for the six compartments surely deriving from a single re-table, is proved correct [11] by a comparison with the works of Llanos at Murcia and with his contributions to the Valencian shutters. The priest and the St. John belong to a type that he reiterates again and again, for instance in the Virgin's handmaid who is farther to the rear in the scene of the Marriage. Many of the figures, particularly the men who have arrested the priest, embody his gaunt specimens of bearded humanity. A soldier in the right background of the episode of the Moorish king's baptism is scarcely differentiated from the standing Roman at the left in the Valencian Resurrection, to whom we have had occasion to allude in discussing the Murcian Adoration of the Shepherds. The actor who had played the part of the spectator between St. Joseph and the officiating ecclesiastic in the Marriage now assumes the rôle of the gesticulating infidel in the religious debate. The effigy of the Eternal Father at the top of the simulated altarpiece before which the messenger displays the chest is formalized in the same fashion as the corresponding representation in the pinnacle of the retable of the Virgin's nuptials. The list of such analogies could be much augmented, but it will not be necessary thus to bore the reader who, having once scrutinized the Murcian paintings, will soon realize

[11] As Mayer recognized: second Spanish edition of his *Geschichte*, 1942, p. 144.

for himself in countless ways that at Caravaca he is in the presence of the same artist. The compositions, as often with Llanos, are dull and unrelieved by the novelties of Yáñez, consisting, for the most part, of a central episode framed in blocks of onlookers; and in the ill-proportioned and badly drawn horse of the foremost mounted Musulman conducting the captive priest, the master falls decidedly below the customary standard of the Fernandos in depicting animals. The old Spanish, decorative accents of gold (and gold of high quality, usually in fine preservation) are maintained to a greater extent than in any of their authenticated productions, for example on the borders of garments, in the canopy over the king interrogating the priest, on the altar of the mass, and on the *baldacchino* in the baptism.

The consideration that two panels manifestly done by Llanos alone and deriving from a retable of St. John Baptist were once to be seen in the Collection of Don Francisco Sanz at Valencia would indicate, but not definitely prove, that they were painted before he betook himself to a more southerly region of the eastern littoral. Since the pieces comprise the central effigy, at my last knowledge in the Lafora Collection at Madrid (Fig. 96), and a narrative compartment depicting St. John's decapitation, the present resting-place of which I have not ascertained,[12] it is scarcely possible that they were parts of the same assemblage as a work once to be seen at Orihuela near Murcia, which appears to have constituted an altarpiece by itself and will subsequently [13] concern us, a large panel of the Baptist's birth capped by a representation of the Trinity. The Christ of Llanos's Resurrection in the Valencian shutters finds almost a replica in the standing Baptist of the principal compartment; the young soldier viewing the decollation affords another example of the type so much favored by the master and used for the priest and St. John Evangelist at Caravaca; both the suffering Baptist and the executioners conform to his often cadaverous conception of his male actors; and his tendency to strained expressiveness distorts the executioner's features with homicidal tension. The noble and lovingly rendered landscape behind the central effigy shows that, when he wished, he could vie with Yáñez in this aspect of their profession and that, like his former comrade, he was prone to experiment in the problem of aërial perspective created by veiling the distance in haze.

---

[12] Illustrated by González Martí in his article in the *Museum*, IV (1914–1916), 396.   [13] P. 269.

FIG. 96. LLANOS. ST. JOHN BAPTIST. LAFORA COLLECTION, MADRID

(*Photo. Archivo Mas*)

Soundly distinguishing the style of Llanos from that of Yáñez, Saralegui [14] has quite as soundly established in the former's production a Last Judgment in the Collection of the Conde de Torrefiel at Valencia (Fig. 97). Although of large dimensions,[15] the panel presents a simplified and monumentally symmetrical treatment of the theme in comparison with the versions by Yáñez, including only Christ, the supplicating Virgin and St. John Evangelist, a pair of trumpeting angels, and a few mortals issuing from their tombs as symbols of the general resurrection at the Last Day. The gestures of the Saviour are the same as in the versions by Yáñez, but His head is well-nigh a replica of that of Llanos's Baptist in the Lafora Collection; St. John possesses the kind of countenance which in the case of the young soldier in the Baptist's decapitation formerly belonging to Don Francisco Sanz I have stressed as one of the most tangible factors for recognizing the separate manner of Llanos; and Saralegui points out the analogy of the risen man in the right foreground to one of the youthful Apostles at the left in the Ascension in the shutters. The phase of the master's style as well as the existence in a Valencian Collection would imply that the Torrefiel panel was executed prior to his Murcian period.

The Corredor Collection at Madrid contributes to our understanding of Valencian art of the early Renaissance not only the Agony in the Garden by Paolo da San Leocadio that we have studied [16] but, still more importantly, what is perhaps the most inventive work of Fernando de Llanos apart from his collaboration on the shutters, a panel of the Flagellation (Fig. 98), equal in its large size, at least in its present condition, to Paolo's painting. The craft of the master is very plain to recognize. Among the most telling tokens are the identity of the brutally impassioned features of the soldier holding a halberd with those of the Baptist's executioner in the Sanz picture, the reappearance, in the helmeted youth at the extreme right, of the profile that is a kind of trade-mark in Fernando's output, and the conformity of the other tormentors at the right to his grim conception of mature masculinity. All his characteristics have assumed the late aspect of his retable at Caravaca. The great interest of the panel lies in the fact that even more than the Adoration of the Shepherds at Murcia it transcends, in the representation of the Ecce Homo in diminished

[14] *Archivo español de arte*, XIX (1946), 136.
[15] About a metre and a half high. [16] P. 45.

FIG. 97. LLANOS. LAST JUDGMENT. TORREFIEL COLLECTION,
VALENCIA
(*Courtesy of Don Leandro de Saralegui*)

Fɪɢ. 98. LLANOS. FLAGELLATION. CORREDOR
COLLECTION, MADRID
(*From an article by Francisco Abbad*)

scale in the background, the hypothetical inferiority of Llanos to
Yáñez in imaginative composition, but at the same time we must
acknowledge that he may be only remembering and developing somewhat farther the piquant arrangement which we have inferred to have
been devised by Yáñez in the partnership for the Virgin's Presentation
in the Valencian shutters. A flight of stone steps cuts across our vision,
as in the Presentation, rising to one of the higher levels with which
Yáñez liked to punctuate his pictures, here a platform on which the
Man of Sorrows stands among a platoon of guards. At the base of the
stairway a wildly gesticulating throng call for Christ, rather than
Barabbas, as a victim, and from their midst — as a striking new
detail in the composition — a Hebrew, even more eager for blood
than the rest, has pushed half-way up the flight, excitedly raising his
arm to accentuate the crowd's demands (thus in the same spot as the
Virgin in the Presentation). According to Yáñez's complication of his
spaces by a series of levels, so Llanos ensconces Herod in a loggia
slightly lower than the elevated platform.

His sure, autographic traces are not hidden by the restoration that
was necessary in the pieces of a predella belonging to a dealer at
Barcelona. They consist of: a central panel representing the frequent
theme for this spot in a retable, Christ of the Passion standing in His
tomb and upheld by a pair of angels; and lateral sections (Fig. 99)
exhibiting half-lengths of saints, in one the ascetics John Baptist and
Onuphrius and in the other canonized bishops, perhaps the Fathers
of the Church, Ambrose and Augustine. Of the two fluffy-haired
angels, the figure at the left is absolutely typical in a certain lankiness
and in the expression of the countenance; the Baptist is a replica of
the upper part of the same saint in the Lafora Collection; and the
bishop at the right furnishes an instance of the master's fondness for
eccentric countenances, if not so much here for eccentric moods. The
landscape backgrounds correspond in appearance and in skilled execution to the vista in the Lafora panel.

FIG. 99. LLANOS. SECTIONS OF A PREDELLA. DEALER, BARCELONA

(Photo. Archivo Mas)

7. Works in which it is Difficult to Decide in Regard to Attributions to One of the Fernandos, to their Followers, or Even to Other Painters.

I was formerly [1] readier than I now am to accept as an achievement of one of the Fernandos a powerfully executed panel which, though within the precincts of the cathedral of Valencia, has received little notice [2] and which, albeit not without injury, came through the terrorism of the civil war, a representation of the good thief, St. Dysmas, hanging upon his cross and worshipped by a kneeling clerical donor, in the chapel on the ambulatory dedicated to this member of the celestial host, who is rarely encountered as a separate theme but enjoyed a special cult at Valencia [3] (Fig. 100). The episodes here introduced into the background incorporate the charming legend [4] of St. Dysmas's connection with the Flight into Egypt, which goes back at least as far as St. Anselm. At the right he and two of his brigands interrupt with threats the travelling Holy Family, and at the left, having been impressed by their sanctity, he shelters them in his cavernous retreat, while the loosed ass grazes quietly at the side.

If either of the Fernandos deserves the credit, it would be necessary to choose Yáñez, but, although the panel does not violate his general technical procedure, it contains no type or detail that *specifically* demands a belief in his authorship. Certainly it is quite worthy of him and at his best, whether we look at the harrowing effect of the robber's physical and mental suffering, combined with the relaxed sense of liberation by death, at the convincing embodiment of aged fervor of devotion in the donor, or at the beauty of the rocky landscape enlivened with the pretty story. Neither the modes nor the talents of any of his imitators, not even in the case of Felipe Pablo who among them would perhaps be the most plausible guess, can be reconciled with what the picture discloses to us. The Valencian painters outside the Fernandos'

[1] Vol. X, p. 370, n. 13.

[2] Tormo (*Levante*, 87) ascribes it only to their school. Sanchis y Sivera (*La catedral de Valencia*, 315) states that it was put in its present place by the canon José Manuel Sanchis de Oribay, who died in 1745, and his language might be misunderstood to signify that he believed the panel of St. Dysmas to have been then painted; but he must mean only that the canon set an older picture in a new architectural frame which he caused to be constructed at this time.

[3] See my vols. VI, pp. 397, 410, and 450, and X, p. 370.

[4] See, for instance, P. Guérin, *Les petits Bollandistes*, III, 637–638, under the feast of St. Dysmas, March 25; and E. J. P. Schmitt, *Dismas, the Good Thief, adapted from the French of L. J. M. Cros, S.J.*, Cincinnati, 1892, p. 7.

FIG. 100. YÁÑEZ OR A MEMBER OF HIS CIRCLE. ST. DYSMAS AND
DONOR. CATHEDRAL, VALENCIA
(*Photo. Archivo Mas*)

immediate circle likewise fail to supply the clue. The landscape and its somewhat elaborate introduction of subordinate incidents find rather close analogies in the Chinchilla Master,[5] in whose recognized works, however, there are no forms comparable with the large figures in the foreground.

While not excluding entirely the possibility of one of the Fernandos' better followers, such as the Alcira Master, it is practically with no misgivings that I classify in our authentic inheritance from Yáñez a vertical panel of St. Michael acquired for the Provincial Museum, Valencia, after the conclusion of the civil war and probably a fragment from a larger assemblage (Fig. 101). The attribution is justified by the similarity to the figure of the archangel in the painting in the Montesinos Collection where he is coupled with St. Jerome and to the angel accompanying the Brauner Madonna. All three profiles exhibit a detached lock of hair falling in front of the ear.

Much significance, by reason of its unusually high quality, attaches to a panel of the Madonna and Child in the cathedral of Burgo de Osma which Berenson[6] has provisionally ascribed to the Fernandos (whose styles he does not distinguish) and which, after much concentration on the problem, I am disposed to claim for Yáñez rather than for any other painter whom I know (Fig. 102), although it is somewhat larger[7] than the master's sure treatments of the subject in the Brauner and Grether Collections. Llanos is out of the question for reasons both of style and of inadequate artistic capacity. We need not be surprised at the presence of a Valencian picture in so distant a spot as Burgo de Osma, for in previous volumes[8] we have seen that the town had harbored earlier examples of the Valencian school, and we shall forthwith register a work of Yáñez or his circle no less far to the north, at Cintruénigo in Navarre, whether any of these productions were actually commissioned for the places where they now exist or were merely imported later by pious donors. I am unable to adduce any Italian follower of Leonardo to sponsor the panel, and the mere fact that so great a connoisseur of the art of Italy as Berenson can discover no painter of this country to whom to relate it constitutes practically sure proof that it is Spanish. Indeed, when I studied the

[5] See above, p. 106.
[6] *Italian Pictures of the Renaissance*, Oxford, Clarendon Press, 1932, p. 289.
[7] The dimensions are 88 centimetres in height by 95 in width, and the panel is now set in a frame of the seventeenth or eighteenth century.
[8] See especially vol. IX, p. 759.

FIG. 101. YÁÑEZ(?). ST. MICHAEL.
PROVINCIAL MUSEUM, VALENCIA

FIG. 102. YÁÑEZ(?). MADONNA AND CHILD.
CATHEDRAL, BURGO DE OSMA
(*Photo. Archivo Mas*)

original, I set down in my notes its Spanish nationality as my final impression. There is, however, another Spaniard whose rights to the honor of the panel's authorship are potent enough to forestall a definite attribution to Yáñez — Juan de Pereda, active at Soria in the modern province of which Burgo de Osma actually lies. I have stated his indebtedness to Leonardo in volume IX,[9] and the panel really exhibits nothing entirely inconsistent with his execution; but on the whole the pendulum seems to me to swing more towards Yáñez's candidacy.

The very Leonardesque Child accords with his standards, especially with the Infant in the Epiphany of the shutters in the cathedral of Valencia, who, like the Madonna, may have been executed by Yáñez in this compartment which is preponderantly the work of Llanos;[10] and, although the type of the Virgin cannot be precisely duplicated in his output, the variation is so slight as to make her entirely compatible with the hypothesis that he painted the figure. It is, nevertheless, the appurtenances of the picture that most clearly bespeak his methods. The sacred pair are relieved against one of his favorite architectural backgrounds executed with his characteristic affection for an illuminator's delicacy of brushwork in the treatment of such settings. A more obvious and more extensive representation of an ancient ruin than the similar structure in the panel of St. Vincent Ferrer and a canonized bishop recently acquired by the Provincial Museum, Valencia,[11] it shows the entablature resting directly upon the pilasters in the classical mode and without the tendency of the Renaissance to interpose an arch beneath the entablature. The Child's seat is a parapet, upon which lie objects of still life, as in the Brauner version of the theme, and at Burgo de Osma there is a simulation, in paint, of a lovely decoration of the parapet by a sculptured frieze of ancient scrolls and *putti*. If the attribution to Yáñez can be maintained, the style reveals that the panel must have been painted at least as early as his first documented works at Valencia from 1506 to 1510, but I am cognizant of no cartoon by Leonardo for the subject that could have been the source.

The composition of the Mother and Child in the Grether Collection is reiterated in a separate panel in the parish church at Cintruénigo, east of Tudela in southern Navarre; but she is now extended to full length, with one of her feet resting upon a constant stage-property of Yáñez, a dais, and to the holy pair there is united, instead of St. Joseph,

[9] P. 700.   [10] See above, p. 190.
[11] See above, p. 217.

Fig. 103. YÁÑEZ OR A FOLLOWER. MADONNA, CHILD, AND
INFANT JOHN. PARISH CHURCH, CINTRUÉNIGO
(*Photo. Archivo Mas*)

the young Baptist, offering the homage of a rose (Fig. 103). It is hard to deny the panel to Yáñez in his Cuenca period when we observe, among other tokens of his late style, that the Child is an actual replica of the corresponding figure in the Grether picture, that His eyes are treated in the same peculiarly staring and not very agreeable way, and that the Virgin, though facially different from the Mother in the panel at Buenos Aires, accords with a Leonardesque type frequently encountered in the Spaniard's output; but I should not put it wholly beyond the bounds of credibility that one of his followers might thus closely have imitated his practices. The gold haloes are of the characteristic Valencian sort, tooled in a design of small bars scalloped at the edges, but appear nowhere else in the production of either partner. If the panel was not a gift of some immigrant from Valencia to the church, it witnesses once again [12] to the wideflung vogue of the Valencian school in the Renaissance as well as in the Middle Ages.

Although the Fernandos' disciple, the Grifo Master, in one of his better moments, cannot be absolutely rejected as the parent of an Epiphany formerly belonging to the M. D. Benzaria Company and sold at New York in 1930 (Fig. 104), I am inclined to believe that Yáñez is a more likely choice to father the picture. More analogous in composition and style to the rendering in the shutters of the high altar of the cathedral at Valencia than to the example at Cuenca but (at least in the present condition of the picture) with the iconographic peculiarity of the absence of St. Joseph, the Benzaria version would belong to the period of his Valencian activity. Figures still lean over a wall behind Our Lady, and the careering horsemen of Leonardo's prototype are retained once more in the left distance; but, although the panel is not a small one, the composition is simpler than in the Epiphany on the shutters and employs somewhat fewer and more monumental forms. The actors in the scene have their stylistic kin in Yáñez's various productions. In particular, Mary differs but slightly from her representation in the Adorations of the Shepherds and of the Wise Men on the shutters; the nearest exact counterpart for the Child is found in the Purification in the same assemblage (a figure that I presume him to have done [13] in this compartment because of the likeness, for one thing, to the Infant in the painting at Buenos Aires); and he was perhaps so satisfied with the proud gentleman he had created on the terrace in the compartment of the Presentation of

---

[12] See above, p. 262.   [13] See above, p. 192.

FIG. 104. YÁÑEZ(?). EPIPHANY. FORMERLY BELONGING
TO THE BENZARIA CO. AND SOLD AT NEW YORK

the Virgin in the shutters that, as at Cuenca, he repeated him in the Benzaria picture in the guise of one of the Kings. The reason for surmising that the Grifo Master might just conceivably have succeeded in approximating so closely the manner of Yáñez is the rather similarly composed treatment of the theme formerly in the possession of Colonel Montesinos at Valencia which we shall eventually [14] ascribe to him.

As offering less material for comparison, a single figure at any given period in the history of art is usually harder to ascribe than an extended composition, and this is particularly true when the figure, as in the case of the St. James Major in the Lázaro Collection at Madrid herewith illustrated (Fig. 105), exhibits analogies to the productions of several Spaniards of the early sixteenth century. I have, however, gradually excluded the other candidates in the several Spanish schools of the time, especially Juan de Borgoña, until after long study I am convinced that the Lázaro panel must have been painted by one of the Valencian Fernandos or by a member of their circle. If either partner was responsible, the evidence seems too slight for determining which; but the still precise draughtsmanship and the retention of a conventional background of a brocade suggest a pristine moment in their careers. The facial type, with double-pointed beard, frequently appears in the works surely or possibly by Yáñez, as in one of the Apostles at the right in the Pentecost of the shutters in the cathedral of Valencia and especially the second Magus from the right in the Benzaria picture. The mannered and almost coy tilt of the head is characteristic of both Fernandos, and no other Spaniard of the period gets just this "humid" intensity of glance, which, despite their general wholesomeness, is touched by Leonardo's morbidity and unpleasantly exemplified, for instance, by the St. Cosmas, ordinarily but perhaps wrongly, in their documented retable, apportioned to Llanos. The halo, though different from those in the Cintruénigo painting, would be as exceptional as they in the output of the twain, whereas it is typical of their imitator, Miguel Esteve, who, if I were obliged to abandon them as possibilities, would be my next choice for a candidate.

Tormo describes as merely in the manner of the Fernandos, and Berenson definitely attributes to one of them (in his general refusal to discriminate between their styles), a large panel of the birth of the Baptist, surmounted by a pinnacle of the Trinity, that used to exist in the church of Montserrat at Orihuela but disappeared during the civil

[14] See below, p. 303.

FIG. 105. YÁÑEZ, LLANOS, OR A MEMBER OF THEIR CIRCLE.
ST. JAMES MAJOR. LÁZARO COLLECTION, MADRID
(*Photo. Archivo Mas*)

war. Although I have never seen the picture on my visits to the city, I was privileged to study it at the Barcelona Exposition of 1929, arriving at the impression that it was worthy of the partners and yet, with the insufficient knowledge of the problem that I then possessed, not attempting to decide between the claims of Yáñez, Llanos, or one of their followers. Without photographs, I can go no further, but, if either of the Fernandos was the author, Llanos, in view of the proximity of Murcia, would be the better bet.[15]

In the sections of a retable in a chapel of the ambulatory in the cathedral of Malaga, the similarities to the modes of Llanos are so intimate as very definitely to force us to ponder the question whether he rather than a close follower may not have been the author. Mayer [16] wrongly placed the panels in the school of Seville and was mistaken also in attaching to the set a Mass of St. Gregory in the same chapel which is indeed an Andalusian or perhaps even a Sevillian work;[17] and, as a matter of fact, it actually is strange that the vogue of the Fernandos' manner should have penetrated so far as Malaga which in general naturally bestowed its artistic commissions upon the artists of Andalusia and particularly of near-lying Granada. Nor is the retable a recent importation into the church like the altarpiece by the Castilian Master of Becerril.[18] The Valencian school in general, however, and, within the school, the modes of the Fernandos possessed an amazing aptitude for penetrating other artistic domains in the peninsula,[19] and Malaga does not lie too far removed from Murcia and particularly is an easy journey by sea for anyone on the east coast.

Of the eight sections of the retable, two divide the Annunciation into halves, but the other six exhibit effigies of saints standing in pleasant landscapes and identified by Spanish inscriptions in their haloes, Cosmas and Damian (Fig. 106), Dominic and Francis (receiving the stigmata, Fig. 107), Cyriacus, the Roman martyr, and Paula, the devotee of St. Jerome. Several canonized personages are named Cyriacus, but the rarely represented deacon and martyr of Rome is here recognizable by his vestment, the dalmatic, and by the lumps of tar upon his head and left shoulder, emblems of the hot pitch that was poured over him as one of his torments when tied, as in the pic-

---

[15] See also above, p. 253, and below, p. 359, n. 8.
[16] *Die Sevillaner Malerschule*, 38.
[17] See my volume X, p. 289.   [18] *Ibid.*, p. 428.
[19] See above, pp. 262 and 267.

FIG. 106. LLANOS OR A FOLLOWER. STS. COSMAS AND DAMIAN,
SECTIONS OF RETABLE. CATHEDRAL, MALAGA

(*Photo. Archivo Mas*)

FIG. 107. LLANOS OR A FOLLOWER. STS. CYRIACUS AND FRANCIS,
SECTIONS OF RETABLE. CATHEDRAL, MALAGA
(*Photo. Archivo Mas*)

ture, to a tree or stake. The Sts. Cosmas and Damian fail to recall very definitely the partners' authenticated representations of these hallowed physicians, and yet the champion of an assignment of the eight panels to Fernando de Llanos might point in them to a number of significant analogies to his other productions. The St. Damian, for instance, is like the angel at the extreme right in the Murcian Adoration of the Shepherds and the priest in the Caravaca series; the companion of St. Francis in the scene of the stigmata possesses a countenance of the same general cast as that of the man between St. Joseph and the cleric in the Marriage of the Virgin at Murcia; and St. Paula is comparable to Our Lady in the Ascension of the Valencian shutters. The similarity of the frames to those of the predella by Llanos belonging to a dealer at Barcelona might suggest the possibility that it was once a part of the Malaga retable, and, if this perchance is true, he would be demonstrated to have done the pieces still *in situ*; but I find it so hard to accommodate the types in the Annunciation to his practices that I must leave his right to the Malaga panels as doubtful. The composition of the stigmatization is the same as that used by the Fernandos' disciple, the Grifo Master, in the retable that gives him his name;[20] but he cannot conceivably be the painter of Malaga, and, if this painter is not Llanos, he is a follower by whom I am at present cognizant of no other works.

Inevitably the question has been raised whether we might owe the copy of the Mona Lisa in the Prado to one of the Fernandos. To me a negative answer seems quite as unreasonable as an affirmative. The frequent actual lifting of *motifs* and figures from Leonardo in their sure productions reveals that, when intending a definite copy, either of them might conceivably have approached as close as this to the teacher to whom they joined with so many others in giving little less than the homage due to a god. We should have to postulate that the Fernando in question made the copy in the period of study in Italy, since he could not have achieved such faithfulness to the prototype through mere memory, and that he brought it back with him to Spain, where a miraculous chance preserved it. Indeed Tormo[21] guesses that, if we are justified in accepting it as a creation of either Fernando, the absence of the landscape might be explained by the supposition that Leonardo had not yet put it into his original when the copy was under-

[20] See below, p. 299.
[21] *Boletín de la Sociedad Española de Excursiones*, XXXII (1924), 39.

taken. The recent Catalogues of the Prado point out that the oak of the panel upon which the copy is painted would indicate a provenience from northern Europe, but so celebrated a scholar as Berenson is quoted by Tormo as at least entertaining the possibility of an attribution to one of the partners.

Decided scepticism, however, seems the only proper attitude to assume towards Berenson's tentative proposal to set under the aegis of the two Fernandos a painting in the Museum at Cadiz representing, in a composition somewhat like that of the Cintruénìgo picture, the Child held by the Madonna and receiving a flower from an angel.[22] The Virgin, to be sure, approximates types to be met in their well authenticated productions, and the angel recalls partially certain faces peering through the crowds of the Játiva Last Judgment; but the Child and the thickly wooded landscape seen through the window at the left vary widely from the partners' norms. One gets the distinct impression of an Italian imitator of Leonardo, though not, I think, Luini, who has also been suggested for the authorship.

8. WORKS WRONGLY ATTRIBUTED TO THE FERNANDOS

Of the paintings ascribed by Suida [1] to Fernando de Llanos, I know only two, both of which seem to me to lie without the manner of this Fernando and also of Yáñez. On one, a Madonna in the Kunsthaus, Zürich,[2] he would like to read in an inscription an abbreviation of the signature of Llanos; but Sánchez Cantón [3] has anticipated me in doubting this interpretation of the letters, and the style cannot be reconciled with the modes of the two Valencian masters. In the second work, a Madonna with saints that used to be deposited in the storerooms of the Kaiser Friedrich Museum at Berlin,[4] the attribution is precluded, in my opinion, by the human types, especially of the men, which, moreover, are very Italianate.

We have already [5] had occasion seriously to question Tormo's provisional ascription of a fresco in the Roman Church of Sant' Onofrio to the Fernandos, and it is necessary categorically to repudiate his en-

---

[22] Mas photo., no. 46889C.

[1] *Leonardo und sein Kreiss*, Munich, 1929, pp. 251–252.

[2] Fig. 54 of Suida's book. I am glad to find, after my writing of this chapter, that I am supported in my rejection of the attribution by Saralegui, in *Archivo español de arte*, XIX (1946), 137.

[3] *Archivo español de arte y arqueología*, V (1929), 127.

[4] Fig. 335 of Suida's book. [5] P. 177.

deavor [6] to see the hand of Yáñez in a *tondo* of the Virgin and St. Joseph adoring the Holy Child in the Borghese Gallery at Rome,[7] a picture that is generally assigned to Pier di Cosimo or to his immediate vicinity. He is very decidedly right, however, when [8] he himself emphatically dissents from the attribution to Yáñez, in Von Loga's posthumous volume *Die Malerei in Spanien*,[9] of a Circumcision [10] in the Hermitage at Leningrad, which has usually been given to Luis de Carvajal, and the idea that Yáñez could have had anything to do with the picture is indeed so fantastic that he charitably supposes the editors of the manuscript left by the German scholar at his death to have misinterpreted one of his statements.

[6] *Monumentos españoles en Roma, y de portugueses é hispano-americanos*, Madrid, 1942, II, 189.

[7] No. 439 of the Gallery. Illustrated by Van Marle, *The Development of the Italian Schools of Painting*, XIII, Fig. 253 (although he wrongly gives the number in the Gallery as 335).

[8] *Boletín de la Sociedad Española de Excursiones*, XXXII (1924), 37.

[9] P. 82.

[10] *Catalogue de la Galérie des Tableaux, Les écoles d'Italie et d'Espagne*, Leningrad, 1891, p. 184, no. 407, and the book of illustrations of the Italian and Spanish schools published at Leningrad in 1912, p. 311.

CHAPTER VIII

THE SCHOOL OF YÁÑEZ AND LLANOS

THE attempt to distinguish in general by which of the two Fernandos each of their followers was formed or to which at least each owed the more would be a difficult or even an impossible task. Probably, indeed, they did not in all instances actually study under Yáñez and Llanos but simply were impressed by the works of these masters and sought to imitate them as best they could, not heeding which executed the various paintings. By tedious application and by analyzing every detail in the productions of the Fernandos' school we might arrive at a tentative opinion in regard to the distribution of each disciple's admiration between the partners, and the result would probably be to the advantage of Yáñez as the more dominating spirit in the twain; but the endeavor would fail to repay the pedantic effort, since we should not thus understand better the style of the disciple or his modifications of the Leonardesque fashions that the two associates had imported into Spain. In the one instance, nevertheless, of Martín Gómez we shall find very definitely that it was Yáñez, rather than Llanos, who deserves the credit of having been the instructor.

1. FELIPE PABLO

It is by the name of Felipe Pablo de San Leocadio that an outstanding follower of the Fernandos has ordinarily been known, and he is regularly put down as a son of Paolo da San Leocadio. The only dissenting voice is that of Max von Boehn, who in his article on Paolo da San Leocadio in the Thieme-Becker *Lexikon* [1] questions whether we ought to recognize a son of his in the Felipe Pablo de Santa Leocadia documented as having done the retable over the high altar of the church of Sto. Domingo at Valencia, the work that is the starting-point, because in part preserved, for our reconstruction of the personality who now concerns us. Felipe Pablo's contract to undertake the commission has not been discovered or at least published, but it is summarized by the great Valencian antiquarian of the end of the

[1] Vol. II, under the entry, *Aregio, Pablo de.*

eighteenth century, José Teixidor, in his book, *Capillas y sepulturas del Convento de Santo Domingo*, which until recently existed only in a manuscript of the Library of the University of Valencia but was printed in 1949 in a private edition of which I have been unable to obtain a copy. Even before the book was brought out, Don Leandro de Saralegui increased my already heavy debt to him by reproducing for me from the manuscript the apposite passage. The following is a translation. "The second [2] retable over the high altar was executed in the year 1525. For all of it the contract was made with Felipe Pablo de Santa Leocadia (*sic*), a Burgundian by race and a most celebrated painter, who undertook to paint it in oil and to gild it for the price of 15500 *sueldos* (?) [3] within six years, during which he was to be given the 15500 *sueldos* that were provided entirely by the illustrious Don Francisco Ausías Carbonell, a son of this monastery and auxiliary bishop of Valencia." Teixidor goes on to date the contract on February 19, 1525, but Villanueva, in epitomizing the document much more briefly in his book of the early nineteenth century, the *Viaje literario*,[4] gives the day of the month as February 9 and prints the name as Felipe Paulo de Santa Leucalia. Since, however, Villanueva acknowledges that he is merely reporting what has been told him about the contract by others, it is more likely that Teixidor's spelling and figures are correct.

There is indeed good reason to concur in Von Boehn's scepticism in regard to Felipe Pablo's parentage. Considering the loose spellings of *San Leocadio* in the documents referring to Paolo, we could accept *Santa Leocadia* or *Santa Leucalia* as corruptions of the surname, and we should thus be justified in surmising Felipe to have been a son or at least some relative of Paolo da San Leocadio, though not the infant son, Pedro Pablo, whom he mentions in his will of 1478; [5] but, on the other hand, there are towns called Santa Leocadia in Spain which might have been Felipe's birthplace, one of them actually in the adjacent province of Murcia. Both Teixidor and Villanueva, however, quote the document as adding to Felipe's name an adjective, *borgoñón*, which interjects a very serious obstacle to discerning in him any kinship with Paolo or derivation from a Spanish town of Santa Leocadia.

---

[2] See below, p. 279.
[3] The monetary unit after the numeral is indicated by a character that Saralegui has grave reservations in interpreting as a symbol for *sueldos*.
[4] I, 39.   [5] See above, p. 11.

Borgoñón means *Burgundian,* and, although the adjectives *Lombard* and *Latin* are applied to Paolo in the documents to describe his Italian extraction, we cannot wrest *Burgundian* into this significance, so that we are faced with the virtual impossibility of perceiving any blood relationship between the two artists. The only forlorn hope would be the assumption that the notary who drew up the document or Felipe Pablo's patrons made a mistake in regard to the painter's nationality. It would not be incredible, however, that he received the surname of *San Leocadio* merely because he was Paolo's pupil, in the same way as Ghiberti (often described as Lorenzo di Bartoluccio in the records) and Verrocchio were called after their first teachers; but, if Felipe obtained his earliest instruction from Paolo, he was untrue to him, since his recognizable works are entirely dependent upon the modes that the two Fernandos had popularized at Valencia. Inasmuch, therefore, as so much doubt attaches to the surname and its meaning, the safer course is to designate the painter merely as Felipe Pablo.

Tramoyeres Blasco [6] states that the last mention of "Felipe Pablo de San Leocadio," an entry in the Valencian tax register of 1542, would indicate that the artist was then in straitened circumstances, but, since Tramoyeres does not reproduce the actual entry, we cannot determine whether he only guessed that the name should be printed in the form *de San Leocadio.* It can scarcely be questioned that our master is identical with the man whom the Barón de Alcahalí [7] records under the simple title of Felipe Pablo, with no further name, as doing in 1532 an illumination in the book of the *Fueros de la Generalidad de Valencia.*

Although demolished in 1663 to give place to a new retable over the high altar of Sto. Domingo,[8] the work of Felipe Pablo was itself a substitute for an earlier altarpiece by Pedro Nicoláu, three sections from the predella of which are in the Provincial Museum at Valencia,[9] and it is no mere chance that two of the six compartments of Felipe Pablo's structure preserved in the same Museum reiterate the themes of his predecessor's extant fragments, the dream of St. Dominic's mother and the triumph of his orthodox book over the Albigensian writings in the trial by fire. Indeed it is impossible to doubt that

[6] *Cultura española,* IX (1908), 143, n.1.
[7] *Diccionario biográfico de artistas valencianos,* Valencia, 1897, p. 116.
[8] See Saralegui in *Boletín de la Sociedad Española de Excursiones,* L (1942), 104.
[9] See my vols. VII, pp. 104–106, and IX, p. 759.

Felipe was asked, or himself chose, to follow closely Nicoláu's proto-types, upon which the two later compositions are plainly based. In the case of both artists, even the story of the child Dominic's leaving his bed to sleep on the bare ground is strangely telescoped with the mother's dream of the flame-breathing hound, and the representation of the trial by fire includes the unusual detail of an inscription upon the saint's book adapted from the Epistle to the Ephesians, IV, 5–6, "Unus deus, una fides, unum baptisma." The version of the latter scene by Felipe Pablo, however, contains an addition to Nicoláu's composition that I am unable to explain, the saint, with another Dominican, repeated in diminished scale in the background beneath the levitating book and raising his hand in benediction.

Of the other four compartments, one depicts the theme of which the Spaniards were so fond and which they called the Patrocinio de la Virgen, Our Lady offering to Christ Sts. Dominic and Francis as champions of virtue to prevent Him from destroying the world with His three darts,[10] but Felipe Pablo has amplified the usual composi-tion by introducing as balances to the pair of champions actual per-sonifications of the three vices that had aroused the divine anger, Pride as a sinister hag, Lust as a buxom wench prinking before a mirror that she carries, and Avarice likewise as a seductive hussy grasping a money-bag (Fig. 108). The next panel displays the scene that was treated by Pedro Berruguete,[11] Dominic saving from the pyre of execution the Albigensian Raymond for future conversion. There follows the frequently encountered episode of the two angels serving Dominic and his brethren at supper in the monastery of Santa Sabina at Rome, and the final compartment is devoted to the saint's funeral, with the vision of the Brescian prior at the left beholding him transported to heaven by angels on ladders let down by the Saviour and His mother.[12]

[10] Vol. VII, p. 691.
[11] Vol. IX, p. 58.
[12] Vol. VII, p. 691. Tormo, in his register of the constituents of the retable (*Valencia: los Museos, 51*), gives only five compartments as preserved, thus failing to include the panel of the angels in the refectory and provisionally attributing it instead to the follower of Juan de Juanes, Cristóbal Lloréns (*op. cit.*, p. 62, no. 628). The present distinguished and scholarly director of the Provincial Museum at Valencia, Don Manuel González Martí, however, having rightly perceived that the panel can be by no one else than Felipe Pablo and that it must belong to the retable from Santo Domingo, has informed me of his discovery in a letter, with his habitual magnanimity. I myself had not perceived the affiliation, but it is necessary only to compare the friars at their meal with the types in the funeral ceremony of St. Dominic in order to

FIG. 108. FELIPE PABLO. THE *PATROCINIO DE LA VIRGEN*, SECTION
OF RETABLE. PROVINCIAL MUSEUM, VALENCIA
(*Photo. Archivo Mas*)

Teixidor, in the extract from his book so kindly copied for me by
Saralegui, goes on to itemize the lost constituents of the retable besides the panels from St. Dominic's life (like Villanueva, without a
specification of the themes of these panels), using partly as his source
an unpublished work, the *Historia del Convento de Predicadores de
la Ciudad de Valencia* written by the Dominican Fray Francisco Sala,
who, since he lived at the end of the sixteenth and beginning of the
seventeenth century, would have seen the structure in place before it
gave way in 1663 to its baroque successor. The main body of the retable
comprised statues, St. Dominic at the centre and four other luminaries
of the Order at the sides, Sts. Peter Martyr, Antonine, Thomas
Aquinas, and Vincent Ferrer, but Sala speaks of two additional paintings, Sts. Peter and Paul in their frequent function as decorations of the
doors at either side of the altar. Teixidor affirms on his own authority
that the retable included also four more panels by Felipe Pablo, scenes
from the Passion of Christ, which we may therefore guess to have
belonged to the predella. When he quotes the contract to the effect
that Felipe agreed to do all the retable, Teixidor can scarcely mean
that he assumed the task of the sculpture as well, although the mention
of gilding may refer to the polychromy of the statues. Saralegui further informs me that Teixidor, in another work actually still remaining
in manuscript, the *Libro de Memorias*, states that in 1756 the six extant panels from St. Dominic's story were freshened by restorations
and, in frames of reduced size, placed in the Capilla de los Reyes in the
church of Sto. Domingo, whence in 1765 they were transferred to the
Sala Capitular, the spot where Villanueva saw them.

The style reveals itself as almost slavishly dependent upon the
Fernandos but as incorporating a slightly harsher and sterner inter-

---

be entirely convinced that González Martí has keenly discerned the truth. Moreover,
even in his group of five Tormo lists a compartment of Innocent III's dream of St.
Dominic as a support to a collapsing church, a theme that is not the *main* subject of
any panel of this period in the Museum, whereas he should have classified as this fifth
compartment the Patrocinio de la Virgen, which even Tramoyeres y Blasco (*Guía del
Museo de Bellas Artes de Valencia*, 1915, p. 41) had recognized as a relic of the retable
from Santo Domingo. The dream of Innocent III appears as a subordinate incident
in small scale in the background of a picture of the confirmation of the Dominican
Order in the Museum, but Tormo himself (*op. cit.*, p. 51, no. 488) correctly ascribes
this picture to Cristóbal Lloréns, which is therefore a section of another retable of
St. Dominic, done by Lloréns for the Dominican monastery of S. Onofre at Játiva,
four further pieces of which are in the Museum of Valencia (*ibid.*, pp. 63 and 64, nos.
653, 654, 656, and 665–666: to these he would evidently and wrongly wish to add
the compartment of the angels appearing to Dominic and his brethren at supper).

FIG. 109. FELIPE PABLO. MADONNA WITH STS. COSMAS AND
DAMIAN. PROVINCIAL MUSEUM, VALENCIA
(*Photo. Archivo Mas*)

pretation of their manner. The bony structure of the countenances is likely to be much emphasized and, as in the St. Dominic and the Pride of the Patrocinio de la Virgen, to be combined with a dourness of expression. There is evident also a keen interest in detailed views of cities and castles, which are brought well forward so as almost to intrude upon the main action at the front of the compositions. Although not a performer of the first rank, Felipe Pablo is distinguished by a rather sharp and incisive draughtsmanship.

In a small panel in the same Museum exhibiting the Madonna seated between Sts. Cosmas and Damian (Fig. 109), his peculiar asperity of modelling emerges so plainly in the visage of the former canonized physician (at the left) as to be in itself sufficient to ensconce the picture among the master's authentic works. Other evidence, however, is not lacking, for example the analogy of the very prominent walled and towered city and the mountains behind it in the landscape to the setting of the Patrocinio de la Virgen in the documented retable. González Martí [13] has pointed out the close resemblance of the Damian in attitude (though not in countenance) to the representation of the same saint, now in the Prado, by Fernando Yáñez. The similarity extends even to the box of medicaments that he holds, and González justly deduces that his companion, whose emblem is here a surgeon's instrument, probably should be taken as a guide in reconstructing in the mind's eye the general appearance of the lost St. Cosmas who must have originally balanced Fernando's St. Damian.

We may perhaps dignify with the title of Felipe's masterpiece an Adoration of the Shepherds in the Geri Collection at Florence, embodying one of the themes to which the two Fernandos and their followers returned again and again (Fig. 110). He himself has been generous enough to authenticate the picture for us by actually repeating two of the figures that we have seen in his other productions. The friar gazing down at St. Dominic's corpse in the documented retable reappears in the rôle of the standing shepherd at the left, and the face of the man raising his hand to his head above the Albigensians one of whom St. Dominic rescues from the fire is employed for the kneeling and ecstatic countryman. The baldpate beside the magistrate in this Albigensian scene is also recalled by the St. Joseph on the other side of the Geri panel. The Eternal Father hovers above the stable of the Nativity in clouds precisely like those through which the celestial

[13] *Museum*, IV (1914–1916), 400, n.23.

FIG. 110. FELIPE PABLO. ADORATION OF THE SHEPHERDS.
GERI COLLECTION, FLORENCE

assemblage is distributed in the scene of the Patrocinio de la Virgen; the group of infantile angels doing homage to the newborn Saviour are very similar to the *putti* beneath the angry Christ in the compartment of the Patrocinio; and Bethlehem, partly hidden by the Virgin's head, has become one of the mediaeval towns that Felipe Pablo is fond of placing at the front 'of his landscapes. The Virgin herself scarcely differs in features and coiffure from the representation of Our Lady between Sts. Cosmas and Damian in the Provincial Museum at Valencia. The St. Joseph and particularly the kneeling shepherd continue the desire for animated, facial expression that we have discovered in certain figures by the Fernandos at Cuenca and Murcia, but the ass, which is debased into no more than a gigantic sheep, betrays that Felipe had not inherited his teachers' preëminence in the delineation of animals.

The characteristic marks of his method stand forth to my eyes with practically convincing clarity in a retable's fragments in the Provincial Museum at Valencia, deriving from the church of S. Agustín in this city, effigies of the Augustinian saints, Augustine and Nicholas of Tolentino (Fig. 111), as well as a Crucifixion (Fig. 112).[14] The facial structure and tragic outlook upon life, for instance, which we have singled out in the St. Dominic of the Patrocinio de la Virgen in the documented cycle are repeated in the St. Nicholas, whose countenance should be compared also with that of the man seen above St. Dominic's arm in the compartment of the trial of the books. The old predilections of the Spanish school are still maintained in such devotional images, an ostentatious textile behind St. Nicholas and a brilliantly brocaded cope upon St. Augustine's shoulders.

I feel myself on much less sure ground when even tentatively I set in my pages on Felipe Pablo a Madonna in one of the rooms attached to the edifice at Valencia that used to be called the church of the Congregación but has now been taken over by the parish of Sto. Tomás

---

[14] Saralegui in a letter generously informs me of what I am confident that he has rightly perceived, namely that this Crucifixion belongs to the same retable as the figures of the two Augustinian saints. I am sorry, however, to be obliged to disagree with my friend (for once!) in his attribution of the fragments from S. Agustín to the Grifo Master (*Boletín de la Sociedad Española de Excursiones*, LII, 1944, p. 34). For the Grifo Master, see below, p. 296. The fragments are too late in style to have anything to do with a retable for the church of S. Agustín that Pedro Cabanes in 1483 contracted to paint, honoring principally St. Catherine of Alexandria and her namesake of Siena but including a figure of St. Augustine (Sánchez y Sivera, *Pintores medievales en Valencia*, 194).

Fig. 111. FELIPE PABLO. STS. AUGUSTINE AND NICHOLAS OF
TOLENTINO, FRAGMENTS OF RETABLE. PROVINCIAL
MUSEUM, VALENCIA

(*Photo. Archivo Mas*)

FIG. 112. FELIPE PABLO. CRUCIFIXION, FRAGMENT OF SAME
RETABLE AS FIG. 111. PROVINCIAL MUSEUM,
VALENCIA

(*Photo. Archivo Mas*)

(Fig. 113). In the group formed by the Fernandos and their circle, however, no one but Felipe has created works exhibiting affinities to the picture that are really provocative for the attribution. The closest analogues in his achievements for the Virgin and Child are found in the Adoration of the Geri Collection, but both types are fairly frequent phenomena in his other paintings, for example in the scene of the dream of St. Dominic's mother. The composition does not follow exactly the lines of any extant version of the theme by the Fernandos, nor does it accord so precisely with the renderings by Leonardo as to require the assumption that the author had been in Italy.

After a good deal of wavering, I have finally been persuaded by Saralegui [15] that Felipe Pablo provides a safer port than Miguel Esteve [16] for the collocation of a panel of Sts. Roch and Sebastian which has entered the Provincial Museum at Valencia from the Collection of Doña Luisa Viver in the city (Fig. 114) and the forms and composition of which recall to a certain degree the compartment of the same two sacred personages in the retable that gives the Borbotó Master his name.[17] The ties with Esteve, such as the resemblance of the St. Roch to the Santiago in the predella of his retable at Lucena del Cid and to his St. Matthew in the Ayuntamiento of Valencia, are too tangible to allow us to make the attribution to Felipe Pablo categorical, and yet the latter's claims are strongly supported by the analogy of St. Sebastian's head to that of the figure of Lust in the compartment of the Patrocinio de la Virgen in the documented altarpiece, by the general conformity of the types to Felipe's more masculine feeling, and by the specific correspondences which Saralegui amasses.

2. THE ALCIRA MASTER

The anonymous pupil of the Fernandos for whom I have chosen the sobriquet of the Alcira Master is less faithful than Felipe Pablo to his teachers and at the same time less gifted, though not without a certain freshness and originality. He takes his name from the town that houses his most comprehensive, extant [1] work, Alcira, where in the chapel of the Communion at the right of the nave in the church of S. Agustín the panels of a retable of the Virgin by his hand have

[15] Archivo español de arte, XXIII (1950), 196.
[16] See below, p. 307.
[17] Vol. VI, pp. 330–331.
[1] At least until the civil war: I have not learned whether the panels survived this catastrophe.

FIG. 113. FELIPE PABLO(?). MADONNA AND CHILD.
CHURCH OF THE CONGREGACIÓN, VALENCIA
(*Photo. Sanchis*)

Fig. 114. FELIPE PABLO(?). STS. ROCH AND
SEBASTIAN. PROVINCIAL MUSEUM,
VALENCIA

been incorporated in the frames of a modern altarpiece. From the body of the original structure there remain the narrative compartments of the Nativity of Christ, the Epiphany (Fig. 115), the Resurrection, the Dormition (in which the painter strained his ability by struggling, less successfully than Paolo da San Leocadio,[2] with the foreshortening of the bed inwards), the Pentecost, and the Coronation. In the predella, where his talents show to better advantage as more suited to a style like that of an illuminator, the subjects, now in a disturbed order, are the Meeting at the Golden Gate, the Marriage of the Virgin, the Annunciation, and the Ascension, which, like the example in the retable of the Puridad in the Provincial Museum at Valencia,[3] departs from the usual treatment of the theme and exhibits a composition off centre. With the exception of the veronica at the summit, the *guardapolvos* are reserved for Prophets and (not very common in Spain) Sibyls, and under the figure of David among the Prophets the inscription, 1527, happily dates for us the retable.

Many of the types witness to the tremendous stir that the Fernandos made in the Valencian artistic atmosphere, for instance, all the participants in the Nativity and, in the Epiphany, the young Magus at the right, in whom the Master has imitated the prominence that they are wont to give to a powerful form at the front of their versions of the subject; but now and again, as in the boy bending his head in the group at the left of the Epiphany and in the Delphic Sibyl,[4] his figures are less contaminated with Leonardesque idiosyncracies and incorporate a more serene and classic beauty, possibly influenced by the creations of Paolo da San Leocadio. His Leonardesque persons are less subtle in expression than those by Felipe Pablo, however much, as in the young Magus of the Epiphany, he endeavors to bestow upon them an intensity of the eyes meant to reproduce the great Florentine's stress upon psychology; and he has a way of disposing the hair in corkscrew curls, thus providing us with one of the Morellian tokens by which his works can be recognized. The more normal types of humanity that he often creates include sometimes bearded men in early middle age and particularly youths whose prettiness perhaps makes them stand forth with a conspicuousness that their subordinate rôles as actors do not justify.

---

[2] See above, p. 41.   [3] Vol. VI, p. 374.
[4] She is encircled with a banderole carrying the inscriptions "S. Delphica" and "Nascetur ex virgine."

FIG. 115. THE ALCIRA MASTER. EPIPHANY, SECTION OF RETABLE.
S. AGUSTÍN, ALCIRA

(*Photo. Archivo Mas*)

It required only brief examination to perceive that he was undeniably the author of the now destroyed wings of a triptych of the Magdalene which reached the Diocesan Museum [5] at Valencia from the same convent of Servite nuns at Sagunto that supplied the Museum with a triptych by the Cabanyes Master.[6] The centre of the Alcira Master's triptych, whether a statue or painted effigy of the Magdalene, had disappeared before the wings suffered in the civil war the same sad fate as the majority of the Museum's treasures. The subject of the interior of one wing was her washing of Christ's feet (Fig. 116), and the other depicted the *Noli me tangere*. The high narrow spaces that the Alcira Master was obliged to cover in the wings made it necessary for him to devise modes for extending the compositions vertically. The masses of pompous architecture of the Renaissance which he so much affected and which represented the house of Simon, where the Magdalene performed her humble act of devoted love, were projected at the bottom as a stage for the *genre* of a cat-and-dog fight and as space for the scattered still life of fruit, foliage, and a rose; and a loggia rose above the dinner-table to provide a setting for the incongruous introduction of two angelic but sportive *putti*. In the other wing, the lower foreground, beyond the garden of the *Noli me tangere*, was filled with rocks, vegetation, shells, and birds somewhat as in Giovanni Bellini's Transfiguration at Naples. The series of ascending planes behind the actual encounter of the Magdalene with her Lord unfolded to us, first, two of the holy women listening to the proclamation of the Resurrection by an angel who was enveloped in Leonardesque shadow within the Sepulchre; then an eery forest likewise in Leonardo's mode; next, a square and bridge of a city; and finally a mountainous landscape. One of the houses on the urban square seemed to be toppling over — a detail that I cannot explain unless it was merely a defect of draughtsmanship or an attempt, since monks are gazing excitedly at the edifice, to symbolize the earthquake that accompanied the Crucifixion. In the four spaces on the exteriors of the wings there were represented in monochrome the actors in the Annunciation and Sts. Peter and Paul.

No one but the Alcira Master himself could have so nearly repeated

---

[5] Nos. 40 and 41. It is absolutely impossible to see on what conceivable grounds Tormo (*Valencia: los Museos*, 126) could propose a date as early as about 1490 and an attribution to the central Italian master, Lorenzo da San Severino, the younger (whom he wrongly calls Ludovico da San Severino).

[6] Vol. VI, p. 406.

FIG. 116. THE ALCIRA MASTER. THE MAGDALENE WASHING CHRIST'S
FEET, DETAIL OF WING OF TRIPTYCH. DIOCESAN MUSEUM,
VALENCIA

(*Photo. Archivo Mas*)

the young Magus of the Alcira Epiphany in the two figures of the Magdalene, particularly as she washed Christ's feet. In the *Noli me tangere*, furthermore, the Saviour wore the painter's formalized curls, and the St. John at the feast of Simon was one of his characteristic comely youths. The bold brocades of the earlier days of the Spanish school managed to maintain themselves in the dress of the Magdalene and in the hangings of Simon's mansion. As in the case of Felipe Pablo, his helplessness as an *animalier* ought to have warned him against cluttering the Sagunto pieces with his mere simulacra of the dumb creation.

Among the imitators of the Fernandos at Valencia, the Alcira Master is the most likely sponsor for a small Presentation of the Virgin in the Carvalho Collection in the Château de Villandry (Fig. 117). Because of the resemblance in frames and in size (due doubtless to a reprehensible cutting down of one or both panels for the sake of correspondence), it might for a moment wrongly give the impression of constituting a companion-piece to a Flemish Nativity of the early sixteenth century in the same Collection. The adolescent Virgin is exactly the feminine type embodied in the Sagunto representations of the Magdalene, and the vendor of animals for the sacrifice, a figure of *genre* in the lower left corner, reappears, with a negro's face, as an attendant of the youthful Magus in the Alcira Epiphany, looking out at us with precisely the same glance.

3. THE GRIFO MASTER

Tormo [1] has thus christened one of the least tolerable among the satellites of the Fernandos, taking the name from the heraldic griffin prominent in the unidentified escutcheons on his most considerable extant work, a retable of the Dominican St. Vincent Ferrer in the Provincial Museum at Valencia; and, instead of translating and calling him the Griffin Master, I preserve the Spanish *Grifo* in the sobriquet for the sake of avoiding misapprehension by different titles, however synonymous in the two languages. From the confusion in the records in regard to the provenience of the retable Saralegui [2] has elicited the probability that it derives from the Dominican monastery of S. Onofre at Museros (just north of Valencia) or from the institution of the

[1] *Valencia: los Museos*, 19.
[2] *Boletín de la Sociedad Española de Excursiones*, LII (1944), 34–35.

FIG. 117. THE ALCIRA MASTER(?). PRESENTATION OF THE VIRGIN
IN THE TEMPLE. CHÂTEAU OF VILLANDRY
(*Photo. Giraudon*)

same religious Order at Játiva also dedicated to S. Onofre rather than from Sto. Domingo at Valencia itself. One of the saints in the predella is certainly either Onuphrius (Onofre) or Paul the Hermit, and, if the former was intended, we should be provided with further proof that it was for a foundation under his patronage that the paintings were done.

The visit that I made to Museros in 1934 supplied me with some slight but far from conclusive evidence favoring the hypothesis of the provenience of the retable in the Valencian Museum from the monastery of S. Onofre in this place. The altarpiece in the present parish church which I had occasion to mention in volume VI [3] as commissioned by the Order of Santiago, to whom Museros belonged, but which was destroyed in the recent civil war struck me, in the brief examination that I had time to devote to it, as possibly a creation of the Grifo Master, thus suggesting that, since an artist, having been given one task in a town, often as a result there obtained others, our painter might have carried out at Museros a retable also in S. Onofre. As a matter of fact, the priest of the parish church told me that the actual source of the then extant altarpiece of the Order of Santiago was the monastery of S. Onofre, the remains of which had become a mere farm, so that, if the retable in the Museum of Valencia also hailed from the monastery, the Grifo Master would have executed two works not only in the same town but in the same edifice. Sanchis y Sivera,[4] however, though wrongly dating the altarpiece of the Order of Santiago, states it to have once decorated the old parish church that gave place to the present edifice, thus contradicting the priest's information; but in any case, without photographs of the lost altarpiece, I can by no means trust my fleeting impression that the Grifo Master painted it, and consequently I am really able to contribute very little to the supposition that his retable in the Valencian Museum was also formerly to be seen at Museros.

Its sections are practically all preserved and have now been assembled in the Museum, reconstituting the original altarpiece, al-

---

[3] Pp. 306, n.1, and 420, n.2. M. Baudouin de Gaiffier, in reviewing my volume VII (*Analecta Bollandiana*, LVII, 1939, p. 204), agrees with me that the Macarius depicted in the altarpiece and in other Spanish paintings must be the more famous saint of this name, called "of Egypt" or "of Scété," the Libyan desert to which he retired.

[4] *Nomenclator geográfico-eclesiástico de los pueblos de la diócesis de Valencia*, Valencia, 1922, p. 309.

though probably not in every instance with the compartments in their proper locations. The central effigy of St. Vincent Ferrer conforms to the long-established Spanish iconography for the theme [5] and is archaically relieved against a golden plaque above a parapet. Of the four lateral, narrative panels, Saralegui [6] has identified the first as the delivery of some one of the many sermons that he successfully directed towards the conversion of the Jews (Fig. 118). The next two compartments embody miracles each of which he often performed, and I see no means of determining which of the examples is intended. One depicts his frequent imitation of Christ in a multiplication of loaves of bread and wine,[7] and the other his quite as customary liberation of a man from demoniac possession.[8] In the last of the narrative panels his obsequies take place, while in the foreground another victim of devils, naturalistically clamped in a strait jacket, is exorcised through touching the saint's Dominican habit. The Crucifixion in the central pinnacle of the structure includes only the forms of Christ, the Virgin, and the kneeling Magdalene. About the dead Saviour supported by two angels in the middle of the predella there are ranged in four compartments St. John Baptist in the wilds, St. Francis receiving the stigmata, the penitent St. Jerome, and St. Onuphrius or St. Paul the Hermit [9] beneath a palm tree and fed by a raven.[10] The *guardapolvos* exhibit: at the summit, the blessing Eternal Father between the heads of two angels (a panel recently discovered in the Museum from which bits at the sides are apparently the only missing parts of the structure); next, flanking the top of the Crucifixion, the standing Sts. Christopher and Michael; then, on cross-pieces, busts of Balaam and Jeremiah; and finally, on the uprights beside the main division of the retable, full-length figures, at the left St. Joseph above St. Paul and at the right St. Dominic above

[5] Vol. VI, p. 101.   [6] *Op. cit.*, p. 36.

[7] P. Guérin, *Les petits Bollandistes*, IV, 229 (under the feast of St. Vincent Ferrer on April 5).

[8] S. M. Hogan, *St. Vincent Ferrer*, London, 1911, p. 101.

[9] The argument against St. Onuphrius would be that he was ordinarily said to have been brought supernatural food by an angel; but a figure who is surely Onuphrius has the raven as an emblem in a retable in the church of Sta. Catalina, Saragossa (vol. VIII, p. 470). Antón Becerra was guilty of the reverse confusion in depicting St. Paul the Hermit as receiving bread, not from a raven, but from an angel (vol. X, p. 222).

[10] The Trinity from the retable that gives the Perea Master his name was once wrongly thought to belong to the Grifo Master's altarpiece of St. Vincent Ferrer: see vol. VI, p. 270, n.3.

Fig. 118. THE GRIFO MASTER. ST. VINCENT FERRER
PREACHING, SECTION OF RETABLE. PROVINCIAL
MUSEUM, VALENCIA

(*Photo. Archivo Mas*)

St. Peter (the two Apostles probably interchanged, in the present set-up, from their pristine positions). The panels ensconcing Sts. Peter and Paul include over each of their heads the shields with the charge of the griffin, but in the former's compartment the field of the escutch-eon is divided between the griffin at the left and an as yet also unrecog-nized charge at the right, the whole being surmounted by an episcopal mitre and a stole.

The intrinsic aesthetic appeal of the Grifo Master is almost nil, but he possesses the archaeological interest of having started probably in the shop of the Artés Master and of then adding an allegiance to Yáñez and Llanos. Among numerous examples of types apparently derived from the Artés Master, some of the most obvious are the bishop beside the cardinal in the scene of the funeral, the St. Dominic on the *guardapolvos*, the Magdalene in the Crucifixion, the angel at the right in the Pietà of the predella, and the Balaam. The counte-nances, however, are often modified by Leonardesque facial traits and chiaroscuro learned at second hand from the Fernandos, and the retable contains many out-and-out imitations of figures by the partners, for instance especially the Baptist of the predella. In a futile endeavor to reproduce Leonardo's intensity of gaze the Grifo Master, as particu-larly in the episodes of the sermon to the Jews and the miracle of the bread and wine, impresses upon his actors an unfortunate effect of strabismus. In general, a defective draughtsman and an uninteresting composer, he is no credit to any of the men under whose influence he fell.

After one has surveyed the retable of St. Vincent Ferrer, he will detect forthwith and indubitably the craft of the Grifo Master in panels of the Epiphany (Fig. 119) and of the young Christ in the Temple set above the credences [11] beside the high altar of the church of Sto. Tomás (also called the church of the Congregación) [12] at Valen-cia. Although the composition of the Epiphany is not closely imitated from any single example among the Fernandos' preserved treatments of the theme, it profited by suggestions from their renderings, and details are actually lifted from more than one compartment of their cycle in the cathedral. The boy holding a casket of gifts is copied from

[11] At my last knowledge, they had been removed, because of the process of recondi-tioning the edifice, and hung high in the sacristy, but I presume that they will eventually be returned to their former functions.
[12] See above, p. 286.

FIG. 119. THE GRIFO MASTER. EPIPHANY. CHURCH OF THE
CONGREGACIÓN, VALENCIA

(*Photo. Sanchis*)

the peering lad in the Epiphany in this cycle, and the two figures next to him repeat the correspondingly placed spectators at the upper level in the Presentation of the Virgin. In setting the two figures and some of the other actors on a raised platform, the Grifo Master borrows the Fernandos' affection for varied elevations in their paintings and thus relieves his ordinary dullness of composition. Indeed it may be said of the panels in the church of the Congregación that they come nearer than any other productions of the Grifo Master to endowing him with respectable rank as an artist.

Even before I knew these panels, I had perceived that stylistic evidence demanded that we ascribe to him another version of the Epiphany which, from the Collection formerly belonging to Colonel Montesinos at Valencia, I was privileged to study in 1933 in the house of one of his heirs, Don José Montesinos (Fig. 120); and the ascription is borne out by the fact that the picture turns out to be merely a variant of the example that we have analyzed in the last paragraph.

An absolutely clear case can be made out for the Grifo Master's claims to a panel in the parish church of Torrente, just west of Valencia, displaying the paired figures of Sts. Bernard and Sebastian (Fig. 121). The former repeats a type commonly encountered in the retable of the Valencian Museum, for instance in the St. Vincent Ferrer multiplying the bread and wine; his habit is made of the heavy stuffs and arranged in the kind of folds that the Master affects; and the St. Sebastian fixes us with the glance and widely separated eyes of the Baptist in the retable's predella.

On the other hand, it is with the proviso of a point of interrogation that we must catalogue under the Grifo Master's name the wings of a triptych which until the civil war existed in the parish church at Lucena del Cid, north of Castellón de la Plana (Fig. 122). The centre consisted of a sculptured Epiphany, evidently coetaneous with the paintings, the subjects of which were standing effigies of St. Honoratus of Lérins [13] and a royal martyr whom I shall have to leave to better iconographers than I to recognize with surety. His emblem was a plate containing what looked like two pieces of bread; he wore a Mussulman's turban; the honor of martyrdom was signified by a palm that he carried; and a sceptre lying upon the ground revealed his kingly status. It is not out of the question that the objects in the plate were hailstones and that we therefore have to do with one of the

[13] Vol. VI, p. 61.

FIG. 120. THE GRIFO MASTER. EPIPHANY. COLLECTION OF
DON JOSÉ MONTESINOS, VALENCIA

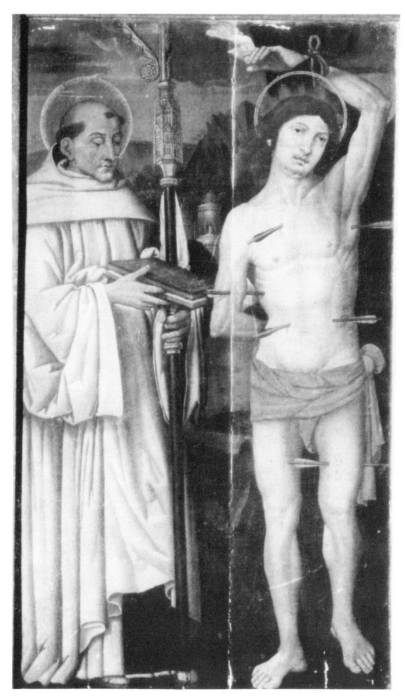

FIG. 121. THE GRIFO MASTER. STS. BERNARD AND
SEBASTIAN. PARISH CHURCH, TORRENTE
(*Photo. Archivo Mas*)

Fig. 122. TRIPTYCH, WITH WINGS BY THE GRIFO MASTER(?). PARISH CHURCH, LUCENA DEL CID

(*Photo. Archivo Mas*)

royal Persian pair, Sts. Abdon and Sennen,[14] the turban merely symbolizing the Orient. The painter cannot be Miguel Esteve who did a retable in the church, and, in addition to a kind of general agreement with the Grifo Master's not too elevated attainments, his authorship is argued particularly by the resemblance of the martyr to several of the participants in St. Vincent's miracle of the bread and wine, although without distortion of the eyes.

4. MIGUEL ESTEVE AND MIGUEL DEL PRADO

These two artists are recorded by documents as having done between 1518 and 1520 in collaboration certain frescoes in the chapel of the Ayuntamiento at Valencia. Since the frescoes are partially preserved, the character of the authors' style is securely established, but, inasmuch as no separate documented painting by either has survived, it is unhappily impossible to disentangle the manner of one partner from that of the other. Indeed, the style of the frescoes is uniform throughout, tending to justify the hypothesis that it is the creation of one of the two painters, whom we shall find to have been in all probability Miguel Esteve, and that the other merely reproduced this style in a servile fashion, perhaps working upon his associate's sketches and laying on the colors under his direct supervision. The situation is peculiarly unfortunate because the style is exactly that of the personality to whom Tormo [1] has given the sobriquet of the Master of the Miracle of Cologne, but we rescue this Master from anonymity only to bestow upon him two real names! And yet the confusion is not quite so desperate, for several considerations strongly imply that Esteve was the creator of the style and the one of the twain endowed with originality, permitting us to identify him with the Master of the Miracle of Cologne. Although the language of the document, dated April 9, 1519, in which Esteve specifies the financial arrangements for Miguel del Prado's collaboration does not make it absolutely clear that the latter had not been joined with him from the beginning of the enterprise, yet it was Esteve alone who, on September 18, 1518,

[14] Vols. VI, p. 130, and VII, p. 53. It would have been natural in this case that the other one of the pair should have been depicted on the reverse of the wing; but the disappearance or destruction of the triptych prevents verification of this possibility, and the distinguished authority on the art of the province of Castellón de la Plana, Don Ángel Sánchez Gozalbo, kindly reports that he does not remember that the reverses of the wings ever contained any paintings of figures.

[1] *Levante*, 111.

first received the commission for the whole cycle of mural paintings, and it was also only he who, after a succession of payments to them both, is declared on May 23, 1520, to have brought the undertaking to a conclusion.[2] Moreover, Miguel del Prado may be deduced to have played a very secondary rôle in the Valencian school of the period, since he appears nowhere else in the records; but Esteve is mentioned on July 12, 1510, as one of a group of artists who served as witnesses on behalf of the Forment atelier of sculpture in a difficulty in which the latter had become involved,[3] and there is a further allusion to him in 1513 as residing in the parish of San Martín at Valencia, though paying a tax not considerable enough to indicate that he had yet emerged as a leading master.[4] I will therefore arbitrarily in the text describe as by Miguel Esteve the works that reproduce precisely the manner of the frescoes of the Ayuntamiento, and I will place his name as a caption under the illustrations in order to avoid such cumbersome phraseology as "by Miguel Esteve or by Miguel del Prado or by the two in collaboration"; but in the case of the illustrations I will set quotation marks about his name as a means of showing that I well realize the possibility of Miguel del Prado's collaboration also in these other works or even of his separate execution.

The chapel of the Ayuntamiento in the ornamentation of which the partners joined with other artists was a new structure of the early Renaissance begun in 1517 to take the place of a Gothic edifice on the spot. The frescoes that the contract called upon them to paint were to comprise: in the round arches made at the tops of the walls by the ribs of the vaulting, the Pantocrator in a nimbus of cherubim over the altar and the Apostles in the corresponding spaces along the walls, each of these saints to be seated on a bench hung with a textile, or standing against such a bench, and holding in one hand the emblem of his martyrdom and in the other a book; in the spandrels of the arches, angels with instruments of music; and at the four corners beneath the vaulting of the chapel, smaller angels carrying banderoles adorned with the symbols of the Passion. The models for the Pantocrator, Apostles, and musical angels were to be the now destroyed frescoes by Paolo da San Leocadio and Francesco Pagano in the apse

[2] For the documents in the case, see the fundamental article by L. Tramoyeres Blasco in *Archivo de arte valenciano*, V (1919), 92 ff.
[3] See an article by X. de Salas in *Anales y Boletín de los Museos de Arte de Barcelona*, I, 2 (1942), 38–39 and 75; and also above, p. 181.
[4] Tramoyeres Blasco, *op. cit.*, 90.

of the cathedral, so that, since the paintings in the Ayuntamiento are partly preserved, we are assisted in reconstructing the lost achievements by the Italian masters.[5] The Ayuntamiento, with its chapel, suffered the fate of so many ancient landmarks, being ruthlessly torn down in 1860 as no longer an object of interest, but a number of the lunettes were providentially saved, transferred to canvas, and deposited in the present town hall, where they survived the cataclysm of the civil war. The majority of the extant lunettes display single figures of seated Apostles, Sts. Peter, Paul (Fig. 123), John (Fig. 124), James Major, and Philip (or, despite the fact that the emblem is a Latin cross,[6] perhaps Andrew); but the other pieces reveal that in some cases they were paired within one space, since Sts. Bartholomew and Matthew[7] are thus ensconced together, and the less well preserved St. Thaddaeus and an Apostle whose attribute I have been unable to make out[8] were originally also united, though now dissociated from each other. When I studied the paintings on the spot in 1926, I did not find the fragments, a half-length of an angel and a bust of the Virgin illustrated by Tramoyeres in his article on the chapel,[9] nor are they mentioned by Tormo in his account of the present Ayuntamiento in his book of 1923, *Levante*;[10] but they are registered in Antonio Beltrán's recent volume dealing with Valencia in the series *Guías artísticas de España*,[11] and, on the basis of Tramoyeres's illustration, I am willing to accept the angel as a relic of the cycle by Miguel Esteve and Miguel del Prado.

The greater number of the Apostles seem to indicate that Esteve and his partner (if he is not a mere echo of Esteve) had first learned their art from Paolo da San Leocadio, but the Sts. John and Matthew imply the quite definite cognizance of the rival strain started in the Valencian school by Yáñez and Llanos that we shall often be able to

---

[5] See above, p. 12.

[6] Andrew not infrequently is distinguished by a Latin cross rather than by the kind named after him: see, for example, the effigy by the Torralba Master in vol. IV, fig. 260, and cf. vol. VII, p. 820.

[7] Tramoyeres so designates him, probably because his sole attribute is a book, and Matthew, like John, was not only an Apostle but the writer of one of the Gospels.

[8] Neither of Tramoyeres's identifications for these two figures can be correct, since St. Mark, for whom he mistakes St. Thaddaeus, was not an Apostle and the attribute of the other is certainly not the fuller's club of St. James Minor, whatever else it may be. St. Thaddaeus is here recognized through his emblem of the halberd, and his natural companion would be St. Simon, since they are both honored on October 28.

[9] See above, p. 308, n. 2.

[10] P. 137.   [11] Barcelona, 1945, p. 108.

FIG. 123. MIGUEL ESTEVE AND MIGUEL DEL PRADO. ST. PAUL,
FRESCO. AYUNTAMIENTO, VALENCIA
(*Photo. Archivo Mas*)

Fig. 124. MIGUEL ESTEVE AND MIGUEL DEL PRADO. ST. JOHN
EVANGELIST, FRESCO. AYUNTAMIENTO, VALENCIA

(*Photo. Archivo Mas*)

discern in Esteve's other productions. The conspicuousness of the commission in the town hall of the capital, Valencia, inspired him to put forth greater effort and to rise here to the stature of a respectable artist, but ordinarily in his works the manners of Paolo da San Leocadio and of the two Fernandos are washed out into a rather debilitated, incompetent, and generalized Italianism of the early Cinquecento. One of his peculiarities is a fondness for swathing his figures in thick folds of unusually heavy draperies. The walls of the loggias in which the Apostles sit are hung with the brilliantly brocaded fabrics beloved by the elder Spanish school and actually prescribed in the contract for the frescoes, but their gold, as even sometimes in the mediaeval paintings of the country, is only simulated in yellow pigment.

Before examining the picture from which Tormo chose the title, the Master of the Miracle of Cologne, we had best study a work that is justly ascribed to this Master by the Spanish scholar [12] and clearly reveals his identity with Esteve, a retable at the west end of the parochial church of Lucena del Cid, north of Castellón de la Plana. Its ordinance appears to have been suggested by Paolo da San Leocadio's altarpiece of the Saviour at Villarreal. Three standing effigies, relieved against patterned gold, fill the principal section, St. Anthony Abbot at the centre, Sts. Peter and Paul in the lateral compartments (Fig. 125). The pinnacle of the structure is occupied by the Madonna of the Rosary, also upon a gold background. The Christ of the Mass of St. Gregory is set in the middle of the predella, flanked by the seated Mother, St. John Evangelist, Santiago, and the Baptist. On the partially preserved [13] *guardapolvos*, beneath the blessing Eternal Father at the top, there are marshalled full-lengths of a canonized bishop and St. Joseph (rare as a separate image at this time except in the Valencian school),[14] half-lengths of Sts. Agatha and Ursula, and the standing form of St. Lucy. The identity of authorship with the frescoes of the Ayuntamiento at Valencia is rendered unmistakable even by the single fact of the practical equality existing between the two representations of St. Paul; but, in addition to the general similarity to the frescoes throughout the altarpiece in modes of drawing and coloring and in the draperies, there are further, striking analogies in types. The St. Peter

[12] *Levante*, 47.

[13] Before the civil war: I have not learned whether the retable or any of its parts survived.

[14] See vol. VI, pp. 290, 298, and 386.

FIG. 125. "MIGUEL ESTEVE." STS. ANTHONY ABBOT AND PAUL,
SECTION OF RETABLE. PARISH CHURCH, LUCENA DEL CID
(*Photo. Archivo Mas*)

at Lucena is like the St. Bartholomew in the town hall; the Sts. Agatha and Lucy are derived from the same model as the St. John; and the Santiago of the predella recalls the St. Matthew. The Sts. Anthony and Paul very plainly display their origin in Paolo da San Leocadio's precedents, and it is difficult to understand the Leonardesque character of the Santiago and the Baptist apart from an absorption of the phase of Italianism introduced into Valencia by the Fernandos.

The painting from which Esteve derived his former sobriquet of the Master of the Miracle of Cologne is a small panel of undiscovered provenience in the Colegio del Patriarca at Valencia (Fig. 126). The theme that it embodies in glorification of the Rosary I have discussed in former volumes [15] when describing other versions. The gentleman of Cologne, kneeling in the lower right corner, is saved from the assassin's knife by an apparition of Our Lady of the Rosary. He already wears upon his head the garland of roses that she has given him, and, as in other representations of the subject, she is also handing him a specimen of this flower. The man about to strike the blow must be a hired bravo, for the vengeful brother of the victim whom the gentleman of Cologne had slain stands on the left side of the panel awed into a reconciliation by the supernatural vision, holding his sword reversed in a sign of peace, and, with the same intention, abandoning his iron gauntlet upon the pavement beside the cap that his enemy has discarded for the heavenly wreath. A retainer gesticulates in surprise behind the brother, and, in transformation of the scene into the formal composition as of an altarpiece, the Virgin is accompanied by the two lights of the Order that is most intimately connected with the Rosary, Sts. Dominic and Catherine of Siena. The romantically inclined may wish to familiarize themselves with the ingenious interpretation from the sanguinary history of the Borgias read into the picture by Bertaux,[16] who was not conversant with the sensational tale of the gentleman of Cologne. Not only must we discard Bertaux's idea, but it is more than doubtful whether the author meant to introduce into this frequent subject of Spanish iconography even a covert reference to Cesare Borgia's alleged murder of his brother Giovanni and his subsequent humiliation. The untooled gold background looks as if it had been modernized.

The evidence supplied by the little panel would perhaps not in

---

[15] VII, pp. 260 and 501–503; VIII, p. 185; and IX, p. 825.
[16] *Gazette des beaux-arts*, 1908, I, 216–220.

FIG. 126. "MIGUEL ESTEVE." MIRACLE OF THE GENTLEMAN OF
COLOGNE. COLEGIO DEL PATRIARCA, VALENCIA
(*Photo. Archivo Mas*)

itself have been sufficient to reveal the same authorship as the frescoes of the Ayuntamiento, although the countenance of the younger man at the lower left is very like that of the St. John; but the Lucena retable furnishes the intermediate and conclusive link between the three works, since, as Tormo recognized, it incorporates precisely the style of the picture in the Colegio del Patriarca. Returning, for instance, to the theme of the Madonna of the Rosary, Esteve literally repeats, except for the standing posture in this picture, the figure in the *remate* at Lucena. The dependence upon Paolo da San Leocadio is not quite so tangible as in some of his other works, and yet the four actors in the foreground and the Virgin are only more than customarily weak descendants of his types. Indeed, were it not for the interest of the subject, the panel would have slight value, betraying Esteve at his worst. The forms are deficient in "tactile values"; the characteristically heavy draperies are here stiff and unpleasant in their lines; and the rigid and feebly unconvincing posture of the assassin is a measure of the painter's shortcomings. The feminine and young masculine types are so similar to those of the Cabanyes Master that the phenomenon is scarcely to be explained only by a joint debt [17] to Paolo da San Leocadio, and we must assume the influence of one of the two debtors upon the other, probably of the Cabanyes Master, who is the better technician, upon Esteve. The visage of the assassin is the only passage reminiscent of the art of the Fernandos.

Bertaux [18] wished to discover in the panel's author Paolo da San Leocadio's son, Pedro Pablo, whom we do not even know to have become a painter; [19] but the French scholar evidently confused Pedro Pablo with Felipe Pablo who may or may not have been another son of Paolo, who really did follow the pictorial profession, and in whom Mayer [20] proposed to recognize the personality called the Master of the Miracle of Cologne. The documented retable of St. Dominic by Felipe Pablo, [21] however, reveals that he possessed a style very different not only from Esteve's manner but also from Paolo's modes and that he owed much more than Esteve to the Leonardesque strain in Valencian art of the period.

[17] Vol. VI, pp. 395 and 400.
[18] In Michel's *Histoire de l'art*, IV, 2, pp. 910–911.
[19] See above, p. 11.
[20] *Geschichte*, edition of 1922, p. 112.
[21] See above, p. 279.

Tormo, in his book, *Levante*,[22] of 1923, mentions as a possible creation of his Master of the Miracle of Cologne a retable, once more devoted to Our Lady of the Rosary, in an Ermita del Rosario near Caudete (close to Villena and just off the road between Albacete and Alicante), but in my visit to Caudete in 1930 I could not find that any such Ermita or its retable still existed.

Both the Lucena altarpiece and the painting of the Miracle of Cologne are dull performances, but the love of prettiness and sweetness embodied in Esteve's feminine types assumes a pleasant aspect when it affects his imagination, causing him to interpret the early narrative of the Gospels in the rather charming terms of tender domestic *genre*. One example is a small panel hanging on the wall of the entrance to the chapel of the Blessed Sacrament in the parish church of La Jana, just west of Vinaroz (Fig. 127), proving that his popularity in the province of Castellón de la Plana extended beyond Lucena del Cid. The subject is the Dream of St. Joseph, beside whom kneels the angel with a banderole upon which are inscribed in Latin the words from the first chapter of St. Matthew's Gospel, "Joseph, thou son of David, fear not to take unto thee Mary thy wife, for that which is conceived in her is of the Holy Ghost"; but, as in Dello Delli's version of the theme at Salamanca,[23] the interest of the painter is really in the quiet beauty of life within the sacred household. Our Lady has the greater prominence, startled from her reading by perceiving, like her mother, St. Anne, at her side, the supernatural experience of her sleeping spouse, and to the right of the Casa Santa another woman sits spinning at the entrance to an urban street, in the delightful delineation of which Esteve quite surprises us. The face of the Virgin is enough to authenticate the panel as his achievement, comparable especially to the countenances of the martyred maidens in the Lucena altarpiece, but there is much additional evidence, were it necessary, for instance the analogy of the St. Anne to the St. Catherine of Siena in the panel of the Colegio del Patriarca. His leanings towards the Leonardesque movement in the contemporary Valencian school are now incorporated particularly in the St. Joseph and in the spinner.[24]

The second of the pictures belongs to the Provincial Museum at Valencia but is of unstated provenience. Similar in mood and compo-

---

[22] P. 254.　　　　　　　　[23] Vol. III, p. 242.

[24] It is pleasant to discover that I am supported in the attribution to Esteve by the potent authority of Saralegui (*Archivo español de arte*, XIX, 1946, p. 139).

Fig. 127. "MIGUEL ESTEVE." DREAM OF ST. JOSEPH. PARISH CHURCH, LA JANA

sition to the panel at La Jana, it depicts, however, no definite event from the New Testament but transforms the subject of the Holy Family into a dulcet representation of the unostentatious existence in the carpenter's shop during the infancy of Our Lord (Fig. 128). Mary sits at the centre interrupting her needlework, with exactly the same posture and gesture as at La Jana, to watch her Son playing with the symbolic lamb held by the young Baptist, behind whom his mother, St. Elizabeth, intently peruses a book. The *genre* of Our Lady's sewing basket and of her pot of lilies is much featured in the foreground, and further back in the house's loggia at the right St. Joseph plies his trade watched by his dog, which atones for lack of zoological correctness by the sense of alert affection that the artist has succeeded in bestowing upon the pet of the establishment. At the gate stand an elderly gentleman and his wife, probably Sts. Joachim and Anne, relieved against another engaging view of a section of a city, a lagoon with its esplanade and bridges framed in a setting of rocky hills. The vista is filled with the small figures and episodes of every-day activities that enliven the backgrounds of Paolo da San Leocadio and Rodrigo de Osona the younger — among them, in a shepherd's flock, even two rams butting each other. Once more the Virgin's countenance renders the authorship obvious, and the St. Joachim virtually repeats the reconciled brother in the painting of the Miracle of Cologne. The actors most plainly exhibiting the influence of the Fernandos are the Sts. Joseph and Elizabeth. The types of the children and the general note of sweetness in most of Esteve's production but especially here make us wonder whether he may not have added to the inheritance from Leonardo some acquaintance with the seductive models created by Correggio.

The Virgin's face in the Holy Family of the Museum is taken and accommodated to that of a man for the representation of Our Lord in a small panel of the Resurrection that has reached the same collection from an undiscovered source (Fig. 129). The standing Roman soldier at the right also proves the picture to be indisputably a work of Esteve, since even more closely than the St. Joachim in the Holy Family he reiterates the reconciled brother in the Miracle of Cologne. For the composition Esteve drew both upon the version of the theme from Sta. Clara at Gandía by Paolo da San Leocadio and the examples by Llanos and Yáñez.

The aspect of his art that depends most heavily upon the Fernandos

FIG. 128. "MIGUEL ESTEVE." HOLY FAMILY. PROVINCIAL MUSEUM,
VALENCIA

(*Photo. Archivo Mas*)

Fig. 129. "MIGUEL ESTEVE." RESURRECTION.
PROVINCIAL MUSEUM, VALENCIA
(*Photo. Archivo Mas*)

is illustrated by an Annunciation in the Provincial Museum at Valencia (Fig. 130) that Saralegui, among his many brilliant suggestions to me in letters, is almost certainly right in divining to have once formed a part of the retable from which the Resurrection derives. The shape of the panel of the Annunciation is the same, and the dimensions are negligibly less; but Saralegui bases his conclusion also upon such considerations as the similarity of the wood, of the binding irons, and of the phase of Esteve's color. We need not, however, resort to the panel's unity with the Resurrection to authenticate it as a production of Esteve, when style and especially the type of the Virgin are enough to establish it in our inheritance from him. Her face agrees with his general conception of women and youths but more as it appears in the frescoed St. John in the Ayuntamiento of Valencia than in the Madonna in the Holy Family of the Museum.

Still another work by Esteve swells the Museum's possessions, a St. Michael coming from no less a place than the chapel dedicated to him in the larger cloister of the Castillo de Montesa (Fig. 131).[25] We perceive again more of the Leonardesque shape of countenance and chiaroscuro that Esteve owed to the Fernandos, and the archangel's resemblance to the St. John of the Ayuntamiento now reaches almost identity. The curious halo, with its big inner star, is often duplicated at Lucena. Esteve's failure to measure up to the standard of Paolo da San Leocadio has already called for our comment, and a status secondary likewise to that of Yáñez is betrayed by a comparison with the handsome and spirited effigy of St. Michael in his retable of the Last Judgment formerly at Játiva.

A panel of the Madonna, Child, and young St. John by Esteve in the Collection of Carlos Tolrá at Barcelona (Fig. 132) has the double interest of revealing him as more dominated than ordinarily by Yáñez and Llanos and of perhaps reflecting a treatment of the theme by one of them in a lost work. We need look no farther than at the Virgin in order to realize that the panel is Esteve's creation, since the type is a constant in his production and appears at La Jana in a practically identical aspect. Under Italian influence Yáñez did such Madonna-pictures, and it is likely that Esteve, although he may have visited the sister peninsula, got his inspiration in this case from the examples by Fernando, as more immediately at hand, rather than from the foreign

---

[25] Like so much else, I owe my knowledge of its provenience to the friendly offices of Don Leandro de Saralegui.

FIG. 130. "MIGUEL ESTEVE." ANNUNCIATION. PROVINCIAL MUSEUM, VALENCIA

(*Photo. Archivo Mas*)

FIG. 131. "MIGUEL ESTEVE." ST. MICHAEL. PROVINCIAL MUSEUM,
VALENCIA

(*Photo. Archivo Mas*)

FIG. 132. "MIGUEL ESTEVE." MADONNA, CHILD, AND YOUNG ST.
JOHN. TOLRÁ COLLECTION, BARCELONA

(*Photo. Archivo Mas*)

models. The panel is not a copy of either of Yáñez's preserved works of the sort, but, since the somewhat provincial Esteve would hardly have improvised on Leonardesque *motifs*, he may here be translating into his own terms a non-extant painting that one of the Fernandos had executed. The Virgin herself is almost a repetition of the corresponding figure in the Flight into Egypt in their shutters for the retable of the cathedral of Valencia. The composition does not reproduce accurately any known cartoon by Leonardo, but, although the children are elevated to a parapet behind which the Virgin is sitting, the types and arrangement derive ultimately from the Italian's studies and final ideas for the St. Anne of the Louvre.

Saralegui [26] has published, as at least once in private possession at Valencia, what seems to be a practical reproduction of the Tolrá panel, finding it impossible to decide to his own satisfaction whether the few slight variations mean that Esteve made a scarcely changed replica or that the two panels are really one and the same, with the scarcely perceptible differences to be explained by repainting or its removal. A repainter might have been responsible for the alteration in the activity of the Virgin's left hand, which in the Tolrá panel is somewhat less close to the prototype in the Flight into Egypt of the shutters, but it is doubtful whether he would have made the unimportant and almost purposeless modifications in her halo and in bits of the trees in the background, so that I am inclined to believe that Esteve did two nearly identical treatments of the subject.

After the study of this series of works, the student will require no further verification of Esteve's handicraft in a small retable now in the Collection of Mr. George A. Cluett at Sea Island, Georgia, but once belonging to M. Émile Pares at Paris (Fig. 133). The whole body of the structure is taken up with the scene of the Adoration of the Shepherds, and the only other narrative piece is consigned to the *remate*, the theme so popular in the Valencian school, Christ presenting to His mother the redeemed of the Old Testament, in this instance almost duplicating in composition the Cabanyes Master's versions in his retables of Sts. Dionysius and Margaret formerly in the church of S. Juan del Hospital at Valencia and of St. Peter in the church of S. Esteban in the same city. [27] On the *guardapolvos*, the summit displays,

[26] *Archivo español de arte*, XIX (1946), 139–140.

[27] Vol. VI, pp. 397 and 412. One of the Barón de San Petrillo's many valuable contributions to our knowledge of Valencian art through his historical and heraldic

FIG. 133. "MIGUEL ESTEVE." RETABLE OF ADORATION OF THE
SHEPHERDS. CLUETT COLLECTION, SEA ISLAND,
GEORGIA, U.S.A.

as at Lucena del Cid, the blessing Father, and at the next level are the standing figures of the Virgin and angel of the Annunciation. The other parts of the right side of the *guardapolvos* are modern, but the corresponding sections at the left belong to the original structure, a bust of St. Francis on the cross-piece and then full-lengths of the Magdalene and the Baptist. The predella, if it ever existed, has been lost. Once more the Virgin in the Adoration of the Shepherds patently incorporates Esteve's favorite and easily recognizable type of femininity, and he accommodatingly nearly reproduces for us, in the piping youth at the left, the reconciled brother's associate in the panel of the Colegio del Patriarca. For the St. Joseph he employed the same model that served for the St. Bartholomew in the frescoes of the Valencian town hall. The most Leonardesque figure is the shepherd between the piper and St. Joseph, but the entire composition is directly lifted from the rendering on the Fernandos' shutters of the retable over the high altar of the cathedral of Valencia.

Among the works that cannot with surety be attributed to Miguel Esteve, the two most significant are a Pentecost in the possession of Don Ignacio Lacuadra at Valencia and a Dormition in the Collection of Don Vicente Lassala in the same city, probably deriving from a single original retable of the Seven Joys of the Virgin like the altarpieces by Paolo da San Leocadio. The paintings have been generally ascribed to the Fernandos,[28] and I myself long clung to this attribution; but, gradually persuaded by the keen perception of Don Leandro de Saralegui,[29] I am now disposed to remove them from the roster of their authentic achievements and to credit them to Miguel Esteve in a phase of his output when he was following their manner more closely than usual and almost succeeded in attaining their technical level. It is in the Dormition (Fig. 134) that the ties with Esteve are most tangible. We do not find in the Fernandos types quite like the Apostle in the lower right corner or the St. John, with the palm, above the Vir-

erudition is his discovery that on May 26, 1523, a notary, Pedro Luis Mercader, founded a benefice of St. Peter in the church of S. Esteban and that, since the retable bears escutcheons both of Mercader and his wife, it must have been commissioned by them and so would be dated in 1523 or shortly thereafter. The name of the wife, Jerónima de Villa, would help to account for the presence of St. Jerome in the predella. See the Barón's article in *Archivo español de arte*, XIV (1940–1941), 206–207. The retable perished in the disturbances of the Spanish civil war.

[28] See Tramoyeres Blasco in *Archivo de arte valenciano*, V (1919), 87 and 96, and González Martí in *Museum* (Barcelona), IV (1914–1916), 402.

[29] *Archivo español de arte*, XVIII (1945), 21.

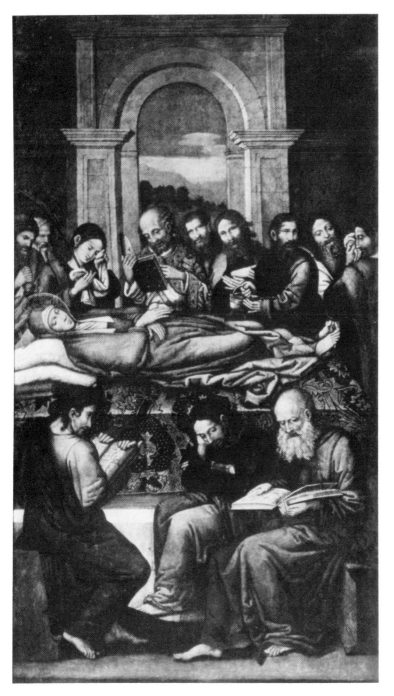

FIG. 134. "MIGUEL ESTEVE(?)." DORMITION. LASSALA COLLECTION,
VALENCIA

(*Photo. Archivo Mas*)

gin's head; but the former is highly and almost peculiarly characteristic of Esteve, as in the St. Philip in the Ayuntamiento at Valencia,
and the latter should be compared with the mode in which Esteve
represented him also in the series of the Ayuntamiento. In the Santiago and Baptist of the predella in the Lucena retable, he gets almost
as near to certain unhealthily staring countenances by the Fernandos
as in the two Apostles next to St. Peter in the Lassala Dormition. The
execution has less of the *sfumatezza* of the artists whom he was imitating and is marked by a kind of smoothness alien to them. The two
fine studies of seated Apostles in the foreground of the Dormition by
Yáñez in the shutters of the cathedral are repeated in the Lassala
version with slight variations, which, however, make them somewhat
less trenchant. As many as two brilliant brocades linger on from
the past of Spanish art — over Our Lady's couch and in St. Peter's
cope.

The provenience of the Lacuadra Pentecost (Fig. 135) from the
same retable is strongly implied by the identical phase of the presumptive Miguel Esteve's style, by the analogous shape of the picture, and
by the general correspondence in the architectural background. If it
were not for this connection, one would be less inclined to detach the
Pentecost from the group of the Fernandos' own works, since the
approximation to their fashions is more pronounced and the tokens of
Esteve's manner less concrete. The audacious innovations in the conception of the scene that Yáñez essayed on the shutters in the cathedral are, to be sure, renounced, but, although there is a reversion to
the traditional Spanish composition, originality is still exhibited by
breaking somewhat the usual regularity in the masses of figures and
by the way in which the manifestations of spiritual afflatus are varied
in the Apostles. The St. John is more Leonardesque than any figure
indubitably by Esteve, and the strange psychology of the Virgin in
the rendering of the theme in the cathedral is almost reiterated in the
countenance bestowed upon her in the Lacuadra panel. Furthermore,
there are technical ventures in the panel that one would scarcely have
expected of the rather unambitious Esteve. As in the representation
of the Baptist's decollation at Marchena by Alejo Fernández, the
interest is increased by a cross lighting from a large window at the
left, and the zoological alertness of the Fernandos is suggested by
the fact that the dove of the Holy Spirit is much less of a symbol even
than in the treatment of Pentecost in the shutters.

FIG. 135. "MIGUEL ESTEVE(?)." PENTECOST.
LACUADRA COLLECTION, VALENCIA

Nevertheless, it is not only because of the above-mentioned relations with the Dormition that we should perhaps — but only *perhaps* — transfer the Lacuadra panel from the Fernandos to the count of Miguel Esteve. Close correspondences with his types are not entirely lacking. The aged Apostle who, just to the left of the Virgin, is looking up at the dove almost duplicates the St. Paul in the Ayuntamiento of Valencia, and it seems impossible that two different artists should have executed faces so nearly identical as those of the Apostle whose head is framed by the door in the Pentecost and the figure second from St. Peter at the right in the Dormition. The explanation may be that in the retable from which the Lassala and Lacuadra compartments derive Esteve was working under the Fernandos' immediate supervision.

It is difficult to select from the followers of Yáñez and Llanos the individual to whom there should be assigned a panel of Santiago that until the civil war could be seen in the Diocesan Museum at Valencia, having entered the institution from the church of S. Bartolomé in this city (Fig. 136), but the resemblance to the St. James Major of the Lucena retable and the character of the drapery make Miguel Esteve the safest bet. The figure was relieved against one of the old gold backgrounds, rising above a parapet and tooled, in variation from the usual Valencian practice, throughout its expanse.

5. The Alcoraz Master

The follower of Yáñez and Llanos whom we linger here to examine is so much more handicapped than the Grifo Master by technical shortcomings that he would scarcely merit our consideration, if it were not for the sake of the completeness at which these volumes aim and if he did not partially compensate for his failure to give us aesthetic pleasure by piquing our interest through iconographic peculiarities and through the archaizing employment of his craft, in one instance, for a kind of ecclesiastical decoration that belongs chiefly to the Middle Ages. His activity, so far as I have been able to discover its examples, was centered at Teruel, where, by reason of the geographical location of the city, Valencian and Aragonese artists disputed patronage. The chief work by him that has come within my cognizance is a retable of St. George in the church, at Teruel, dedicated to St. Michael. Of the compartments, which are still set in their original Plateresque frames,

FIG. 136. "MIGUEL ESTEVE(?)." ST. JAMES MAJOR. DIOCESAN
MUSEUM, VALENCIA
(*Photo. Archivo Mas*)

the principal one and its two flanking sections incorporate the story of St. George's miraculous appearance, in 1096, to help Peter I of Aragon win the battle of Alcoraz (near Huesca) against the Moors, thus supplying me with the pseudonym for the painter that I have used above as a heading. The manifestation of the great warrior saint to assist the Christians to a victory over the infidels we have found to be more than once a constituent of retables of St. George, but we have been bothered by the question whether in the early Valencian retables of the Centenar de la Pluma and at Jérica it was the battle of Alcoraz that was intended or the corresponding Valencian defeat of the Moslems, with the same supernatural aid, at El Puig de Enesa in 1237.[1] In the Teruel altarpiece the representations in the lateral sections leave no doubt that it is the fight at Alcoraz with which we have to do, since they are not related of the combat at El Puig; and, in distinction from the two other retables, the subject is given the importance of expansion over three compartments.

St. George upon his steed dominates the scene of the struggle in the principal compartment; behind him there charge onward the Christian knights carrying a banner adorned with the heraldic bars of Aragon; and on the earth lie three of the four royal Moorish heads alleged to have been picked up on the field after the victory. I have not discovered in the accounts of the battle a reference to the cross rising from a tree on a hill in the distance. A cross set upon an eminence is said to have once commemorated the fight at El Puig de Enesa, but this one consideration will not counterbalance the sure allusions to the battle of Alcoraz in the lateral compartments. The panel at the left side displays St. George proceeding to the encounter with the warrior mounted behind him on the same horse who is reputed to have miraculously appeared to accompany him and is described either as a nobleman of the Moncada family or as a German emperor's son, marvelously transported by St. George from the battle of Antioch, fought on the same day as Alcoraz, to the Spanish arena of conflict. In the panel at the right we see the Christian barons presenting to Peter I the heads of the four slain Moorish kings and the shield, with the blazon of a white ground crossed with red, that had been carried

---

[1] See my vol. VI, pp. 582–583. Ricardo del Arco has recently championed anew the identification of the battle of Alcoraz in the retable of the Centenar de la Pluma (*Boletín de la Sociedad Española de Excursiones*, LI, 1943, pp. 296 ff.), but Saralegui takes the cudgels up against him, maintaining that it is rather the battle of El Puig de Enesa which is depicted (*Arte español*, XV, 1944, p. 54, n. 1).

by St. George, prophetic of the fact that among the insignia of the Aragonese sovereigns there was henceforth to be included a flag in which each of the four parts made by a cross was occupied by one of the heads.[2]

With iconographic harmony the subjects and their arrangement at the higher level of the retable correspond to the scenes of Alcoraz below. St. George's fight with the dragon is placed directly above the principal compartment, which exhibits his prowess in the Aragonese battle, and at the sides are two related themes, the princess leading the conquered monster with her girdle and the saint within the city giving it the *coup de grâce* in the presence of the king, queen, and their daughter. The Lamentation over the Dead Christ at the centre of the predella is set between further episodes of the martyr's story. At the left are two tortures which I have not found in any of the other Spanish cycles devoted to St. George, despite their multiple gory representations of his extended agonies,[3] but the first of the pair of subjects, his insertion in a heated bull of metal, is included in the late Gothic, Flemish altarpiece by Jan Borremans in the Musée des Arts Décoratifs at Brussels.[4] The second panel (Fig. 137) shows him suffering the amputation of his feet while his already severed hands are cooking in a pan in the foreground! The corresponding scenes at the right of the Pietà are his ultimate decapitation and the interment of his body, clad in a shroud ornamented with his red cross and lowered into a tomb likewise marked with his escutcheon, as an angel bears his soul to heaven.

The types of humanity and pictorial modes plainly declare their derivation from the current in Valencian painting set in motion by the Fernandos, particularly in the cases of the princess conducting the dragon, the St. George undergoing amputation, and the aged spectator of this atrocity; but the models created by the Alcoraz Master's inspirers have degenerated, in his hands, almost to the level of rusticity.

Together with the interest of his iconography, he has the adventitious significance of continuing the representation of figured subjects in frontals, whereas this early mediaeval custom had generally by the

---

[2] For an account of these prodigies of the battle of Alcoraz, see the article by Del Arco already cited and the entry in the *Diccionario enciclopédico hispano-americano*, admirable, like the other articles in this publication, for its compression of accurate information.

[3] Vols. II, p. 398; III, p. 62; and VI, p. 583.

[4] See my *History of European and American Sculpture*, I, fig. 42.

FIG. 137. THE ALCORAZ MASTER. AMPUTATION OF ST. GEORGE'S
FEET, SECTION OF RETABLE. S. MIGUEL, TERUEL

(*Photo. Archivo Mas*)

beginning of the sixteenth century yielded in antependia to mere pure design. The proof is a frontal of wood on the altar of the chapel in the cathedral of Teruel that contains the retable by the Florida Master.[5] Even in this instance the body of the antependium is adorned with an expanse of merely decorative patterns, which, however, give way at the centre to a small version of the Purification (Fig. 138). Execution by the hand of the author of the retable in S. Miguel is obvious not only in the chiaroscuro and indeed in the whole stylistic procedure but also in the emergence of the retable's very types. The Virgin, for example, should be compared with the princess leading the dragon, and the St. Joseph with the old man gloating over St. George's dismemberment. The Alcoraz Master's right to be numbered, albeit humbly, among the disciples of Yáñez and Llanos is even more apparent than in the retable of St. George, for the woman holding the candles is directly copied from such figures by the partners as the Marys in the Lamentation of the cathedral at Valencia.

6. Martín Gómez the Elder

It is curious that this painter has received little or no consideration from historians of art when his style is soundly established by the existence of at least one documented production and turns out to be not only a partial but also a competent adaptation of the manner that Fernando Yáñez displayed at Cuenca. He deserves rescue from oblivion likewise because he won so much appreciation in this city that in the third quarter of the sixteenth century he was the principal painter for the cathedral, executing in the edifice from *c.* 1552 to *c.* 1574 [1] a whole series of achievements. The reason for appending the designation, "the elder," to his name is that there was a slightly later painter also called Martín Gómez whom we know through his traceable activity in the Escorial from 1598 to 1601. Ceán Bermúdez [2] and succeeding writers have generally confused the two masters, but the documented works in the Escorial [3] indisputably demonstrate that, as Tormo [4] has the credit of suspecting, their author was a different individual from Yáñez's follower and inferior to him in craft.

[5] Vol. VIII, p. 474.   [1] See the following paragraph and p. 348.
[2] *Diccionario*, II, 203.
[3] Julián Zarco Cuevas, *Pintores españoles en San Lorenzo el Real de El Escorial*, Madrid, 1931, p. 131.
[4] *Archivo español de arte y arqueología*, VIII (1932), 87.

FIG. 138. THE ALCORAZ MASTER. PURIFICATION, CENTRE OF FRONTAL. CATHEDRAL, TERUEL

(Photo. Archivo Mas)

We arrive at the personality and style of Martín Gómez I through a statement of Ceán Bermúdez,[5] based on the archives of the cathedral of Cuenca, to the effect that he painted in 1552 Sts. Matthew, Lawrence, and Michael in a retable on the *trascoro* of the church. The retable exists in the chapel of St. Matthew at this place in the edifice but only with the paired effigies of the Evangelist and St. Lawrence; and, since they are set in their original frame and entirely accommodated to it, without any room for a St. Michael, and since no visitor to Cuenca, not even Ponz, publishing his third volume[6] in 1774, records a St. Michael in the altarpiece, we are confronted with a difficult problem. The document may have specified a figure of St. Michael which by a change of program was never carried out, and Ceán perhaps did no more than read the document, not taking the trouble to verify whether the extant retable conformed in all points; or above the large compartment of the coupled Sts. Matthew and Lawrence, which now constitutes the whole retable, there might have been originally a separately framed pinnacle with a representation of the archangel that early disappeared, and as a matter of fact such pinnacles, with various themes, surmount all the other altarpieces by Martín Gómez in the cathedral. Inasmuch, moreover, as the church contains a chapel of St. Michael, though not on the *trascoro* but opening on the nave, it is conceivable that Gómez executed his figure for this destination and that Ceán misinterpreted the document's language in regard to the picture's location, but in any case no painting of the archangel by the master is now to be seen in the chapel or indeed elsewhere in the cathedral's precincts. It is significant indeed that, in declaring the sculptor and architect Jamete to have carved the frame of the retable by Gómez, Ceán[7] describes it merely as of Sts. Matthew and Lawrence, with no mention of a St. Michael.

José Mariá Quadrado and Vicente de la Fuente[8] state that the records of the cathedral of Cuenca show Martín Gómez to have painted for the church three works which by reason of the writers' tantalizing lack of precision cannot be really identified, an altarpiece of Santiago, another retable for the chapter of canons, and "an image that stood at the entrance of the main portal." The last of these

---

[5] *Op. cit.*, II, 203.

[6] *Viaje de España*, III, *Carta primera*, paragraph 42.

[7] *Op. cit.*, VI, 4.

[8] *Castilla la Nueva* (in the series *España, sus monumentos y artes*), Barcelona, II, 1886, p. 277, n. 2.

commissions apparently consisted merely in the polychromy of a statue that no longer exists, and, since the altarpiece of Santiago also seems not to be preserved, we have no means of determining whether here likewise Gómez only colored a sculptured monument or whether he did for it actual pictures. We perhaps but far from certainly ought to recognize as fragments of the retable for the chapter of canons two panels of the Birth of Christ and Purification which internal evidence proves him surely to have executed and which at least as early as the end of the eighteenth century have been known as decorating the Sala Capitular de Invierno.

Although other works of Gómez expand our understanding of his capabilities in subordinate characteristics, the essence of his style is quite adequately set forth even in the restricted limits of his securely documented retable which consists only of standing figures of St. Matthew, with the angel as his regular attribute, and of St. Lawrence (Fig. 139).[9] We can at once define the style concisely as a worthy offshoot from the manner of Fernando Yáñez modified by the increasing technical knowledge of the Renaissance. The origins of the types of humanity are found in Fernando's works at Cuenca, but we shall later adduce evidence suggesting that Gómez may well have been conversant even with his Valencian productions. St. Lawrence combines the emphasis of Yáñez upon the bony structure of the countenance, as in the St. Dominic of the Albornoz Crucifixion, with this master's addiction to piously upturned faces; the St. Matthew derives from such figures as the Prophets at the sides and the Sts. Peter and Paul in the predella of the Crucifixion; and the *putto* who acts the part of the Evangelist's angel belongs in the class of the children who relieve in the predella the horror of St. Catherine's decollation. One of Martín's individual peculiarities is illustrated by the St. Matthew, his predilection for wind-blown hair; and in general the inheritance from Yáñez is so far translated into his follower's own distinctive terms that no artist's hand is more easily recognizable. Another of these terms is his treatment of draperies: he takes the multiplied, narrow folds in which his teacher liked to dispose fabrics and twists them into more numerous and pronounced curves, thus signalizing, as in some other respects, a further advance toward mannerism. In accordance with the undulating tendency, he depicts the end of Lawrence's dalmatic as bending forth to rest on the saint's emblem, the

[9] The dimensions are 1.90 metres in height by 1.00 in width.

FIG. 139. MARTÍN GÓMEZ THE ELDER. STS. MATTHEW AND
LAWRENCE. CATHEDRAL, CUENCA

(*Photo. Pando*)

FIG. 140. MARTÍN GÓMEZ THE ELDER. PURIFICATION, FRAGMENT
OF RETABLE. CATHEDRAL, CUENCA
(*Photo. Pando*)

gridiron, but the combination of the gridiron and the vestment has also another purpose, the rationalization, so to speak, of the emblem, so that it is more than an arbitrary symbol and performs an actual function. Correspondingly the angel, St. Matthew's attribute, not only serves as a lectern for him but obligingly holds his inkwell and supports his own foot upon another volume of the Evangelist's writings. In a formal composition for an altarpiece such as this, Gómez still retains the old convention of a gold background, diapering it with vertical bands of Plateresque *motifs*. It is difficult to detect either in the altarpiece or elsewhere in his output any trace of a perpetuation of his teacher's interest in Raphael.

Next in order, as just conceivably documented achievements [10] of Martín Gómez, we turn naturally to the large [11] panels of the Birth of Christ and Purification (Fig. 140) in the Sala Capitular de Invierno in the cathedral of Cuenca, in any case demonstrated by internal evidence to be autographic productions of his and possibly remaining to us from a single, otherwise lost altarpiece. We remember the panels chiefly because the Purification strongly implies that he had carefully examined the shutters done by Yáñez and Llanos for the retable of the cathedral of Valencia. The whole left half of the picture is nearly a replica of the corresponding section in the version in the shutters, and, unless we stretch our imaginations to guess that Yáñez had repeated the composition in a non-extant rendering in Cuenca or the region, we are bound to believe that Gómez had studied under him during the earlier years of the sixteenth century in Valencia or at least had made at some time of his life a journey to the city. The woman at the left with the basket of doves upon her head reiterates virtually line by line the correspondingly placed handmaid in the Valencian panel. Like so much else in Gómez's art, the nature of her face goes back, through Yáñez, to Leonardo, with whose creations there is no reason for assuming that Gómez had any direct contact, but the slight alteration of the prototype afforded by Yáñez, which derives from the Mona Lisa, results in a kind of feminine countenance that peculiarly belongs to our master and is employed by him more than once.

In a prominent spot at the extreme left of the Nativity he intro-

[10] See above, p. 340.
[11] Both are 1.10 metres wide, and the heights are nearly equal, 1.60 metres for the Birth and 1.80 for the Purification.

duces a favorite figure of both Fernandos, the shepherd carrying a lamb upon his shoulders, whom Yáñez had depicted in the background even of his version of the theme at the top of the principal retable in the Albornoz chapel in the cathedral of Cuenca, but I cannot perceive any other debts to this version in Gómez's panel. The careering horseman in the left background is closer to the cavaliers in the Epiphany of the Valencian shutters than to those in the rendering by Yáñez over a lateral altar of the Albornoz chapel. Neither in the steed nor in the beasts of the shepherds in the central background nor in the ox and ass in the right foreground nor elsewhere in his paintings does Gómez show himself by any means the peer of the Fernandos as an *animalier*. The two standing shepherds in the background exhibit his fondness for flying locks of hair; and the whole picture not only exemplifies his general attainment of more closely knit compositions than those of his inspirer, but it also is more elaborate than Yáñez's manipulations of the subject. The manger of the Infant Jesus is surrounded by a bevy of child-angels dropping flowers on Him, while other blossoms and petals, as well as multiplied banderoles inscribed with *Gloria in excelsis*, flutter down from the skies. Over the parapet behind, there lean three shepherds, who embody something of the inventiveness of Yáñez in effective poses.

Both the Nativity and the Purification illustrate a recurrent characteristic of Gómez that fails to emerge in the retable of Sts. Matthew and Lawrence, a relaxation of the legacy from his teacher into greater suavity.

The most comprehensive work that the style shows him indubitably to have painted in the cathedral of Cuenca is the retable of the Coronation over the altar of a chapel on the ambulatory. The principal piece represents the Trinity placing the crown upon the head of the Virgin as she rises into the heavens amidst supporting angels (Fig. 141), and round about, in subordinate compartments, are seven scenes from her story, the Meeting at the Golden Gate, her Nativity, the Annunciation, Visitation, Birth of Christ, Epiphany, and Purification. In a pinnacle, as so frequently in Valencian altarpieces, God the Father bestows His benediction. The figures in the predella are half-lengths: in the central panel, the blessing Christ of the Eucharist between Sts. Peter and Paul; in the left compartment, Sts. Matthew, Thomas (with the emblem of the carpenter's rule), and John Evangelist; and in the balancing division at the right, Sts. James Major, Andrew, and

Fig. 141. MARTÍN GÓMEZ THE ELDER. CORONATION AND BITS OF
LATERAL COMPARTMENTS, SECTION OF RETABLE.
CATHEDRAL, CUENCA

(*Photo. Pando*)

Bartholomew. Of these Apostles, St. Matthew has the distinction of being singled out by carrying a banderole inscribed in Castilian with his name, probably because he enjoyed a special cult in a chapel [12] dedicated to him in the church.

The undertaking seems to have been regarded by Gómez as a matter of routine and not to have stimulated him to any great exertion. The compositions of the lateral scenes from the life of the Virgin are traditional, with almost no reminiscences of the treatments of the events by Yáñez, however much the types of actors are indebted to him. In the Purification Gómez now preserves from the rendering in the Valencian shutters only the handmaid carrying the basket, literally repeating his conception of her in the panel of the Sala Capitular; and his own adaptation of the face of the Mona Lisa incorporated in her countenance appears in the retable also in the attendants in the Meeting at the Golden Gate and the Visitation (as may be seen in the bits of the episodes comprised in the illustration, Fig. 141, in the former case at the lower left and in the latter at the upper right). The Meeting at the Golden Gate includes another of the lamb-bearing shepherds taken over from Yáñez, who, however, introduces no such actor into his version of the subject at Valencia. In the Purification Gómez reverts even more conspicuously to the practices of mediaeval Spanish painting than in the retention of a diapered gold background in his altarpiece of Sts. Matthew and Lawrence, for not only does he garb the priest in one of the brilliant, old auric brocades but he follows the frequent habit of his predecessors by emphasizing the frankly decorative function of the brocade through presenting its pattern in bald frontality.

He appears to have spent still less effort upon the retable in the chapel of the Pozo family, also in the ambulatory, perhaps turning over some of the execution to his shop, for instance the pinnacle of the Crucifixion. The chief compartment, beneath the pinnacle, represents the Assumption (Fig. 142, telescoped, as often, with the Coronation, which, however, is more subordinated than in the example discussed in the last paragraph). The main body of the structure consists, in addition, only of four narrow panels set between pilasters at the sides and depicting pairs of standing saints, Cosmas and Damian at the upper level and the Catherines of Alexandria and Siena at the lower, all relieved against gold backgrounds. In the predella, the Epiphany

[12] See above, p. 339.

Fig. 142. MARTÍN GÓMEZ THE ELDER. ASSUMPTION, CENTRE OF
RETABLE, CHAPEL OF THE POZO FAMILY, CATHEDRAL, CUENCA
(*Photo. Pando*)

is spread out, by the inclusion of the Magi's suite, to cover the long, horizontal space of the central division; and the smaller, lateral sections are adorned with half-lengths of sacred personages, at the left the Baptist, whose hair flutters forth in the mode that Gómez preferred, and at the right the figure who provides really the principal interest of the retable, the patron bishop of Cuenca, a St. Julian, who occupied the see at the beginning of the thirteenth century. The interest is an iconographic one because he is so rarely encountered and because the picture embodies the most distinctive fact about him, since he is seen plying, with the aid of his servant, the industry by which he humbly earned their livelihood, basket-making.[13]

At the east end of the cathedral there is still another chapel containing a retable proclaimed by stylistic evidence to be an achievement of Martín Gómez, in this instance honoring the two St. Johns (Fig. 143).[14] Its importance lies in the fact that a Castilian inscription on the base dates it in 1574, thus carrying the master to the latest moment of his life that we know. The words of the inscription state that the retable was set up in 1574 [15] as a memorial to the canon and dean of the cathedral, Juan de Barreda, who died at the beginning of July in this year at the advanced age of ninety-five and who provided by an endowment for the recitation of the *Salve, Regina* in the church on Saturdays and on certain feasts. The paintings, set in the customary handsome Plateresque frames that enhance the beauty of Gómez's creations, comprise only: two panels with effigies of the St. Johns standing in landscapes the winds of which, as regularly, have tousled their locks; and a semicircular *remate* of the Crucifixion.

He was manifestly the author also of an analogous, simple retable [16] of unascertained provenience and now in the Museo Diocesano attached to the cathedral of Cuenca, which exhibits as its central theme the Last Supper, composed, according to one of the old Spanish schemes for the subject, about a round table (Fig. 144). The narrow lateral compartments display for our veneration between sculptured, Plateresque colonnettes, St. Vincent (with one of his ordinary emblems, a raven) and St. Christopher; and the structure includes, be-

---

[13] Different, of course, from the more famous layman, St. Julian Hospitator. For the episcopal St. Julian of Cuenca, see the Bollandists under the day of his feast, January 28, and P. Guérin, *Les petits Bollandistes*, II, 88.

[14] The dimensions are approximately 3 metres in height by 2.30 in width.

[15] Quadrado and De la Fuente (*op. cit.*, II, 288, n. 1) have misread the date as 1624.

[16] The dimensions are 2.10 metres in height by 1.86 in width.

Fig. 143. MARTÍN GÓMEZ THE ELDER. RETABLE OF THE TWO
ST. JOHNS. CATHEDRAL, CUENCA

(*Photo. Pando*)

FIG. 144. MARTÍN GÓMEZ THE ELDER. RETABLE OF LAST SUPPER.
DIOCESAN MUSEUM, CUENCA
(*Photo. Pando*)

FIG. 145. MARTÍN GÓMEZ THE ELDER. ST. JOHN EVANGELIST BOILED
IN OIL. DIOCESAN MUSEUM, CUENCA

(*Photo. Pando*)

sides, a pinnacle of the Annunciation. The genesis of the style of Gómez in Yáñez's creations is illustrated — to choose just one example — by the vivid resemblance of the hieratic Saviour in the Last Supper to Fernando's superb Christ in the panel of the Cremer Collection.[17] On the dalmatic of St. Vincent, as on the cope of the priest in the Purification in the retable of the Coronation, Gómez still clings to the mediaeval convention of refusing to sacrifice the ornamental effect of the bold pattern in the fabric by giving it the lines that it would naturally assume.

The Museo Diocesano of Cuenca, harbors a panel [18] again plainly by Gómez and depicting St. John Evangelist boiled in oil, probably the relic of a retable whose original location has been forgotten (Fig. 145). One of his characteristically compact compositions, it not only exemplifies his fondness, a legacy from Yáñez, for introducing children in the rôles of spectators (as in the Purification in the Sala Capitular), but also affords a final instance of direct lifting of an actor from his master's production, the executioner at the right holding a halberd, whose attitude was inspired by such figures of Fernando as the shepherd resting upon a staff with head bowed at a piquant angle in the Meeting at the Golden Gate in the Valencian shutters and the similarly posed St. Joseph in the Cuenca Epiphany.

7. PAINTINGS IN THE SCHOOL OF THE FERNANDOS NOT ATTRIBUTABLE TO ANY DEFINED PERSONALITIES

The most important work of this class is a retable in the church of S. Juan Bautista at Albacete, which, of two such altarpieces in the edifice that were first properly treated by Tormo, alone escaped the havoc of the Spanish civil war. Its significance lies in the fact that it was painted by a late follower of the Fernandos who, like Martín Gómez the Elder, has practically passed into the modes of the High Renaissance and who indeed is stylistically related to Gómez, though not identical with him. In the course of my further studies in Spanish art it is quite possible that I shall come upon other productions by his hand, discovering his actual name or creating, for him, a sobriquet, a distinction that he well merits as a pleasantly capable performer in his profession.

---

[17] See above, p. 227.
[18] The dimensions are 1.48 metres in height by 1.31 in width.

At the time of my visit to Albacete in 1930, the retable that still remains to us adorned the westernmost chapel on the Epistle side of the church [1] and seemed to have kept its original frames for the painted panels, which were grouped about a probably later statue of the risen Christ at the centre. In the main body of the structure, the two lower panels depicted the Annunciation and the Nativity, and the two upper, the Agony in the Garden and the Resurrection (Fig. 146). The predella marshalled in pairs Sts. James Major and Andrew, Isaiah and Solomon, and Sts. Agatha and Barbara; but I believe that the Apostles and virgin martyrs disappeared in the war, although fortunately the rest of the paintings were saved. The inscription on the scroll accompanying Isaiah is the familiar prophecy of the virgin birth in the fourteenth verse of his seventh chapter, and the words on Solomon's banderole are the second verse of the second chapter of the Song of Songs.

Tormo [2] once assigned all the panels to a pupil of the Fernandos, but his later dictum [3] was that they came largely from the brush of the anonymous artist who did the frescoes in the fully developed style of the Renaissance in the sacristy of the church and that only the Annunciation and Nativity were executed by a painter of the beginning of the Cinquecento, whom he no longer declared the partners to have influenced. I am confident that his earlier opinion was the correct one and that all the panels emanated from a single shop which continued the Fernandos' manner but in which the (no longer extant?) Sts. James, Andrew, Agatha, and Barbara might possibly have been handed over to an assistant.

The still Leonardesque types stem from the Fernandos, though less markedly than do those of Martín Gómez, and it may be that the Albacete painter derived them largely at second hand from Gómez, of whom much suggests that he was perhaps a disciple. He appears, however, to have known directly productions of the partners and their circle, which the advice of Gómez might have led him to examine. In the Resurrection, the postures of Christ and of the guardsman raising his shield have actual counterparts in the version in the Valencian

[1] Tormo in 1908 (*Cultura española*, XI, p. 778) first set this retable in an apsidal chapel, but in his *Levante* of 1923 (p. 310) he describes it as in the place that I have specified. I do not know where in the church, after the war, the panels now are or how they have been put together.

[2] *Cultura española*, XI (1908), 778.

[3] *Levante*, 1923, p. 310.

FIG. 146. SCHOOL OF YÁÑEZ AND LLANOS. RESURRECTION, SECTION
OF RETABLE. S. JUAN BAUTISTA, ALBACETE

shutters (although the Saviour is thus depicted by Yáñez also in the Albornoz retable at Cuenca), and we ought possibly to seek in the Valencian version less close sources for the attitudes of the other soldiers, who may derive likewise from the rendering [4] by a painter under the Fernandos' influence, Miguel Esteve. For the Virgin and St. Joseph of the Nativity, the master could have had vaguely in mind the precedents in the treatment in the cathedral of Valencia, even, for instance, copying the detail of the carefully studied, foreshortened hand of Christ's foster-father according to one of Yáñez's special technical interests; but he was conceivably familiar also with the Benzaria Epiphany of which we have conjectured Yáñez to have been the author.[5] Except for the difference in sex, the profile Virgin at Albacete is more similar to the kneeling Magus in this Epiphany than to Our Lady in the Nativity of the shutters; two shepherds lean over a parapet at the left like the spectators of the Adoration of the Wise Men (and more analogously than in Martín Gómez's Nativity in the Sala Capitular at Cuenca); and the sacred event takes place at Albacete and in the Benzaria picture against the setting of a ruin the formation of which is practically identical, opening at the upper left to a vista over the hillsides where in the Nativity the shepherds are amazed by the angelic proclamation and where in the Epiphany the suite of the Magi are waiting.

The style of the Albacete painter is intimately affiliated, as I have already implied, with that of Martín Gómez but more placid, less forceful in its types of human beings, and not quite so sympathetic with mannerism. I once played with the hypothesis that he might be merely a later phase of the Alcira Master, to whom he exhibits some resemblances, as in the fashion of the hair, but the divergences are so much more conspicuous than the similarities that I balk at making the equation. The old habits of the Spanish school persist in the very pronounced decorative detail of a handsome, brocaded golden canopy behind the Virgin of the Annunciation.

For the mere sad sake of a memory I will set down the pertinent data about the other, now lost retable in the church. Its panels were built into a baroque structure over the altar in the third chapel from the west on the Gospel side of the edifice. The bottom zone of the structure contained two wretched canvases of the seventeenth or eighteenth century, and the compartments of the first half of the Cinque-

---

[4] See above, p. 319.   [5] See above, p. 267.

cento occupied only the upper tiers, at the top the Annunciation (with much the same composition as in the other retable) and the Nativity and at the next, lower level the Epiphany and Purification. Here again Tormo changed his opinion. In 1908 [6] he attributed all four panels to a pupil of the Fernandos, but in 1923 [7] he claimed the Annunciation and Nativity for Yáñez himself and gave the other two pieces to a not very faithful imitator of Llanos. The judgments which I find recorded in my notes of 1930 are that I was not entirely unwilling to accept a difference in authorship in the two tiers but that I could not bring myself to believe that either of the Fernandos executed the Annunciation and Nativity. The compartments of the Epiphany and Purification, slightly darker in tonality, seemed to me the creation of some follower of theirs less expert than the author of the other two sections, indulging in more elongated forms and a prettier, more Correggesque type of Virgin. In both pairs the traits of the Fernandos and their school emerged clearly. For instance, the St. Joseph of the Nativity was the same Leonardesque sort of bald-headed old man, in the great, swelling, classic robes of Fra Bartolommeo, as the Virgin's husband in the rendering of the theme on the shutters of the cathedral of Valencia and as many another figure in this whole phase of Valencian painting; and in the Purification the face of the person behind Our Lady betrayed the violent contrasts of light and shadow in which the partners sometimes showed less allegiance to Leonardo than to Pier di Cosimo. As in the other retable, the Virgin of the Annunciation still knelt in front of a *baldacchino* of gold.

Two further works in the province of Albacete, though tributaries of the stream that sprang from Yáñez and Llanos, appear to have been executed neither by the author of the retable preserved in the church of S. Juan Bautista nor even by a single painter. A seeming dependence upon the composition of the Nativity in this retable is about all that is left of the partners' tradition in a version of the subject in the *parroquia* at Chinchilla de Monte-Aragón (Fig. 147); but in the second work, a pair of panels depicting Sts. Christopher and James Major in the church of the Trinidad at Alcaraz (Fig. 148) in the part of Spain where Yáñez was born and found patronage at the end of his life, the countenance of Santiago still clearly witnesses to a type of person introduced into Spanish art by the Fernandos, and their

---

[6] *Cultura española*, XI, 778.
[7] *Levante*, 310.

FIG. 147. SCHOOL OF YÁÑEZ AND LLANOS. NATIVITY. PARISH
CHURCH, CHINCHILLA DE MONTE-ARAGÓN
(*Photo. Archivo Mas*)

FIG. 148. SCHOOL OF YÁÑEZ AND LLANOS. STS. CHRISTOPHER AND
JAMES MAJOR. CHURCH OF THE TRINIDAD, ALCARAZ
(*Photo. Archivo Mas*)

Leonardesque fondness for equestrian *motifs* in backgrounds persists in a representation, behind the Apostle's effigy, of his discomfiture of the Moors.

A not too highly endowed but loyal follower of theirs was responsible for an altarpiece retaining its original Plateresque frames and now in the Mateu Collection at Barcelona (Fig. 149). The principal theme should probably be interpreted as the birth of the Baptist rather than of the Virgin because the preternaturally mature infant seems distinctly a boy and because an effigy of the Forerunner occupies one of the two flanking compartments as a pendant to St. James Major at the right. In the circular *remate*, the actors in the Annunciation surround a *tondo* of the blessing Eternal Father, and the predella is constituted by busts of virgin martyrs, (reading from left to right) Apollonia, Catherine, Lucy, and Agatha.[8] Since the general formation and frames of the retable recall the altarpiece of the Last Supper in the Diocesan Museum at Cuenca by Yáñez's pupil, Martín Gómez,[9] it is possible that the Mateu specimen hails from the same region, where Yáñez himself was employed, but the craftsman is not Gómez or anyone else in the *entourage* of the Fernandos with whom I am familiar.

In the case of a fragment of a predella in the possession of French and Co. at New York (Fig. 150), the evidence is not sufficient for determining whether the author might be the painter of the Mateu retable, the Grifo Master, the Alcoraz Master, or some other secondary member of the Fernandos' circle. The preserved parts include: the central piece of the Resurrection, a simplification of the versions by Llanos in the retable in the cathedral of Valencia and by Yáñez in the panel of the Provincial Museum in the same city; and the left section, with half-length pairs of Apostles in three compartments, (reading from right to left) Paul, Peter, James Major, Thomas, Andrew, and a figure who, since he carries the attribute of a spear or lance, may be Thaddaeus, Matthias, or even Matthew.

At a visit to Albarracín, west of Teruel, in 1928, I saw in a chapel at the right of the nave in the church of Santiago the remains of a retable that struck me as an offshoot of the manner of the Fernandos. The situation of the town in the district of Teruel, the focus of the

[8] The subjects of the subordinate parts of the retable show, of course, that it is not the altarpiece once at Orihuela: see above, p. 269.

[9] See above, p. 348.

FIG. 149. SCHOOL OF YÁÑEZ AND LLANOS. RETABLE. MATEU
COLLECTION, BARCELONA

(*Photo. Archivo Mas*)

FIG. 150. SCHOOL OF YÁÑEZ AND LLANOS. PREDELLA. FRENCH AND CO., NEW YORK

(*Courtesy of the owners*)

activity of their follower, the Alcoraz Master, would create a presupposition in favor of his authorship; but possessing neither photographs nor an adequate memory of the panels and not even informed
that they survived the Spanish civil war, I cannot say whether the
style substantiated the presupposition or whether, instead, they were
painted by another exponent of the Fernandos' widely disseminated
fashions. St. Sebastian constituted the subject of the principal compartment, only the upper part of which was visible, either because the
rest had been destroyed or was hidden by later accretions.[10] The two
flanking compartments in the main body of the retable depicted at the
left St. Roch and at the right St. Sebastian's frequent iconographical
companion, St. Fabian. Above this principal section were representations of the Trinity and the two actors in the Annunciation. The best
pieces seemed to me the five virgin martyrs of the predella, Lucy,
Apollonia, Catherine, Barbara, and Agatha. Gold backgrounds were
archaistically retained for the sacred effigies throughout the retable, as
well as gold accents in their attire.

[10] A modern picture of the souls in Purgatory beseeching the Madonna's aid was
inserted in the retable.

CHAPTER IX

VALENCIAN PAINTINGS OF THE EARLY
RENAISSANCE BUT OF UNCERTAIN
AFFILIATIONS

To SPONSOR a veronica in the Sala Capitular of the cathedral of Barcelona, obviously belonging to the Valencian rather than the Catalan school (Fig. 151), I can discover no artist so likely as Paolo da San Leocadio. The form that the checkering of the gold background assumes is a trade-mark of Vicente Juan Masip, the father of Juan de Juanes, and does not occur in Paolo's known works, since the lozenges in the backgrounds of the predella formerly owned by Mrs. Francisca Reyes at New York and provisionally ascribed to him are simpler in their pattern; but the type and style of the bust itself can scarcely be reconciled with Masip's norms. The evidence, however, is not sufficient for a categorical assignment even to Paolo, and it is quite possible that I stupidly fail to recognize the brush of some other Valencian painter of the first years of the sixteenth century.

I have tried to discern Paolo's hand also in an Agony in the Garden that is in the possession of Doña Pilar Aleu at Barcelona and was there shown at the Exposition of the Art of the Passion in 1945; [1] but I can uncover no definite proof of such an affiliation, and on the whole the authorship of the Cabanyes Master seems more probable. Although judgment is hampered by the panel's loss of pieces at both sides, the composition in what remains is more akin to the Cabanyes Master's version in the predella of the retable of Sts. Dionysius and Margaret than to Paolo's treatments of the theme, and the types and draperies, particularly in the case of Christ, are quite otherwise than a deterrent to the Cabanyes Master's claims. The setting includes one of his favorite forked trees; but quite unusually two large birds sit upon its branches, and just as anomalous in his production is the fact that an adjoining tree turns out to be a palm. The principal obstacle to making him responsible for the picture is found in the somewhat harder lines of its draughtsmanship as compared to his customary *sfumatezza.*

[1] No. 8 of the Catalogue of the Exposition by Manuel Trens.

Fig. 151. VALENCIAN SCHOOL, SIXTEENTH CENTURY. VERONICA.
CATHEDRAL, BARCELONA
(*Photo. Archivo Mas*)

Not only by reason of the place where it is located but also to some extent on account of the style, Vicente Juan Masip is a tempting candidate for election as the painter of a panel of St. Peter which, since it is now in the episcopal palace at Segorbe, must come from the town or its territory, although there is no longer anyone living who can specify the exact provenience (Fig. 152); and yet he has so many other possible rivals in the contest that his victory at the polls of connoisseurship is by no means a foregone conclusion. The attribution to Masip could be upheld on the basis of such arguments as the facial resemblance to the old shepherd peering from behind the column in the Nativity of the artist's retable also at Segorbe, although the archaisms would assign the St. Peter to an early moment in his career; but, no sooner do we begin to be persuaded than we are inhibited by stylistic analogies to the Fernandos, to members of their circle, for instance Felipe Pablo, or even to the Borbotó Master, who participated in the strain in the Valencian school that the Perea Master had founded.

An insoluble puzzle is presented to me by a panel in the Museum of Catalan Art at Barcelona depicting the Lamentation over the Dead Christ (Fig. 153). I find it difficult to subscribe to either of the two opinions of Don Leandro de Saralegui, who first [2] ensconced it in the circle of the Osonas and subsequently [3] attributed it to the author of the two St. Vincents in the cathedral of Valencia, a painter who for me is none other than Vicente Juan Masip.[4] The composition and one or two of the types, such as the Virgin and the holy woman just above the Magdalene, seem derived from the Játiva Master, and I have sometimes wondered whether it could not be a repainted work by this artist; but the likelihood is that it should be classified in the period just after him and that it was made by someone who was conversant with his productions and with those of the Martínez Master's circle to which he belonged but who had ameliorated their lingering, primitive hardness through contact with the idealizing tendencies of Paolo da San Leocadio and the early Valencian Renaissance in general. Indeed we probably owe the panel to a painter of whom no other works have yet been recognized but who through later discoveries may eventually emerge as a distinct individuality.

[2] *Boletín de la Sociedad Española de Excursiones,* XL (1932), 51.

[3] *Ibid.,* LII (1944), 29.

[4] See above, p. 60.

FIG. 152. VALENCIAN SCHOOL, SIXTEENTH CENTURY.
ST. PETER. EPISCOPAL PALACE, SEGORBE
(*Photo. Archivo Mas*)

Fig. 153. VALENCIAN SCHOOL, SIXTEENTH CENTURY.
LAMENTATION OVER THE DEAD CHRIST. MUSEUM
OF CATALAN ART, BARCELONA

(From an article by Saralegui)

FIG. 154. YÁÑEZ, LLANOS, OR A MEMBER OF THEIR CIRCLE(?).
ST. SEBASTIAN. NAVARRO ALCÁCER COLLECTION, VALENCIA
(*Photo. Archivo Mas*)

The large [5] and impressive rendering of the Dormition in the Ayuntamiento of Guadalest, north of Alicante, seems to be executed in the style of the partners Requena and Rubiales; but there is not enough concrete proof to bring it definitely into connection with them.

I had arrived at the conclusion that a St. Sebastian in the Navarro Alcácer Collection at Valencia (Fig. 154) probably ought to be assigned to Llanos, Yáñez, or an artist in their clique, when I was glad to be confirmed in the surmise by Saralegui who in a letter to me tentatively proposed the same allocation; but the peculiar traits of the atelier are so little marked, especially the Leonardesque proclivities, and slight resemblances to other masters of the time and place so disturbing, for instance to Requena and Rubiales, that I have lacked the courage to discuss the panel in the sections of this book which deal with the Fernandos or even with their followers. Somewhat varied from the Montesinos example by Yáñez and revealing apparently a closer dependence upon Peruginesque or similar prototypes, the picture belongs to a slightly more mature moment of the Renaissance both in anatomy and general style, so that, if either of the Fernandos was the author, we should have to suppose that he painted it at a rather tardy date in his career. Counterparts in their production are not lacking, such as the young, standing Apostle above the Virgin in the Ascension of the shutters in the Valencian cathedral, but we can certainly not set aside the possibility of execution by their disciple at Cuenca, Martín Gómez.

[5] There is a tolerable reproduction in the Espasa Encyclopaedia, XXVI, p. 1504: the dimensions are three metres in height by two in width. At my visit to this region in 1934, I found that the triptych recorded by Tormo (*Levante*, 280) at Benimantell has disappeared.

APPENDIX

APPENDIX

ADDITIONS TO VOLUMES I–X

Ramón Destorrents (the Iravalls Master)

In volume IX [1] we registered Verrié's ingenious deduction that the Catalan painter known through the records as active in the mid-fourteenth century, Ramón Destorrents, might well be identical with the personality embodying an early aspect of the Serras' style whom he and Gudiol Ricart had isolated and to whom I gave the name of the Iravalls Master; and he has now conclusively demonstrated the truth of his deduction in an article [2] that is a model of scientific and aesthetic method for other historians of art to emulate. The pith of the proof is as follows. Through the subject of the panel of St. Anne by the Iravalls Master in the Lisbon Museum and through its heraldry, Verrié definitively establishes the fact that it was the principal compartment of a retable ordered by Peter IV of Aragon for the chapel of the royal palace of the Almudaina at Palma in his recently acquired domain of the Balearic Isles, and he puts the seal upon this portion of the evidence by recognizing as the retable's pinnacle a Crucifixion that still exists actually at Palma in the Museo Arqueológico (Luliano). The equation of the author of the St. Anne and the Crucifixion, namely the Iravalls Master, with Ramón Destorrents is achieved by Verrié on the basis of a document in which on March 26, 1353,[3] Pedro IV authorizes payment to the artist for a retable that was to be placed in the royal chapel at Palma as well as for another, now lost altarpiece at Valencia. The exact date of Ramón's completion of the order has not been ascertained, but the retable was not shipped from Barcelona to Majorca until 1358, according to another document which Verrié includes in his article and in which it is stated that some injuries suffered by the panels during the voyage were repaired by our old friend, the Balearic painter, Juan Daurer.[4] The commission for the retable had originally been given by Peter IV to Ferrer Bassa, but this master's death at the end of the forties of the Trecento and the sovereign's concern with other matters delayed the accomplishment of the project and resulted in Ramón's eventual obtainment of the distinguished task.[5]

[1] P. 741.

[2] *Anales y Boletín de los Museos de Arte de Barcelona*, VI, 3–4 (1948), 321–340.

[3] He thus has to abandon his former dating of the retable in 1347–1348.

[4] I had already referred to this document in volume III, p. 148, as furnishing the first known date in Daurer's life, but I did not state its contents: cf. G. Llabrés in *Bolletí de la Societat Arqueològica Luliana*, XIX (1922–1923) 187. For Daurer, see also below, p. 387.

[5] Verrié (p. 337) believes that between 1458 and 1465 the retable by Rafael Moger was substituted for the one by Destorrents, but Moger's work was not, like his prede-

The works that have been brought into connection with the Iravalls Master may thus happily be placed under the name of Ramón Destorrents, whom we found in volume IX to deserve perhaps the honor of having been the Serras' teacher. Among the sure works, the panel of Sts. Clara and Catherine in the cathedral of Barcelona is just conceivably documented, as Verrié realizes, by an entry of August 28, 1351, which he publishes from the church's archives and in which Ramón acknowledges the receipt of something, probably remuneration for a painting, from a lady whose Christian name, Catherine, alone is included but who therefore may have desired her celestial homonym to be represented in the picture.

The Serras and Their Circle

I shall have to leave it to my perceptive Catalan friends to determine precisely where under the above heading to place a fragment of a Last Supper in the Collection of Mrs. Edith Bennett at Washington (Fig. 155), for it obtrudes one of the cases in which, by reason of the closely interrelated manners of the Serras and their followers, the evidence is not copious or clear enough to allow my poor eyes to arrive at a definite conclusion that satisfies me. Only three Apostles are preserved in the fragment, Bartholomew, James Minor, and Philip, with their names inscribed beside them in Catalan.[1] The affiliations with Jaime Serra himself in types and style are extremely close, particularly in his phase embodied in the retable of Abella de la Conca,[2] but, since there are resemblances to the works of such contemporaries as the Master of St. Mark and the Rusiñol Master,[3] we must give them also at least some consideration in the question of attribution. Moreover, the composition and general modes are different in the Last Supper in the predella of the retable from Sijena in the Museum of Catalan

---

cessor's, done for the main altar of the chapel of St. Anne but for the lateral altar dedicated to St. Praxedes: cf. my vol. VII, p. 649, and Enrique Sureda, *De la corte de los señores reyes de Mallorca*, Madrid, 1914, p. 43. We cannot, therefore, say just when Ramón's altarpiece was discarded from the chapel of St. Anne, but Llabrés (*op. cit.*, 187) asserts that it was probably in the eighteenth century.

[1] The dimensions are 54 centimetres in length by 50 in height. Bartholomew's name is spelled *Bertomeu* (or perhaps to be read rather *Bertomau*), less frequent than the other Catalan form *Bartomeu*. In each case the name is on one side of the head, and *S*, an abbreviation for the Catalan *Sant*, on the other. The appellation beside the figure that I identify as James Minor is so far erased that I cannot be certain that it is *Jaume*, but he would be a natural Apostle to couple with Philip, because they are both commemorated by the Church on May 1.

[2] Vol. II, p. 464.

[3] In the Castilian edition of his book, *Historia de la pintura gótica en Cataluña*, Barcelona, 1944, p. 30, Gudiol Ricart makes it plain that he considers parts of a single retable the panels by the Rusiñol Master about which his statement was not quite clear in the earlier Catalan edition: see my volume VIII, p. 565. The Dupont Nativity in this set of panels and a Burial of the Virgin, which was not hitherto known to me but obviously derives from the same assemblage, belonged at last report to Don Apolinar Sánchez of Madrid and have been recognized as creations of the Rusiñol Master by Saralegui independently of me: see his article in the *Archivo español de arte*, XXIV (1951), 213.

FIG. 155. CIRCLE OF THE SERRAS. FRAGMENT OF LAST SUPPER.
COLLECTION OF MRS. EDITH BENNETT, WASHINGTON
(*Courtesy of the owner*)

Art, Barcelona,[4] which may have been painted by Jaime, although at a later moment in his career than the period to which the Bennett fragment would be assigned.

THE RUBIÓ MASTER

In an illuminating article [1] the distinguished Catalan scholar, Juan Ainaud de Lasarte, has amplified our comprehension of this painter by revealing that there survived the civil war and still exist in the *parroquia* at Rubió all the other sections of the capacious retable that hitherto I had known only through the central compartment, the Coronation,[2] in the church and through the predella of the Passion in the Vich Museum.[3] The Coronation, capped by the usual Crucifixion, is set between lateral compartments of the other six Joys of the Virgin, and the uprights and pinnacles contain small effigies of Prophets and Apostles. Although Ainaud accepts the predella of Sts. Cosmas and Damian in the Vich Museum and the Oppenheim retable of St. Anthony Abbot,[4] now acquired by the Museum of Catalan Art, Barcelona, that I have assigned to the Rubió Master, he decides in favor of the Master of St. Mark in the case of a predella with scenes from the story of St. Stephen two of which have passed from the Junyent Collection at Barcelona to the Torelló Collection in the same city and a third of which, depicting his dispute with the Jews and hitherto unnoticed by me, has also eventually entered from the Masriera Collection, Barcelona, the Museum of Catalan Art. Even I [5] had seriously hesitated between the claims of the Master of St. Mark and the Rubió Master; but, spurred on to a careful reëxamination of the problem by my consciousness of Ainaud's discerning eye, I am willing now to switch to his opinion. I have pressed my pedantic analysis to the Morellian point of finding that the rounder ears are more characteristic of the Master of St. Mark. Since Ainaud does not mention another work that I have ascribed to the Rubió Master, the panel of the two St. Johns in the Sloan Collection, New York,[6] I gather that he has not come to a definite opinion about the attribution; but once involved through his article in the question of the Master's authentic productions, I myself have considered the attribution again. As usually happens in reviewing one's past judgments, I am now inclined to be less dogmatic; and yet the Sloan picture is extremely similar in style to the Rubió Master's achievements, and I have still to find another painter of the time to whom it can be so reasonably allocated.

[4] See my vol. II, p. 234.
[1] *El retaule de Rubió dintre la pintura catalana del siglo XIV*, published by the Biblioteca del Centro de Estudios Comarcales, Igualada, 1949.
[2] Vol. X, p. 300.
[3] Vol. VIII, p. 567.
[4] Vol. IX, p. 744.
[5] Vol. VIII, pp. 568–570.
[6] *Ibid.*, p. 570.

JUAN MATES

With the critical acumen to which he has accustomed us, Ainaud [1] has made important accretions to the considerable deposit that this outstanding member of Borrassá's [2] general circle has left us. Publishing the beginning of Mates's contract of September 15, 1422, and receipt of December 31 in the same year for the first payment for a retable to decorate the high altar of the parish church of Sta. María at Vilarrodona, north of Tarragona,[3] he justly discovers relics of the monument in two panels, a Crucifixion and a fragment of a Coronation that were to be seen in the sacristy of the edifice until the revolutionary disturbances of 1936 but are now preserved only in photographs. Ainaud's second feat of detection is particularly a credit to his connoisseurship, the recognition of a work of Mates in the last place where one would expect to find it, the Museum of the Seminario at Venice. Donated to the institution in 1925, it was once the large, central compartment of a retable and embodies a rather unusual piece of iconography. The subject of the enthroned Madonna serenaded by angels is common enough, but the Child here leans forth to crown the patroness of Barcelona, St. Eulalia (identified by the emblem of the *eculeus* behind her). The final paintings that Ainaud assigns to Mates, a pair of small pinnacles from a retable depicting the Annunciation and Resurrection (in the presence of the Virgin, as often in Catalan iconography), I have long known as once in the Perriollat Collection, Paris, and now belonging to Monsieur L. P. Bresset at Marseilles. Although I had considered the possibility of Mates's authorship, I had hesitated to make the attribution because the stylistic evidence did not seem to me quite concrete enough; but the weight of the Spanish scholar's opinion has induced me to review the question, with the consequence that I am convinced of the accuracy of his perception. He may even be right in the suggestion that the panels might derive from the same original assemblage as the Nativity that from the possession of Mrs. Dohan at Darling, Pennsylvania,[4] has passed into the Otero Vizcarrondo Collection at Carracas, Venezuela.

BERNARDO MARTORELL

Emergence of a hitherto unrecognized work by this principal Catalan exponent of the most typical aspects of the international movement is always an event, particularly when the work turns out to be a further section of a retable from which other pieces had already been discovered. Such is the happy truth about an Annunciation belonging to Mr. F. Cleveland Morgan

[1] *Anales y Boletín de los Museos de Arte de Barcelona*, VI, 3–4 (1948), 341.
[2] In the *Art Quarterly* (Detroit), XIV (1951), 108, I have published a retable of St. Michael in the Pardo Collection, Paris, by a follower of Borrassá whom I do not recognize.
[3] The documents had already been summarized by J. M. Madurell in *Anales y Boletín de los Museos de Arte de Barcelona*, III, 4 (1945), 315.
[4] See my vol. VIII, p. 600.

FIG. 156. BERNARDO MARTORELL. ANNUNCIATION. MORGAN
COLLECTION, MONTREAL

at Montreal (Fig. 156), every element in which bespeaks Martorell's craft at one of its loveliest, presumably early moments and the frame and dimensions of which, as well as the figuration of the haloes, establish derivation from the same retable of the Virgin, whichever that retable was,[1] as the Nativity of the Lippmann Collection, Berlin, and the Coronation of the Traumann Collection, Madrid.[2] The composition is scarcely varied from that of his miniature of the Annunciation in the Book of Offices in the Apeles Mestres Collection at Barcelona.[3]

My recent acquaintance with the charming Collection of Mr. Marius de Zayas at Stamford, Connecticut, has disclosed as one of its treasures a panel of the Ascension[4] (probably a fragment of some other retable) which, again plainly a creation of Martorell, would be unhesitatingly judged, because of the broadening of the style beyond the more precise draughtsmanship of many of his productions, to have been painted at the end of his career, unless we had found that such a criterion is not in his case too sure a chronological touchstone (Fig. 157).[5] By retaining the stereotyped Catalan composition for the subject (except that, like his follower at Bañolas,[6] he represents Christ as ascending with His back towards us), he denies himself latitude for much invention, but in the figures themselves he succeeds in giving us some of the most incisive embodiments of his captivating types.

[1] Vol. VIII, p. 623.

[2] *Ibid.*, p. 629. The dimensions of the Annunciation are about 80 centimetres in height by 50 in width; for the corresponding measurements of the other two panels, see vols. VI, p. 552, and VIII, p. 626. The Traumann Coronation is now in the Collection of Don Ricardo Viñas Barcelona.

[3] Vols. VII, fig. 289, and VIII, p. 628.

[4] The dimensions are 32 inches in height by 25¼ in width.

[5] Vol. IX, p. 758. Nevertheless, Gudiol Ricart and his collaborators in the *Catálogo monumental de España, Ciudad de Barcelona*, 127, explain the discrepancy between the year of the contract for the two panels in Sta. María del Mar, 1435, and their apparently late manner on the supposition that Martorell did not actually carry them out until *c*. 1450, the date that I had proposed for them before the publication of the document.

[6] See my vol. VIII, p. 634. In his book *Dos obras maestras del arte gótico en Bañolas* (Barcelona, 1947), Luis G. Constans suggests, though not arriving at absolute certainty, that this retable of the Virgin by a follower of Martorell in the church of S. Esteban at Bañolas originally decorated a much hallowed altar of Nuestra Señora de la Scala, which was located at the extreme east end of the building behind and at a loftier level than the high altar, a consideration that would explain so important a retable in an edifice under the invocation of St. Stephen. Eventually the retable was relegated to a secondary chapel, but it now graces the high altar. Of the sections that I did not specify in volume VIII, the central compartment is so big that it must have been intended for a larger effigy of Our Lady, whether carved or painted, than the earlier statue of her, dating from the fourteenth century, that it now contains; the panel of Christ of the Passion from the middle of the predella seems to be the only piece of the structure which has been lost; on the uprights the artist depicted twelve of Mary's ancestors; and in the pinnacles four Prophets.

Fig. 157. BERNARDO MARTORELL. ASCENSION. DE ZAYAS
COLLECTION, STAMFORD, CONNECTICUT
(*Courtesy of the owner*)

The School of Majorca in the Fourteenth and First Half of the Fifteenth Century

Among many problems in Spanish painting which cry for investigation and some of which my retirement from teaching has given me long desired leisure for studying, one is the question whether, with the help of the copious photographs recently taken of works of art in Majorca, it was possible not only to augment there our inheritance from exponents of the Italo-Gothic and international styles whom we have already isolated but also to segregate further personalities of the sort by making groups of the productions that in my previous volumes I was obliged to leave unattached because forced to rely merely on visual memory. Despite the confusingly interrelated manners of the Majorcan painters in the fourteenth and first half of the fifteenth century, a considerable measure of success has attended my efforts, enabling me even to parcel out works that have come to light only in the last years; and yet a certain number of panels remain for which I cannot specify the authors but some of which may well have been executed by the defined personalities, although the evidence is not sufficient to ascribe them conclusively. I cannot afford the space for the detailed comparisons by which I have arrived at the attributions, when my volumes are already too crowded with such boring analyses, but I beg the reader to believe that I have devoted long, frequent, and careful labor to the task.

1. *The Loert Master*

The new photographs have dispelled the doubts that I expressed in volume III [1] in regard to a single authorship for the retables of St. Quiteria in the Museo Arqueológico (Luliano) at Palma and of St. Eulalia now in the Museo Episcopal which has been made in one of the Salas Capitulares of the cathedral, although the former may have been executed some years prior to the latter. In the struggle to find a distinctive denomination for this painter of the middle of the fourteenth century, I can hit upon nothing better than the Loert Master, since there is a chance that he might be identical with a Juan Loert [2] whom we know, however, only in slightly earlier documents and who is connected by no record with either altarpiece.

Subsequently to the time when I wrote volume III and had at my disposal no more lengthy account of St. Quiteria's sensational story than the summary of her *Acta* in the Bollandists under May 22, further sources both literary and pictorial [3] have come to my attention, joining with the photographs to enable me to specify more exactly the narrative themes in her Majorcan retable. The first scene is her birth, according to one tradition, in Portugal,[4] but the painter, with unexpected restraint, foregoes the opportunity to depict the prodigious miracle said to have marked the event, namely,

---

[1] Pp. 141–144.   [2] *Ibid.*, p. 144.
[3] See my vols. IV, p. 636, and VIII, p. 325.
[4] G. Cardoso, *Agiologio lusitano*, Lisbon, III (1666), 354.

that she was one of nine daughters brought forth at a single parturition. Next, a grown Christian maiden, she is arraigned before her pagan father, from whom she had temporarily escaped.[5] Permitted by him to retire with thirty girls and other devotees to the valley of Aufragia for pious exercises, she is shown, in the third episode, denouncing to the apostate king of this region, Lentimanus, a dragon on Mount Galganus and a demon on Mount Ungulus. Then we see her and the girls consoled by angels during the incarceration to which they have been subjected by the monarch, and in a fifth section of the retable she baptizes her jailers converted by the supernatural opening of the prison. In the following two sections she restores sight to Lentimanus, who has been stricken with blindness for his intent to slay her, and she leads to him the subjugated demon. Having finally recovered their faith, the king and his two renegade bishops unite themselves to St. Quiteria in deeds of charity. The ninth section I still cannot elucidate, a scene in which a haloed maiden watches another standing in a pool: one of them would be Quiteria and the other probably the outstanding virgin among her companions, Columbina, but I do not know which is which. The last three sections represent: Quiteria's decapitation at the hands of a minion of her disappointed suitor, Germanus; the angel who had been her constant, close associate carrying the martyr's head (instead of the usual version, which declared that, like another Saint Denis, she transported it herself); and the ceremony of her burial.

2. *The Inca Master*

To this painter whose activity must have fallen mainly within the second half of the fourteenth century and whom, in the appendix of volume VI,[1] we eventually segregated, we can now assign, among works that I have formerly mentioned, the St. Christopher, capped by a pinnacle of the resurrected Saviour, in the church of Sta. Cruz at Palma, once the central section of an otherwise lost retable.[2] The stylistic proof is corroborated by the similarities in frame that my lamented friend and mentor, the distinguished Majorcan scholar, Don Rafael Ysasi, pointed out[3] in the principal compartment of an already recognized achievement of the Inca Master, the altarpiece of the Virgin of Mercy from the ruined monastery of Sto. Domingo at Palma preserved in the Museo de la Lonja. I have now perceived that the subject of this compartment is really the favorite Spanish iconographical theme, the Patrocinio de la Virgen,[4] but that by exception St. Peter Martyr, instead of St. Francis, is joined to St. Dominic and Our Lady of Mercy in supplication for mankind against divine wrath, that in

[5] In the marvel of her birth and in her experiences with her father, her tale significantly parallels that of another Portuguese virgin, St. Liberata: cf. my vol. IX, p. 698.
[1] P. 586.
[2] Vol. III, p. 152.
[3] *Bolletí de la Societat Arqueològica Luliana*, XXV (1934), 245–246.
[4] See above, p. 280.

FIG. 158. THE INCA MASTER. ST. CATHERINE OF ALEXANDRIA.
CONVENTO DE LA CONCEPCIÓN, PALMA
(*Photo. Tous*)

the surmounting panel the angels round the Trinity and not Christ hurl the arrows of God's anger, and that the prostrate king and knight are unrescued victims.

The second work now attributable to the Inca Master that I have registered in a former volume [5] consists in the fragments of a predella of the Passion in the church of Sta. María del Puig at Pollensa, which turns out to be a part of none of the other assemblages of panels in the edifice.[6] The photographs show that in the Agony in the Garden a number of Apostles and not three only are depicted as asleep and that the whole representation of Christ before Pilate is extant.

Of paintings by the Master hitherto unknown to me, the finest is a standing effigy of St. Catherine of Alexandria, probably once the centre of an altarpiece, which belongs to the treasures lately found in the Convento de la Concepción, Palma (Fig. 158). Less significant examples of his craft by reason of their sadly battered condition can be seen in fragments from the story of St. Margaret in the Museo Episcopal in the same city, two of them bits of a scene or scenes of her tortures and the other pair in their original state exhibiting her in prayer before her execution and then the answer to her supplications in the appearance of the Hand of God in the heavens.

The accumulation of all this additional material for comparison forces me to retract the misgivings that I expressed in volume II [7] about the attribution of the triptych of the Madonna, St. George, and St. Martin in Fenway Court, Boston, to the Inca Master and to classify it definitely among his most winsome achievements.

3. The Campos Master

The *floruit* of the painter whom I thus christen from his altarpiece of the Virgin in the Ermita of S. Blas near Campos [1] (Fig. 159) on the island perhaps stretched into the early years of the fifteenth century. In volume IV [2] I had already divined what the photographs now confirm, i.e., that he executed also the retable of the archangels at Pollensa in the church of Sta. María del Puig (Fig. 160). Furthermore, the photographs disclose that the saint in the predella of the Pollensa retable about whose identity I was in doubt is Damian and not Cosmas, that, as we have just noted, the fragments of the Passion in the church do not derive from the retable of the archangels but were done by the Inca Master, and that the medallions of three Apostles likewise there preserved are the sole remains of some other assemblage.[3]

[5] IV, p. 620.
[6] See below, under the Campos Master.
[7] P. 313.
[1] Vol. IV, p. 616.
[2] P. 618.
[3] See below, p. 390.

Fig. 159. THE CAMPOS MASTER. ANNUNCIATION, SECTION OF
RETABLE. ERMITA DE S. BLAS, CAMPOS
(*Photo. Archivo Mas*)

Fig. 160. THE CAMPOS MASTER. APPEARANCE OF ST. MICHAEL ON
THE CASTEL SANT' ANGELO, SECTION OF RETABLE. STA.
MARÍA DEL PUIG, POLLENSA

(*Photo. Archivo Mas*)

4. *The Castellig Master and Juan Daurer*

The phase of painting headed on the mainland by Luis Borrassá is most nearly paralleled at Majorca by the artist for whom his retable of Sts. Peter and Paul at Castellig [1] supplies a sobriquet. Considerable interest attaches to him because he proves either to have collaborated with or succeeded Juan Daurer [2] in the creation of the important retable of St. Nicholas from Portopí now in the Museo Arqueológico at Palma. Before indicating the partition of the labor between them, it is necessary to specify, as I failed to do in volume III,[3] the subjects of the six lateral compartments relating some of St. Nicholas's deeds. The scenes at the left are his charity to the three indigent sisters, his rescue of the young cupbearer from the palace of the heathen king, and his restoration of this boy to his parents;[4] the balancing triad at the right depict his lecture to the thieves of the goods belonging to the Jew who had made a statue of the saint (Fig. 161), the sailors admonished by him to pour out from the ship the inflammable oil presented by the she-devil,[5] and his resuscitation of the three butchered lads. It is very obvious that these compartments at the right and the adjoining large effigy of St. Clara were done by Juan Daurer, who, since his manner seems to antedate somewhat that of the Castellig Master, probably died before he completed the order, leaving all the rest to be carrried out by his successor. The *genre* of the international movement begins to affect the Castellig Master's production in that the heathen king's palace is represented as the residence of a Moorish potentate in which two men are engaged in playing chess (Fig. 162). My suggestion in volume III that pinnacles of the Eternal Father and four Prophets in the Museo Arqueológico might have been parts of the same altarpiece may now be definitely dismissed.

Manifestly the Castellig Master deserves the credit of another well known monument of the Majorcan school, the Dormition in the Palma church of Sta. Eulalia.[6]

On account of its dilapidated condition I have not yet included in these volumes what must have been originally a charming specimen of his attainments, expressing, as his creations often do, the peculiarly Majorcan delicacy at its loveliest, a retable of St. Ursula which remains to us only in a fragment in the Museo Arqueológico at Palma comprising no more than a bit of a predella with scenes from the virgin martyr's romantic tale and of a subpredella with medallions of Apostles. Time has spared even only a very small section of the predella, the (half-effaced) episode of St. Ursula and her maidens bidding farewell to her father and bridegroom, the Pope Cyriacus in the midst of his retinue welcoming the bevy of girls at Rome, and a seg-

[1] Vol. IV, p. 614.
[2] For Daurer, see also above, p. 373. I cannot believe that Verrié (*Anales y Boletín de los Museos de Arte de Barcelona*, VI, 3–4, 1948, p. 336) will hold to the opinion that Daurer is identical with the Inca Master, particularly after he has examined the works that I have now added to the latter's corpus.
[3] P. 160.
[4] See my vol. IV, p. 252.
[5] Vol. VIII, p. 13.
[6] Vol. III, p. 162.

FIG. 161. JUAN DAURER. THE LECTURE OF ST. NICHOLAS TO THE THIEVES, SECTION OF RETABLE OF ST. NICHOLAS. MUSEO ARQUEOLÓGICO, PALMA

(*Photo. Archivo Mas*)

FIG. 162. THE CASTELLIG MASTER. RESCUE OF THE YOUNG CUP-
BEARER BY ST. NICHOLAS, SECTION OF RETABLE OF ST. NICHOLAS.
MUSEO ARQUEOLÓGICO, PALMA

(*Photo. Archivo Mas*)

ment of the compartment depicting their slaughter. The hall of St. Ursula's parent (Fig. 163) is paved with precisely the same pattern as the oriental dwelling from which St. Nicholas saved the cupbearer! The Museo Arqueológico houses also the merest shred of a panel by the Castellig Master representing the death of a monk who, if he was a saint, exhibits no halo and whom from his habit and that of his brothers in the religious life I should judge to have been a Hieronymite (Fig. 164).[7] The medallions of three Apostles in Sta. María del Puig at Pollensa that I have mentioned above [8] obtrude one of the doubtful cases which I described at the beginning of this section of the appendix as suggesting but not establishing an attribution to a known personality, since we may just conceivably owe them to the Castellig Master's brush.

My renewed examination of the later panels at the bottom of his retable at Castellig, as well as of the mutilated bits of a Resurrection and Pentecost (Fig. 165) having the same provenience and now in the Museo Arqueológico, Palma,[9] demonstrates that they should unquestionably be added to our scant, certain legacy from the Majorcan painter of the second half of the fifteenth century, Rafael Moger.

5. The Alcudia Master

The disclosure of the works of art possessed by the Convento de la Concepción at Palma enables us to extricate the personality of a manipulator of the fully evolved international style on the island of Majorca, to whom I will give the name of the Alcudia Master on the basis of the first achievements by him with which I became acquainted, the panels of the Dormition and of St. Thomas's reception of the Virgin's girdle (Fig. 166) at Alcudia in the house of the rector of the parish church.[1] The paintings in the Convento de la Concepción manifestly by the same hand seem to be likewise fragments of a single retable, a pinnacle of the Crucifixion and a compartment depicting the guardian angel of the monastery of Sts. María del Puig at Pollensa spreading his protecting arms over the mountain of this religious institution and its buildings (Fig. 167). To realize the unity of authorship with the Alcudia panels, one need do no more than note such precise analogies as exist between the angel and the St. John at the head of the bier in the Dormition or between Longinus wounding Christ's side in the Crucifixion and St. Thomas extending his hands to grasp the girdle. The style is an insular counterpart of the modes of Bernardo Martorell on the Catalan mainland, even somewhat gentler by reason of Majorcan aesthetic standards and, although showing less technical proficiency than Bernardo, yet superior to the general average of the local school. The fluffy treatment of masses of hair creates a resemblance to the figures of the Barcelona painter, Juan Mates,[2] who, however, cannot be equated with the

[7] Not a Franciscan, as is usually stated.
[8] P. 384.
[1] Vol. IV, p. 622.

[9] Vol. IV, p. 615.
[2] See above, p. 377.

FIG. 163. THE CASTELLIG MASTER. ST. URSULA'S FATHER, A
RETAINER, AND HER BRIDEGROOM, PART OF SCENE OF HER
FAREWELL, SECTION OF PREDELLA. MUSEO
ARQUEOLÓGICO, PALMA

(*Photo. Archivo Mas*)

FIG. 164. THE CASTELLIG MASTER. FRAGMENT OF A PANEL
REPRESENTING THE DEATH OF A MONK. MUSEO
ARQUEOLÓGICO, PALMA

(*Photo. Archivo Mas*)

FIG. 165. RAFAEL MOGER. FRAGMENT OF PENTECOST. MUSEO ARQUEOLÓGICO, PALMA

(Photo. Archivo Mas)

FIG. 166. THE ALCUDIA MASTER. ST. THOMAS'S RECEPTION OF THE
VIRGIN'S GIRDLE. RECTOR'S HOUSE, ALCUDIA
(*Photo. Tous*)

FIG. 167. THE ALCUDIA MASTER. GUARDIAN ANGEL OF MONASTERY
OF STA. MARÍA DEL PUIG, POLLENSA, FRAGMENT OF RETABLE.
CONVENTO DE LA CONCEPCIÓN, PALMA

(*Photo. Tous*)

Alcudia Master or thus proved to have included Majorca, as well as Sardinia, in the wide sphere of his activity.

The emergence of the Alcudia Master's personality now finally solves an old problem of connoisseurship, for he turns out to be the artist who did the fine, double veronica of Christ and the Virgin in the Museo Arqueológico, Palma, and for whom we have so long been searching (Fig. 168).[3] The attribution would perhaps be adequately established by the virtual identity of Our Lord's countenance in the Crucifixion in the Convento de la Concepción, and corroboratory evidence could be found in Mary's facial similarity to the sorrowing Mother on Calvary and the soldier whose helmet is surmounted by a crescent; but the conclusive argument is added by the fact that the curious stylization of the projecting wisps of the Saviour's hair in the panel of the Museum can be detected at the lower left edge of His locks as He hangs upon the cross. The provenience of the veronica from the Majorcan monastery of Valldemosa[4] spoke in the first place for an insular author, and the Alcudia Master is a sufficiently capable performer not to oblige us to seek a candidate any longer in the generally more competent schools of the mainland. There still remains unelucidated, however, the question of the relationship of the bust of the Virgin to the very exact replica in the Museum of Vich, and I must confess that I am less disposed than formerly[5] to agree with the elder Gudiol in assigning the replica to a later date, whether or not it was made by the Alcudia Master himself.

THE ARGUIS MASTER

In the case of an effigy of St. John Baptist, manifestly once the principal compartment of a retable and now in the Bauzá Collection at Madrid (Fig. 169), it has taken some looking on my part to discern the author, but I am confident that I have finally hit upon the truth. The panel is seen forthwith to incorporate the height of the international movement in Spain, and the choice eventually narrows down to its outstanding and not uninteresting Aragonese exponent, the Arguis Master. The reasons for my failure to recognize immediately his hand are that the painters of the time did not ordinarily reveal their distinctive traits in the large figures of saints petrified into cult-images at the centres of altarpieces, that the Baptist in such instances was represented by all artists in much the same way, and that no other sizable forms of this saint by the Arguis Master have been identified with which to compare the example in the Bauzá Collection. We have to rely, therefore, upon the appurtenances in the picture for our proof. In the foreground and throughout the elaborate, rising landscape of the background, which, even more than was usual in the works of the international style, is crammed with little figures engaged in the pursuits of every-day life, we perceive the heaped-up rocks so peculiarly characteristic of the Arguis

[3] Vol. III, p. 162. [4] Ibid.
[5] Ibid. The only pronounced difference in the replica is that a background of simple color takes the place of the exquisitely patterned gold in the picture at Palma.

Fig. 168. THE ALCUDIA MASTER. DOUBLE VERONICA. MUSEO ARQUEOLÓGICO, PALMA

(*Photo. Archivo Mas*)

FIG. 169. THE ARGUIS MASTER. ST. JOHN BAPTIST.
BAUZÁ COLLECTION, MADRID
(*Photo. Archivo Mas*)

Master, assuming jagged and other strange geological formations, overspread by a capricious chiaroscuro, and one of them, at the beginning of the road's turn at the highest elevation on the right, actually given the beehive's shape with which he is fantastically prone to endow them.[1] Quite as telling is the reappearance of the pebbles that he likes to scatter about the soil and rocks, and again one of these, at the top of the crag framing St. John at the left, is twisted, according to his frequent whim, into the resemblance of a molasses drop. All over the heights are perched his imaginative interpretations of the romantic castles of international landscape, as in his retable at Alquézar.[2] Among the figures of *genre* in the background, two who at the city-gate are close enough to us to be clearly descried exhibit precisely the kind of haggard countenance that he so often affects, for example in a number of the participants in the procession to the Castel Sant' Angelo in the set of panels in the Prado; and the younger of the twain tilts up his head at the Master's favorite pertness of angle. I have saved, however, until the end the detail that seals the attribution, the *exact* repetition of the jewelled edging of St. Gregory's cope in the panels at Baltimore [3] upon the border of the Baptist's mantle.

Correspondingly it has gradually dawned upon me that we owe to the Arguis Master two panels now in the Collection of Dr. Ferrando on the island of Majorca, each with a pair of Apostles, evidently the remains of one of the usual Spanish representations of the whole college of Twelve. Sts. James Major and John stand in one panel, and Philip and Thomas in the other (Fig. 170), the four holding banderoles inscribed, as so frequently, with verses of the Apostles' Creed.[4] In the actual figures, the most unescapable evidence of the authorship is found in the head of Philip, which reiterates not only the characteristic tilt that I have specified in the last paragraph but also a type often used by the Master, especially for the Paul in the Prado retable; and the Thomas should likewise be compared with the so-called Matthias in the Baltimore shrine. As in the case, however, of the Bauzá Baptist, the appurtenances of the panels contribute to the proof, for the Apostles are not set directly upon the floor, as the figures ordinarily are in the paintings of interiors at the period, but upon a platform, according to an idiosyncrasy of the Arguis Master that may be verified in almost all

[1] Vol. III, p. 199.

[2] *Ibid.*, p. 200.

[3] Vol. VIII, p. 677.

[4] The verses are, of course, in Latin, but the scrolls contain also the names of the Apostles in Castilian, except in the case of James, who lacks any such designation. The form for Philip is *Felip*, which might be thought Catalan instead of the Castilian *Felipe*, but the final *e* was probably conceived as hidden by the turn of the scroll, since John's name seems plainly the Castilian *Juan* and not the Catalan *Joan*. *Tomas* is the same in both languages. The verses ordinarily assigned to Philip and Thomas in such assemblages are here interchanged, but a more serious blunder is the bestowal upon Philip of the emblem of James Minor, the fuller's club, the origin of the error perhaps being that these two Apostles are commemorated on the same day, May 1.

Fig. 170. THE ARGUIS MASTER. STS. PHILIP AND THOMAS.
COLLECTION OF DR. FERRANDO, MAJORCA
(*Photo. Archivo Mas*)

his achievements. The gold backgrounds are tooled with the sort of bold foliate pattern common in the Aragonese works of the international style.

NICOLÁS SOLANA

Ever since we first [1] defined the personality of this other Aragonese member of the international movement, who indulges in stylization at least as capricious as that of the Arguis Master, though somewhat different in its character, almost each succeeding volume has yielded important accretions to the corpus of his works, especially volume X [2] with the whole retable of St. Peter at Daroca; and we are here fortunately able to maintain the precedent by securely crediting to him a pair of panels in the Museum at Bilbao representing the *Noli me tangere* (Fig. 171) and the Ascension, the relics of an altarpiece. Despite the obviousness of the attribution I will take the space to enumerate some of the proofs, inasmuch as there are very few, even among the lovers of Spanish painting, who have studied him sufficiently to recognize his hand with readiness. In the Ascension, the Virgin reiterates a favorite but curiously simpering type of his, illustrated, for instance, by the St. Apollonia at Daroca; [3] the Apostle behind her, with the whimsical headdress, scarcely differs from the angel in the Gallery of Kansas City; [4] the personage just above her belongs to the same class of humanity as the figure at the left in Solana's signed panel in the Juñer Collection at Barcelona; [5] and the Apostle at the right whose nose is elongated to agree with the late Gothic velleity for caricature finds more than one exact counterpart among the Hebrews in the Crucifixion that the Juñer Collection also numbers among its possessions. [6] The artist even dares thus to distort with uglily pointed nostrils the countenance of the Magdalene in the *Noli me tangere* and to employ for the Christ in this compartment precisely the foppishly bearded and moustached sort of face utilized for the Daroca St. Barnabas. [7] As he carried to an extreme the addiction of the ultimate phase of the Gothic period to eccentric and even ill-favored specimens of mankind, so he exaggerated the fondness of the international movement for *genre*, almost sacrilegiously too much concerned with making the garden of the *Noli me tangere* into a veritable bird sanctuary in which multiplied members of the feathered creation engage in varied, characteristic activities, some of them pursuing magnified insects. Even the Magdalene's box of ointment is so fantastically enlarged that it looks like a fountain, according to the desire of "international" painters to dot their landscapes with pretty objects that will catch and delight the eye.

[1] Vol. V, p. 306. [2] P. 323.
[3] Vol. VI, fig. 265. [4] Vol. V, fig. 97.
[5] *Ibid.*, fig. 94. [6] *Ibid.*, fig. 96.
[7] Vol. VI, fig. 265.

FIG. 171. NICOLÁS SOLANA. *NOLI ME TANGERE*.
MUSEUM, BILBAO
(*Photo. Archivo Mas*)

GHERARDO STARNINA

I should long since have pondered the question whether any new light is shed upon the problem of attributions of extant works in Spain to this late Giottesco by the studies that Ugo Procacci has devoted to him, published in a series of three articles in the *Rivista d'arte* beginning in 1933,[1] the very year that I last discussed the artist in my volume IV [2] and before, thus, I was acquainted with the results of the Italian scholar's investigations. Relying upon the trustworthiness of Vasari's immediate predecessors in writing upon the art of their country, who, as well as the famous Aretine, ascribe to Starnina the frescoes of the chapel of St. Jerome in the church of the Carmine at Florence, Procacci accepts as the starting-point for the reconstruction of the master's personality the scanty fragments of the frescoes that are preserved but were hidden behind a brick wall of the seventeenth century until at Procacci's insistence they were uncovered. We should feel on surer ground if we had a document of Starnina's own time proving that he was the author, but the unanimous consent of the writers of the sixteenth century makes it practically a certainty. Procacci has found a record showing that the frescoes of the chapel of St. Jerome were completed by October 2, 1404, and through comparisons with these works he claims for Starnina, among the mural paintings in the Castellani Chapel in S. Croce, Florence, all of which had often been conjecturally assigned to the artist, only those having to do with St. Anthony Abbot. On like internal evidence he revives an old attribution to Starnina in the case of a panel, No. 447 of the Uffizi, depicting the activities of hermits in the Thebaid, to which in recent times connoisseurs have enjoyed the sport of attaching the names of all sorts of masters.

In the problems of Starnina's biography and chronology, Procacci sets aside, too lightly as it seems to me, what is at least the possibility of a first sojourn in Spain [3] on the artist's part before the earliest mention of his presence at Florence in 1387. Treating his certain but perhaps second residence in Spain and knowing merely the articles of Sanchis y Sivera on *Pintores medievales en Valencia* brought out in 1912 and 1913 in the *Estudis universitaris catalans* and not his subsequent publication of the articles, with additions, as a monograph in 1930, the Italian scholar does not place Starnina definitely in the Iberian peninsula until 1398; but the monograph would have revealed to Procacci that he is thrice recorded at Valencia already in 1395 and first on June 22.[4] His return to Florence must have occurred, as we have seen, early enough to have permitted him to finish the decoration of the chapel of St. Jerome by October 2, 1404. Deriving my information from Van Marle, I had taken February 6, 1408, as the last recorded date in Starnina's life, but Procacci has shown that the year of this

---

[1] For the exact references, see the bibliography at the end of the present volume.
[2] Pp. 644–649.
[3] See my vol. III, p. 8.
[4] The monograph, p. 45, and my vol. III, p. 8.

February 6 was really 1409, when the artist was engaged upon a commission at Empoli. He must have died between this time and October 28, 1413, the date of an entry unearthed by Procacci in a Florentine municipal record referring to his heirs.

Among paintings in Spain, it was only in certain works in the cathedral of Toledo that, when I wrote my volumes III [5] and IV,[6] I stated Starnina's authorship to be at least conceivable; and the fragments in the chapel of St. Jerome at Florence, which Procacci has so persuasively assigned to him, as well as the additional evidence supplied by the sections in the Castellani chapel and by the panel of the Thebaid, in both of which with a considerable degree of probability we ought to discern his craft, render me now very much more willing to ascribe some of the works at Toledo to his hand. The predella in the baptismal chapel and the canvas of St. Nicholas [7] in the chapel of the Trinity may be excluded as Spanish imitations of the Italian manner; but, as I look at the reproductions of the paintings in Italy attributed to Starnina by Procacci, I find it very hard to escape the conviction that he did also the retable in the chapel of S. Eugenio, the upper zone of frescoes in the chapel of S. Blas, and the two saints in the chapel of Sto. Sepulcro, whom from the first [8] I have been disposed to believe that he executed. His style seems to me to emerge in certain passages in the retable that are not wholly concealed by the very extensive repainting of Juan de Borgoña in the early sixteenth century.[9] In particular there should be singled out as suggestive of Starnina's brush the St. Joseph, priest, and (just behind him) Simeon in the Purification, the St. Peter and the bearded Jew at the left in the Betrayal, and (Fig. 172) the Pilate washing his hands, who persuasively resembles the best preserved figure in the Carmine cycle, the St. Benedict. Internal evidence would therefore confirm the guess that the retable in the chapel of S. Eugenio might have been thither moved from the chapel of the Epiphany and thus be an actual documented work of Starnina.[10]

In order to attribute to him the upper zone of frescoes in the chapel of S. Blas, we should have to return to the old theory which I was once inclined to discard,[11] namely, that Rodríguez de Toledo did only the practically obliterated lower zone, and we should be obliged to accept the idea which I have never entirely renounced,[12] i.e., that we owe the upper zone to the same master as the retable in the chapel of S. Eugenio. Among the many details that I might choose to illustrate the closeness to the mode of the paintings in the Carmine, the Hebrew who faces us in the group listening at the door of the chamber of Pentecost (Fig. 173) finds a·striking counterpart again in the St. Benedict, and the young Apostle receiving the

---

[5] Chapter XXXIX.   [6] Pp. 644–649.

[7] When I wrote volume III (p. 233), I had not perceived that it was a canvas instead of a panel or that the saint was Nicholas.

[8] Vol. IV, p. 646.

[9] Vol. IX, p. 171.   [10] Vol. IV, pp. 644–645.

[11] Vol. III, p. 226.   [12] *Ibid.*, p. 231.

FIG. 172. STARNINA(?). CHRIST BEFORE PILATE, SECTION OF
RETABLE (REPAINTED BY JUAN DE BORGOÑA). CHAPEL
OF S. EUGENIO, CATHEDRAL, TOLEDO

(*Photo. Archivo Mas*)

FIG. 173. STARNINA(?). PENTECOST, SECTION OF FRESCOES IN
CHAPEL OF S. BLAS, CATHEDRAL, TOLEDO
(*Photo. Archivo Mas*)

gift of the Holy Spirit at the centre recalls a decorative head published by Procacci on page 183 of his first article. If Starnina does indeed deserve the credit of all these works in the cathedral of Toledo, I myself cannot discern so clearly the subtle steps in stylistic evolution that Procacci analyzes in his Italian career as to attempt to specify whether he did the cycles in Spain during the hypothetical first journey or in his residence there subsequently to 1387. We have noted in volume IV [13] that there is some reason, unhappily inconclusive, for assigning the retable in the chapel of S. Eugenio to the year 1393.

THE VILLAMEDIANA MASTER

It has been a long trek to find the real, original location of the panels from St. Ursula's story of which four are in the Leverhulme Gallery at Port Sunlight and another quartet passed from the Gorostiza Collection, Bilbao, into the world of dealing. Perceiving that they were products of the international movement, we started [1] by refusing to seek them, with certain critics, in the school of Nice and by turning to Spain, where, however, from the first we doubted Bertaux to have been right in affiliating them with Catalonia. Renewed study of the style through the discovery of the Gorostiza set diverted us more and more from the eastern Spanish littoral towards the west.[2] Next,[3] in examining the course of the international movement in the region of Palencia in the western part of the peninsula, we became practically convinced that here must have been the seat of the activity of the painter whom we were trailing. Certainty was achieved when we succeeded [4] in grouping the cycle of St. Ursula and a number of other Palencian works as creations of a single personality and in giving him the name of the Villamediana Master. In the present volume we reach at last the final station in our journey by coming upon the actual edifice that contained the Leverhulme and Gorostiza panels, for I have unearthed an old photograph [5] of the retable in which they were incorporated, a structure over an altar now dedicated to the pope, St. Pius V, in the Dominican church of S. Pablo in the city of Palencia itself.

The photograph shows a baroque altarpiece with a statue of St. Pius at the centre but with the panels of the fifteenth century built into its sides, whether done originally for this spot in the church or moved hither from another place in the edifice to form an incongruous section of the later assemblage. The Gorostiza set constituted an upper tier, and the Leverhulme series a lower; but another exciting revelation of the photograph is that, as I have suspected,[6] there belonged to the retable of St. Ursula the smaller compartments of seated saints now distributed through the Johnson

---

[13] P. 646.
[2] Vol. IV, p. 564.
[4] Vol. IX, p. 790.
[5] No. 2005 of the photographs taken by the Madrid firm then called Laurent and Co. but now Ruiz Vernacci.

[1] Vol. II, p. 448.
[3] Vol. VI, p. 614.
[6] Vol. II, p. 450, n. 1.

Collection at Philadelphia,[7] the Zorn Museum at Mora, Sweden,[8] and a public or private gallery [9] that I have not yet ascertained. Four of these compartments made a kind of predella, as again I had surmised, but another set of the same number and size filled the space between the tiers honoring St. Ursula. Two of the four Johnson panels were in this space at the upper left, and the other pair at the right in the predella; the St. Dominic now in unascertained possession was at the extreme right at the upper level; and the pair of Zorn pieces occupied the predella's left. Only one compartment, next to St. Dominic, is thus unaccounted for, and the photograph proves that already this panel of the Villamediana Master's retable had disappeared from the spot and that there had been substituted another, the nature and period of which the reproduction is not clear enough to disclose.

THE PALANQUINOS MASTER

Don Raimundo Ruiz of Madrid has recently acquired four panels from a retable of St. James Major that not only were most patently executed by this generously preserved leader in the Hispano-Flemish movement in the school of Leon but incorporate the highest attainments of which he was capable. Of undiscovered original provenience,[1] they depict scenes from the Apostle's story, of which three are often encountered, his sermonizing, decapitation (together with his convert, Josias), and the transportation of his body in the bull-drawn cart to Queen Lupa's palace. Although the subject of the fourth compartment figures in the account of St. James in the *Golden Legend,* I do not recall having met it before in art, the bridge giving way to drown the pursuers of the Apostle's disciples, who had escaped from the prison into which they had been cast at the instance of the still mistrustful Lupa prior to her reception of his relics (Fig. 174). Contrary to the Master's usual but not unvarying practice, real skies take the place of elaborately patterned gold.

In a panel in private possession at Barcelona, representing St. Catherine's ordeal of the wheels (Fig. 175), all elements point to the Palanquinos Master, but I have refrained from making the attribution categorical until now the Ruiz cycle of St. James has provided absolute counterparts for the two old, shaggily haired and bearded spectators of the virgin martyr's gruesome experience in a man who at the extreme right views the Apostle's decapitation and in another who through a window peers at the bulls carting his body into Queen Lupa's presence. The gold background, though not incised with any of his frequent Moorish figurations, exhibits a diaper of flowered lozenges, also characteristic of his altarpieces. I am sorry to

[7] *Ibid.,* p. 448.　　　　　　　　　　[8] Vol. X, p. 330.
[9] Vol. IX, p. 790 and fig. 329.
[1] They do not seem to be mentioned anywhere in Gómez-Moreno's *Catálogos monumentales* of the provinces of Leon and Zamora, where we should expect to find them, nor can they, of course, belong to the series by the Astorga Master once in the chapel of the Astorga cemetery: see my vol. IX, p. 557. The dimensions of the panels are 114 centimetres in height by 89 in width.

FIG. 174. THE PALANQUINOS MASTER. PURSUERS OF ST. JAMES
MAJOR'S DISCIPLES DROWNED BY COLLAPSE OF BRIDGE, SECTION
OF RETABLE. COLLECTION OF RAIMUNDO RUIZ, MADRID
(*Courtesy of the owner*)

FIG. 175. THE PALANQUINOS MASTER. ST. CATHERINE'S
ORDEAL OF THE WHEELS. PRIVATE COLLECTION,
BARCELONA

(*Photo. Archivo Mas*)

stigmatize the Palanquinos Master with one of the rare instances of pruriency in mediaeval Spanish art, the all too evident salacious delight that he has taken in the excuse offered by the theme for reducing the maiden's costume to the point of leaving few of her rather opulent, naked charms to the imagination.

Among the works that in former volumes I have left without definite ascription, we may now transfer to this painter's count the Betrayal that from the Manzi Collection [2] has passed into the possession of Mr. Charles S. Wakefield-Mori at Monte Carlo. I have hitherto hesitated to return to the picture because the homogeneity with his manner is not entirely obvious, but by adding one detail of correspondence to another we arrive, I have finally decided, at enough cumulative evidence to justify the attribution. I confess that it was probably the *mudéjar* design in the gold background, virtually confined to the Palanquinos Master in Hispano-Flemish painting, which first led me to weigh the possibility of his authorship and then to perceive that in general style there was nothing discordant with the idea. The next detailed proof, after the background, is found in the head of the soldier raising his arm, since the countenance conforms to a type and to a kind of modelling in chiaroscuro peculiarly characteristic of the Master, as in the lover and his two companions visiting the imprisoned St. Marina in the Mayorga retable,[3] and since the loosely gathered locks of hair are likewise a distinguishing trait of his figures, illustrated also by the same three actors in this altarpiece. In one of the subordinate episodes depicted in the offing, Judas, leading the soldiers for the arrest, provides a further example of this kind of person, and he wears the pointed cap that is among the Master's favorite articles of costume. The angel in another of these episodes, the Agony in the Garden, resembles closely the celestial spirit crowning the St. Damian of the cathedral at Leon.[4] The Saviour, seized in the foreground by His captors, is very different from His representation in the version of the theme at Mayorga; but you cannot confine a painter to a single norm, and facial resemblances of a certain degree occur in the Christ of the Entombment and in the St. Andrew in the Mayorga retable. If we could state with entire confidence that the Isaiah formerly belonging to Kleinberger and Co. at Paris [5] was done by the Palanquinos Master, we should be provided with an achievement of his displaying a countenance decidedly analogous to that of Our Lord in the Betrayal.

[2] Vol. IV, p. 468, fig. 181. The dimensions are 1.27 metres in height by .85 in width. I should now be much less disposed to discern affiliations with the Assumption that I illustrated as fig. 180 in the same volume.

[3] Vol. IV, fig. 40.

[4] Vol. IV, fig. 39.

[5] Vol. VII, p. 843. The cleaning of the Kleinberger panel has revealed that the face had not, as I once suspected, been retouched. There has also emerged, after the cleaning, an inscription on the base of the parapet, "El es Isiais, Rei," betraying in his name the general, defective spelling of the period and exemplifying the curious and not infrequent custom of denominating the Prophets as Kings: cf. vol. IX, p. 84, n. 15.

The Milá Master

At last there has appeared *in situ* a work by this pleasing Hispano-Flemish painter for whom I have eventually adopted the title of the Milá Master,[1] a panel in no less a place than the great Cistercian convent of Las Huelgas at Burgos, representing the Virgin of Mercy spreading her mantle at the right over nuns of the Order and at the left over Ferdinand, Isabella, three of their children, and the cardinal-primate of Spain, Pedro de Mendoza (Fig. 176). It would seem that we could thus localize the artist's activity in the province of Burgos, and we have noted [2] that there is a tradition that another production by him, the Garnelo Mass of St. Gregory, comes from this region; but such reports of provenience are far from trustworthy, and the picture at Las Huelgas, with personages so important as the royal family, might have been executed elsewhere at their order or the cardinal's and dispatched to the convent, or they might have sent the painter from another spot to the convent to carry out the commission. Indeed, we have had occasion in former volumes to conjecture on stylistic evidence that the Milá Master's focus was the adjoining province of Palencia.

His authorship of the panel at Las Huelgas can be detected in every one of its aspects, as has been perceived by Diego Angulo,[3] who rightly identifies the children as the eldest daughter named after her mother, Prince John, and the future Joanna the Mad, deducing from their ages a date in the middle of the eighties of the fifteenth century. Ferdinand's head has been lost in the injuries suffered by the panel, and the other countenances can scarcely be taken as anything like accurate portraits since they are adapted to the Master's few, often repeated types. Princess Isabella, for instance, is no more than one of his characteristic maidens, such as the girl warming the cloth in the Adanero Birth of the Virgin; and the cardinal has a nondescript face not at all similar to the obviously better likeness in the contemporary cycle by the Luna Master in S. Ginés, Guadalajara.[4] With the substitution of two symmetrically disposed demons hurling the arrows of wrath against which Our Lady is the protectress, instead of the more usual and blasphemous introduction of the Deity as manipulator of the shafts, the composition is really a variant of the theme called by the Spaniards the Patrocinio de la Virgin.[5]

Saralegui [6] has augmented our comprehension of the Milá Master not only in the past by correct attributions but more recently by a work quite as indisputably in the same category, a panel in a private collection at Madrid depicting the sermon of an Apostle (or Evangelist?) in whom he would tentatively like to recognize St. Peter exalted to his cathedra at Antioch. I am sorry, however, for once to be obliged to take decided exception to

---

[1] Vol. X, pp. 331–335.   [2] Vol. IV, p. 296.

[3] In the publication, *Iconografía española*, Cuaderno 1, Madrid, 1945, pp. 5–7.

[4] Vol. VII, fig. 348.

[5] *Ibid.*, p. 691.

[6] *Archivo español de arte*, XXIII (1950), 200.

FIG. 176. THE MILÁ MASTER. VIRGIN OF MERCY WITH FERDINAND,
ISABELLA, THREE OF THEIR CHILDREN, PEDRO DE MENDOZA,
AND CISTERCIAN NUNS. CONVENT OF LAS HUELGAS,
BURGOS

(*Photo. Photo Club*)

another contention of his, the belief that the Milá Master is identical with my Frómista Master. Their styles and types are related, bcause the Milá Master also was very probably active in the province of Palencia, and I would not put it beyond the bounds of credibility that here and there, as in the Pentecost, he might have assisted on the retable that gives the other painter his name and so have been trained by him; but in general the Frómista Master is clearly distinguishable, for example in the greater masculinity and bluffness of his productions.

To Saralegui's and Angulo's important accretions to our stock of the Milá Master's works I am glad now humbly to make two contributions of my own. In the first, a panel at least once in the Echaurren Collection at Madrid depicting the arrest of a hallowed deacon other than the well known Sts. Stephen, Lawrence, or Vincent [7] (Fig. 177), the most determinative factor for the ascription is the captor at the left who embodies a characteristic and frequent, bearded type of the Master, as especially in the St. Joachim of the Presentation of the Virgin in the Chicago Art Institute.[8] The St. Gregory in the picture of the Garnelo Collection [9] and St. Anne in the triptych of the Mateu Collection [10] are variants of the kind of countenance that he uses for the deacon. The landscape also constitutes an important item in the proof since it manifestly accords with this element in his paintings and is even practically a replica of the setting in the Flight into Egypt in the Gor Collection.

It is the careful review of the Milá Master's qualities necessitated by the study of the Echaurren panel that has revealed him as very probably the author of a work which puzzled me when I wrote volume IV and has continued to be an enigma ever since, the Dream of Jacob in the Provincial Museum at Seville.[11] No single factor is perhaps sufficient to enforce the attribution, but the aggregation of a number of close similarities to his manner creates a strong presumption in its favor. The nearest thing in the picture to an absolute reproduction of elements in his other achievements is the distinctive landscape, the counterparts for which may be seen in the Echaurren panel and again in the Gor Flight into Egypt. Furthermore, I scarcely understand how I should not have been struck before by the agreement of the Jacob with the bearded sort of face which I have stressed in the last paragraph, particularly with that of the man with the spear (Longinus?) among the symbols of the Passion in the Garnelo Mass of St. Gregory. The likeness of the angels to those of the Prado Assumption is not complete; but the disparities are by no means so wide as not to have been bridged by one artist, and in both pictures these figures share the de-

---

[7] Since the arrest takes place in the country, he cannot be Stephen or Lawrence who were apprehended in the city; and St. Vincent is regularly and properly represented as taken prisoner together with his bishop, St. Valerius. The shield of the soldier at the left is edged with a conglomeration of letters that are legible but, as so often in similar inscriptions on the Spanish paintings of the period, make no sense, at least to our minds of the twentieth century.

[8] Vol. VII, fig. 341.   [9] Vol. IV, fig. 109.

[10] Vol. VI, fig. 282.   [11] Vol. IV, p. 474, and fig. 184.

FIG. 177. THE MILÁ MASTER. ARREST OF A
HALLOWED DEACON. ECHAURREN
COLLECTION, MADRID

(*Photo. Moreno*)

lightful vernal freshness with which the Master is wont to imbue his youthful actors. As a matter of fact, the angel hovering over Sts. Joachim and Anne in the Meeting at the Golden Gate in the Mateu triptych varies somewhat from his brothers in the Prado Assumption and provides a partial analogue for the two celestial spirits above Jacob. The angel at the right exemplifies a pert-nosed type of profile often employed by our painter, as in the Virgin's handmaid in the Visitation of the Milá Collection.

THE AVILA MASTER

In three fragments of a retable that belong to the Museum at Vitoria, depicting the Madonna standing between Sts. Dominic and Thomas Aquinas (Fig. 178), I doubt whether I should have recognized the hand of the Avila Master if the Virgin were not practically duplicated by her representation in the Epiphany of the Dupont Collection, Barcelona, which it was only in my most recent volume [1] that I was able to attach to him. Neither of these figures of Our Lady conforms facially to his conceptions of her in other works, and in the Dupont panel we had to resort to different factors to establish the attribution. We thus arrive at the correct collocation of the Vitoria triad by a bridge in which the Dupont Epiphany is tied to the Master's better known productions and the triad is linked to the Epiphany. The affinity to the Virgin of the Epiphany extends to the unusual audacity, for Spain, of a costume decidedly décolleté. When we have once become certain that we are in the presence of the Avila Master, we discern analogies that ought to have been apparent to us from the first. If we are able to find a counterpart for the Virgin only in his treatment of her in the Dupont picture, it requires no more than a little closer look to see the same sort of countenance in some of the angels who flutter above the sacred personages in the triptych of the Lázaro Collection. The sour-visaged Dominican saints merely accentuate the unsparing sternness with which the Master was wont to stress the virility of his men, as in the prostrate shepherd of the triptych's left wing or St. Joachim's companion in the panel in S. Vicente, Avila; and we ought not to forget that it is likely that he approximated all the types in the many works that he must have painted beside the mere handful that have come down to us. St. Thomas Aquinas is distinguished not only, as a Doctor of the Church, by the regular emblem of a small ecclesiastical edifice illumined with rays from his hand but also by the rare, though not unparalleled, attribute of a jewelled border to his black mantle, according to the splendor in which he appeared to Brother Albert. [2] The introduction of Sts. Dominic and Thomas Aquinas probably means that the panels once graced an institution of the Black Friars, but, since they may have entered the Museum from a private collection, we possess no proof that the institution lay near Vitoria, from the district of which the Museum's contents mostly derive, or that the activity of the artist thus stretched far north of his focus, Avila.

[1] Vol. X, p. 349.   [2] See my vol. IX, p. 37.

FIG. 178. THE AVILA MASTER. MADONNA WITH STS. DOMINIC AND
THOMAS AQUINAS. MUSEUM, VITORIA

(*Photo. Archivo Mas*)

The Master of El Parral

Certain Hispano-Flemish paintings that because of my defective visual memory I was obliged in volume IV [1] to leave without definite attribution are revealed in the photographs lately made by the Mas Archive to incorporate the craft of a single artist, to whom we may give the name of the Master of El Parral since his activity, so far as we know it, seems to have centered at this Hieronymite monastery, close to the city of Segovia. About contemporary in the latter part of the fifteenth century with his perhaps somewhat less technically gifted rival in this region whom I have called the Segovia Master,[2] he asserts himself characteristically and at his best in two panels that from El Parral have passed into the near-lying city's Provincial Museum and depict the Lamentation over the Dead Christ and the Assumption (Figs. 179 and 180).[3] Probably once sections of the same retable, at least they are shown indisputably to be one personality's achievements, even if the critic goes no further than a comparison of the Magdalene in the Lamentation and the uppermost angel at the left assisting the Virgin to heaven or than a glance at the peculiarly stringy tresses of all these three figures. The Master is very cognizant of his Flemish precedents, as especially in the appealing angels in the Assumption; but he adapts his actors to Iberian ethnic standards, and his own rather melancholy individuality affects his production, causing him, as in the case of the soaring Virgin, to impart a mournful expression to countenances on which we should have expected elation. This proclivity stands him in good stead in the Lamentation, where the intense, sincere, and even beautiful embodiment of grief would be hard to duplicate among his contemporaries in the profession. I have not overlooked the possibility that he might be identical with some one of these contemporaries, although not exhibiting the most typical manner of such a painter, but the considerable study that I have devoted to the problem has failed to convince me of any equation of the sort. The Lamentation, for example, shows a few analogies to the panel of the miracle of Sts. Cosmas and Damian, now in the Prado, for which an attribution to Fernando del Rincón has very tentatively been proposed;[4] but the links with this panel are far from sufficient to establish the same authorship, which, indeed, could be argued only on the supposition that the artist might have executed the two Segovia pictures at an early stage in his career before he turned into the ways of the Renaissance that the Prado picture illustrates.

The Master of El Parral provides the sponsor of another pair of works for which, when I wrote volume IV,[5] I could find no sure attachments, the curious paintings on cloth in the Museum of Segovia that, again deriving from the monastery of El Parral, represent, in one case, St. Jerome leading monks of his Order and, in the other, his follower St. Paula with her

[1] Pp. 455–456.
[2] Ibid., p. 451.
[3] Ibid., p. 456, where I have described the Lamentation as a Deposition.
[4] Vol. IX, p. 271.   [5] P. 455.

Fig. 179. THE MASTER OF EL PARRAL. LAMENTATION OVER THE
DEAD CHRIST. PROVINCIAL MUSEUM, SEGOVIA
(*Photo. Archivo Mas*)

FIG. 180. THE MASTER OF EL PARRAL. ASSUMPTION.
PROVINCIAL MUSEUM, SEGOVIA
(*Photo. Unturbe*)

daughter Eustochium surrounded by Hieronymite nuns (Fig. 181). The proof of the attribution is not far to seek. Between St. Paula and her daughter, a nun repeats the face of the Virgin of the Assumption, and the type is scarcely varied in two other Hieronymite ladies farther in the background; Eustochium looks upward with exactly the pertness and with very much the same countenance as the lowest angel at the right in the Assumption; the profile of the uppermost angel at the right is used for the nun behind Eustochium; a monk bending his head among St. Jerome's disciples wears the unnecessarily woebegone expression that our Master cultivates; and the rayed haloes of the Lamentation reappear, except that those of Sts. Jerome, Paula, and Eustochium add the queer inner figuration which, for some reason that I have not yet fathomed, seems to have been associated with the Hieronymite Order.[6]

The photographs demonstrate not only that my visual memory was less faulty than usual when I related [7] to this pair of paintings the panel in the Lázaro Collection, Madrid, depicting St. Jerome in his study aided by his brothers in religion but also that indeed the panel was actually executed by our Master and may well have been originally a part of the same assemblage. It is hardly possible that even a single artist in separate efforts should have created personages marked by such identity as exists in the two representations of St. Jerome and his monastic companions. I had guessed that the paintings on cloth might have been organ-shutters, but it is just as likely that they were the wings for an altarpiece of which the Lázaro panel constituted a section.

THE PEREA MASTER

The ferreting about among the possessions of the Provincial Museum at Valencia occasioned by its admirable reconstitution has resulted in the discovery of the true [1] capping piece of the *guardapolvos* in the retable that gives the Perea Master his name, a panel depicting only two adoring angels.

In my sixth volume [2] I outlined the knotty problem involved in the retable of St. Anne in the Colegiata at Játiva, which unhappily perished in the civil war, namely whether we ought to see in it an early work of the Perea Master or postulate as its author a hypothetical teacher of his; and in a recent monograph,[3] as remarkable for its delicate connoisseurship and discrimination as for its profound erudition, Don Leandro de Saralegui has championed the second alternative, creating for the teacher the sobriquet of the Master of St. Anne. The Spanish scholar's potent authority naturally demanded that I review carefully and in detail the whole evidence once more, but the result has been that the affiliations of the St. Anne retable

[6] See my vol. V, p. 12.
[7] Vol. IV, pp. 455–457, where the panel is illustrated.
[1] Vol. VI, p. 272.
[2] Pp. 274–275.
[3] *El Maestro de Sta. Ana y su escuela*, published by the Institución Alfonso el Magnánimo, Valencia, 1950.

FIG. 181. THE MASTER OF EL PARRAL. STS. JEROME AND PAULA
WITH FOLLOWERS. PROVINCIAL MUSEUM, SEGOVIA
(*Photo. Archivo Mas*)

with the Perea Master's works seem to me so close and the differences so few and so little pronounced that, for my own peace of mind, I still do not *dare* to go beyond the conclusions at which I arrived in volume VI, i.e., that the data at our disposal really fail to justify a decision one way or the other but that, if I were absolutely forced to choose, I should prefer to think of the Perea Master himself as executing the retable at an earlier moment in his career than the period to which the majority of his extant achievements belong. The panel of the Madonna of Mercy in the Martínez Aloy Collection at Valencia, which I had assigned to the Perea Master's putative beginnings,[4] and the St. Cosmas in the Ledyard Collection, New York, which [5] I had given to the same artist by perceiving a similarity to this panel, are logically attributed by Saralegui to his Master of St. Anne, and in a letter to me, after he had read my volume X, he adds to the list the painting of Christ before Pilate in a Swiss collection that I there [6] published, as well as consequently the Via Dolorosa in the Leger Collection, London,[7] about which in his monograph he was still hesitant; but again I must confess with humiliation that my eyes refuse to discern clearly the St. Anne Master's or even the Perea Master's hand in another work that he brings into the same category, the *Anna selbdritt* which has passed from the Bosch Collection [8] to the Barcelona Museum and which he adduces cogent arguments to suggest as the possible long lost principal compartment of the Játiva altarpiece. Since my books have abundantly shown how often I have been guided and even corrected by Saralegui, I particularly regret these shades of divergence from his opinions, as also my pigheaded loathness to alter my classifications of the Visitation in a private collection at Madrid [9] and the Sts. Lucy and Agatha in the church of the Hospital at Villarreal [10] (blessedly preserved in the civil war), paintings that with reservations he includes under the Master of St. Anne's name.

If he is right in segregating this Master (and be it understood finally that I am far from definitely rejecting his contention), it would appear reasonable, as he claims, to make the author of the retable of St. Anne the fountainhead of the broad stream in the Valencian school that I have traced to the Perea Master; but, even if we grant the separate existence of the St. Anne Master, I should still maintain that the stream derived its actual flow from the Perea Master who, so far as may be judged from the extant remains, was a much more forceful personality.

Nor can he persuade me, in the above-mentioned letter, to transfer to the Artés Master two works that I have assigned in volume X [11] to the Perea Master, the Entry into Jerusalem and the panel in which I had followed the Bollandists in recognizing St. Dysmas's murder of his father. The question of an attribution to either of these artists, who so closely resemble each other, lapses into insignificance in comparison with the

[4] Vol. VI, p. 282.
[5] Vol. IX, p. 831.
[6] P. 366.
[7] Vol. VI, p. 285.
[8] *Ibid.*, p. 116.
[9] *Ibid.*, p. 369.
[10] *Ibid.*, p. 440.
[11] P. 366.

iconographic importance of Saralegui's brilliant discovery of the real subject of the second of the pictures. He has revealed his discovery to me in the letter and graciously permits me to publish it. The theme is a common one in representations of the story of the Holy Cross, the Byzantine emperor, Heraclius, killing the Persian king, Chosroës, after defeating him in battle and thereby recovering the sacred relic. The painter has conformed closely to the account of the assassination in the chapter on the feast of the Exaltation of the Cross in the *Golden Legend,* thus introducing details some of which had puzzled me in attempting to apply them to the redeemed malefactor. Chosroës is clad with a magnificence and sits upon a splendid throne that befit his august state; in his desire "that he should be called god of all the people" he has "set the tree of the Cross on his right side instead of the sun, and a cock on the left side instead of the Holy Ghost"; and above the walls of the room we see the "images of the sun and of the moon and of the stars" that ornamented the tower which he had caused to be constructed as a symbol of his claim to divine prerogatives. Saralegui explains Chosroës's lack of a crown by his delegation of earthly power to his son and points out to me that Heraclius properly wears an imperial diadem; and I am no more troubled than is the Spanish scholar by the bestowal of a halo upon the emperor who at least in his rôle of champion of the Cross would have been deemed a Christian hero and, as Saralegui calls to my attention in a second letter, is actually given a halo by the Aragonese painter, Miguel Jiménez.[12] Another Valencian artist, the Gil Master, had long before depicted the slaying of Chosroës with almost exactly the same composition and details.[13]

In *Archivo español de arte,* XIX (1946), 142, Saralegui assigns to his St. Anne Master a small Madonna in the Collection of Doña Elena Pascual Boldún at Valencia, but the editors of the periodical, misinterpreting his statements, placed under the illustration of the picture the caption "Maestro de Játiva" as if he were ascribing it to my Játiva Master, whereas he used the words "Maestro de Játiva" only as another designation of the St. Anne Master who also was employed in this town. In a subsequent letter to me, he has confirmed his choice of the St. Anne Master as the author.

With his customary visual keenness Angulo [14] has placed in the school of the Perea Master a panel of the Madonna enthroned between two angels in the Toma Stelian Museum at Bucharest, which probably itself constituted a whole retable, since it possesses *guardapolvos* truncated at the bottom with curving incisions according to the mode in which they were treated at the lowest ends of altarpieces; and, as has not infrequently happened in the past, I have the audacity to go beyond his admirable caution and set the picture among the astoundingly large number of works by the Master himself that have been handed down to us. Since the painting exists in a collec-

---

[12] See my vol. VIII, fig. 35.
[13] Vol. VII, p. 793.
[14] *Archivo español de arte,* XIV (1940–1941), 319.

tion too remote for most of us to visit and since the Catalogue of the Museum, which includes a reproduction, will not be found in many libraries, I take the space to publish an illustration (Fig. 182).

The Artés Master and the Játiva Master

Further sections of the retable of St. Jerome by the Artés Master, from which I published two pieces in vol. VI,[1] have been recognized by Saralegui,[2] the central effigy of this Father of the Church and two narrative themes, his youthful flagellation by angels and his penitence in the wilds. All five panels may be argued to have come from a single, original retable since they were formerly in the Collection of Colonel Montesinos at Valencia and are now distributed in the city among his heirs: the two that I identified belong to his widow; the effigy and flagellation to the sons of Don Francisco Gómez Fos; and the penitence to the estate of the Condesa de la Vallesa de Mandor. I quite concur also in Saralegui's attribution to the Artés Master of a small panel of St. John Evangelist in the Navarro Alcácer Collection, Valencia, but I have not seen even a photograph of the Coronation in the Almolda Collection at San Sebastian, which he classifies as a work of the same painter. In his monograph on El Maestro de Sta. Ana[3] he is manifestly right in adding another panel to these important accretions to our understanding of the Artés Master, a Madonna that from the town of Bocairente and probably from its parish church has reached the Museum at Játiva; and he properly ventures the guess that the picture may have been a part of the retable from which sections, also once at Bocairente, though not in the parish church, now grace the Calabuig Collection, Valencia (in whatever edifice at Bocairente the retable originally existed).[4] He hesitates[5] between the Artés Master, the Játiva Master, or a collaboration of the two for the authorship of a large Flagellation lately presented to the church of Sto. Tomás (formerly called the church of the Congregación)[6] at Valencia, even questioning whether after all they may not be one and the same individual (Fig. 183); but I believe that I can distinguish two personalities and that it is the Artés Master to whom the Flagellation should be assigned. With acute perception,[7] however, he has transferred to the Artés Master the medallions of Sts. Cosmas and Damian in the cathedral, Valencia, that I,[8] though with misgivings, had attached to Rodrigo de Osona the younger; and, because they appear to be retouched by the same hand as the other pieces by the Artés Master in the church,

[1] P. 314.
[2] Arte español, XVII (1947), 38, n. 13, and Archivo español de arte, XXI (1948), 276 ff.
[3] Published by the Institución Alfonso el Magnánimo, Valencia, 1950, p. 44, n. 1.
[4] See my vol. VI, p. 304.
[5] Monograph on El Maestro de Santa Ana, 34, n. 1.
[6] See above, p. 286.
[7] Archivo español de arte, XXI (1948), 287.
[8] Vol. VI, p. 212.

FIG. 182. THE PEREA MASTER. MADONNA AND ANGELS.
TOMA STELIAN MUSEUM, BUCHAREST
(*From the Catalogue of the Museum*)

FIG. 183. THE ARTÉS MASTER. FLAGELLATION. CHURCH OF
THE CONGREGACIÓN, VALENCIA

(*Photo. Archivo Mas*)

depicting Sts. Barnabas, Anthony of Padua, and the Crucifixion,[9] he suspects that the whole set of five might have once helped to constitute a single assemblage. The size of the medallions (49 centimetres in diameter) tends to make him discard the hypothesis that they could have been the decorations of a reliquary of Sts. Cosmas and Damian recorded to have been painted for the cathedral in 1506 by a Master Vicente and an Onofre Alemany, one of whom otherwise would have proved to be the Artés Master!

Among the many paintings that Saralegui's unflagging research and discerning eye are constantly calling forth from their hiding-places and allocating for us and posterity, there is a panel of the paired and half-length figures of Sts. Francis and Bernard belonging to the Caballé Collection at Valencia, in which he is probably right in recognizing the Játiva Master's rather than the Artés Master's craft.[10] No less interesting is his provisional but tempting suggestion that the panel may be a fragment of the now lacking central compartment of the Master's retable in S. Pedro at Játiva[11] where the effigies would originally have been depicted at full length. The principal objection to the acceptance of the proposition is that we should have expected St. Gerald instead of St. Francis to have been coupled with St. Bernard in accord with the fact that scenes from the lives of St. Gerald (the patron of the donor, Guerau de Castelvert Ripoll)[12] and of St. Bernard are included in the retable's lateral sections, nor is the objection quite removed by Saralegui's argument that the name of Francis, as well as of Bernard, occurs in the donor's family.

It is believed by Saralegui[13] that, if the Játiva Master and the Artés Master are not one and the same, the former inspired the latter, but I should prefer to think of the bolder and more vigorous Artés Master as the teacher.

My own augmentation of this phase of Valencian art begins with an attractive panel of the Nativity, belonging to the Koetser Gallery at New York (Fig. 184), which involves a delicate problem of connoisseurship, since it lies so near to the border-line between the affiliated manners of the Játiva and Artés Masters that in provisionally deciding for the former I can plead little more than my own general feeling for his style, bred by long intimacy with his achievements. The head of the Virgin is the only element that perhaps does not accord entirely with his norms, but in the original picture she looks less unlike his other women than in the illustration, and as a matter of fact there exist a number of close parallels in his authenticated productions, for instance the angel of the Annunciation in the retable that, fortunately surviving the civil war, has been transferred

[9] *Ibid.*, p. 306.
[10] *Archivo español de arte*, XXIII (1950), 189.
[11] Vol. VI, p. 346. The retable is another of the works of art at Játiva not destroyed in the war.
[12] Vol. VII, p. 713, n. 2.
[13] Monograph on *El Maestro de Santa Ana*, 32.

FIG. 184. THE JÁTIVA MASTER(?). NATIVITY.
KOETSER GALLERY, NEW YORK
(*Courtesy of the Gallery*)

from S. Francisco at Játiva [14] to the Colegiata. The ear emerging conspicuously from the Virgin's parted hair is a peculiarity of the Perea Master [15] rather than of his followers, the Játiva and Artés Masters, and might be interpreted as assigning the Koetser panel to an early date in the Játiva Master's career. The background displays not only his distinction in the realm of landscape but also precisely the contrast of rocky eminences with pleasant valleys that is characteristic of his settings; [16] and the taurine proclivities of the Spaniards which so often punctuate the paintings of the Valencian school here manifest themselves in the reservation of the champaign for the grazing of a herd of bulls. The Epiphany in the Museum at Toledo, Ohio, [17] appears to come from the same phase of the Játiva Master's output and even exhibits the corresponding rayed haloes, but the much smaller size forestalls the possibility that it was a companion-piece of the Koetser Nativity. [18]

On the other hand, I am disposed to support the candidacy of the Artés Master rather than of the Játiva Master in the case of two large [19] panels depicting the Prophets Jeremiah and Isaiah which were offered for sale at the Kende Galleries, New York, in October, 1951 (Fig. 185), and which recall, even in the character of the accompanying banderoles and of their lettering, the worthies of the old dispensation on the *guardapolvos* of his retable in the Provincial Museum, Valencia. [20] In addition to the Prophets' appellations, the banderoles bear in the inscriptions sentences from their writings with reference to the Passion: for Jeremiah, from Lamentations, IV, 20, "Christus Dominus captus est in peccatis nostris"; and for Isaiah, from his fifty-third chapter, verse 12, "Cum sceleratis deputatus est."

Our perplexities in the matter of attribution end when finally we encounter the fragments of a retable in the Cruilles Collection, Barcelona, in which the claims of the Artés Master over the Játiva Master appear to me incontestable (Fig. 186). Standing effigies of the Baptist and St. Sebastian are capped by a Crucifixion scarcely differing from the version in the assemblage of panels from Agullent by the Artés Master that until the holocausts of the Spanish war could be seen in the Diocesan Museum at Valencia; [21] and behind St. Sebastian there unfolds one of the rather luxuriant landscapes to which he sometimes treats us. A comparison with the very similar figures of the same sacred personages by the Borbotó

[14] Vol. VI, p. 345.

[15] *Ibid.*, p. 269.

[16] *Ibid.*, p. 354.

[17] Vol. VIII, p. 719.

[18] The dimensions of the Toledo panel are 12½ inches in height by 9¼ in width; those of the Nativity, 25½ inches by 17.

[19] The measurements of each are 32½ inches in height by 13 in width.

[20] Vol. VI, p. 298.

[21] Vol. VI, p. 301. If Saralegui has published the practically identical Crucifixion by the Artés Master in the Collection of Don Manuel González Martí at Valencia, I have stupidly overlooked what he may have said of it.

FIG. 185. THE ARTÉS MASTER. JEREMIAH AND ISAIAH. OFFERED
FOR SALE AT THE KENDE GALLERIES, NEW YORK, IN 1951

FIG. 186. THE ARTÉS MASTER. ST. JOHN BAPTIST, ST. SEBASTIAN,
AND CRUCIFIXION, FRAGMENTS OF RETABLE. CRUILLES
COLLECTION, BARCELONA

(*Photo. Archivo Mas*)

Master in the retable that gives him his name [22] graphically emphasizes the slight but distinct shades of difference that made of this occasional collaborator with the Artés Master more of an adherent to the tendencies of the Renaissance.

ARNALDO GASSIES (THE ELNE MASTER)

To the periodic rewards for my pedantic labors in isolating artistic personalities whose real appellations I did not know, there has been added another example in Marcel Durliat's [1] perception that Arnaldo (in Catalan, Arnau) Gassies was the name of the painter of Roussillon for whom in volume VII [2] I was obliged to coin the sobriquet of the Elne Master. The satisfaction that I might naturally feel, however, is curtailed by the consideration that the information through which Durliat reached his conclusion had long been at hand for me to use, Paul Masnou's [3] reference, as early as 1925, to a contract with Gassies, dated March 21, 1454, to do the paintings of the Elne Master's principal extant work, the retable of Sts. Michael and Hippolytus at Palau del Vidre. Masnou apparently was not cognizant of the existence of the retable for which Gassies contracted, and it remained for Durliat to make the connection. My only consolation for my oversight is that the number of the rare review, *Ruscino*, in which Masnou published the information was not to be found anywhere in the United States, but I ought, of course, to have learned of the article's existence and to have sought it out in a foreign library. The contract discloses also the identity of the donor, a Pedro Montroig, who is represented on his knees in the central compartment, the section of the altarpiece that was reserved for sculpture, executed by an artist whose name has not yet been discovered.

Durliat summarizes, from Masnou, the rather extensive data that we possess in regard to the career of Arnaldo Gassies, which, nevertheless, fail to attach him securely to any other extant work. We first hear of him on November 17, 1434, when, evidently still a young man, he married and was residing in Perpignan. Already or soon he served as apprentice to the painter of Perpignan, Andrés Mates, the father of the Juan Mates of Roussillon [4] and the grandfather of Huguet's pupil, Jorge Mates,[5] but in 1437 he betook himself to the centre of Catalan art, Barcelona, to study under an otherwise unrecorded painter, Pedro Tortos. We need not register his lost achievements after his return to Roussillon at least by 1440, which are itemized by Durliat, but it should be noted that in 1448 he

---

[22] *Ibid.*, p. 330 and fig. 134.

[1] See his article in *Revue des études roussillonnaises*, I (1951), 197–214.

[2] P. 559.

[3] See his articles on *Quelques peintres roussillonnais du XVe siècle*, in the periodical *Ruscino*, XV (1925), 103–107. Durliat merely epitomizes the contract, actually quoting no more than one clause from it.

[4] Not identical with the now well defined Juan Mates of Barcelona: cf. my vol. IX, p. 752, and above, p. 377.

[5] Vol. VII, p. 562.

agreed to do a retable of Sts. Andrew and Bartholomew for the town of St. Laurent de la Salanque (northeast of Perpignan) of which the scene from the former's history in the Basel Museum that I have ascribed to the Elne Master [6] might conceivably be a fragment. Arnaldo must have died shortly before August 11, 1456, when his widow initiated the legal proceedings necessitated by his decease. A painter, Arnau Gassies, just conceivably identical with the homonym in Roussillon, is recorded on September 17, 1432, as an assistant doing minor passages in the paintings of Apostles in the cathedral of Valencia.[7]

For the retable at Palau del Vidre I proposed, in volume VII,[8] a date not later than the sixties of the Quattrocento, and it turns out that the contract for the enterprise was signed in 1453, still a tardy enough moment for Gassies, at some second visit to Barcelona, to have seen, as I have surmised,[9] the first works that Huguet carried out in the city and its region, as well as the productions of the artists by whom Huguet was then surrounded. Nor does the year of the contract disprove my hypothesis that the author of the Palau del Vidre retable may have based the composition for the compartment depicting the archangel's miracle at Mont St. Michel upon the version in Huguet's retable of the Revendedores (now in the Museum of Catalan Art, Barcelona), which may come from a time prior to the usually assigned but conjectural date, 1455, and, moreover, the actual completion of the altarpiece by Gassies might have dragged on until his death in 1456. Indeed, although his retable for St. Laurent de la Salangue was ordered in 1448, we have the definite record that the final payment had not been made by November 18, 1450.

It is only after the many years since I wrote volume VII, and, by a strange coincidence, at the same time as the Elne Master's true name has been revealed, that I am able to add another work to the scant number of paintings which I have credited to him. The panel with which we have to do, formerly in the possession of Madame Marguerite Mengin at Paris (Fig. 187),[10] continues a composition for Pentecost, especially in the two emotionally excited Apostles in the foreground, that goes back in the Catalan school to at least as early a moment as the activity of the shop of the Serras [11] in the fourteenth century. Anyone who has long scrutinized the achievements of Gassies feels at once that the panel has brought him into the artist's presence, but detailed identities are not far to seek. The majority of the Apostles have the odd, snooping noses so characteristic of the artist, as in the figures behind St. Hippolytus in the scene of his

---

[6] *Ibid.*, p. 564.

[7] Sanchis y Sivera, *La catedral de Valencia*, 534, and *Pintores medievales en Valencia*, 119; and M. González Martí, *Cerámica del Levante Español*, III, Barcelona, 1952, pp. 540 and 542, n. 1.

[8] P. 562.

[9] *Ibid.*

[10] The dimensions are 115 centimetres in height by 92 in width.

[11] See my vol. II, fig. 161.

Fig. 187. ARNALDO GASSIES. PENTECOST.
MENGIN COLLECTION, PARIS
(*Courtesy of the owner*)

benediction of his household in the retable at Palau del Vidre; the St. John in the lower left corner displays a profile and a treatment of the hair that Arnaldo is prone to use in his representation of youths, for example in the first of the persons accompanying St. Hippolytus and in two of the actors in the painting in the Basel Museum; we perceive once again not only his tendency, as in the episode of St. Hippolytus's baptism, to vary the designs of the haloes, within a single compartment, between checkered and foliate patterns but also his avoidance of embossings in these nimbuses, contrary to the developing Catalan practice; and the garments are generally trimmed with his favorite pearls.

MARTÍN BERNAT AND MIGUEL JIMÉNEZ

A private collection at Lisbon contains the relics of an altarpiece that possesses the interest of affording an example of the collaboration of these Aragonese partners and followers of Bermejo in which the contributions of each may be pretty clearly distinguished (Fig. 188). Of the four compartments, the Ascension and Pentecost must have been executed by Bernat and turn out indeed to be no more than slightly varied treatments of the renderings of the themes in his documented retable at Tarazona.[1] The Nativity and Epiphany are just as plainly achievements, in the main, of Jiménez, although the less competent brush of his associate may have intruded here and there, as in the representations of St. Joseph.

We may number among the handsomest creations of Jiménez two large panels of the standing Sts. Michael and Sebastian in the possession of Don Apolinar Sánchez at Madrid [2] (Fig. 189). The figures of these two sacred personages are composed in a very similar way in the altarpiece from Pastriz in the Saragossa Museum,[3] although the master did not actually repeat the countenances.

Don Federico Balaguer [4] has unearthed records having to do with Martín de Larraz who assisted Miguel Jiménez on the retable of Tamarite de Litera [5] (destroyed in the civil war) and to whom in one of these documents Miguel's heirs are shown to have been indebted for 400 sueldos as late as 1513, ten years after the retable had been completed. The sum is thought by the Spanish scholar to be so considerable as to mean that Martín actually executed certain of the compartments, for instance the Flagellation that I have attributed to Miguel's son, Juan, but, since the amount is really paltry in comparison with the 12000 sueldos [6] that Miguel and Juan received for the undertaking, I am still disposed to believe that,

[1] Vol. VIII, p. 49.
[2] Without collusion (!), Don Leandro de Saralegui (*Archivo español de arte*, XXIV, 1951, p. 215) and I have arrived at the same conclusion about the attribution.
[3] Vol. VIII, p. 102.
[4] *Aragón*, January-March, 1950, p. 16.
[5] See my vol. VIII, p. 81.
[6] See the documents published by Merigó in the *Boletín del Museo Provincial de Zaragoza*, segunda época, I (1934), 36 and 38.

FIG. 188. MARTÍN BERNAT AND MIGUEL JIMÉNEZ. SECTIONS OF A
RETABLE. PRIVATE COLLECTION, LISBON

FIG. 189. MIGUEL JIMÉNEZ. STS. MICHAEL AND SEBASTIAN.
COLLECTION OF APOLINAR SÁNCHEZ, MADRID
(*Courtesy of the owner*)

of the two styles which alone are clearly distinguishable in the retable, we owe one, the lion's share, to the father and the other, for the reasons adduced in my volume VIII,[7] to the son and that Martín de Larraz's collaboration was of the most subordinate nature, not revealing itself tangibly in the paintings. Balaguer, however, summarizes a document that shows Martín to have been an independent master, his receipt of May 25, 1514, acknowledging payment for a retable that he did at the town of Yaso, east of Huesca, but, as the panels are lost, we are here balked in an attempt to arrive at a conception of his separate manner. It is also suggestive that, although in the records he is sometimes described as a citizen of Huesca, the contract of 1500 for the retable of Tamarite states him at least then to be residing at San Esteban de Litera, near Tamarite, for there were once to be seen in the church of San Esteban de Litera fragments, said to be in the style of Miguel Jiménez and Bernat, from a retable that had formerly decorated the high altar. If these fragments could ever be found, they might turn out to incorporate such modifications of the modes of Jiménez and Bernat as we should expect Martín de Larraz to embody.

THE OSLO MASTER

In Bermejo's extensive Aragonese following, a hitherto unrecognized personality may now be segregated and given the name of the Oslo Master from the odd circumstance of the existence of one of his productions, an Epiphany, in so unlikely a place as the National Gallery at the capital of Norway (Fig. 190). I am unhappily forced thus to resort to a foreign sobriquet for him because I have discovered no achievement of his in its original location in a town in Spain. Similarities to his style are detectable both in the retable of St. Romanus from Castro which was saved in the civil war and at my last knowledge deposited in the Lonja at Saragossa, perhaps eventually to find a permanent home in the Huesca Museum, and in the retable of Sts. Michael, John Baptist, and Sebastian that from the Lázaro Collection, Madrid, has passed into the Torelló Collection, Barcelona, two works that I now consider to be by a single painter;[1] but, after much study of the problem, I seriously doubt the equation of this painter with the Oslo Master.

The artist in the Aragonese strain deriving from Bermejo who perhaps exhibits the nearest stylistic kinship to the Oslo Master is Martín Bernat, but the creator of the panel now in Norway turns out to be a slightly more careful and vigorous craftsman, although making no great demands upon our admiration. The figure in the Epiphany most clearly exhibiting resemblances both to Bermejo and Bernat is the standing Caucasian Magus, but, of course, either through contact with other exponents of this phase of Aragonese painting or merely through participation in the same tendency our Master does not fail to show relationships to colleagues besides Bernat,

[7] Pp. 81 and 85.
[1] For both these retables, see my vol. VIII, p. 507.

FIG. 190. THE OSLO MASTER. EPIPHANY.
NATIONAL GALLERY, OSLO
(*Courtesy of the Frick Art Reference Library*)

for instance, in the old king, to Miguel Jiménez. Even if he had in general no higher aims than giving good, honest value to his pious clients and kept for the most part within the established formulae of the Aragonese coterie to which he belonged, yet occasionally he permitted himself relieving and inventive details. The curious posture of the old king is not, I think, the result of an inability to represent convincingly the attitude of kneeling but was meant to approximate the more fervid ritualistic act of prostration, in accord with the successfully delineated expression of intense devotion in the countenance. Likewise, the Oslo Master appears to have sensed a colored man's fondness for gay costume in clothing Balthasar not only in a surcoat of one of the usual conspicuous brocades common in Spanish painting of the period but also in loudly striped trousers. Nevertheless, he is not so lavish in the gold appurtenances of his panels as the majority of his rivals in this region of Spain. It was, to be sure, the general practice of Aragon at the time to eschew the Catalan embossings of gold backgrounds and to treat them, as in the panel at Oslo, merely with an incised pattern; but, in distinction from the other, contemporary Aragonese painters, our Master avoids also the accentuation of such accessories as borders of garments, crowns, and the like by raised and gilded stucco and restricts himself in his embossings to two rings of the simplest kind of halo, perhaps partly because his *floruit* may have fallen towards the end of the Middle Ages, c. 1500, when the taste for sumptuous enhancement of altarpieces was beginning to give way to the chastening influence of the Renaissance. The religious emotion that we have remarked in the old king is more ardent than the ordinary standard of Christian sentiment in Aragon of the period as incorporated in the art and constitutes a marked characteristic of the Oslo Master's modes.

We are unmistakably in the presence of these modes when we look at a Pentecost belonging to Madame Marguerite Mengin at Paris (Fig. 191).[2] The bearded Wise Man is practically repeated in one of the Apostles at the left, who gazes upward in ecstatic subjection to the divine will; the similarly devout, aged Apostle behind the Virgin at the right exhibits, as in the St. Joseph in the Oslo Epiphany, a peculiar stylization of the beard into stiff locks; the young St. John kneeling at the lower left scarcely differs in his countenance and its modelling from the Oslo Madonna; we perceive once more the Master's strange reversion to the thin, spidery hands of Byzantine art; and the haloes and gold backgrounds, seen through the arches of the setting, reiterate the treatment that we have analyzed in the picture in Norway. There are perhaps no details in the architecture of this setting that could not be explained as Gothic, but they are manipulated in a sober, classical way which again suggests that the Master may have survived to know something of the dawning Renaissance. His resort to bits of inventiveness for the sake of alleviating traditional compositions here takes the form of the punctuation of the edifice by an emphasized oculus through

---

[2] The dimensions are 172 centimetres in height by 90 in width.

FIG. 191. THE OSLO MASTER. PENTECOST.
MENGIN COLLECTION, PARIS
(*Courtesy of the owner*)

which has flown the symmetrically schematized dove of the Holy Spirit —
an architectural detail that prophesies the round window in the Visitation
in the Museum of Huesca by the Aragonese painter of the early Renaissance, the Sijena Master.

The Resurrection formerly owned by Miss Dean at Riverdale and now
in the Collection of Mr. C. O. von Kienbusch, New York, provides one of
a number of instances in which, by eventually discovering the real author,
I have been rewarded for refraining from an attribution on insufficient
evidence, since the panel, which I labelled in volume VIII [3] no more
exactly than as produced by an Aragonese disciple of Bermejo, obtains a
definite sponsor in the Oslo Master, whom I have recently isolated. In the
midst of a general agreement with his manner, he is shown to have painted
the panel by such specific facial identities as exist between the risen Christ
and the ecstatic Apostle in the Pentecost or between the upgazing guard
at the lower left and the Virgin in Madame Mengin's picture. It is to be
noted also that the design in the embossed ends of the cross in Christ's halo
is precisely duplicated in the nimbus of the Holy Child in the Oslo Epiphany.
More than in any other figure by our Master, the visages of the two soldiers
slumbering on the sarcophagus imply that the works of Miguel Jiménez
had come within his cognizance.

A Crucifixion in the Eyzaguirre Collection at Paris, when all the evidence that it affords is added together, can safely be placed among the
works which the Oslo Master has left us (Fig. 192). The heads are varied
from the types that we have found in his other paintings only by the expression of agony, the Christ, for instance, suggesting comparison with the
Apostle in the Mengin Pentecost whom I have singled out in the preceding
paragraph and the St. John recalling the way he is represented in the same
picture. Other factors also accord with the attribution, the elongated
fingers, the nature of the drapery's rigid stylization, the foliate design in the
gold background, and the figuration of the haloes, including the peculiar
extremities of the cross in the Saviour's nimbus that have demanded our
comment in two of the artist's other panels. Even the stones on the ground
are delineated in his characteristic mode, and a few small, round ones are
scattered along the path that leads to Jerusalem in the background exactly
as they appear under the negroid Magus in the Oslo Epiphany.

PEDRO BERRUGUETE

The most important event that has recently occurred in our study of this
forerunner of the Spanish Renaissance is the discovery of one of his most
delightful and competent achievements in a heap of abandoned pieces of old
wood and carvings in the City Hall of Madrid! A small panel depicting the

---

[3] P. 238 and fig. 106. The Oslo Master proves not to be identifiable with either
of the candidates that I proposed in volume VIII as possibilities for the authorship of
the Resurrection, the painter of a predella in the church of Nuestra Señora de la Peña
at Ágreda and the follower of Jiménez to whom in my volume on the early Aragonese
Renaissance I shall give the name of the Huesca Master.

Fig. 192. THE OSLO MASTER. CRUCIFIXION.
EYZAGUIRRE COLLECTION, PARIS
(*Photo. Giraudon*)

Madonna of the Milk seated in the back of an elaborate shrine in which, according to the Spanish architectural fashions of the time, Gothic and *mudéjar* elements are combined with prognostications of the Renaissance, the picture has been so thoroughly analyzed by Gómez-Moreno [1] as to dispense me from anything more than a few remarks in connection with what I have written about the master in volume IX.[2] It adds to the example in the diptych at Palencia another representation of the Virgin in full length holding the Child, and Gómez-Moreno stresses, perhaps a little too much, the analogies to the version in half length belonging to the Vizconde de Roda at Madrid; but in actual style and in the introduction of simulated statuettes to decorate the architecture the panel resembles most the Annunciation in the Cartuja de Miraflores. Amidst the general problem of the chronology of Berruguete's works in Spain, the date of the Annunciation remains in doubt [3] and therefore that of the Madrid Madonna; nor are we assisted in the question by any knowledge of the panel's ultimate provenience. A study of the composition has revealed to me that it is an adaptation of Roger van der Weyden's rendering of the theme in the Thyssen Collection at Lugano; but, since we possess no information about the history of this rendering, we cannot say whether Pedro saw it in Spain, Italy, or, not incredibly, Flanders, and there is also the chance that he had encountered only a copy which has not come to light. Likewise, in discussing in volume IX [4] the treatment in the Palencian diptych, I ought to have noted as possible sources Jan van Eyck's Melbourne Madonna or the Flemish master's lost painting which, known through a copy at Covarrubias, must early have reached Spain,[5] where Pedro could have examined it. In any case, these considerations should perhaps lead me to admit more direct contact on Berruguete's part with the art of the Low Countries than I have hitherto been inclined to discern.[6]

Of productions by him that have come to my own attention since the publication of volume IX, a most characteristically executed panel of the Assumption (Fig. 193), in an unnamed private collection at Barcelona, varies but slightly the composition of the rendering that at least once was in the possession of the Ruiz brothers at Madrid,[7] but it cannot be demonstrated, so far as I can ascertain, to have belonged to any of the cycles by his hand that we have hitherto registered.

More memorable, for the light that it throws upon his general production as well as for its intrinsic beauty, is a Pietà said to come from Palencia, one of the seats of the master's activity, and now owned at Barcelona by Don José Gudiol Ricart. Revealed by the shape of the panel to have formed the pinnacle of a retable, it constitutes an example of the rare substitution of this theme for the Crucifixion usual at the top of altarpieces in the Spanish school of the Middle Ages and Renaissance. Not only do the

[1] *Archivo español de arte*, XXIV (1951), 1–4.
[2] Chapter II.
[3] *Ibid.*, pp. 104–107.
[4] P. 99.
[5] Vol. IV, pp. 18–20.
[6] Vol. IX, pp. 44–48.
[7] *Ibid.*, fig. 31.

FIG. 193. PEDRO BERRUGUETE. ASSUMPTION.
PRIVATE COLLECTION, BARCELONA
(*Photo. Archivo Mas*)

types, every touch of the brush, and particularly the peculiarly individual chiaroscuro accord entirely with Pedro Berruguete's procedure and with this procedure at its best, but the composition is largely made up of elements that we have found in his versions of the subject in the predella of the retable at Becerril de Campos and in the diptych of the Palencian cathedral. As often in his works, he clings to the older practice of setting his figures against a background of brocaded gold. The panel casts its first ray of new light upon the Pietà in the Parcent Collection at Madrid, which, from the doubtful status that I was obliged to give to it in volume IX,[8] is elevated to the rank of a practically certain achievement of Berruguete through the similarity of the two Magdalenes. Still more significant is the illumination of his career in Italy, corroborating his execution of the Liberal Arts painted for Federico da Montefeltro by the impressive, exact analogy of the allegorical figure of Dialectic to the holy woman supporting the Saviour's head, by the *general* facial resemblance of the Virgin to the Music, and by the obvious attainment of the distinguished technical level of the productions of his Italian period, which a few critics — in my opinion, wrongly — have refused to see in at least the majority of his works done for Spain, using this supposed inferiority as a reason for denying to him the Montefeltro cycle.[9] Another detail that should not be passed over is the identity of Christ's head in the Gudiol panel and in the treatment of the subject that Berruguete did at Venice, now in the Brera Gallery at Milan.[10]

Of the remains of his retable from Frechilla,[11] the two wrecked pieces, the Via Dolorosa and the Entry into Jerusalem, having been restored and filled in with modern additions, found themselves, at my last knowledge, in the Barcelona market; and the fragments comprising a section of the Flagellation and two maidens from the scene of the Virgin's Presentation were owned by Don José Gudiol Ricart in the same city.

FRANCISCO DE COMONTES

The photographs recently taken by the Mas Archive of the paintings on cloth in the Ermita de S. Eugenio at Toledo, documented as works of Francisco de Comontes, help to supplement the statements about them that I made in volume IX,[1] writing from notes made on the spot and without the aid of reproductions. In regard to iconography, they reveal that the demoniacal subject cannot possibly be the Temptation of Christ but probably should be interpreted, according to Parro's surmise, as an encounter of

[8] P. 124.
[9] Writing in 1945, before the publication of my volume IX, Martin Davies (*Early Netherlandish School, National Gallery, London*, pp. 45–53) joined the small group of those still attributing the Liberal Arts to Joos van Gent, and he proposed that they might derive, not from Urbino, but from a lesser Montefeltro palace at Gubbio.
[10] Vol. IX, fig. 46. Subsequently to my writing of this paragraph and independently of me, Angulo has also published the Gudiol Pietà in *Archivo español de arte*, XXIV (1951), 165–166.
[11] Vol. IX, p. 96.   [1] Pp. 342 and 345.

Satan with Job in conformity with the implication of the first two chapters of the patriarch's Book in the Old Testament, although no verse specifically describes such a meeting.[2] The intimate relationship between Comontes and Correa [3] is exemplified in the Visitation by the anomalous consignment of Zacharias to an upper window, as in one of the latter artist's panels at Meco.[4] The paintings of the young Christ in the Temple and of the Marriage at Cana betray that Comontes was no composer of large narrative scenes and that in these instances he filled his spaces with uninteresting throngs, endeavoring to save the nuptial feast from dullness by the insertion of incongruous bits of *genre* consisting of greedy children and the activities of the household pets.

He adds another instance to the circulation of artists between the regions of Toledo and Guadalajara that we have before remarked in these volumes, since he manifestly executed a Lamentation over the Dead Christ, painted on cloth, in the cathedral of Sigüenza, which lies within the province of the latter city (Fig. 194). With rather unusual iconography, two Prophets, instead of angels, hover in the air, holding banderoles inscribed with verses from their writings that I do not remember having seen in other versions of the subject. Jeremiah quotes from his Lamentations, V, 15, "Defecit gaudium cordis nostri: versus est in luctum chorus noster";[5] and Nahum repeats a part of the seventh verse of his third chapter, "Unde quaeram consolatorem tibi?" From the copious and obvious evidence for the attribution, we may select for emphasis the similarity of the Magdalene to Francisco's type of young woman, the reappearance of his norms for elderly men in the Joseph of Arimathaea in the right background, the general character of the narrow, winding folds of drapery, and, above all, in the St. John, as in two of the shepherds in the Nativity in the cathedral of Toledo, his interpretation of a kind of youthful countenance inherited from his teacher, Juan de Borgoña.

The easily recognizable feminine type that he prefers, the mannered twist of the body, the nature of the landscape, and all other factors put the unmistakable stamp of his handicraft upon a panel of the standing St. Catherine in the Milicua Collection at Barcelona (Fig. 195). With some slight variation of his more ritualistic effigy of her in the cathedral of Toledo,[6] she not only, as commonly, tramples upon Maximin but, too graphically, she presses her emblem of the sword into one of his eyes; and the background is partially filled with a fierce storm as the divine means, rather than the usual angel, of breaking the wheels intended for her torture and of thus destroying the pagans.

---

[2] Could the object that the devil is handing to Job be a crab, *cancer*, a symbol of the skin diseases with which he afflicted the patriarch?

[3] Vol. IX, pp. 314 and 352.

[4] Vol. X, p. 413.

[5] Does this mean that the picture was done to decorate the *coro* of the cathedral?

[6] Vol. IX, p. 350.

FIG. 194. FRANCISCO DE COMONTES. LAMENTATION OVER THE
DEAD CHRIST. CATHEDRAL, SIGÜENZA

(*Photo. Archivo Mas*)

FIG. 195. FRANCISCO DE COMONTES. ST. CATHERINE OF ALEXANDRIA.
MILICUA COLLECTION, BARCELONA
(*Photo. Archivo Mas*)

The Riofrío Master

It is always a gratification to be able to confirm through new evidence, after the lapse of years, my segregation of the personality of an artist, especially if his works are sparsely preserved as in the case of the painter of the very early Renaissance to whom I have given the name of the Riofrío Master and whose activity appears to have centered at Avila.[1] The new evidence is provided by a Lamentation over the Dead Christ which, since it belongs to the Museum of Segovia, must come from some place in the province of this city and therefore near enough to Avila to have fallen within the radius of the Master's vogue (Fig. 196). So shaped and so large as to suggest that it once constituted the decoration of a sepulchral niche, the panel includes a clerical donor, still in the reduced proportions assigned to these figures in the Middle Ages, and at the bottom an inscription in Gothic characters effaced to such an extent that it has become, at least to my eyes, indecipherable.[2] In addition to the usual participants in the scene, there is anomalously introduced, above the donor, an armored old man holding a spear and piously clasping his hands. Of the same size as the other personages, although, like Joseph of Arimathaea and Nicodemus, without a halo, he probably was intended as Longinus, who pierced Our Lord's side, perhaps finding a place in the picture because the donor entertained for him a special devotion.

No more abundant proof of an attribution could be desired. The Magdalene's head, for example, exactly repeats that of the Virgin in the Purification in the cathedral of Avila; Nicodemus, who with a direct naturalism but not without a touch of bathos is depicted as using a handkerchief to wipe away his tears, conforms to an aged type, wearing a striped hat, that, often employed by the Riofrío Master, is well illustrated by one of the Prophets in the paintings at Avila in the church of S. Pedro; the St. John Evangelist scarcely differs from the treatment of this Apostle in the S. Pedro series; the Joseph of Arimathaea (with the ladder) recalls the Baptist in S. Pedro; and the backgrounds of the retable in the Musée de Cluny, Paris, unfold similar landscapes. Apparently, however, expending less care upon the execution than was his wont, he did not take much pains with the problem of a long, horizontal composition, but, finding that he had not correctly planned the space, he arbitrarily filled the lower right section by absurdly elongating and posing the Magdalene's body.

B. del Castro

When I ascribed in volume IX[1] two figures of Hebrews to this master, whose initial we established in volume X[2] as a B and whom we were able

---

[1] Vol. IX, p. 383.

[2] The donor's name is said to be Contreras, probably because someone has been able to read the word in the inscription.

[1] P. 422.   [2] P. 424.

Fig. 196. THE RIOFRÍO MASTER. LAMENTATION OVER THE DEAD
CHRIST. PROVINCIAL MUSEUM, SEGOVIA
(*Photo. Archivo Mas*)

to localize at least for a part of his career in the province of Palencia, I expressed the hope that further members of the same series might be discovered in order to clarify the underlying idea of the aggregation; and I have now come upon such another pair in the Allen R. Hite Art Institute, Louisville, Kentucky (Fig. 197), panels that not only suggest what the general unifying theme of the series was but also strongly support the attribution. I have not been able to ferret out in concordances to the Vulgate the names of the two additional Jewish personages which, as in the case of the twain with whom I was already familiar, are inscribed on ledges at the bottom of the pictures, Zemeyas and Joeth, but it is to be surmised that they also are the appellations of obscure characters in the Old Testament, here given a Latinization different from the forms that the Vulgate uses. The banderole above Zemeyas reads:

"Lex scripta est ut jus serviret [3] cuique. Nocentes plectendi. Offendit. Ergo necandus erit."
(The law has been written so that justice shall serve everyone. The guilty are to be punished. He has offended. Therefore he must be put to death.)

The words on the corresponding scroll of Joeth are:

"Quin simulare juvat. Certe hunc damnare veremur insontem. Hinc torquet pectora nostra timor."
(Verily [4] it is advantageous to simulate. Surely we are afraid of condemning him innocent. For this reason fear torments our breasts.)

My friend, the distinguished classical scholar, Dr. Alston H. Chase, has perceived that the lines constitute in each case good elegiac distichs,[5] and it is certain that the inscriptions accompanying the two figures whom I discussed in volume IX would also prove to be cast in this metre, if they could be deciphered accurately. The sentences on the banderole of the Zadok in the Georgi Collection, New York, form themselves into an elegiac distich when we include the two as yet undeciphered words, and the reason that the scroll of the Gomer in the Harris Collection, London, cannot be thus scanned is undoubtedly the modern tampering with the inscription that my struggle in volume IX to elicit meaning from it appears to betray.

The important likelihoods which may be deduced from the evidence furnished by the sentiments on the four banderoles, taken in conjunction, are that the personages represent some of "the chief priests and elders and all the council" debating the question of putting Christ to death and that the painter was using as a source for depicting this subject a mystery play or a poem which I leave to others more conversant with Christian literature in Latin to identify. It is apparent that the writer, whoever he was, selected

---

[3] The *i* of *serviret* is out of place, according to a not infrequent kind of error in inscriptions of the period.

[4] Or perhaps *Quin* should be translated, "Nay, rather."

[5] The second line of the first distich begins with "plectendi"; of the second distich, with "insontem."

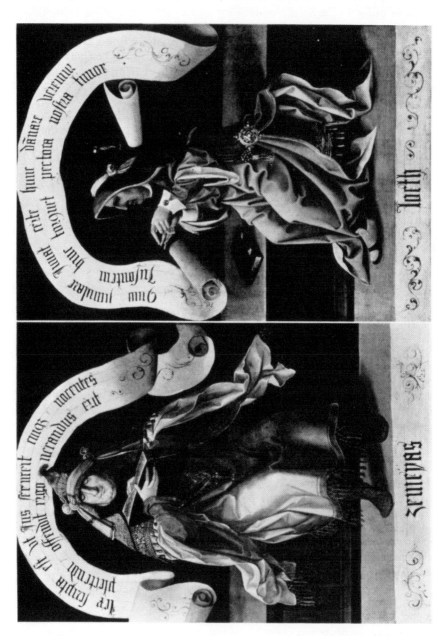

Fig. 197. B. DEL CASTRO(?). ZEMEYAS AND JOETH.
ALLEN R. HITE ART INSTITUTE, LOUISVILLE, KENTUCKY

names for his "scribes and Pharisees" from characters who in the Old Testament were only casually mentioned.

The new stylistic evidence provided by the panels in the Louisville Institute seems to me practically to confirm the ascription of the series to Castro, for instance the intimate facial resemblance of Zemeyas to the Innocent III in the painting of the confirmation of the Franciscan Order in the Johnson Collection at Philadelphia.

ANDRÉS LÓPEZ AND ANTONIO DE VEGA

We should have expected that a fragment of a retable of the early Renaissance in the sacristy of the cathedral of Sigüenza depicting in half length Sts. Paul and Andrew (Fig. 198) as well as the mere bust of another Apostle, who has no identifying emblem, would have turned out to be works of Juan de Pereda, the painter who has left us in the church the important altarpiece of the period dedicated to St. Liberata, but the style seems to me indisputably the same as that which I have connected with the above-mentioned partners.[1] Since the activities of artists were often at this time confined within the limits of dioceses, it is somewhat surprising to find employed at Sigüenza painters whom otherwise we know only as active in Segovia and its district, but the two cities are not geographically far distant from each other. Doubts in regard to the authorship disappear to my eyes when I observe the analogy, in type and chiaroscuro, of the St. Paul to the St. Joachim of the Meeting at the Golden Gate in the church of the Trinidad at Segovia and of the St. Andrew to the St. Joachim and two of his aged friends in the Presentation of the Virgin that has now been acquired for the Torelló Collection at Barcelona.[2] The head of the unrecognizable Apostle also more or less conforms to the latter conception of the Virgin's father. The partners' affection for the old Hispano-Flemish, decorative brilliancy is embodied in the retention of gold backgrounds diapered with a conspicuous pattern.

The handicraft which we associate with them emerges so much more clearly in a similar series of four half-lengths in the Museum at Lisbon that I am ashamed not to have recognized the panels' affiliations before. The worthies of the Old Testament, David and Isaiah, are the subjects of two of the set, and the other pair depict the Apostles Sts. Andrew and John (Fig. 199). The Catalogue of the exhibition in 1940 of Spanish paintings of the fifteenth and sixteenth centuries belonging to the Museum describes the panels, which are roughly equal in measurements, as sections of a predella; but it would be curious that Prophets and Apostles together should have been included in such a part of a retable, and I imagine that, despite the restricted size,[3] at least one of the pairs derives from some other loca-

[1] Vols. IX, p. 706, and X, p. 456.
[2] Vol. X, fig. 196. The companion-piece of the Virgin sewing (*ibid.*, p. 456) has also entered the same Collection.
[3] The dimensions are about 50 centimetres in height by 40 in width.

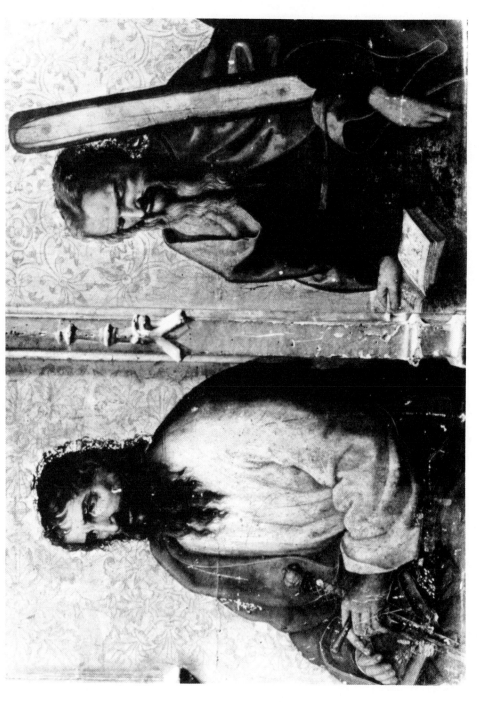

FIG. 198. ANDRÉS LÓPEZ AND ANTONIO DE VEGA. STS. PAUL AND ANDREW.

Fig. 199. ANDRÉS LÓPEZ AND ANTONIO DE VEGA. ISAIAH AND ST. JOHN EVANGELIST. MUSEUM, LISBON

(Courtesy of the Museum)

tion in the assemblage. The banderoles held by David and Isaiah contain their names followed by the words,[4] "Miserere mei," appropriate enough for the former because the petition occurs so often in the Psalms, but oddly repeated for Isaiah in whose Prophecy there is found only the analogous clause, "Miserere nostri" (XXXIII, 2).[5] The St. Andrew and the Isaiah once more incorporate, though in a somewhat less elderly phase, the type of St. Joachim and his two companions in the panel of the Virgin's Presentation to which I have referred in the last paragraph; the St. John actually echoes in gesture as well as countenance the same Evangelist in the altarpiece in the Trinidad at Segovia; and the figures are relieved against still more ostentatiously designed gold than the Sigüenza Apostles.

The pattern in the gold backgrounds of the Lisbon series, the type of the David and Isaiah, and even the nature of the banderoles are so exactly reproduced in a panel of a Prophet in private possession at Madrid that we are bound to predicate that it was a compartment of the same original retable (Fig. 200). Despite the effort that I have devoted to the matter, I have been able to decipher satisfactorily neither the name inscribed in the halo nor the words on the banderole, and I suspect that, as sometimes happened, they have been garbled by a restorer: in any case I cannot identify what personage of the Old Testament was intended. Were it necessary, further proof of the panel's proper allocation would be afforded by the considerations that the Prophet displays precisely the same hat as the Isaiah, that he wears one of the brightly brocaded garments for which López and Vega had such a lingering fondness, and that his visage, if deprived of the beard, finds an absolute analogue in the spectator between St. Lucy and the magistrate in the scene of her decollation in the Feder Collection at New York.[6]

The photographs recently taken by the Mas Archive in Segovia establish the justice of claiming for the partners two works in the Provincial Museum of the town that I mentioned in volume IX [7] as given to them by others, the Virgin of Sorrows ascribed by the Marqués de Lozoya and the Baptism attributed by Angulo, the latter a hastily executed panel but authenticated by the kind of landscape as well as by the types of the actors.

I am not sure that I have hit upon the truth in assigning to Andrés López and his associate a large panel of St. Sebastian in the Collection of Mrs.

<hr />

[4] Only partly visible in the case of David.

[5] I attach no significance to what looks like the spelling *Xuan* in St. John's halo, since *J* and *X* were interchangeable in Castilian of the period.

[6] Vol. X, fig. 200.

[7] Pp. 711–712. The photographs do not include the pieces that the Marqués de Lozoya states to have been parts of the same original assemblage as the Virgin of Sorrows and to belong to the Museum, a representation of St. Jerome in his study, which I do not find entered in my notes as there existing, and, from the predella, two Fathers-of-the-Church. I wonder whether he could be referring to the panel of St. Jerome in his study which is now to be seen in the Lázaro Collection, Madrid, but may have been once in the Segovia Museum, a work, however, that was certainly painted by the Master of El Parral: see above, p. 421.

Fig. 200. ANDRÉS LÓPEZ AND ANTONIO DE VEGA. PROPHET.
PRIVATE COLLECTION, MADRID
(*Photo. Moreno*)

FIG. 201. ANDRÉS LÓPEZ AND ANTONIO DE VEGA(?). ST. SEBASTIAN.
COLLECTION OF MRS. MIRA SALOMON, NEW YORK

FIG. 202. ANTÓN BECERRA. STS. JOHN EVANGELIST AND
MICHAEL. CATHEDRAL, CIUDAD REAL
(*Photo. Archivo Mas*)

Mira Salomon at New York, originally the principal compartment or at least one of the main sections in a retable (Fig. 201);[8] but it exhibits many intimate affinities to their style, and there is no other master of the period in any part of Spain with whose production it so neatly accords. The kind of visage, with narrow, somewhat pointed nose and generally sharp features, is of a cast often met in their output, as in several of the heads in the scene of the amputation of St. Lucy's breasts in the Feder Collection and especially in the magistrate ordering her decollation in the companion-piece; and the facial chiaroscuro is manipulated in a way that we constantly observe in their works, for example in a St. Sebastian belonging to a dealer at Barcelona.[9] The Salomon representation of this saint is conceived rather differently from the Barcelona figure, as well as from the effigy in their retable in the church of the Trinidad at Segovia; but a moment's inspection reveals that in the Barcelona rendering the folds of the drapery are very similar, that the footwear is much the same, and that even the diversity in the countenances is almost negligible. We must indeed allow to any artist as great a degree of latitude in the treatment of an identical theme. Corroboratory evidence is not lacking in such details as the delineation of the hands, the masonry of the parapet,[10] and the conspicuousness of the auric brocades.

A recently published summary of a document [11] extends the span of life of the second partner, Antonio de Vega, to 1527, when he collaborated with the carver, Sancho de León, in a (lost) retable for the church of San Marcos at Buitrago, east of Segovia.

ANTÓN BECERRA

The photographing by the Mas Archive of two panels of the life-size figures of Sts. John Evangelist and Michael built into a later retable in a chapel in the cathedral of Ciudad Real (Fig. 202) brings me great satisfaction not only because, although I have long known of the existence of the paintings, I have never been able to include a visit to them in my travels in Spain, but also because they prove to be unmistakable achievements of the Andalusian artist, Antón Becerra, by whom so few works are preserved or at least recognized.[1] Deriving from a retable in a chapel of St. Michael that once existed in the edifice,[2] they are found in a city so close to the borders of Andalusia that it would be a likely spot to have engaged Becerra's services.

In the midst of a general and often detailed agreement with his manner, it is especially the St. John that makes the attribution imperative, for I submit that no one else could have executed a figure so similar in stocky proportions of the body, posture, inclination of the head, breadth of drapery,

[8] The panel is now set in an alien frame, within which the dimensions are 44 inches in height by 28 in width.
[9] Vol. X, fig. 199.
[10] *Ibid.*, fig. 196.
[11] *Estudios segovianos*, I (1949), 130.
[1] Vol. X, p. 222.
[2] Rafael Ramírez de Arellano, *Ciudad-Real Artística*, Ciudad Real, 1893, p. 33.

FIG. 203. ANTÓN BECERRA. ST. JAMES
MAJOR, SECTION OF RETABLE.
MUSEO ARQUEOLÓGICO,
MADRID

and the nature of the folds to the Santiago of his signed retable in the Archaeological Museum at Madrid (Fig. 203).[3] Each of the following single, detailed proofs is not in itself determinative, but, when all are added together, they acquire a cumulative force and both separately and in conjunction ratify Becerra's authorship. The Evangelist's countenance is modelled in the same way as that of the Virgin in the signed retable; the lids of his eyes, as also in the St. Michael, are lowered in precisely the fashion that the retable shows us in several of its personages; the bottom of his tunic takes exactly the rigid, pipe-like folds of the corresponding section of the costume of Becerra's St. Paul at Baeza;[4] just at the left of St. John the same interest is manifested in filling a space with pieces of masonry as beside the Baeza St. Peter;[5] and the painter's retention of the mediaeval practice of hanging plaques of textiles behind sacred figures is also illustrated in the case of the Beloved Disciple, who stands before a fabric even very similar in design to the specimens in Becerra's other works and almost identical with the example on the throne of the Virgin at Madrid. In the episode depicted in diminished scale on a kind of viaduct in the left background, the cure of the lame man by St. John and St. Peter (the latter of whom can just be seen within the gate of the Temple), the artist has given to the Evangelist, in distinction from the main effigy, the silky undulations of hair that he so often affects.

We should hardly have recognized the St. Michael as a creation of Becerra because we have so sparse a number of works with which to compare it, but, taught that as a companion-piece to the St. John the archangel must have been executed by him, we soon perceive how well the panel fits into his manner. The figure, for instance, possesses something of the broad and heavy canon for the human form that we have stressed in the Evangelist; the face is almost a profile version of Mary's countenance in the Madrid retable; St. Michael's fingers recall those of the Madrid Santiago's and the Baeza St. Peter's left hand; and the woman whom he is weighing in the scales exhibits the typical wavy tresses. The paintings at Ciudad Real reveal a facet in Becerra's personality for which in his other extant productions he did not give himself an opportunity, the charm that he shared with so many of his Spanish contemporaries in the landscapes of backgrounds. At the right of St. John he has been able to express his appreciation for the beauties of a receding valley, but it is particularly in the vista at St. Michael's left that he adequately unfolds to us his pleasure in the varied wonders of nature, depicting the side of a mountain with romantic Gothic buildings at its several levels, with peopled terraces opening before the edifices, and the whole outlook culminating at the top in a towering and forbidding mass of jagged rock.

[3] The proportions and breadth of the Santiago were partly caused, as we have seen in volume X, by the dependence upon Cranach's St. James in his series of woodcuts of Apostles, but, since the St. John scarcely seems to have been suggested by the German's representation of him in the series, Becerra himself may have liked to endow some of his figures with these characteristics.

[4] Vol. X, fig. 82.

[5] I am not referring, of course, to the parti-colored architecture at the top of the panel of St. Peter.

ADDITIONAL BIBLIOGRAPHY

ADDITIONAL BIBLIOGRAPHY
FOR
VOLUMES I–X

Ainaud de Lasarte, Juan, *El retaule de Rubió dintre la pintura catalana del segle XIV*, published by the Biblioteca del Centro de Estudios Comarcales, Igualada, 1949.

—— *Tabla de la Resurrección procedente de Santes Creus*, Anales y Boletín de los Museos de Arte de Barcelona, IV, 3–4 (1946), 499–505.

—— *Tablas inéditas de Juan Mates*, Anales y Boletín de los Museos de Arte de Barcelona, VI, 3–4 (1948), 341–344.

Angulo Íñiguez, Diego, La *"Adoración de los Reyes,"* del Museo de Bayona, atribuída á Rodrigo de Osona, Archivo español de arte, XVIII (1945), 383.

—— *Una nueva obra de Pedro Berruguete*, Archivo español de arte, XXIV (1951), 165–166.

—— *Una tabla valenciana en Bucarest*, Archivo español de arte, XIV (1940–1941), 319.

Balaguer, Federico, *El antiguo retablo mayor de la Colegiata de Tamarite, y el pintor Martín de Larraz*, Aragón, January to March, 1950, p. 16.

Camón Aznar, José, *La Pasión de Cristo en el arte español*, vol. III in the series *Los grandes temas del arte cristiano en España*, Madrid, 1949.

Davies, Martin, *Early Netherlandish School, National Gallery, London*, London, 1945 (for Pedro Berruguete).

Delogu, Raffaello, *Chiosa al "Maestro di Peñafel,"* Annali della Facoltà di Lettere, Filosofia e Magistero della Università di Cagliari, XIII (1946), 3–12.

Durán y Sanpere, Agustín, *Viaje alrededor de una miniatura*, Barcelona, 1950.

Durliat, Marcel, *Arnaud Gassies, peintre perpignanais du quinzième siècle*, Revue des études roussillonnaises, I (1951), 197–214.

—— *L'atelier de Maître Alexandre en Roussillon et en Cerdagne*, Revue des études roussillonnaises, I (1951), 103–119.

Durruty, Inés, *El retablo de Santa Ana en el Seminario Conciliar de Valladolid*, Boletín del Seminario de Estudios de Arte y Arqueología, Universidad de Valladolid, Fascículos XXVIII–XXX (1941–1942), 219–237.

García Guinea, Miguel-Ángel, *El retablo del palacio arzobispal de Valladolid*, Boletín del Seminario de Estudios de Arte y Arqueología, Universidad de Valladolid, Fascículos LII–LIV (1950), 151–167.

Gómez-Moreno, Manuel, *La joya del Ayuntamiento Madrileño, ahora descubierta* (a Madonna by Pedro Berruguete), *Archivo español de arte*, XXIV (1951), 1–4.

González Martí, Manuel, *Cerámicas valencianas en las pinturas de retablos*, Chapter IX in volume III of his monumental work, *Cerámica del Levante Español*, Barcelona, 1952.

Grau, Mariano, *Obras perdidas u olvidadas*, Estudios segovianos, I (1949), 128–130.

Hernández Manero, Elda, and Cariñena Gil, Margarita, and Aznar Dolz, Amparo, *Estudio monográfico de las pinturas setabenses de tema mariano*, in the publication *Ecos de la Papelera de San Jorge*, Játiva, 1948.

Layna Serrano, Francisco, *La Parroquia de Mondéjar; sus retablos y el del convento de Almonacid de Zorita*, Boletín de la Sociedad Española de Excursiones, XLIII (1935), 265–290.

Martín González, Juan José, *Guía histórico-artística de Valladolid*, Valladolid, 1949.

Procacci, Ugo, *Gherardo Starnina*, Rivista d'arte, XV (1933), 151–190; XVII (1935), 333–384; XVIII (1936), 77–94.

Ramírez de Arellano, Rafael, *Ciudad-Real artística*, Ciudad Real, 1893.

Sánchez Cantón, Francisco Javier, *Los retratos de los reyes de España*, Barcelona, 1948.

Saralegui, Leandro de, *El Maestro de Sta. Ana y su escuela*, published by the Institución Alfonso el Magnánimo, Valencia, 1950.

—— *Sobre algunas pinturas españolas del XIV al XVI*, Archivo español de arte, XXIV (1951), 209–224.

—— *Una tabla inédita de Jacomart* (??), Boletín de la Sociedad Castellonense de Cultura, XXV (1949), Cuaderno jubilar, 507–509.

Uranga, José E., *El sepulcro de Mosén Francés* (de Villaespesa), Príncipe de Viana, X (1949), 227–240.

Verrié, F. P., *Iconografía de la Natividad á través de la pintura catalana medioeval*, Barcelona, 1942.

—— *Una obra documentada de Ramón Destorrents*, Anales y Boletín de los Museos de Arte de Barcelona, VI, 3–4 (1948), 321–340.

Ysasi, Rafael, *Parte central de un retablo de San Cristóbal*, Bolletí de la Societat Arqueològica Luliana, XXV (1934), 245–246.

INDICES

INDEX OF NAMES OF ARTISTS

In cases where there are two or more entries after a name, italics indicate the pages on which the principal discussions of the artists in question may be found; for masters who are mentioned only incidentally, italics have not been used in such instances.

INDEX OF PLACES

In cases where there are two or more numerical references after an entry, italics indicate the pages on which the principal discussions of the paintings in question may be found. Asterisks denote the presence of illustrations.